GCSE AQA English
Language & Literature

You'll be ready to smash your English Language and Literature exams with this brilliant CGP book by your side!

It's packed with clear study notes, exam practice questions and CGP's expert exam advice. Plus, we've included knowledge organisers to make revising as easy as possible — including one for *every* set text on the AQA Literature exam.

And it doesn't stop there — CGP RevisionHub is full of online summary tests, video walkthroughs and an Online Edition to get you fully prepared. What could be better?

Unlock CGP RevisionHub

Just scan a QR code in the book to access the CGP RevisionHub.
Or go to **cgpbooks.co.uk/revise** and enter this code!

1324 7620 4527 7260

By the way, this code only works for one person. If somebody else has used this book before you, they might have already claimed the code.

Complete
Revision & Practice
with new CGP RevisionHub

Contents

How To Use This Book 1

Section One — Exam Basics

Planning Answers 2
Structuring Paragraphs 4
Using Evidence 5
Reading with Insight 6
Writing Well 7
Spelling, Punctuation and Grammar 8
Exam Basics — Knowledge Organiser 9
    Revision Summary Test for Section One 10

Section Two — Introduction to English Language

Exam Structure 11
The Assessment Objectives 12
Paper 1 — Questions 1 and 2 13
Paper 1 — Questions 3 and 4 14
Paper 1 — Question 5 15
Paper 2 — Questions 1 and 2 16
Paper 2 — Questions 3 and 4 17
Paper 2 — Question 5 18
English Language Exams — Knowledge Organiser 19

Section Three — English Language: Understanding Texts

Information and Ideas 20
Summarising and Linking 21
Audience 22
Writer's Purpose 23
Informative Texts 24
Entertaining Texts 25
Texts that Argue or Persuade 26
Texts that Advise 27
    Warm-Up Questions 28
    Exam-Style Questions 29
Writer's Viewpoint and Attitude 31
Literary Fiction 32
Literary Non-Fiction 33
19th-Century Texts 34
Understanding Texts — Knowledge Organiser 36
    Worked Answer 38
    Exam-Style Questions 40
    Revision Summary Test for Section Three 41

Section Four — English Language: Language & Structure

Tone 42
Style and Register 43
Words and Phrases 44
Figurative Language 46
    Warm-Up Questions 47
    Exam-Style Questions 48
Alliteration and Onomatopoeia 49
Irony 50
Sarcasm 51
Rhetoric 52
Bias 53
Descriptive Language 54
Other Language Techniques 55
    Warm-Up Questions 56
    Exam-Style Questions 57
Narrative Viewpoint 59
Structure — Whole Texts 60
Sentence Forms 64
Language & Structure — Knowledge Organiser 66
    Worked Answer 68
    Exam-Style Questions 70
    Revision Summary Test for Section Four 71

Section Five — English Language: Writing

Writing with Purpose 72
Writing for an Audience 74
Writing Stories 76
Writing Descriptions 79
    Warm-Up Questions 80
    Exam-Style Questions 81
Writing Newspaper Articles 82
Writing Leaflets 84
Writing Essays 85
Writing Speeches 86
Writing Letters 87
Writing — Knowledge Organiser 88
    Worked Answer 90
    Exam-Style Questions 92
    Revision Summary Test for Section Five 93

Section Six — English Language: Sample Exams & Graded Answers

Sample Exam — Paper 1 94
Exam Text 96
Graded Answers — Paper 1, Question 1 97
Graded Answers — Paper 1, Question 2 98
Graded Answers — Paper 1, Question 3 100
Graded Answers — Paper 1, Question 4 102
Graded Answers — Paper 1, Question 5 104
Sample Exam — Paper 2 106
Exam Text A 108
Exam Text B 109
Graded Answers — Paper 2, Question 1 110
Graded Answers — Paper 2, Question 2 112
Graded Answers — Paper 2, Question 3 114
Graded Answers — Paper 2, Question 4 116
Graded Answers — Paper 2, Question 5 118

Introduction to English Literature 120

Section Seven — English Literature: Prose & Drama

Writing About Prose and Drama 121
Writing About Characters 122
The Writer's Techniques 124
Context 127
Themes and the Writer's Message 128
Using Quotations 129
   Warm-Up Questions 130
   Exam-Style Questions 132
   Revision Summary Test for Section Seven 133

Section Eight — English Literature: Drama

Reading Plays 134
Writing About Plays 136
Writing About Modern Plays 138
Writing About Shakespeare 140
Shakespeare's Language 142
The Structure of Shakespeare's Plays 144
   Warm-Up Questions 145
   Worked Exam-Style Question — Paper 1 146
   Worked Exam-Style Question — Paper 2 148
   Exam-Style Questions 150

Section Nine — English Literature: Prose

Writing About Prose 151
Analysing Narrators 153
19th-Century Fiction 154
   Warm-Up Questions 157
   Worked Exam-Style Question — Paper 1 158
   Worked Exam-Style Question — Paper 2 160
   Exam-Style Questions 162

Section Ten — English Literature: Poetry

Poetry — What You Have To Do 163
Form and Structure 164
Poetic Techniques 165
Comparing Poems 170
   Warm-Up Questions 171
   Revision Summary Test for Section Ten 172

Section Eleven — English Literature: Poetry Anthology

The Poetry Anthology 173
How to Structure Your Answer 174
How to Answer the Question 175
How to Write a Top Grade Answer 178
   Warm-Up Questions 179
   Worked Exam-Style Question
   — Love and Relationships 180
   Worked Exam-Style Question
   — Power and Conflict 182
   Worked Exam-Style Question
   — Worlds and Lives 184
   Exam-Style Questions 186

Section Twelve — English Literature: Unseen Poetry

Five Steps to Analysing a Poem 187
   Worked Exam-Style Question 188
Comparing Two Poems 191
   Worked Exam-Style Question 192
   Warm-Up Questions 194
   Exam-Style Questions 195

Section Thirteen — English Literature: Knowledge Organisers

Blood Brothers — Knowledge Organiser 197
A Christmas Carol — Knowledge Organiser 198
An Inspector Calls — Knowledge Organiser 199
Dr Jekyll and Mr Hyde — Knowledge Organiser 200
Macbeth — Knowledge Organiser 201
Power and Conflict — Knowledge Organiser ... 202
Romeo and Juliet — Knowledge Organiser 204

Practice Papers — English Language

Paper 1 205
Paper 2 209

Practice Papers — English Literature

Paper 1 214
Paper 2 228

Answers 238
Glossary 264
Index 267

Published by CGP

Editors:
Siân Butler
Emma Duffee
Rebecca Greaves
Nathan Leach
Delicia Ong
Kirsty Sweetman
Matt Topping

With thanks to Emma Crighton and Nathan Mair for the proofreading
and Jade Sim for the copyright research.

Acknowledgements:

This book does not include any official AQA questions and is not endorsed by AQA.

*Letter on page 35 to Princess (later Queen) Victoria from King Leopold I of Belgium,
August 1832, from The Letters of Queen Victoria, Volume 1 (of 3), 1837-1843.*

*Extract used on page 96 from The Snow Child by Eowyn Ivey. Copyright © 2012 Eowyn Ivey. Reproduced with permission
of the Licensor through PLSclear and by permission of Reagan Arthur Books, an imprint of Hachette Book Group, Inc.*

*First interview on page 109 adapted from "Of the life of an orphan girl, a street-seller",
London Labour and the London Poor, volume 1 by Henry Mayhew, published in the 1840s.*

*Second interview on page 109 adapted from "Of children sent out as street-sellers by their parents",
London Labour and the London Poor, volume 1 by Henry Mayhew, published in the 1840s.*

Poem used on page 192 'Ghosts' by Robert Service. Used by courtesy of Anne Longepe, Robert W. Service Estate

*Poem used on page 195: 'At Sea'. The poem was published in 2003 by
Arrowhead Press in Jennifer Copley's collection 'House by the Sea'.*

Article entitled 'Confessions of a Nanny' on page 210 © Copyright Guardian News & Media Ltd 2025

*Letter written by Charlotte Brontë on page 211 from "Charlotte Brontë and
Her Circle", by Clement K. Shorter, 1896 (pages 80-82).*

*Poem used on page 236: For a Five-Year Old by Fleur Adcock from Poems 1960-2000 (Bloodaxe Books, 2000).
Reproduced with permission of Bloodaxe Books www.bloodaxebooks.com*

Poem used on page 237 from 'The Beautiful Lie' by Sheenagh Pugh (Seren, 2009)

ISBN: 978 1 78908 876 2

Clipart from Corel®
Printed by Elanders Ltd, Newcastle upon Tyne.

Based on the classic CGP style created by Richard Parsons.

Text, design, layout and original illustrations © Coordination Group Publications Ltd. (CGP) 2025
All rights reserved.

Photocopying more than one section of this book is not permitted, even if you have a CLA licence.
Extra copies are available from CGP with next day delivery • 0800 1712 712 • www.cgpbooks.co.uk

How To Use This Book

This book tells you how to deal with even the trickiest English questions that might come up in your GCSEs.

Check whether you're doing **one** English GCSE or **two**

1) Everybody has to study English Language. Section Two explains what you'll have to do in the exam.

2) You might also take a GCSE in English Literature. If you do, you'll read and analyse prose, drama and poetry — page 120 has information on what you'll study and how you'll be assessed.

3) This book will help you prepare for both GCSEs. Section One gives advice on how to plan and write answers for English Language and English Literature.

4) To get top grades, you need to know the correct technical terms (rhetoric, alliteration, stanza, etc.). There's a handy glossary at the back of the book that defines all the terms you'll need.

Get to grips with the **AQA English Language** course

- Section Three is about how to read, understand and select information from different types of texts.

- Section Four digs deeper into the techniques that writers use — it shows you how to pick out different features of language and structure and analyse their effects.

- Section Five guides you through how to write your own creative and non-fiction texts, such as how to structure your writing, the sort of things to include and what language to use.

- Section Six contains a sample exam and annotated graded answers for both papers 1 and 2 — it shows you what you need to do to achieve a certain mark for every question type.

- There are practice papers (with answers) for both English Language exams at the back of the book.

Get ready for the **AQA English Literature** exams

- Section Seven gives you advice on what to look for when you're studying a prose or drama text.

- Section Eight is all about the specific things you need to think about if you're reading a play, and Section Nine covers the different elements of prose texts.

- Section Ten talks you through analysing poetry, including how to compare poems.

- Section Eleven shows you how to get to grips with the poems in your Poetry Anthology, and Section Twelve is all about how to understand and analyse a poem you haven't read before.

- At the end of the book, you'll find practice papers, with answers, for both English Literature exams.

Use the **resources** in the **CGP RevisionHub** too

1) The RevisionHub has videos giving tips on how to answer each English Language practice question from Section Six. Plus, there are full-length, annotated versions of question 5 answers for both papers.

2) There are also Knowledge Organisers online for all the English Literature set texts (some of these can be found in Section Thirteen too).

3) The Revision Summary Tests in this book can also be completed online. There, you can find sample answers, assess your progress and easily keep track of the areas you need to work on.

Throughout the book there are QR codes you can scan to access your digital extras. Or if you're on a computer, go to www.cgpbooks.co.uk/blurb.

Find the CGP RevisionHub at cgpbooks.co.uk/blurb

Section One — Exam Basics

Planning Answers

Time is precious in exams. But I promise, if you take a few minutes to plan your answers, you won't regret it.

Read the question Carefully and Calmly

1) Give yourself time to read through the questions and any texts or extracts at the start of the exam.
2) Always read the questions before the texts or extracts — that way, you'll know what to look out for.
3) Make sure you're clear about what the questions are asking you to do by underlining the key words.

> What are the differences between the two main characters?

Think Critically and Pick Out key quotes

1) If you're given a text or extract, it's not enough to just read it — you need to think about the writer's choices. Here are some questions to keep in mind as you read:

- What are the writer's intentions?
- What is the overall tone?
- What is the overall structure?

Think about the form, language, audience and purpose as you read a text or extract — this will help you plan your answers.

2) It's also a good idea to pick out key words and phrases from the text that link to the question.

3) For example, if you were given a question on romantic love in your English Literature exam about the extract below, you should highlight all the quotes that show how love is portrayed:

> Romeo: If I profane with my unworthiest hand
> This holy shrine, the gentle sin is this:
> My lips, two blushing pilgrims ready stand,
> To smooth that rough touch with a tender kiss.
>
> *Romeo and Juliet* Act 1, Scene 5

Extracts in the exams will be longer than this one.

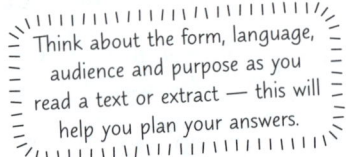

The highlighted quotes use religious imagery to portray Romeo's love, so they can be used to illustrate how romantic love is presented as sacred.

4) You should think about what these highlighted quotes tell you about the question topic. Then use this to form the basis of your exam answer.

5) Don't spend ages annotating — just focus on the bits that are most relevant to the questions.

Jot down your Main Ideas before you start writing

1) A clear plan will help you organise your ideas and make you less likely to forget something important.

2) Don't spend too long on your plan. It's only rough work, so you don't need to write in full sentences — for example, you could use a spider diagram:

3) If the question is only worth a few marks you might not need to do a plan — just jot down a few ideas.

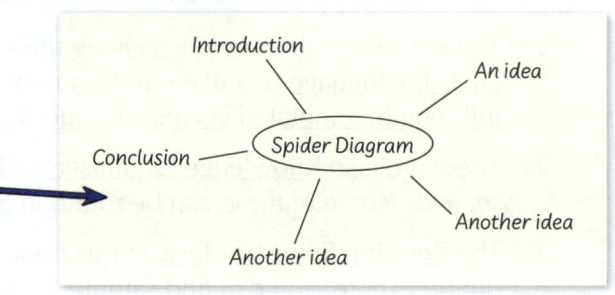

Planning Answers

Plan the Structure of your English Literature Essays

1) You'll need to write essays for both English Literature exam papers. It's important to plan the structure of each essay before you start writing so it has a clear introduction, argument and conclusion.

2) Your introduction should briefly answer the question you're writing about. It needs to make clear how you're going to tackle the topic.

3) The middle section of your essay should explain your answer in detail and back up your points with evidence.

4) Write a paragraph for each point you make. Make sure you comment on your evidence and explain how it supports your point.

5) Remember to write a conclusion — this is a paragraph at the end which sums up your main points. This will make your argument really clear to the examiner.

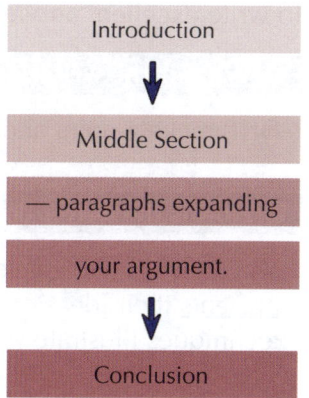

Make a Detailed Plan for Longer English Language Questions

1) You don't need to do a detailed plan for the shorter English Language questions, but you should plan longer answers. This will make sure your responses have a clear, logical structure that the examiner can follow easily.

2) The writing questions (question 5 on both English Language papers) are worth the most marks, so you should spend more time planning them.

There are marks in question 5 for how well you organise your response.

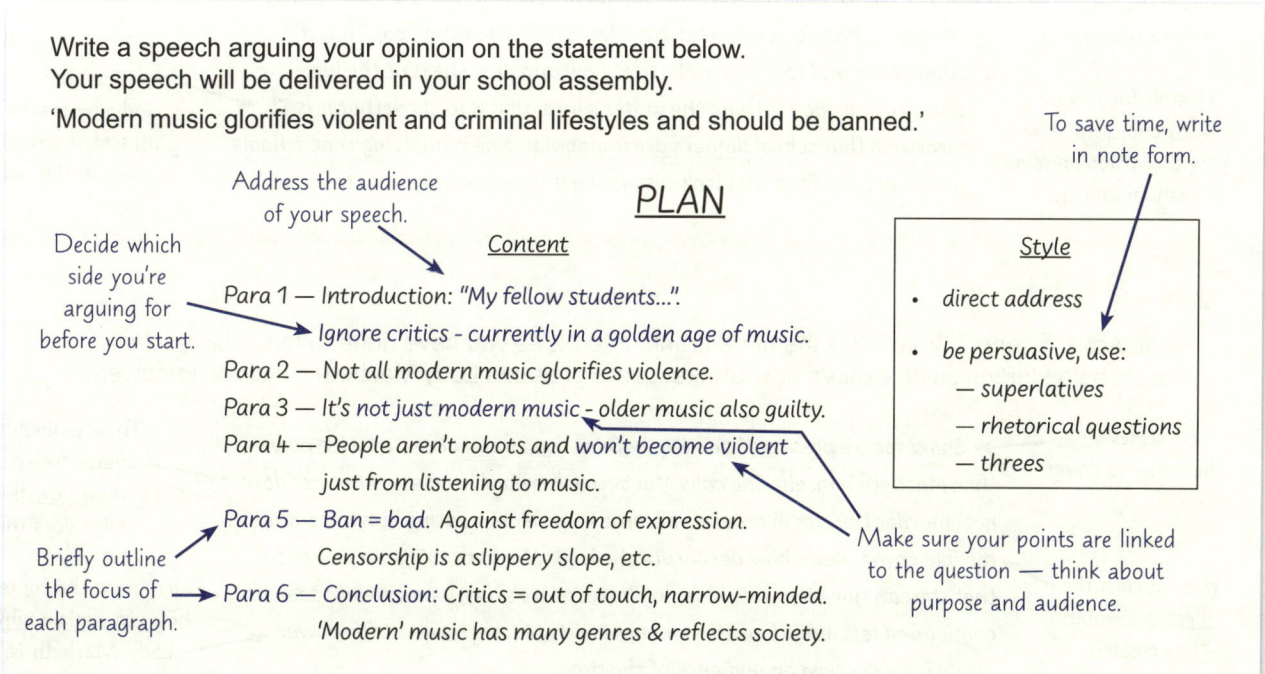

You don't need to plan every answer in these exams...

You won't need a plan for every question, but make a brief plan to help you with some of the longer questions. It'll help you to organise your ideas. Leave time to check your work at the end, too.

Structuring Paragraphs

Well-structured paragraphs help you stay on topic and pick up marks. It's important to master them.

Each Paragraph should answer What, How and Why

To write excellent answers for both English Language and English Literature, just think What How Why.

1. What is the writer doing?

First, make a point about what the writer's message is or what they're trying to say or show in the text.

2. How is the writer doing it?

You then need to give evidence to support your point, showing how the writer presents their ideas or information. Think about how language or structure techniques illustrate your point, and how the writer's methods create an effect.

3. Why is the writer doing it?

Finally, explain why the writer might have used those methods. You could think about what the effect on the reader is, what the writer's intention is, or what the purpose of the text is.

> Don't worry if you've been taught a different structure, like P.E.A., P.E.E.D. or P.E.T.A.L. As long as you're considering what the writer is doing, how the ideas are presented and why they're writing, then you're on the right track.

In each paragraph, make sure you discuss how and why the writer creates effects. This will show the examiner that you really understand and have thought about the text. Here are a couple of examples:

Explain how the writer uses language to describe school dinners.

This states what the writer's message is. → The writer believes that the quality of school dinners is inadequate. She says school food is "pallid, tasteless pap". The word "pap" has a disgusted sound to it. It emphasises how appalled she is at the low quality of the food. I think the writer's intention is to show that it isn't surprising that school dinners are unpopular. She is implying that schools should provide food that isn't disgusting if they want children to eat it.

This bit focuses on a word choice to show how the writer presents school dinners.

This bit explores the writer's intentions and why they've presented school dinners in this way.

Read Act 1, Scene 7, from "Was the hope drunk..." to "... as you have done to this." Using this extract as a starting point, explore how Shakespeare presents Lady Macbeth's attitude to power.

This states what the writer is doing. → Shakespeare presents Lady Macbeth as even more obsessed with power than Macbeth himself. She calls Macbeth a "coward" and says that he "dare not" murder Duncan in order to become king. Manipulating him to commit a terrible crime shows how desperate she is for Macbeth to attain power so that she can rule alongside him. In Shakespeare's day, women were seen as gentler and less ambitious than men, so Lady Macbeth's quest for power would have shocked an audience of the time.

This explains the effect the writer has created.

These embedded quotes (see p.5) show how the writer does this.

Referencing the context helps to explain why Lady Macbeth is presented in this way.

Your paragraphs should follow a clear structure...

Stick with a solid paragraph structure like What How Why to help your answers stay focused on the exam question. There are lots of other helpful structures out there too — use the one you've been taught.

Using Evidence

Good answers are fully supported by specific details from the text. Here are some tips on how to do that:

Use **Evidence** from the text to **Back Up** your points

1) Whenever you make a new point, you need to use details from the text to back it up.
2) You should try to use a mix of different sorts of evidence.
3) If you're using quotes, try to keep them short. It'll really impress the examiner if you embed them in a sentence, like this:

> *The writer refers to the situation as "indefensible", suggesting that he is extremely critical of the way it has been handled.*

Using short quotes can show that you've carefully selected your evidence. Embedding them helps your analysis flow better and sound more sophisticated.

4) Paraphrased details from the text also work well as evidence. You just need to describe one of the writer's techniques, or one of the text's features, in your own words, like this:

> *Tennyson uses a rhetorical question in the final stanza, which emphasises the heroism of the Light Brigade.*

5) Here are a couple of examples to show you how to include evidence from the text in your answer:

Explain how the writer uses language to describe the fire.

Embedded quotes show that you've carefully considered your answer.

> The writer uses various linguistic devices to demonstrate how powerful the fire is. At the start of the extract, he paints a vivid picture of the fire as a "pageant" of colour. He then uses a metaphor to equate the destructive power of the fire with that of a beast that is tearing down the workshop and "devouring" it. All of these images make the fire seem impressive and potent.

Your evidence could just be a description of one of the writer's techniques.

Read Act 2, Scene 1, from "If this were true..." to "And not my husband's secrets?". Using this extract as a starting point, write about how Shakespeare presents femininity in *Julius Caesar*.

Embedding short quotes will help your answer to flow smoothly.

> In 'Julius Caesar', femininity appears to be defined by its weakness. For example, in Act 2, Scene 1, Portia believes that she is a strong person despite her gender rather than because of it. She states: "I grant I am a woman, but withal / A woman that Lord Brutus took to wife". The verb "grant" shows that she sees being a woman as a failing, which is only overcome by her position as Brutus's "wife" and also as "Cato's daughter". It is clear she believes these men in her life are the primary source of her strength: it is because of how she is "fathered" and "husbanded" that she is able to be "stronger than" other women. This shows that she considers femininity to be inherently weaker than masculinity.

If you use a longer quote, make sure you copy it correctly and use the correct punctuation.

Use quotes and paraphrased details to support your points...

Referencing specific details from the text is really important because it'll help you to explore what the writer is trying to show. Just make sure that you go on to explain how the evidence supports your point as well.

Reading with Insight

To get the top grades, you need to show that you can 'read with insight' — you've got to make it clear that you understand more than just the obvious things. You can think of it as 'reading between the lines'.

You need to look Beyond what's Obvious

1) You may understand what happens in a text, or what it's about, but you'll need to write about more than just that in your answers.

2) You can show insight if you work out what the writer's intentions are and how they want the reader to feel.

Looking beyond what's obvious will help you explore why the writer has used certain methods — look back at p.4 for more on this.

3) Here's an example of the kind of thing you could write:

> *The rhetorical questions make the reader doubt whether homework is a good thing. The writer seems to want to make readers feel guilty.*

Think about the reasons why the writer has included certain features — show you've understood their intended effect on the reader.

4) Remember to include examples from the text to support your interpretation:

> *Darcy is portrayed as an unlikeable character in this extract. He is described as "above being pleased", hinting at his arrogance and haughtiness. However, the swiftness with which the ball-goers change their opinion of him shows their fickleness and hints that their judgement is not to be trusted.*

Try to explain how the writer creates a particular impression of a character or event. Examiners love it if you can give alternative interpretations that go beyond the obvious.

Inference means working things out from Clues

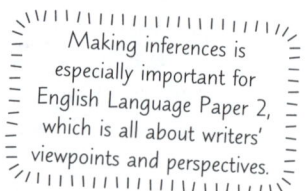

Making inferences is especially important for English Language Paper 2, which is all about writers' viewpoints and perspectives.

1) Writers don't usually make things obvious — but you can use evidence from the text to make an inference about what the writer really wants us to think.

2) You need to analyse details from the text to show what they reveal about the writer's intentions:

> *The writer uses words like "endless" and "unoriginal", which imply that he did not enjoy the film.*

The writer's language indicates their emotions and attitude.

> *In 'The Emigrée', Rumens uses irony when describing the "free city" she has moved to, emphasising that, for her, it is a restrictive place.*

The writer will often use tone to imply what they really mean — look out for irony or sarcasm.

3) You could use phrases like these to show that you've made an inference:

| The writer gives a sense of... | The writer appears to be... | This suggests that... |

Think about the effect the writer wants to create...

Everything in a text has been carefully crafted by the writer, so look for clues that reveal their intentions. Demonstrate that you understand what the writer is showing you, not just what they're telling you.

Writing Well

In these exams, it's not just what you write that's important — it's how you write as well.

Keep your writing Formal but Interesting

1) For these exams, it's important that you write in Standard English.
2) Standard English is the version of English you should use for formal writing. There are a few simple rules that you can follow to make sure you're writing in Standard English:

- Avoid using informal words and phrases (e.g. putting 'like' after sentences).
- Avoid using slang or local dialect words that some people might not understand.
- Use correct spelling, punctuation and grammar (have a look at page 8).

Use clear Explaining Words and Phrases

1) You should use explaining words and phrases to make your answers easy to follow.

- This signifies that...
- This highlights the fact that...
- This imagery reflects...
- This is reminiscent of...
- Furthermore...
- This continues the idea of...

2) Using words and phrases like these makes your writing sound more professional.
3) They're also really useful for structuring your paragraphs (see page 4). They help you to link your analysis of the writer's methods and their effects to your key idea.

Use Paragraphs to structure your answer

1) Your points need to be clearly organised and linked together. To do that you need to write in paragraphs.
2) You can use different paragraph structures to organise your points in different ways. For example:

- You could write a paragraph for every idea you want to discuss.
- You could discuss two ideas that contrast or agree with each other within a paragraph — this can be useful when comparing two texts.
- You could focus on one idea and link together lots of examples with different explanations within a paragraph.

However you structure your paragraphs, make sure you're analysing the writer's methods and the effects or intentions.

3) Linking your paragraphs together smoothly makes your writing sound confident and considered. You could use linking words like these to help you do this:

- However...
- In contrast...
- On the other hand...
- Equally...
- In the same way...
- In addition...
- Alternatively...
- Conversely...

Your answer needs to have a clear structure...
Organise your ideas into paragraphs, and use the phrases on this page to link them together smoothly. A clear structure will show the examiner that you've thought about your answer, and make it easier to read.

Spelling, Punctuation and Grammar

There are some marks available for correct use of spelling, punctuation and grammar, or SPaG, in both the English Language and Literature exams. This page should help you to avoid the most common SPaG errors...

Watch Out for these SPaG errors

You'll be marked on SPaG in Section A of both English Literature papers and Section B of the English Language papers.

Spelling

1) Avoid common spelling mistakes, like 'their', 'they're' and 'there' or 'where', 'were' and 'wear'.
2) Remember that 'affect' is a verb, but 'effect' is a noun, e.g. 'the sound effect affects the reader'.
3) Always write words out in full — avoid abbreviations like 'etc.' and 'e.g.'.
4) Make sure any information taken from the extract, including the writer's name, is spelt correctly.

Punctuation

1) Commas can be used to separate items in a list or when you've used more than one adjective. A pair of commas can also be used to separate extra information in a sentence.
2) Colons can be used to introduce a list or to add a piece of information that explains your sentence.
3) Semi-colons can separate longer phrases in a list, or they can be used to join two sentences together — as long as both sentences are about the same thing and make sense on their own.

Grammar

1) Don't change tenses in your writing by mistake.
2) Don't use double negatives, e.g. 'There wasn't no reason' should be 'There wasn't any reason'.
3) Remember 'it's' (with an apostrophe) is short for 'it is' or 'it has'. 'Its' (without an apostrophe) means 'belonging to it'.
4) Never write 'should of' — it's always 'should have', 'would have', 'could have'.
5) Start a new paragraph for each point — begin a new line and leave an indent before each paragraph.

This is how you should Correct any Mistakes

You should leave a few minutes at the end of the exams to check your work and correct any errors.

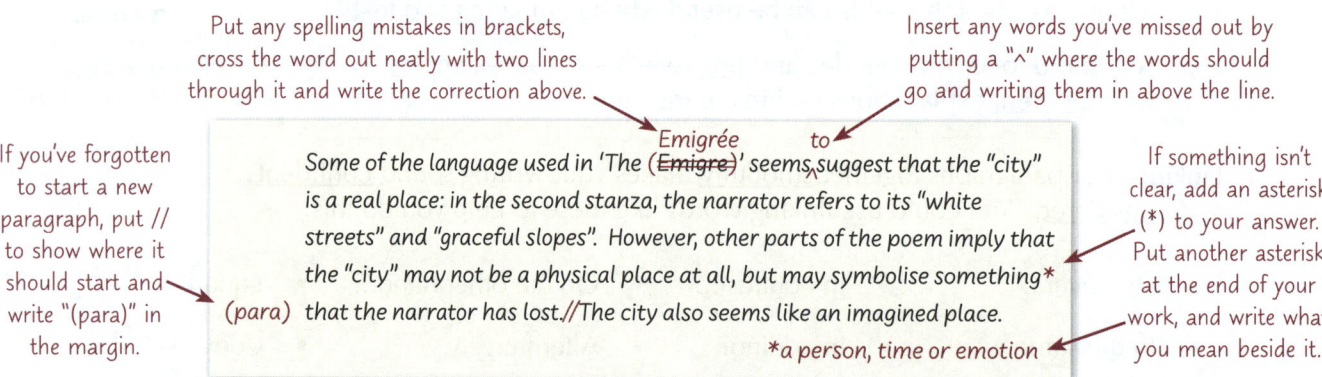

Put any spelling mistakes in brackets, cross the word out neatly with two lines through it and write the correction above.

Insert any words you've missed out by putting a "^" where the words should go and writing them in above the line.

If you've forgotten to start a new paragraph, put // to show where it should start and write "(para)" in the margin.

If something isn't clear, add an asterisk (*) to your answer. Put another asterisk at the end of your work, and write what you mean beside it.

Make sure you can spell subject-specific words...

Some of the marks in your exams are for using subject terminology (e.g. metaphor, onomatopoeia). When you're using these, you need to get the spelling correct — so make sure you learn those pesky words.

Section One — Exam Basics

Exam Basics — Knowledge Organiser

There's a lot to remember when you're doing your English exams, but luckily all the essentials are summarised on this page.

Planning Answers

Think critically as you read:
- What are the writer's intentions?
- What is the text's tone?
- What is the text's structure?

Highlight key quotes in a text.

Plan longer answers — but don't spend too much time planning. Jot down:
- Main ideas — So you don't leave anything out.
- Structure — To make sure your answer is organised.

Structuring Paragraphs

What is the writer doing? → Make a point.
- What is the writer's message?
- What is the writer trying to say or show?

How is the writer doing it? → Explain how with evidence.
- How are language or structure techniques used?
- How do the writer's methods create an effect?

Why is the writer doing it? → Explain why the writer may have presented their ideas this way. Consider:
- the effect on the reader
- the writer's intention or purpose.

Looking beyond what's obvious will show that you're being perceptive.

Reading with Insight

Think about why a text might have been written.

Make inferences to work out how the writer might want the reader to feel.

Inference — an idea worked out from clues

Analyse textual evidence

Literary features → Think about the intended effect on the reader.

Language → Word choices can indicate a writer's emotions and attitude.

Tone → Consider the feeling you get from a text. Look for bias / sarcasm.

Writing Well

Be formal — Only write in Standard English.
- Avoid slang
- Avoid informal phrases

Be clear — Use explaining words/phrases.
- This signifies...
- This reflects...
- This highlights...
- This implies...

Use paragraphs — Link your points clearly so your answer reads smoothly.
- In addition...
- However...
- Alternatively...

SPaG

Spelling
- Look out for common mistakes.
- Avoid abbreviations.
- Copy source information carefully.

Grammar
- Stay in the same tense.
- Avoid double negatives.
- Use 'its' and 'it's' correctly.
- Start a new paragraph for each new point.

Punctuation
- Don't mix up colons and semi-colons:

Colons introduce lists & add explanatory information. Semi-colons separate items in a list & link sentences.

- Use commas properly. Commas are used when:
  1. Separating items in a list.
  2. Separating extra information in a sentence.

EXAM TIP: Your answers need to be clear and easy to follow...
To get a good mark, your writing has to make sense. So that your longer answers are crystal-clear, make sure that you do a brief plan, structure your points carefully and keep an eye on your SPaG.

Revision Summary Test for Section One

Section One done already — time to test your knowledge of the exam format.
- These questions are **hard**, but they'll really help you see **how well you know your stuff**.
- Tackle the **revision summary test** below, or scan the QR code to do it **online**.
You can **track your progress** online and see **which areas need more work**.
- There are **sample answers** for the test here: www.cgpbooks.co.uk/blurb-answers

Planning, Structuring Paragraphs and Using Evidence (p.2-5)

1) Should you read the questions or the text(s) first in the exam? Why?
2) Is the statement below true or false? Give reasons for your answer.
   You should make a detailed plan for every question in these exams.
3) Describe the purpose of these paragraphs in an English Literature essay:
   a) the introduction
   b) the conclusion
4) Briefly describe how to make a plan for an English Language creative writing question.
5) Explain what you should write for each part of a paragraph that uses the
   What How Why structure.
6) Briefly describe two different ways you can provide evidence to support your answer.

Reading with Insight and Writing Well (p.6-7)

7) Give two examples of things you could comment on to show that you are reading with insight.
8) What does 'inference' mean?
9) Give an example of a phrase you could use to show that you've made an inference.
10) Write down two features of Standard English.
11) List three explaining words or phrases you can use to make your answers easy to follow.
12) Give two examples of linking words or phrases you could use at the start of a paragraph to show:
    a) that the point being made supports the previous paragraph
    b) that the point being made contrasts with the previous paragraph.

Spelling, Punctuation and Grammar (p.8)

13) Which of the following sentences is correct? Explain why.
    a) The metaphor at the start of the second paragraph has a startling effect on the reader.
    b) The metaphor at the start of the second paragraph has a startling affect on the reader.
14) Does the following sentence use a semi-colon correctly? Explain why / why not.
    Gazing out of the window; Tomek dreamt of the day when he would be free from revision.
15) Explain why a comma is needed in each of these sentences:
    a) Elton went to the supermarket to buy bread, milk, tomatoes and cheese.
    b) Becca, who has just turned 17, wants to learn to drive.
16) What is the difference between 'its' and 'it's'?
17) What is the grammatical error in the following sentences? What should each one say instead?
    a) I never told you to use no apostrophes in that sentence.
    b) You could of used a better paragraph structure to improve your answer.
18) Give three common errors you should look out for when you check your answers for:
    a) spelling   b) punctuation   c) grammar
19) Explain how to make a correction in each of the following situations:
    a) When a new paragraph should start
    b) When a word or two is missing
    c) When something isn't clear

Section One — Exam Basics

Section Two — Introduction to English Language

Exam Structure

Understanding the structure of your exams is really important. You need to know what to expect on the day.

You will sit **Two** different English Language papers

1) Paper 1 focuses on fiction and Paper 2 focuses on non-fiction.
2) You will have 1 hour 45 minutes for each paper.
3) Both papers are split into two sections — Section A covers reading, and Section B covers writing.
4) Each paper is worth 50% of the English Language GCSE.

Both papers have **Five** questions...

Have a look at pages 13-18 for more detail on the individual questions on each Language paper.

For paper 1, there will be a question paper and a separate insert containing one extract from a work of literary fiction — it will be from either the twentieth or twenty-first century.

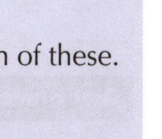

You should spend the first 15 minutes reading through the source and the questions.

Section A: Reading is worth 40 marks. It has four questions:

- Question 1 is worth 4 marks. You should spend about 5 minutes on this.
- Questions 2 and 3 are worth 8 marks each. You should spend about 10 minutes on each of these.
- Question 4 is worth 20 marks. You should spend about 20 minutes on this.

Section B: Writing only has one question (there'll be a choice of tasks, but you only need to do one):

- Question 5 is worth 40 marks. You should spend 45 minutes on this.

For paper 2, there will be a question paper and a separate insert containing two non-fiction sources — one from the nineteenth century and one from either the twentieth or twenty-first century (whichever wasn't used in paper 1).

If you have any time left at the end of the exam, use it to check through your work.

You should spend the first 15 minutes reading through the sources and the questions.

Section A: Reading is worth 40 marks. It has four questions:

- Question 1 is worth 4 marks. You should spend about 5 minutes on this.
- Question 2 is worth 8 marks. You should spend about 8 minutes on this.
- Question 3 is worth 12 marks. You should spend about 12 minutes on this.
- Question 4 is worth 16 marks. You should spend about 20 minutes on this.

Section B: Writing only has one question:

- Question 5 is worth 40 marks. You should spend 45 minutes on this.

You need to know what each paper is going to look like...

Make sure you've really understood this page, especially the number of marks available for each question — if you allow just over one minute per mark, you'll be on track to get everything finished in time.

The Assessment Objectives

Now you understand the basic structure of the English Language exams, it's time to look at each question in more detail. First, here's the background to what the questions are about — the assessment objectives.

Each Assessment Objective refers to a different Skill

1) The assessment objectives are the things that AQA say you need to do to get good marks in the exam.
2) They'll come in handy when you're working out what you need to do for each of the questions — there's more on how each of the assessment objectives apply to the individual questions on pages 13-18.
3) The English Language exams test assessment objectives 1 to 6. Here's a brief description of each of them:

Assessment Objective 1

- Pick out and understand pieces of explicit and implicit information from the texts.
- Collect and put together information from different texts.

Assessment Objective 2

- Explain how writers use language and structure to achieve their purpose and influence readers.
- Use technical terms to support your analysis of language and structure.

Assessment Objective 3

- Compare different writers' ideas and perspectives.
- Compare the methods used by different writers to convey their ideas.

Assessment Objective 4

- Critically evaluate texts, giving a personal opinion about how successful the writing is.
- Provide detailed evidence from the text to support your opinion.

Assessment Objective 5

- Write clearly and imaginatively, adapting your tone and style for various purposes and audiences.
- Organise your writing into a clear structure.

Assessment Objective 6

- Use a wide variety of sentence structures and vocabulary, so that your writing is clear and purposeful.
- Write accurately, paying particular attention to spelling, punctuation and grammar.

Remember what the examiner is looking for...

These assessment objectives are the basis for the Language exams (and their mark schemes), so try to keep them in mind as you revise. The next six pages will show you how to apply them to each of the questions.

Paper 1 — Questions 1 and 2

This section is full of expert advice on answering each exam question. The questions here look a bit different to the ones in the real exam (which you can find on AQA's website), but they'll still help you to get prepared.

You need to Find Information for Question 1

1) Question 1 will test the first part of assessment objective 1 — it will test your ability to find information or ideas in the text.

2) It will be made up of four multiple-choice questions. You will be given three different possible answers each time, and you will have to tick the box next to the correct answer.

3) Most of the information you'll be asked to find will be explicit (it will be obviously written out in the extract), but keep an eye out for implicit information too (information that needs to be worked out from what is said in the text).

4) The question will usually look something like this:

> Q1   Use **lines 1-7** of the text to answer the questions below. ← *The right answers to all four parts of the question are in this section of the text.*
> For each question, tick the correct option.
> There is one correct answer per question.
>
> Q1.1   What is strange about the inside of the house? ← *There will be four questions like this where you'll choose one of the possible answers.*
> 　　　There is no furniture　☐
> 　　　There are no doors　　☐
> 　　　It seems uninhabited　☐
> 　　　　　　　　　　　　　　　**[1 mark]** ← *Each multiple-choice question is worth one mark. In total, there are four marks available.*

PAPER 1 Q1

Question 2 is about the Effects of Language on the Reader

1) This question will test the language part of assessment objective 2 — you'll need to write about how the writer uses language to achieve effects and influence the reader.

   The structure part of assessment objective 2 will be covered in paper 1, question 3 (see page 14).

2) The question will usually look something like this:

PAPER 1 Q2

> *This part of the question will change depending on the purpose of the text.* 　　　*Make sure you only analyse this part of the text.*
>
> Q2   Explain how the writer uses language to describe **the atmosphere in the room** in **lines 11-20**.
>
> You may wish to explore how the writer uses particular language techniques, specific words and phrases, or different types of sentence.
>
> 　　　　　　　　　　　　　　　**[8 marks]**

For questions that ask 'how' the writer has done something, you need to write about the methods the writer has used and their effect on the reader. In this case you need to focus on the effects of the writer's language on the reader.

Make sure your answer includes quotes that demonstrate each of the things listed here.

Try to use technical terms to describe the writer's use of language.

Question 1 is only worth four marks, but it's still important...

Acing question 1 is a good way to gain some easy marks before you have to tackle the more complex analysis questions. For question 2, remember to cover all of the points that are given in the question.

Section Two — Introduction to English Language

Paper 1 — Questions 3 and 4

Question 3 is similar to question 2, except it's about structure rather than language. After that, you have to answer question 4, which is worth 20 marks. You'll need to write more for this.

Question 3 asks about the writer's use of Structure

1) This question will test the structure part of assessment objective 2 — you'll need to write about how the writer uses structure to create an effect.

2) The question will usually look something like this:

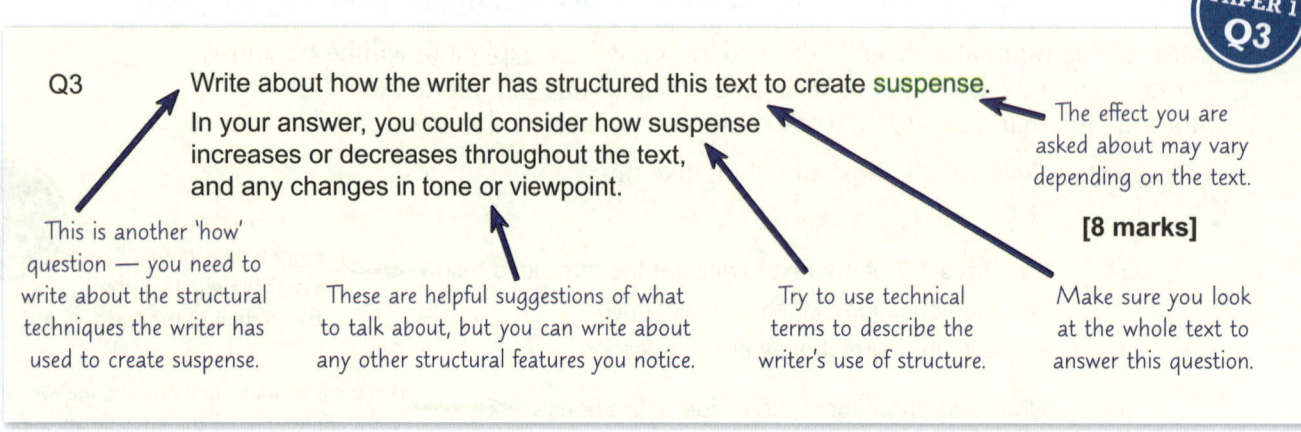

You need to give a Personal Judgement for Question 4

1) This question will test assessment objective 4 — you'll need to evaluate the text critically and give a personal response.

2) The question will usually look something like this:

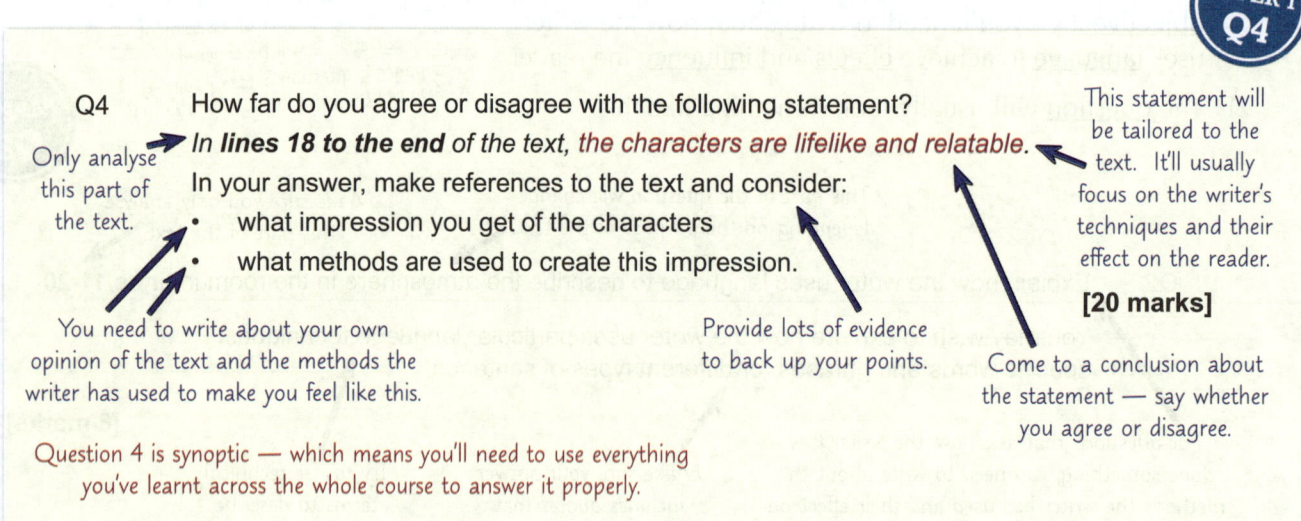

Don't forget to give your opinion in question 4...

To get all the marks for question 4, you need to provide a personal evaluation of the text and back it up with detailed evidence — use a range of short examples from the text to show what you've based your opinion on.

Section Two — Introduction to English Language

Paper 1 — Question 5

Question 5 is the writing question in paper 1, and it's worth 40 marks.

You only need to do One of the tasks for Question 5

1) Question 5 is a creative writing task that will test assessment objectives 5 and 6 — examiners will be looking for you to produce an interesting, well-organised and accurately written piece.

2) There will be a choice of tasks, but you only need to do one.

3) The tasks will usually be on a similar theme to the text from the reading section.

4) The question might look something like this:

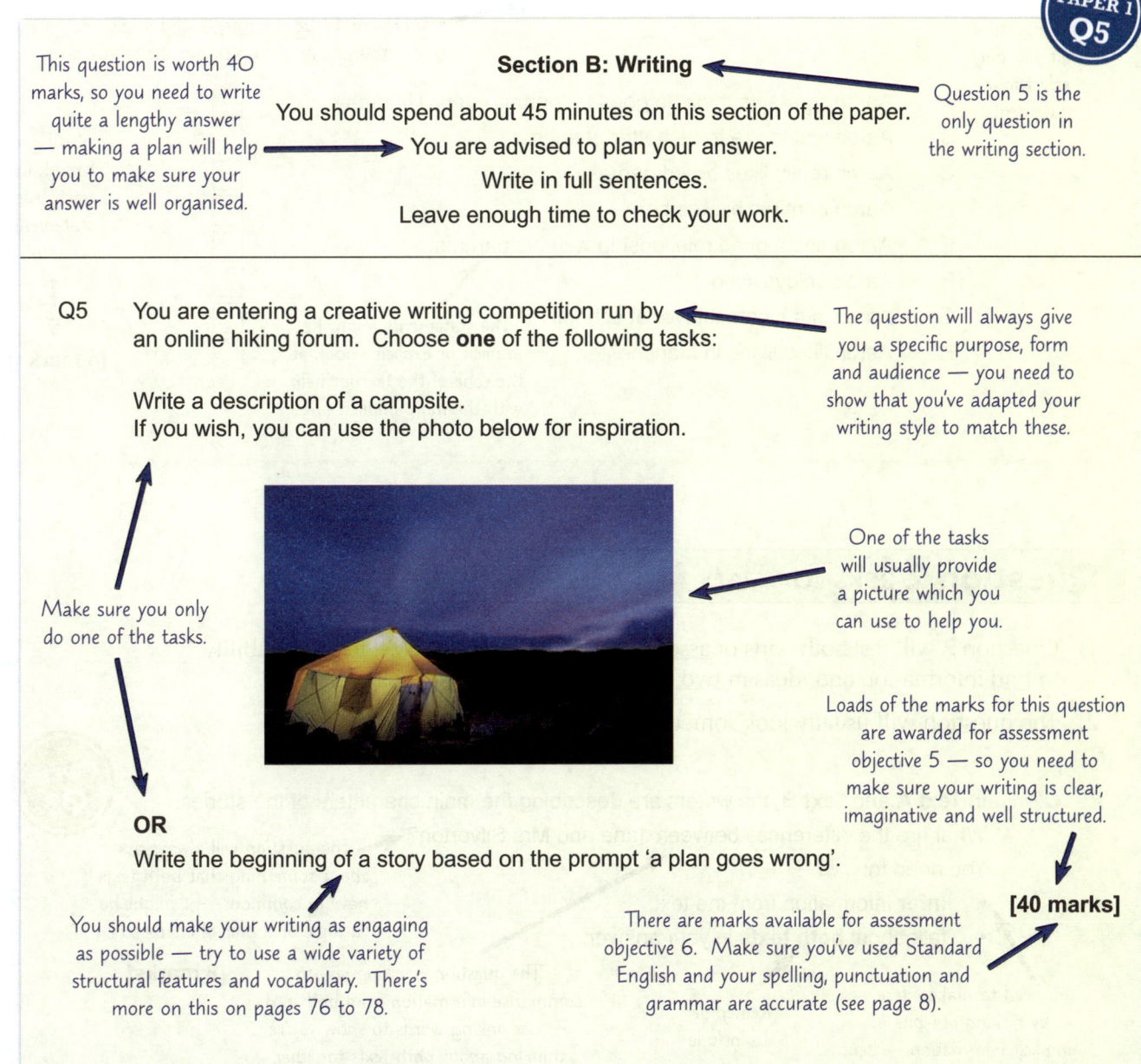

This question is worth 40 marks, so you need to write quite a lengthy answer — making a plan will help you to make sure your answer is well organised.

Section B: Writing

You should spend about 45 minutes on this section of the paper.
You are advised to plan your answer.
Write in full sentences.
Leave enough time to check your work.

Question 5 is the only question in the writing section.

Q5   You are entering a creative writing competition run by an online hiking forum. Choose **one** of the following tasks:

Write a description of a campsite.
If you wish, you can use the photo below for inspiration.

The question will always give you a specific purpose, form and audience — you need to show that you've adapted your writing style to match these.

Make sure you only do one of the tasks.

One of the tasks will usually provide a picture which you can use to help you.

Loads of the marks for this question are awarded for assessment objective 5 — so you need to make sure your writing is clear, imaginative and well structured.

OR

Write the beginning of a story based on the prompt 'a plan goes wrong'.

You should make your writing as engaging as possible — try to use a wide variety of structural features and vocabulary. There's more on this on pages 76 to 78.

There are marks available for assessment objective 6. Make sure you've used Standard English and your spelling, punctuation and grammar are accurate (see page 8).

[40 marks]

Question 5 is focused on your creative writing skills...

In this part of the paper, the examiners want you to show that you can write imaginatively. Make sure you use plenty of descriptive language and try to produce as interesting a piece of writing as you possibly can.

Paper 2 — Questions 1 and 2

Paper 2 starts with two questions that test your ability to find information and ideas in the sources.

Choose **Four True Statements** in **Question 1**

1) This question will test the first part of assessment objective 1 — you will need to show that you can find information or ideas in the text.

2) The question will usually look something like this:

Remember to read the question carefully — in the real exam, you may be asked to shade the boxes, not tick them.

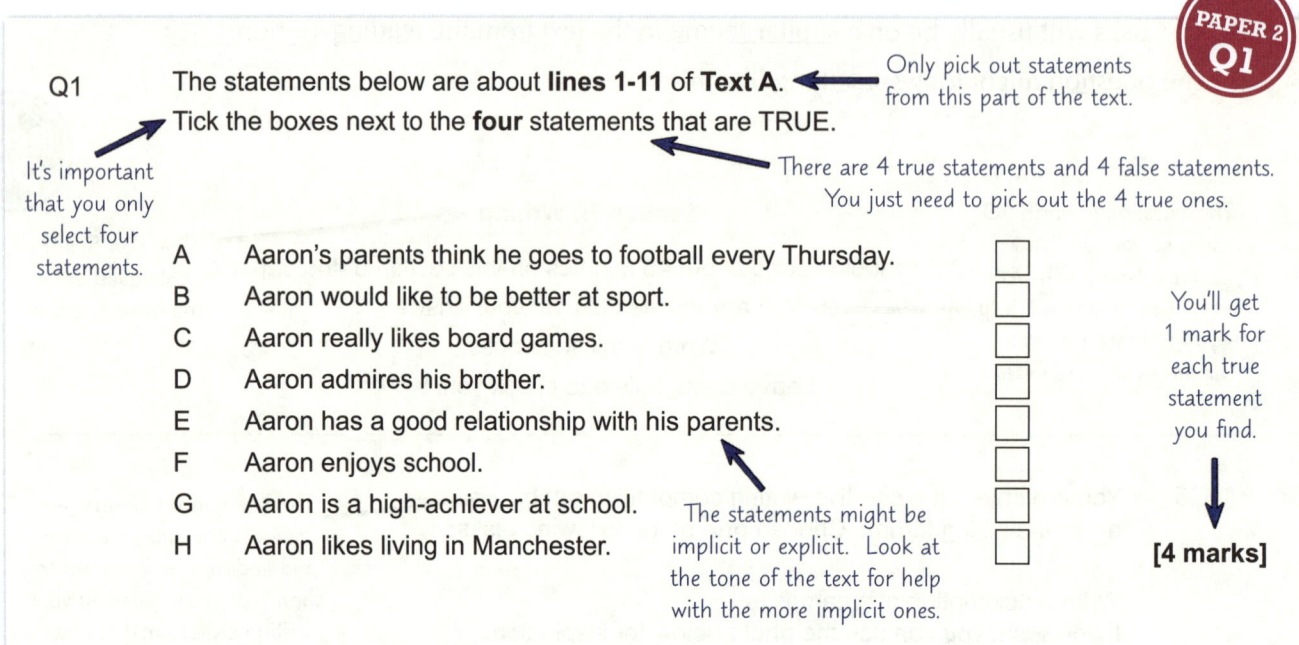

Q1 The statements below are about **lines 1-11** of **Text A**.
Tick the boxes next to the **four** statements that are TRUE.

- *Only pick out statements from this part of the text.*
- *There are 4 true statements and 4 false statements. You just need to pick out the 4 true ones.*
- *It's important that you only select four statements.*

A Aaron's parents think he goes to football every Thursday.
B Aaron would like to be better at sport.
C Aaron really likes board games.
D Aaron admires his brother.
E Aaron has a good relationship with his parents.
F Aaron enjoys school.
G Aaron is a high-achiever at school.
H Aaron likes living in Manchester.

The statements might be implicit or explicit. Look at the tone of the text for help with the more implicit ones.

You'll get 1 mark for each true statement you find.

[4 marks]

Question 2 asks for facts from **Both** sources

1) Question 2 will test both parts of assessment objective 1 — it will test your ability to find information and ideas in two sources and summarise what you find.

2) The question will usually look something like this:

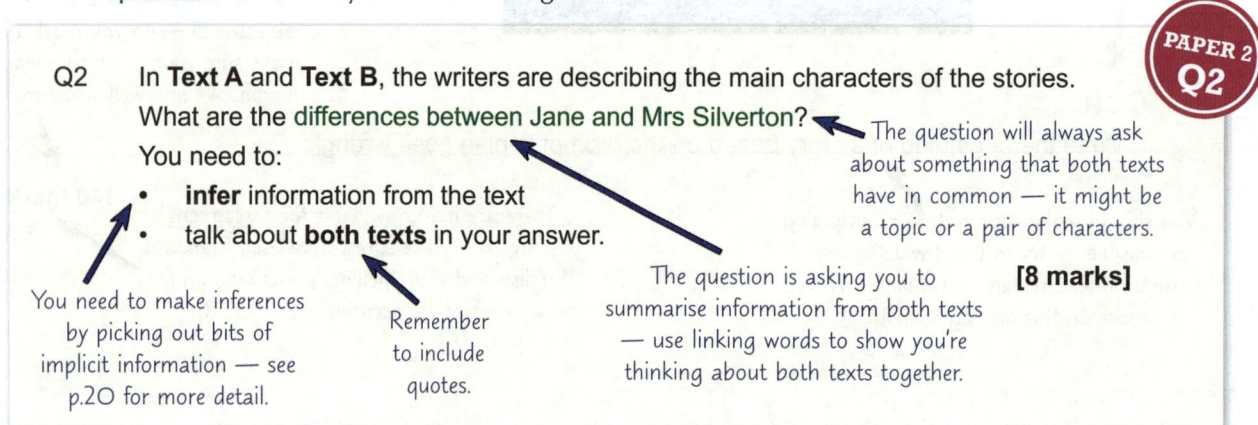

Q2 In **Text A** and **Text B**, the writers are describing the main characters of the stories.
What are the differences between Jane and Mrs Silverton?
You need to:
• **infer** information from the text
• talk about **both texts** in your answer.

The question will always ask about something that both texts have in common — it might be a topic or a pair of characters.

You need to make inferences by picking out bits of implicit information — see p.20 for more detail.

Remember to include quotes.

The question is asking you to summarise information from both texts — use linking words to show you're thinking about both texts together.

[8 marks]

Prove that you know what's going on in the two source texts...

For these two questions, you need to show that you've really understood the texts. In question 1, select the statements you're sure about first. In question 2, try to make perceptive links between the sources.

Section Two — Introduction to English Language

Paper 2 — Questions 3 and 4

Question 3 on paper 2 is pretty similar to question 2 on paper 1 (see page 13) — it's all about how the writer has used language. Question 4 is about two writers' attitudes and how they have conveyed them.

Question 3 covers the Effects of the writer's use of Language

1) This question will test the language part of assessment objective 2 — you'll need to write about how the writer uses language to achieve effects and influence the reader.

2) The question will usually look something like this:

PAPER 2 Q3

Q3 Explain how the writer uses language to describe Jenny's frustration in lines 17-27 of Text B.

[12 marks]

- This is another 'how' question, so you need to write about the techniques the writer has used to achieve their purpose. Have a look at paper 1, questions 2 and 3 for other examples of 'how' questions.
- Your answer should use carefully selected quotes and technical terms to back up your points.
- Try to refer specifically to particular words, phrases, language features and techniques.
- This part of the question will change depending on the content of the text.

Question 4 is synoptic — which means you'll need to use everything you've learnt across the whole course to answer it properly.

Question 4 asks you to Compare Perspectives

1) This question will test assessment objective 3 — you'll need to identify and compare different writers' attitudes and perspectives, and how they're conveyed.

2) The question will usually look something like this:

PAPER 2 Q4

Q4 This question is about Text A and Text B, where both writers talk about healthy eating.

Compare how they convey their different attitudes to healthy eating.
You may wish to explore what the writers' attitudes are and what methods they use to convey their attitudes.
You should use examples from both texts.

[16 marks]

- Make sure you cover everything mentioned here — you need to write about what the writers' attitudes are and how they are similar or different.
- Make sure you give quotes and examples from both sources.
- This part of the question will change depending on the topics covered in the texts.
- Try to identify how the writers have used language and structure to show subtle differences in their attitudes. This will show the examiner that you've really understood the text.

Pay attention to how many marks each question is worth...

Question 3 is very similar to question 2 on paper 1, but don't forget — it's worth quite a few more marks.
Question 4 is your chance to bring all your skills together and really show that you've understood the texts.

Paper 2 — Question 5

Paper 2, question 5 is another 40-mark writing task. This time, you need to give your own perspective on a theme. The theme will be similar to the one that was covered by the two sources in the reading section.

The last question is a **Writing** task

1) Question 5 is a writing task that will test assessment objectives 5 and 6 — examiners will be looking for you to produce an interesting, well-organised and accurately written piece.

2) You'll need to write in the form of a non-fiction text, such as a newspaper article.

3) The question will ask you to give your own perspective on a similar theme to the one covered in the reading section of the paper.

4) The question will usually look something like this:

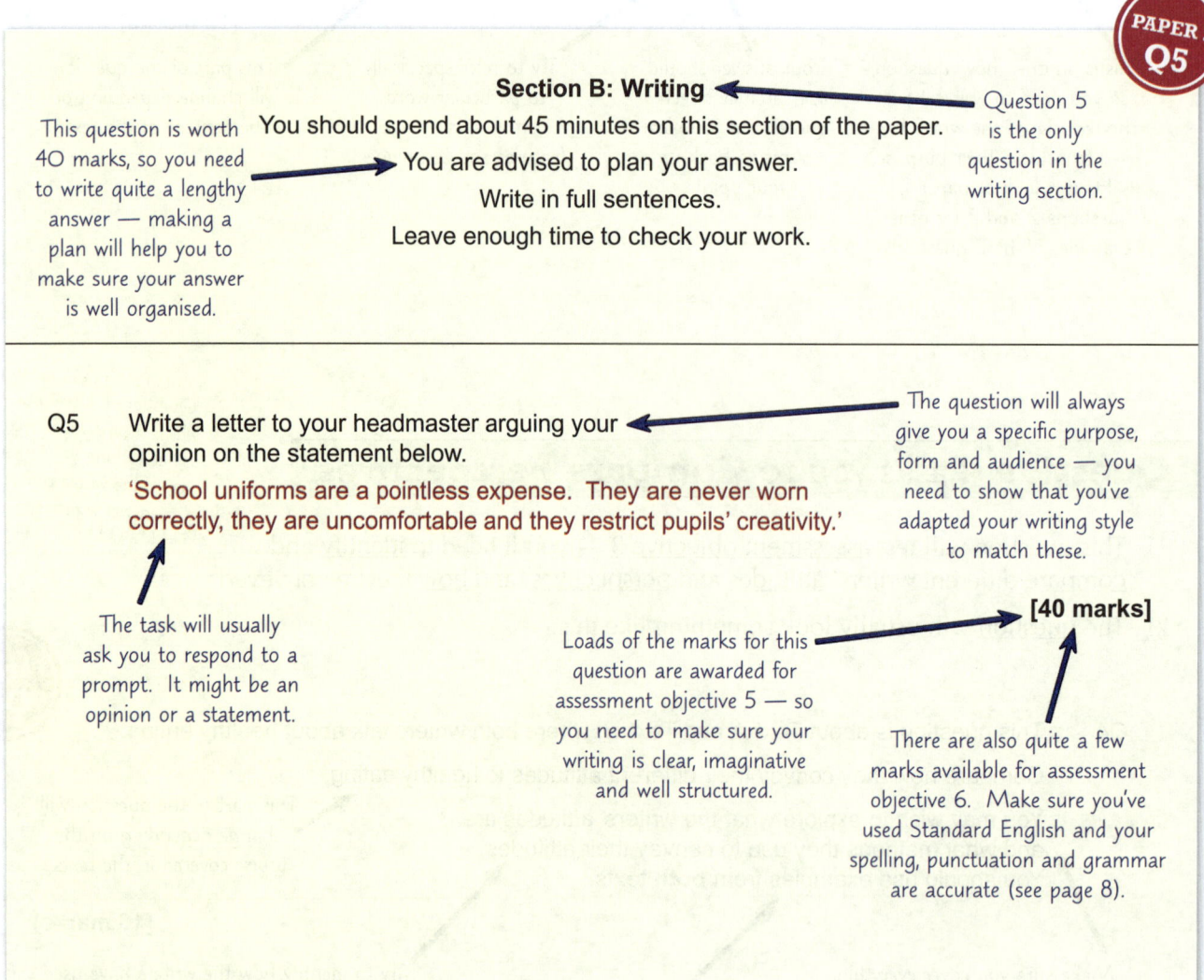

Section B: Writing

You should spend about 45 minutes on this section of the paper.
You are advised to plan your answer.
Write in full sentences.
Leave enough time to check your work.

This question is worth 40 marks, so you need to write quite a lengthy answer — making a plan will help you to make sure your answer is well organised.

Question 5 is the only question in the writing section.

Q5 Write a letter to your headmaster arguing your opinion on the statement below.

'School uniforms are a pointless expense. They are never worn correctly, they are uncomfortable and they restrict pupils' creativity.'

[40 marks]

The task will usually ask you to respond to a prompt. It might be an opinion or a statement.

Loads of the marks for this question are awarded for assessment objective 5 — so you need to make sure your writing is clear, imaginative and well structured.

The question will always give you a specific purpose, form and audience — you need to show that you've adapted your writing style to match these.

There are also quite a few marks available for assessment objective 6. Make sure you've used Standard English and your spelling, punctuation and grammar are accurate (see page 8).

You will need to adapt your tone, style and register...

Your answer to question 5 needs to be well-suited to the purpose, form and audience given in the question, so think carefully about which tone, style and register (see pages 42-43) would be the most appropriate.

English Language Exams — Knowledge Organiser

Phew...that was a lot. Never fear — I've summarised all the key information about the English Language exams on this page.

Exam Structure

Basics

- There are two language papers — each worth 50% of your final mark.
- Each paper lasts 1 hour 45 minutes.
- Each paper is worth 80 marks.
- Both papers have two sections:

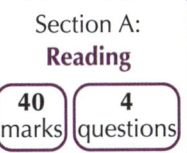 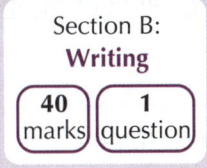

Section A: Reading — 40 marks, 4 questions
Section B: Writing — 40 marks, 1 question

What you'll be given

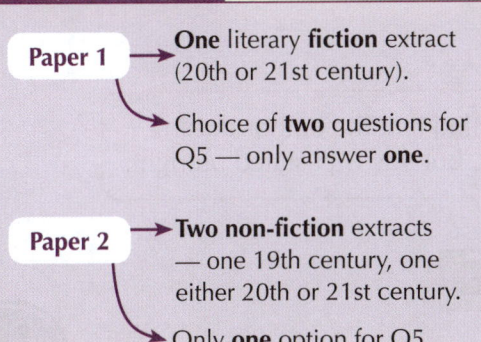

Paper 1 → One literary fiction extract (20th or 21st century).
→ Choice of two questions for Q5 — only answer one.

Paper 2 → Two non-fiction extracts — one 19th century, one either 20th or 21st century.
→ Only one option for Q5.

Assessment Objectives

Not every AO is tested by every question.

» Pick out explicit and implicit information.
» Put together information from different texts.

» Explain how writers use language & structure to achieve a purpose/influence readers.
» Use technical terms to support analysis.

» Compare writers' ideas & perspectives.
» Compare writers' methods.

» Evaluate texts and give opinions.
» Provide evidence to support opinions.

» Write clearly for a specific purpose & audience.
» Structure and carefully organise your response.

» Use a wide variety of sentence structures and vocabulary.
» Write accurately, with good SPaG.

Paper 1

Section	Question	Marks	Suggested time	Question focus	AOs tested
A	1	4	5 mins	Four multiple-choice questions.	AO1
A	2	8	10 mins	The writer's use of language.	AO2
A	3	8	10 mins	The writer's use of structure.	AO2
A	4	20	20 mins	Evaluating a statement.	AO4
B	5	40	45 mins	Responding to one writing prompt.	AO5, AO6

Paper 2

Section	Question	Marks	Suggested time	Question focus	AOs tested
A	1	4	5 mins	Choosing four true statements.	AO1
A	2	8	8 mins	Summarising two texts.	AO1
A	3	12	12 mins	The writer's use of language.	AO2
A	4	16	20 mins	Comparing writers' perspectives.	AO3
B	5	40	45 mins	Responding to a writing prompt.	AO5, AO6

Make sure you know what you need to do in the exam...

If you don't know what examiners are looking for, it's hard to be sure you're meeting the criteria for the top marks. Double-check that you're answering the question and addressing the right AOs.

Section Three — English Language: Understanding Texts

Information and Ideas

These two pages will help you with assessment objective 1 (see page 12). This page is about picking out information from a text, and the next page is about summarising information from two different texts.

Information and ideas can be Explicit or Implicit

1) The first thing you need to be able to do in order to analyse a text is to understand the basic things it's telling you.

2) This will help you to pick up some easy marks for paper 1, question 1 and paper 2, question 1.

3) The information and ideas you need to pick out will either be explicit or implicit.

4) Explicit information is clearly written in the text.

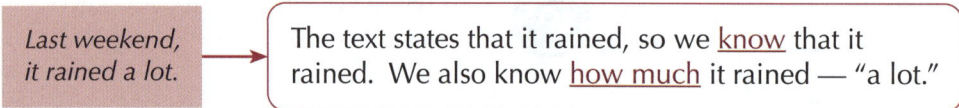

Last weekend, it rained a lot. → The text states that it rained, so we know that it rained. We also know how much it rained — "a lot."

5) Implicit information needs a little more detective work — you'll need to work it out from what is said in the text.

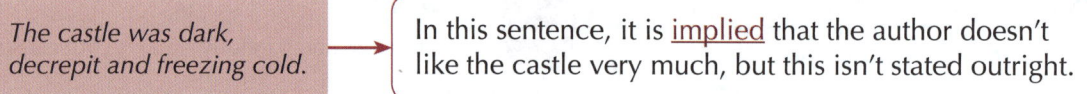

The castle was dark, decrepit and freezing cold. → In this sentence, it is implied that the author doesn't like the castle very much, but this isn't stated outright.

Look for Key Words as you Read the text

PAPER 1 Q1

Q1   Use the extract to answer the questions below.
For each question, tick the correct option. There is one correct answer per question.

> Brian had hated school. He often thought back to the dreary breezeblock walls, the freezing classrooms and the constant drone of the centuries-old plumbing.
> St Mary's had been the closest school to Brian's house, but that was an all-girls school. This meant that every morning Brian had had to withstand the torment of a fifteen-minute bus journey across town to Beeches Hall — the boys' school. This bus journey would have been perfectly tolerable had it not been for the driver: a peculiar, unpleasant man with a severely erratic driving style.

Look for key words from the question to help you find information in the text.

Q1.1 What is the school plumbing like?

Dreary ☐
Cold ☐
Noisy ☑

This fact isn't explicitly written in the text, but it is implied.

Put a tick in one of the answer boxes.

Q1.2 What is Brian's school called?

St Mary's ☐
Beeches Hall ☑
Breezeblock ☐

Be careful. This fact is explicit information but the text gives the name of two schools. You need to work out which one Brian goes to.

Paper 2, question 1 will test finding explicit and implicit information...

Remember — *explicit* information is clearly stated in the text, whereas *implicit* information is implied. You'll need to be able to spot both kinds of information in the texts to meet the criteria for assessment objective 1.

Summarising and Linking

For paper 2, question 2, you need to link ideas from two texts — you can't just point information out.

You'll also need to Summarise information

1) Paper 2, question 2 will ask you to pick out information and ideas on the <u>same topic</u> from two <u>different texts</u>. You might need to make <u>inferences</u> to find information — it won't always be <u>explicitly</u> stated.

2) You'll then need to <u>summarise</u> the <u>similarities</u> or <u>differences</u> in what you've picked out.

3) You'll also need to <u>back up</u> your points with examples from the text.

4) <u>Linking words</u> are essential for writing about similarities and differences, as they show that you've made a <u>comparison</u>.

These are a few examples of linking words, but there are plenty more.

To show similarities:	To show differences:
• Similarly • Likewise • Equally • Also	• Whereas • Although • However • But

Make Links between the texts

PAPER 2 Q2

Q2   In **Text A** and **Text B**, the writers are presenting an interaction between a father and a son.
What are the differences between Andrew and Richard?

Look out for obvious differences between the two texts, e.g. Andrew's and Richard's ages, but don't just limit yourself to explicit details.

Text A — 20th-century diary

Friday 21 March 1947

What a truly miserable afternoon. Daddy shouted at me just for being late to school. "You should be more responsible now you're thirteen, Andrew!" he was yelling. He even said he had half a mind to stop wasting his money on my private education. I know he's angry, but I think his outburst was a bit of an overreaction.

Text B — 19th-century diary

Saturday 12 September 1868

Today was Richard's 16th birthday party, but it was not such a celebration after all. Richard sat quietly all evening, his hands folded in his lap, as Father ranted about how the party was a waste of the little money we have. Richard only broke his silence to acknowledge Father's tirade with a respectful "Yes, Sir".

Use linking words to show that you've thought about how the texts are similar or different.

Richard's body language has shown the reader something about his personality.

Richard seems to be more respectful, whereas Andrew is less so. Andrew is willing to challenge ideas, as he remarks that his father has overreacted. His defensive tone suggests that he feels he knows better than his father. In contrast, Richard seems much meeker and less cheeky. He sits quietly with "his hands folded in his lap", referring to his father as "Sir", even though he's shouting at him. This is perhaps a result of the fact that their situations are very different: Richard is a nineteenth-century boy from a family with "little money", whereas Andrew is a twentieth-century boy who has had an expensive "private education".

This difference has been inferred from the texts — it isn't explicitly stated in them.

You can make more perceptive observations by commenting on the tone of the texts.

Use quotes to support the comparisons you make.

If you master these skills you can pick up some easy marks...

You'll need good observation skills for these kinds of questions. Comment on the explicit differences between the texts, but don't forget to write about implicit ideas too — things that are implied by the writer.

Audience

In the English Language exams, you'll need to think about the audience — the intended readers of the text.

Writers aim their work at **General** or **Specific** audiences

1) The writer will always have a group of people in mind when they write — this is their audience.

2) The audience of a text can be quite general, e.g. adults, or more specific, e.g. parents with children under the age of 3.

3) Some texts will have more than one audience, e.g. children's books will try to appeal to the kids who read them, but also to the parents who will buy them.

Look for **Clues** about the **Target Audience**

1) Sometimes you can work out who the target audience is by the text's content (subject matter):

   | *This latest model is a beautiful car. Its impressive engine can send you shooting from 0-60 mph in less than 8 seconds.* | → | This text is clearly aimed at someone who's interested in high-performance cars. |

2) The vocabulary (choice of words) can tell you about the target audience's age group:

   | *Today, we witnessed a discussion on fox hunting. As one can imagine, this issue, although it has been debated for many years, still managed to elicit mixed emotions from all concerned.* | → | The sophisticated vocabulary, like 'elicit', rather than 'bring out', and the complex sentences show that this text is aimed at adults. |

   | *Dungeon Killer 3 is the hottest new game of the year! There are 52 awesome levels and 6 cool new characters — don't miss out on the wildest gaming experience of your life!* | → | This one uses modern slang and simple sentences, so it's clear that this text is aimed at younger people. |

3) The language can also give you clues about the target audience's level of understanding:

   | *The object of a game of football is to get the ball in the opposing team's goal. Sounds easy, but the other team has the same thing in mind. Also, there are eleven players on the other team trying to stop you.* | → | The simple, general explanations in this text show that it's written for people who don't know much about football. |

   | *The next hole was a par 3 and I hit my tee shot directly onto the green. Sadly, my putting let me down badly, and I ended up getting a bogey.* | → | The technical vocabulary here shows that this is for people who know quite a bit about golf. |

The audience is one of the first things you should look for in a text...

You need to work out who the intended audience of a text is so that you can discuss the writer's purpose, the techniques they use and how successful they are. Keep the audience in mind throughout your answer.

Section Three — English Language: Understanding Texts

Writer's Purpose

Every text you come across in your English Language exams will have been written for a reason.

There are **Four Common Purposes** of writing

1) The <u>purpose</u> of a text is the <u>reason</u> that it's been written — what the writer is <u>trying to do</u>.

2) Most texts are written for <u>one</u> of these reasons:

> *Pages 24-27 tell you how to spot a text's purpose, and how you can discuss this in the exam.*

To Argue or Persuade
- They give the writer's <u>opinion</u>.
- They get the reader to <u>agree</u> with them.

To Advise
- They <u>help</u> the reader to <u>do something</u>.
- They give <u>instructions</u> on what to do.

To Inform
- They <u>tell</u> the reader about something.
- They help the reader to increase their <u>understanding</u> of a subject.

To Entertain
- They are <u>enjoyable</u> to read.
- They make the reader <u>feel</u> something.

3) Lots of texts have <u>more than one</u> purpose, though. E.g. a biographical text could be written to both <u>inform</u> and <u>entertain</u> its audience.

4) In the exams, read the texts carefully and make sure that you think about <u>what</u> the writers are trying to <u>achieve</u> (and <u>how</u> they're achieving it).

5) Look out for super helpful exam questions that actually <u>tell you</u> the writer's purpose. E.g. if the question asks you about how the writer uses language to <u>influence</u> the reader, you know it's about <u>persuading</u>.

Purpose is **More Obvious** in **Non-Fiction** texts

1) The purpose of most <u>non-fiction</u> texts is usually quite <u>obvious</u>. For example:

> If a speech is trying to <u>argue</u> a particular point of view, the writer might make this very <u>clear</u> to make the argument more <u>powerful</u>.

2) Look out for texts where it might be <u>less obvious</u>, though. For example:

> A <u>magazine article</u> is primarily written to <u>entertain</u> its audience, so it might use a <u>chatty</u> tone to engage the reader. This might make it <u>less obvious</u> that it's also trying to <u>argue</u> a particular point of view.

3) A piece of fiction's most obvious purpose is to <u>entertain</u>, but writers sometimes use entertainment to achieve <u>another purpose</u>.

> Lots of fiction texts are <u>entertaining</u> stories on the surface, but they can contain <u>another message</u>. The writer might want to <u>argue</u> their own point of view or <u>inform</u> the reader about something.

You need to know the writer's purpose to write a good answer...

Always make sure you consider a text's purpose. If there's more than one purpose to a text, write about them both. And if you can write about how one purpose is used to achieve another, that's even better.

Informative Texts

Informative texts (like this book, in fact) always have something they're trying to tell you.

Informative writing Tells you something

1) When writing an informative text, the writer's aim is to pass on knowledge to the reader as clearly and effectively as possible.

2) They will adapt their language to match their intended audience, e.g. they might need to write for different age groups, or for people with different levels of understanding.

3) Purely informative texts will present information in a balanced and factual way. They will contain lots of facts and figures, but no opinions.

4) Some informative texts might also be arguing a particular viewpoint, though. For example:

> Many newspapers carefully pick information that supports a particular political party. Even though a newspaper article may not say outright what its opinion is, it can still be biased.

Have a look back at page 22 for more on audience.

Bias is when a piece of writing is influenced by the opinion of its author — see page 53.

Read the passage Carefully

Q1 Tick the boxes next to the **four** statements that are TRUE.

Contains facts like dates and statistics.

Uses clear, direct language.

> The MINI first went on sale in 1959 and is widely regarded as a great icon of British culture. Soon after its release, the MINI became the bestselling car in Europe. Over five million of them were made and many famous people, including The Beatles, bought them.
>
> The MINI is still around today, although it has undergone some major changes. It was originally conceived as an affordable car for the people, but now it is made by BMW and aimed at a different market. Nevertheless, the MINI remains a very popular car to this day.

Formal tone makes the information feel reliable.

A The MINI went on sale in the late 1950s. ✓
B The MINI has sold very well over time. ✓
C The MINI isn't very popular any more. ☐
D BMW have always manufactured MINIs. ☐
E MINIs have changed over time. ✓
F The MINI was the bestselling car in the world. ☐
G The MINI is not aimed at the same market as it used to be. ✓
H The Beatles advertised the MINI. ☐

This is phrased differently in the text, but it's still true.

You can only go on what the text says, and it only mentions that the MINI was the 'bestselling car in Europe', so this must be false.

Look at some examples of informative writing as practice...

You need to be able to recognise informative writing and explain how it's being used. If the information is biased, make sure you comment on that. It will show the examiner that you've really thought about the text.

Section Three — English Language: Understanding Texts

Entertaining Texts

Entertaining texts make you feel something. You need to be able to explain how they do this.

Entertaining writing aims to be Enjoyable to read

1) Entertaining writing is the sort of thing you'd read for pleasure, e.g. literary fiction.

2) Unlike informative texts, they contain few facts. Instead, they try to make you feel something, like scared, excited, or amused.

3) Entertaining writing is often very descriptive, and uses narrative techniques to make texts more enjoyable to read (see pages 54 and 59).

4) Writers also use structural techniques and different sentence forms to create entertaining texts (see pages 60-65). E.g. lots of short, punchy sentences can be used to make a text feel more exciting.

> Writers might use entertaining writing to engage a reader when they have another purpose in mind. E.g. travel books are entertaining non-fiction, but they're also informative.

Think about What makes the text entertaining

PAPER 1 Q2

Q2 Explain how the writer uses language to describe cycling in the extract below.

> He could feel the power of the bike humming beneath him as they both hurtled along. They were an elegant couple skimming the dance floor, whirling past plodding onlookers in their graceless automobiles, twisting around sweeping corners with effortless precision and darting along endless straights as they pushed each other on towards the inevitable conclusion. The bike hit the wall with all its hulking force.

- Lots of energetic verbs make the text entertaining and fast-paced.
- The text uses imagery to make the description come to life.
- Different sentence lengths vary the pace of the text, making it more interesting.

The writer describes cycling with an extended metaphor that personifies the bike as a dance partner. The bike and the rider become an "elegant couple" whose movements contrast with the "plodding" and "graceless" cars, suggesting that cycling is an art form. The writer uses a long sentence to develop this metaphor. This lengthy second sentence contains several verbs that are related to dancing and speed, such as "whirling" and "darting". The cumulative effect of these verbs creates an entertaining sense of pace and tension. It is as if the sentence is rushing and building towards a conclusion. The writer then disperses this tension with the final short sentence. The phrase "hit the wall" is very blunt, which suggests that cycling can become dangerous very quickly. This is emphasised by its contrast to the preceding build-up, adding to the shock and impact of the conclusion.

- Use key words from the question to keep your answer focused.
- Try to identify how the writer uses different parts of speech.
- You need to use technical terms.
- You should analyse the language at both word and sentence level.
- Write about the writer's intentions and the effects of their language on the reader.

Many entertaining texts also have other purposes...

Entertaining writing really helps to keep readers interested. So even if a writer's main purpose is to inform, argue, persuade or advise, they might still want to make their writing entertaining so the reader enjoys it.

Texts that Argue or Persuade

When you write about a text that argues or persuades, you need to be able to say exactly how it does this.

Arguing and Persuading are Similar

1) When people write to argue, they want to make the reader agree with their opinion. They use clear and forceful language to get their points across, and they might use facts and figures to back up points.

2) Persuasive writing tries to get the reader to do something, such as support a charity. It does this with techniques including emotive language that aims to make the reader sympathise with their cause.

3) When writing to persuade, writers might sometimes be more subtle about their aims and opinions, e.g.:

> *It is clear that this is a good school, and that people who attend it do well.*

This writer uses the phrase 'It is clear' to make their opinion sound like fact. This can make the writing sound more informative, when actually it's persuasive.

4) When writing to argue or persuade, writers often use rhetorical devices such as hyperbole, repetition or rhetorical questions (see page 52).

Explain the Effects of the writer's choice of Language

PAPER 2 Q3

Q3 Explain how the writer uses language to describe breakfast in the extract below.

WHY BOTHER WITH BREAKFAST?

David Barowsky, *nutritional analyst*

Eating breakfast improves mental and physical performance. This is a well-known and incontrovertible fact. And yet 20 million of us Britons regularly skip this essential refuelling opportunity. Why is this the case? Are we too busy commuting, getting the kids ready for school, blow-drying our hair? Do you often feel frantic and harassed in the morning? Well, the time has come to change your ways. Allowing your kids to skip breakfast is reckless and irresponsible. You are not providing them with the energy they need to face the day.

The writer uses statements to make their point clearly and forcefully.

Uses rhetorical questions.

Facts and figures are used to back up their argument.

Addresses the reader directly using the pronoun 'you'.

Try to use technical terms wherever you can.

Barowsky uses **exaggerated formal language** to describe breakfast as an "essential refuelling opportunity", emphasising how **important** a meal he thinks it is. This elaborate description of breakfast suggests that Barowsky believes it is a meal to be taken seriously and the word "opportunity" further implies that breakfast is something that should be valued. Barowsky also uses the **personal pronouns** "you" and "we" to establish a connection with the reader, whilst adjectives like **"reckless"** and **"irresponsible"** encourage an emotional response. This connection gives the writer a platform from which he can emphasise the importance of eating breakfast to the reader.

Use wording from the question in your answer.

Analyse the effects of individual words.

Texts that argue or persuade may well come up in paper 2...

If a writer is trying to argue a point or persuade you to do something, they're trying to make you see things from their point of view. It'll be one-sided, with carefully chosen evidence that supports their point of view.

Section Three — English Language: Understanding Texts

Texts that Advise

When writing to advise, a writer uses reassuring and easily understandable language to guide their reader.

Writing to Advise sounds Clear and Calm

1) When writing to advise, writers want their readers to follow their suggestions.

2) The tone will be calm and less emotional than writing that argues or persuades.

3) The advice will usually be clear and direct. For example, it might use:

- Vocabulary that matches the audience's subject knowledge.
- Second-person pronouns (e.g. 'you') to make the advice feel personal.
- A logical structure that makes the advice easy to follow.

4) The register (see page 43) may be formal, e.g. in a letter from a solicitor offering legal advice, or informal, e.g. in a magazine advice column.

Writing to Advise looks Like This

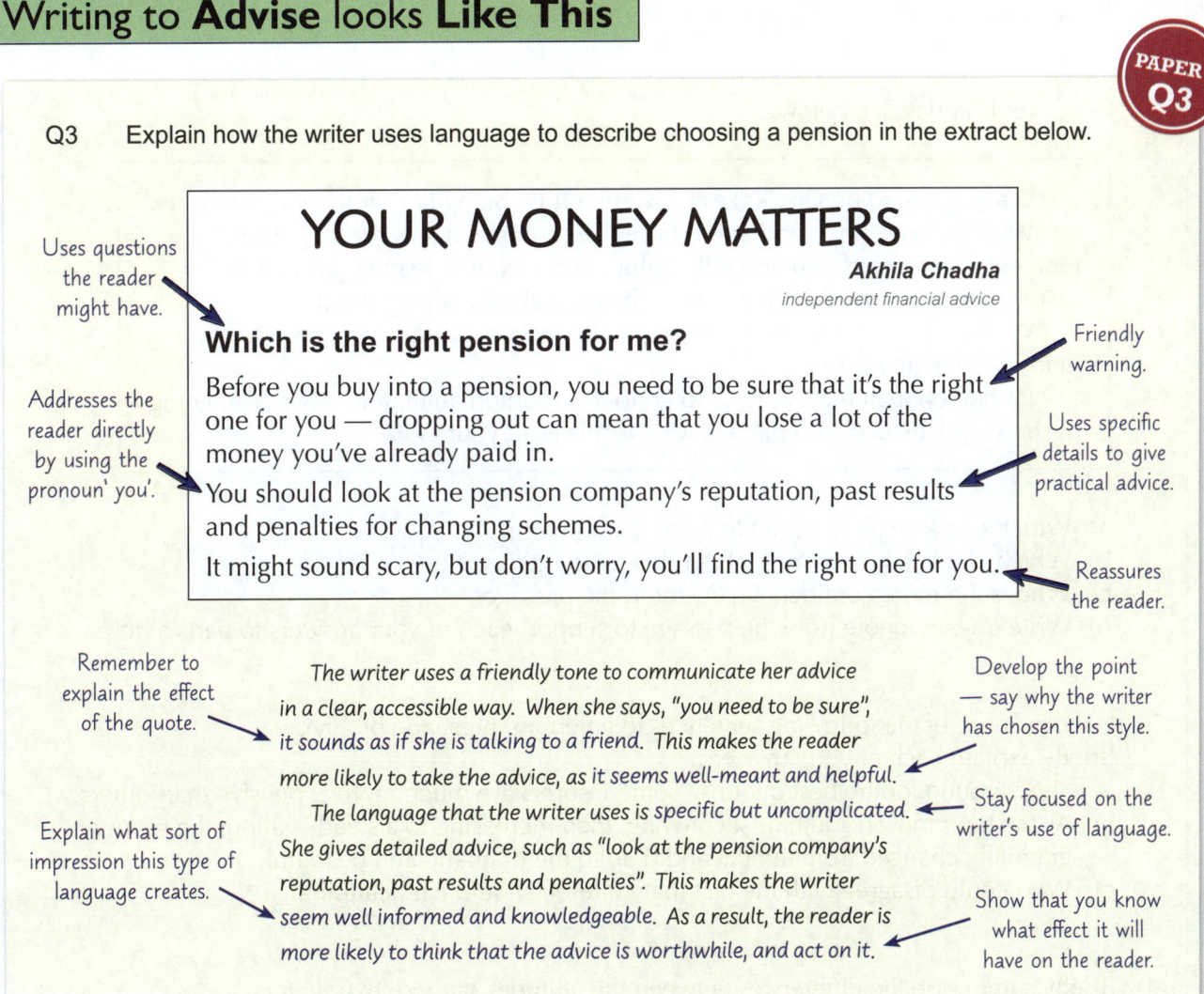

PAPER 2 Q3

Q3 Explain how the writer uses language to describe choosing a pension in the extract below.

YOUR MONEY MATTERS
Akhila Chadha
independent financial advice

Which is the right pension for me?

Before you buy into a pension, you need to be sure that it's the right one for you — dropping out can mean that you lose a lot of the money you've already paid in.

You should look at the pension company's reputation, past results and penalties for changing schemes.

It might sound scary, but don't worry, you'll find the right one for you.

Uses questions the reader might have.

Addresses the reader directly by using the pronoun 'you'.

Friendly warning.

Uses specific details to give practical advice.

Reassures the reader.

Remember to explain the effect of the quote.

Explain what sort of impression this type of language creates.

The writer uses a friendly tone to communicate her advice in a clear, accessible way. When she says, "you need to be sure", it sounds as if she is talking to a friend. This makes the reader more likely to take the advice, as it seems well-meant and helpful.
The language that the writer uses is specific but uncomplicated. She gives detailed advice, such as "look at the pension company's reputation, past results and penalties". This makes the writer seem well informed and knowledgeable. As a result, the reader is more likely to think that the advice is worthwhile, and act on it.

Develop the point — say why the writer has chosen this style.

Stay focused on the writer's use of language.

Show that you know what effect it will have on the reader.

Learn to spot the common features of texts that advise...

Texts that advise can be written for many different audiences, but a lot of the features will stay the same. Look at whether the language is formal or informal — it'll vary depending on the subject and audience.

Warm-Up Questions

To help you to digest everything you've read so far, here's a page of warm-up questions. The questions shouldn't take you too long, but try to write a few sentences for each one. You can check your answers in the back of the book to see how you're getting on. Then, when you're ready, have a look at page 29.

Warm-Up Questions

1) Read the short passage below.

> Dani approached the roller coaster with wide eyes. She had never been a big fan of rides, but her friend Amara had offered to give £20 to charity if Dani agreed to ride the biggest roller coaster in the park — a towering steel beast with four loops and six corkscrew turns. Her stomach churned at the thought.
> "You can do it, Dani," Amara said, squeezing her shoulder. "You might even enjoy it!"

Are the following statements true or false?
a) Dani is nervous about going on the roller coaster.
b) It was Dani's idea to get sponsored to go on the ride.

2) Read the short passage below.

> "We're going to be late, Rakesh," warned Rita, biting her thumbnail nervously.
> "We'll be fine!" insisted Rakesh from the depths of his wardrobe. After a moment he emerged, triumphantly holding his favourite leather jacket aloft.
> Rita glared pointedly at her watch, then at Rakesh, who grinned.
> "We'll be fine," he repeated, trying on the jacket and admiring his reflection in the full-length mirror.
> "It's bad enough that we have to go to this reunion at all, and now we're going to show up late too," complained Rita. "This is all your fault."

a) Which character is reluctant to go to the reunion?
b) Which character cares most about time management?
c) Who is the more confident character in the passage?
d) Write down a quote from the passage to support each of your answers to parts a) to c).

3) Is the purpose of the following sentences to entertain, persuade or advise?
Briefly explain each of your answers.
a) Shop around for the best quote — some insurers are much more expensive than others.
b) As the train moved south, first crawling, then increasing to a steady gallop, the scenery gradually changed from the flat and drab to the dramatic and beautiful.
c) Who could disagree with the fact that children should eat healthily?

4) Briefly summarise the differences between the attitudes of these two writers.
Writer A: *"I've always considered mixed schools to be a barrier to educational progress. We should all stick with traditional, single-sex education."*
Writer B: *"Mixed-sex schools are clearly superior, but parents should have a choice."*

Exam-Style Questions

Now you've learnt some theory, it's time to put it into practice. These questions will help you prepare for the ones in the real exams (although the actual questions might look a bit different). Try to do them without looking back at this section for help. You can mark yourself using the answers in the back of the book.

Q1 Use the following extract from a novel to answer the questions below.

For each question, tick the correct option. There is one correct answer per question.

> The doorbell rang. Someone must have answered it, because moments later I heard George's grinding tones in the hallway.
> "So lovely to be here!" he cried, his voice carrying easily across the living room.
> "Did you invite him?" I hissed, staring desperately at Rosa.
> "I could hardly leave him out," she said coolly. "It would have been too obvious."
> He entered the room. His garish purple suit and elaborate hairstyle made him stand out sharply from the other guests. "George, darling," Rosa cooed. "You made it."
> "Rosa!" he said, presenting her with a bottle of cheap-looking wine. "And Pritha," he said to me with a smirk, extending a greasy hand adorned with several gaudy rings. "Good to see you."
> "You too," I said, forcing a smile and letting go of his hand quickly.

Q1.1 How does George speak?

- Loudly ☐
- In a high-pitched voice ☐
- With a soothing voice ☐

Q1.2 What does Pritha think of George's suit?

- It looks too bright ☐
- The colour is beautiful ☐
- It looks expensive ☐

Q1.3 How does Rosa greet George?

- With shock ☐
- In a friendly way ☐
- With indifference ☐

Q1.4 What does George give to Pritha?

- A handshake ☐
- Alcohol ☐
- A ring ☐

Q2 In **Text A** and **Text B**, the writers are writing about marriage. What are the differences between the behaviour of the wives?

You need to:

- **infer** information from the text
- talk about **both texts** in your answer.

Text A — extract from a 19th-century women's magazine

The secret to our harmonious marriage lies in the willingness of my wife to be amenable to my needs.
My wife does not pester me, nor will she bore me with gossip or domestic trivialities. Instead, she will endeavour to be sweet and charming, always fulfilling my needs. If I wish to complain, she listens; if I seek quiet, she is silent. The home is her sphere, and she strives to make it a haven for me, in which I need not lift a finger.

Text B — extract from a 21st-century newspaper article

In the 21st century, a marriage is a partnership of equals. As both my wife and I work full time, we believe that it is essential for our domestic responsibilities to be shared evenly too. Whilst housework was once considered the domain of women, my wife spurns the idea that she should work full-time and take sole care of a home. In fact, whenever she hands me a mop or a chopping board, she reminds me sweetly that I am just as capable of cleaning and cooking as her.

Exam-Style Questions

Q3 Read the following extract from a review of a holiday park.

> You would need a fortnight to try all the activities at Lowbridge Park. From abseiling to zorbing, the park offers a mind-boggling range of activities. I was only there for a long weekend, so I had to prioritise!
>
> I began with a pony trek. Although it drizzled the entire morning, it was a great way to explore the woodland. In the afternoon I debated between rock climbing and mountain biking. I settled on the former, primarily to stay out of the rain!
>
> The next day, the weather was much better, so my choice fell between canoeing and sailing. I settled for a canoe and headed out on the lake, which was simply stunning early in the morning, clear, calm and blue. The good weather lasted into the afternoon, which meant that I was lucky enough to go paragliding. What an exhilarating experience!
>
> The next morning, I decided to finish my weekend with a spot of archery. Alas, I'm no Robin Hood, but the instructor was patient and funny, and I did improve a little over the course of the morning.

The statements below are about the extract above.

Tick the boxes next to the **four** statements that are TRUE.

- A   The writer went mountain biking. ☐
- B   On the second day, the writer got up early. ☐
- C   The writer had time to try everything. ☐
- D   The writer enjoyed the pony trek. ☐
- E   The weather stayed sunny all weekend. ☐
- F   You can abseil at Lowbridge Park. ☐
- G   The writer liked the archery instructor. ☐
- H   The writer went canoeing down a river. ☐

Q4 Read the following extract from an advice leaflet about an election.

Explain how the writer uses language to describe voting.

> ### It's Decision Time — But Who Do I Vote For?
> Unless you've been living under a rock for the past month, you'll probably have noticed that there's an election coming up. Deciding who to vote for can be a daunting task, but it's also an important one. Luckily, there's plenty of help out there.
>
> **Learn the Lingo**
>
> Firstly, you need to be well-informed on the principles and policies that each party stands for. If you start to feel overwhelmed by all the political lingo in their leaflets, don't panic — have a look online, where there are plenty of websites that break it down for you.
>
> **Choose a Capable Candidate**
>
> It's also a good idea to look into the candidates in your constituency. They represent you in parliament, so you'll want to vote for someone who has a strong voice, and who will stand up for what your area needs.
>
> It's true — choosing who to vote for isn't easy. However, if you take the time to do a bit of research, you will be able to make the right decision for you.

Section Three — English Language: Understanding Texts

Writer's Viewpoint and Attitude

English Language Paper 2 is all about writers' viewpoints and attitudes, especially question 4.

Viewpoint and Attitude are Different to Purpose

1) A writer's purpose is what they're trying to do, but their viewpoint (or attitude) is what they think about the topics that they're writing about.

2) You can work out what a writer's viewpoint might be by looking for clues in the language, tone, style and content of a text. For example:

> *I urge you to visit this truly unique and hidden valley — you must see such beautiful scenery at least once in your life.*

This text's purpose is to persuade its audience to visit a place. The author's viewpoint is their belief that the valley is beautiful and that it should be visited. The writer uses emotive adjectives and an upbeat tone to convey their viewpoint.

Use the writers' Tone to make Inferences about Attitude

PAPER 2 Q4

Q4 Compare how the two writers convey their different attitudes to manners and politeness.

Text A — 19th-century etiquette guide

> The way you behave when out in society is paramount. It is essential that you show the highest level of social refinement possible. For example, if someone offers you their hand, take it. Always remove your hat when entering a building. Be punctual to all social events to which you are invited.

Text B — 21st-century newspaper article

> Anyone who's ever taken a ride on the London Underground will know that there are some real nuisances out there. All too often, I've seen people refusing to give their seat up to an elderly passenger. I mean, it's just common courtesy, isn't it? Is it really so difficult to just be a little more civil towards other people?

Try to make your observations as perceptive as possible. Examiners will be really impressed if you can pick out subtle differences between the writers' attitudes.

The authors of both texts largely agree that being polite is important. However, there are subtle differences in their attitudes. The author of Text A focuses on etiquette in specific situations. They use a confident, assured tone, which is created by the use of imperative verbs such as "take" and "remove". They also give their advice using the pronoun "you", which makes the text sound more like a series of commands than a piece of advice. These things suggest that their ideas about "refinement" are very strict.

This is a useful phrase to use when you're linking the two texts.

By contrast, the author of Text B has a more laid-back attitude towards the need for "common courtesy". Rather than telling the reader how to behave as in Text A, they use an example and rhetorical questions to make the reader think about why people should be "more civil". This is possibly because Text B is from the 21st century, whereas Text A was written in the 19th century — a time when etiquette was considered to be much more important.

Looking at the writer's tone is usually a good place to start.

Use technical terms to discuss the different methods both writers use to convey their attitudes.

Think about the reasons why their attitudes differ — think about when and why they were written.

Comment on how attitudes are conveyed...

You need to go beyond just what the writer's saying and think about how they're expressing their viewpoint. For example, even if two writers have the same opinion, one might express it more strongly than the other.

Literary Fiction

In paper 1, you'll be given an extract from a piece of literary fiction, and you need to be able to analyse it.

Literary fiction **Entertains** the reader

1) Literary fiction, such as a novel or short story, is written to entertain. It might do this by affecting the reader's emotions, describing the atmosphere of a place, using an intriguing structure or developing the personality of a character.

2) All literary fiction has a narrator. It's most often either a first-person (uses 'I' and 'we') or third-person (uses 'he', 'she' and 'they') narrator.

3) Literary fiction uses lots of descriptive and figurative language (e.g. metaphors, similes, analogy and personification) to capture the reader's imagination.

4) Literary fiction is also structured to interest the reader — texts will often build the tension towards a dramatic climax, or they might use repetition and varied sentence structures to change the pace of a text.

5) Dialogue is also often used to move the plot along and give insight into the thoughts and feelings of different characters.

See section 4 for more on all these language and structural features.

Look Closely at the **Language** used in a text

PAPER 1 Q2

Q2 Explain how the writer uses language to describe Edward's surroundings.

Edward hurried down the **dark, smog-filled** alley. The place had become almost completely unrecognisable: the green fields he remembered from his childhood had long since been **drowned in concrete**. The alley became darker, and its bends and turns were increasingly disorientating. **A creak. A whisper. Every noise put him on edge.** But he pressed on.

Eventually, Edward found himself at Dorine's lab. He walked in, stooping to avoid hitting his head on the low door frame. The lab was a large circular room; the walls were lined with **hundreds of tattered books, and half-finished research papers** lay strewn across the many desks.

The books seemed to whisper to each other, as if disconcerted by the presence of an outsider. Edward felt as though they were watching him.

Dorine was poring over some papers in front of her, and hadn't noticed that Edward had arrived. After a few moments, she looked up from her desk and saw Edward waiting. **She could see** the flicker of hope glimmering in his eyes — the hope that they might still be able to turn back the clock.

"I'm afraid it's not looking good, Ed," Dorine murmured.

Edward was beginning to feel as though the endless walls of books were glowering at him in judgement. *My God*, he thought. *How could we have let this happen?*

- These adjectives set the scene as an uninviting place.
- The writer uses Edward's fear to emphasise that his surroundings are frightening.
- The writer uses Dorine's surroundings to tell the reader about her personality.
- This personification makes Edward's surroundings seem hostile and hints that he's feeling guilty.
- The emotive verb 'drowned' creates a negative impression of the concrete.
- The use of very short sentences adds to the feeling of unease and suspense.
- Personification makes it clear that Edward feels uncomfortable in the lab.

You need to practise writing about extracts from literary fiction...

You're always going to have to answer some questions about a piece of literary fiction — it makes up the whole reading section of paper 1. That means you're going to need to know all of this stuff really well.

Section Three — English Language: Understanding Texts

Literary Non-Fiction

Now it's time to look at literary non-fiction — this is what paper 2 will focus on.

Literary non-fiction is **Entertaining** but **Factual**

1) Literary non-fiction texts use literary styles and techniques, but they are based on facts or real events.

2) Non-fiction texts such as biographies, autobiographies, and travel writing will often be written in a similar style to literary fiction.

3) They are written to inform the reader about something, but the writer uses a literary style to make it entertaining too. For example, they might use descriptive language and dialogue to make the information more interesting to the reader.

4) Literary non-fiction is almost always written in the first person, which adds a sense of personality to the text, helping to engage the reader.

Have a look back at the previous page to remind yourself about literary style.

Literary non-fiction tries to **Engage** the **Reader**

Q3 Explain how the writer uses language to describe their time in Paris.

Directly addresses the reader, making them feel more involved.

Dearest reader — I wish today to impart to you some recollections of my summer spent in Paris, a city which over time has played host to a multitude of great thinkers and artists. A hundred years may have passed since the French Revolution, but Paris remains a shining beacon of revolutionary spirit.

Contains facts and refers to real places to inform the reader.

The city of Paris has some **spectacular** specimens of architecture. One bright evening, I took a particularly enjoyable stroll down the **Champs-Élysées**, and was quite amazed by the **stunning** curvature of its **Arc de Triomphe**. **The arch incited within me the strongest feelings of awe and wonderment; it is truly a structure built to inspire.**

The language used in this text is quite formal, which makes the writer seem more authoritative.

Paris has been ever-popular with the gentleman traveller, but this year the city **captures one's imagination** more than ever before, as it hosts the annual 'World's Fair'. There I saw many wonderful artefacts, including a magnificent replica of the Bastille, the famous site of the rebellion which began France's Revolution. The replica was incredibly lifelike, **from the gloomy outer stonework to the banquet hall within.**

Ends with a strong, memorable statement that will stay in the reader's mind.

Although the fortress was a thrilling diversion, it was far from the real star of the fair — that honour belonged to the newly-erected 'Eiffel Tower', said to be the largest building on Earth. The new tower amazed fair-goers with its enormous metallic form (although some were not altogether thrilled by its brash modernity). Whether one marvels at this remarkable feat of engineering, or recoils from its audacious magnitude, **the new tower is assuredly a sight to behold.**

The text uses lots of emotive adjectives to clearly show the writer's viewpoint. Purely informative non-fiction wouldn't use adjectives like these.

The writer's viewpoint gives the description a positive tone.

This description adds detail, which helps things come to life for the reader.

This sentence creates suspense by not revealing what the 'real star' is right away.

Literary non-fiction is not as complicated as it might sound...

Don't let the phrase "literary non-fiction" worry you — it's just a category that describes any factual text that is written in an entertaining way. Have a look at page 57, question 1 for an example of literary non-fiction.

19th-Century Texts

In paper 2, you'll always be given a 19th-century non-fiction text. Here's some information about the period.

19th-century Writing is often quite Formal

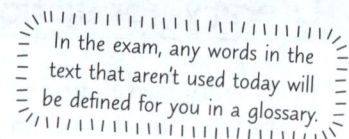
In the exam, any words in the text that aren't used today will be defined for you in a glossary.

1) 19th-century texts can sound a bit different to more modern texts, but you should still be able to understand what's going on.

2) A lot of the texts will use a more formal register (see page 43) than modern writing, even if the audience is quite familiar (see next page for an example of this).

3) The sentences may be quite long and the word order can sometimes be different to modern texts. Try not to worry about this — just re-read any sentences you can't make sense of at first. Here are a couple of examples:

> *Then, Albert being gone and we two left alone, Edward enquired as to whether I might accompany him on a stroll in the garden.*

→ This sentence is written using a formal register, e.g. it uses 'enquired' instead of 'asked'. It might seem a bit confusingly phrased too, but 'Albert being gone and we two left alone' is just another way of saying 'Albert had gone and the two of us were left alone.'

> *I believe it necessary to abandon this foul enterprise.*

→ Sometimes it can seem as if a word has been missed out — modern writers would probably put 'is' after 'it' in this sentence.

19th-century Society was Different to today

1) Knowing about 19th-century society will help you to understand the text better in the exam.

2) It will also help you to compare the viewpoints and perspectives of writers from different time periods (which you need to do for paper 2, question 4).

Social Class

- Early 19th-century society was divided between the rich upper classes (who owned the land) and the poorer working classes.
- Throughout the 19th century, the Industrial Revolution was creating opportunities for more people to make more money.
- This meant that the middle classes grew in number and influence throughout the century.

Education

- In the early 19th century, few children went to school. Children from poor families often worked to help support their families instead.
- In the late 19th century, education reforms made school compulsory for all young children.
- Rich families often sent their children to boarding school, or hired a governess to live with the family and teach the children at home.

Women

- After they got married, most women were expected to be in charge of looking after the home and children.
- Women didn't have as many rights as men — they couldn't vote in elections and they often didn't control their own money and property.

Religion

- Christianity had a big influence — most of the middle and upper classes attended church regularly.
- However, science was starting to challenge some religious ideas, e.g. Darwin's theory of evolution questioned the Bible's account of creation.

19th-Century Texts

Have a look at this piece of 19th-century Writing

This is a letter written to Princess (later Queen) Victoria of the United Kingdom by her uncle, King Leopold I of Belgium. In it, Leopold describes his new wife, Louise Marie.

> Laeken, 31st August 1832.
>
> **MY DEAREST LOVE**,—You told me you wished to have a description of your new Aunt. I therefore shall both mentally and physically describe her to you.
>
> She is extremely gentle and amiable, her actions are always guided by principles. She is at all times ready and disposed to sacrifice her comfort and inclinations to see others happy. She values goodness, merit, and **virtue** much more than beauty, riches, and amusements. With all this she is highly informed and very clever; **she speaks and writes English, German and Italian**; she speaks English very well indeed. In short, my dear Love, you see that I may well recommend her as **an example for all young ladies**, being Princesses or not.
>
> Now to her appearance. She is about Feodore's* height, her hair very fair, light blue eyes, of a very gentle, intelligent and kind expression. A Bourbon** nose and small mouth. The figure is much like Feodore's but rather less stout. **She rides very well**, which she proved to my great alarm the other day, by keeping her seat though a horse of mine ran away with her full speed for at least half a mile. **What she does particularly well is dancing.** Music unfortunately she is not very fond of, though she plays on **the harp**; **I believe there is some idleness in the case**. There exists already great confidence and affection between us; she is desirous of doing everything that can contribute to my happiness, and I study whatever can make her happy and contented.
>
> You will see by these descriptions that though my good little wife is not the tallest Queen, **she is a very great prize which I highly value and cherish**...
>
> **Now it is time I should finish my letter.** Say everything that is kind to good Lehzen***, and believe me ever, **my dearest Love**, your faithful Friend and Uncle,
>
> LEOPOLD R.

Glossary
* Feodore — Victoria's half-sister, Princess Feodora
** Bourbon — the Bourbons were the French royal family
*** Lehzen — Princess Victoria's governess, Louise Lehzen

Annotations (left):
- The tone is affectionate but the register is formal — this is common in 19th-century letters.
- Being 'virtuous' was an important quality in 19th-century society — it means having strong morals.
- This shows the 19th-century viewpoint of what was valued in upper class women.
- You might come across a tricky phrase or sentence. Use the context and the rest of the sentence to work out what's going on. Here, Leopold suggests that Louise Marie doesn't try very hard at playing the harp.
- 19th-century texts often phrase things differently — here, a modern writer might have said "I should end this letter here."

Annotations (right):
- Upper class women were educated in European languages in the 19th century.
- Upper class women were considered to be accomplished by their ability in things like riding, dancing, playing music and speaking languages.
- Women were often seen as belonging to their husbands.
- Superlatives (e.g. 'kindest', 'most gracious') are common in 19th-century writing.

You will definitely have to analyse a 19th-century text in paper 2...

It's important to make sure you're comfortable reading and understanding 19th-century texts. These pages might look more like History than English, but they'll help you to improve some of your answers in paper 2.

Understanding Texts — Knowledge Organiser

Section Three has a lot of information to remember, so here's a helpful summary of the topics that were covered. Read through and check you're confident with everything — if there's anything you're not sure about, have a look back at the relevant pages.

Information & Ideas

Information can be explicit or implicit.

Explicit ideas — clearly stated.

Implicit ideas — not clearly stated. Can be worked out (inferred).

Audience

Audiences can be general or specific.

e.g. adults   e.g. parents of young children

Texts can have multiple target audiences.

You can work out the audience from clues in the text:

Subject matter

A text's content can tell you who might be interested in it — e.g. text about baking is probably aimed at bakers.

Vocabulary

- Sophisticated & complex — adult audience
- Slang — younger audience

Language

- Technical — for experts
- Simple — for inexperienced people

Writer's Viewpoint

- What the writer thinks about a topic.
- It can be worked out from details in the text:
  1. Language
  2. Style
  3. Tone
  4. Content
- Don't just say what writer's viewpoint is — analyse how they express it.

In Paper 2, question 4, you have to compare two writers' viewpoints on a topic, & how they convey their attitudes.

Types of Text

Texts are written to fit their purpose.

Informative texts

- Language adapted to suit target audience — e.g. to match age group or level of expertise.
- Balanced & factual — gives facts, not opinions.
- BUT some informative texts are biased.

Entertaining texts

- Descriptive, with few facts.
- Use narrative & structural techniques.

Texts that argue or persuade

- **Argue** — Use clear, forceful language. Support points with facts & figures.
- **Persuade** — Use emotive language to gain sympathy. Make opinions sound like facts.

Both use rhetorical techniques — e.g. hyperbole, repetition & rhetorical questions.

Writer's Purpose

There are four common reasons why a text is written:

To Argue or Persuade	• Gives the writer's opinion. • Gets reader to agree with them.
To Inform	• Tells reader about something. • Increases reader's understanding.
To Advise	• Gives instructions. • Helps reader to do something.
To Entertain	• Enjoyable to read. • Makes reader feel something.

Texts can have multiple purposes — e.g. a biography can inform *and* entertain.

Sometimes exam questions will tell you the writer's purpose.

A non-fiction text's purpose is usually obvious — e.g. a speech might clearly argue a point of view.

Fiction's purpose is to entertain, but entertainment can be used for other purposes — e.g. to inform.

Texts that advise

- Calm, clear & direct tone.
- Logical structure which is easy to follow.
- Second-person pronouns (e.g. 'you') — advice feels personal.
- Can be formal (e.g. legal letter) or informal (e.g. magazine advice column).

Literary Texts

Literary fiction (AO2)

- ☑ Written to entertain.
- ☑ Always has a narrator — usually first or third-person.

  *First-person: 'I' / 'we'
  Third-person: 'he' / 'she' / 'they'.*

- ☑ Lots of descriptive & figurative language.

  > e.g. metaphors, personification or similes can capture the reader's imagination.

- ☑ Structured to interest reader.

  > e.g. tension can build to a dramatic conclusion, or repetition can change the pace of a text.

- ☑ Dialogue — advances plot & provides insight into characters.

  Paper 1 will contain a piece of literary fiction.

Literary non-fiction

E.g. biographies, autobiographies & travel writing.

- ☑ Written to inform *and* entertain.
- ☑ Use literary styles & techniques, but are based on facts or real events.
- ☑ Normally have a first-person narrator — adds a sense of personality & engages the reader.

One of the texts in Paper 2 will be literary non-fiction.

Summarising & Linking (AO1)

You'll be given a topic and two texts.

1. **Pick out** explicit & implicit information on the topic from each text.
2. **Summarise** similarities or differences between these ideas.
3. **Back up** your points with examples.

Linking words show you've made a comparison:

To show similarities:
- Similarly
- Likewise
- Also
- Equally

Summarising is tested in paper 2 question 2.

To show differences:
- Whereas
- Although
- However
- But

19th-Century Texts (AO2, AO3)

19th-century texts sound different to more modern texts — look out for:

- More formal register than modern writing.
- Long sentences with an unusual word order.
- Unfamiliar words — these should be defined for you in a glossary.

One of the texts in Paper 2 will be from the 19th century. You'll have to compare it to a more modern text.

Social class
- Early 19th century: divide between rich upper classes & poorer working classes.
- The Industrial Revolution increased wealth — middle classes grew in size & influence.

Education
- Early 19th century: few children went to school, many poor children worked.
- Late 19th century: school made compulsory.
- Rich children often sent to boarding school.

19th-century society was different to today

Women
- Expected to marry, have children & run household.
- Had fewer rights than men — couldn't vote.

Religion
- Christianity was important — most people attended church regularly.
- BUT science began challenging religion.

There's a lot to think about when you first read a text...

When you're tackling an unseen text, it's really important to identify its audience and purpose. Then, you can analyse *how* it's adapted to suit them — through its language, content, form or tone.

Worked Answer

It can be hard to know what a good answer looks like, so here's a sample question with a worked answer for you to read. The bullet points on the next page explain how this answer could be improved. Once you've read through it all, you could try rewriting the answer with the improvements on another piece of paper.

Q1 This question is about **Text A** and **Text B**, where both writers are presenting their views on trains and railways.

Text A — 19th-century diary
Dear Diary —
   I've had quite a day today! Daddy and I took a trip to see the new steam train, which was being exhibited in James Square. It was fascinating — a clanking, grinding steel colossus, shiny as a new penny, with a great puff of steam that emerged from its funnel and curled into the summer sky. I've never seen the like — and to think, Daddy says one day they may be able to carry people from one end of the country to the other! I for one cannot wait.

Text B — 21st-century speech
Residents of Station Crescent! I know that you, like me, are plagued day-in, day-out with the sounds, smells and sights of the railway. Like me, many of you moved here at a time when three or four trains a day passed by, barely disturbing us at all. And like me, you've seen our area systematically invaded by a non-stop army of trains, impacting our quality of life — not to mention the price of our homes. The time has come to take a stand against the relentless growth of the railways.

Compare how the writers convey their different attitudes towards rail transport.

You may wish to explore what the writers' attitudes are and what methods they use to convey their attitudes. You should use examples from **both** texts.

---

figurative language — "shiny as a new penny" in A, army metaphor in B
rhetorical devices in B — aims to persuade. A is more descriptive e.g. "curled" bit.
exclamation mark for excitement in A but for emotive effect in B
A wants more trains, B wants fewer trains

You <u>don't</u> need to make a <u>detailed plan</u> for this type of question, but <u>quickly</u> jotting down your <u>ideas</u> (like this) can be helpful.

This is a great opening sentence. It makes a <u>clear point</u> that is focused on the <u>question</u>.

Use <u>linking words and phrases</u> to show that you're making a <u>comparison</u>.

The writers of both texts use figurative language to convey their attitudes to rail transport. In Text A, the train is "shiny as a new penny". This simile suggests that the writer feels the train is exciting because it's so new. In contrast, the figurative language in Text B shows the writer's frustration with trains. He uses a metaphor to compare them to a "non-stop army", which makes them seem like a relentless and aggressive nuisance.

This answer <u>identifies</u> a language technique and then explains its <u>effect</u>.

To make this into a top level paragraph, you could mention <u>why</u> they might have these different attitudes by referring to the <u>contexts</u> of the texts.

Section Three — English Language: Understanding Texts

Worked Answer

It's good to think about how the writer has conveyed their attitude through <u>structure</u>, as well as through language.

The attitudes in Text B are conveyed using rhetorical devices. The writer <u>repeats</u> the phrase "like me" to get the audience on side. The writer also uses direct address, such as "Residents of Station Crescent", to suggest that the audience are a united team, who are able to work together to change things. In Text A <u>the attitudes are conveyed using</u> descriptive language, such as "<u>a great puff of steam that emerged from its funnel and curled into the summer sky</u>". This shows how impressed the writer is by the new trains, feeling they are almost magical.

Phrases like this keep your answer <u>focused</u> on the writer's methods — <u>how</u> attitudes are conveyed...

This quote does <u>support</u> the point, but it would be better to make it much <u>shorter</u> and then explain its effect more <u>specifically</u>.

Both of the writers use exclamation marks to make their attitudes clear. In Text A, they are used by the writer to emphasise their <u>excited attitude</u> to the steam train. On the other hand, in Text B, the writer uses an exclamation mark to show his dedication to the cause and to persuade the audience to agree that <u>the trains are a problem</u>.

...and phrases like these focus on the <u>first</u> bullet point (<u>what</u> the attitudes are and how they're <u>different</u>).

The writer in Text A hopes that there will be more trains. They "cannot wait" for the trains to be able to carry people from one end of the country to the other, and <u>the phrase "I for one"</u> implies that the author believes other people will feel the same. In Text B, the attitude is very different. This writer wants there to be fewer trains, because there used to be "three or four" and they use <u>the phrase "relentless growth"</u> to suggest to the audience that further expansion poses a real danger to the community.

The examiner will want to see that you can analyse the effect of individual words and <u>phrases</u>.

Each <u>paragraph</u> in this answer makes a <u>new comparison</u> between the writers' attitudes. This shows a <u>clear understanding</u> of the differences.

- This is a good answer. It clearly compares the writers' attitudes and it also discusses the writers' methods.
- To get the very top marks, this answer could be improved by:
  - using the different contexts of the texts to comment on why the attitudes might be different.
  - pointing out more subtle differences in the attitudes, e.g. the writer in Text A is writing about seeing one train on one particular day, whereas the writer in Text B is writing about living alongside multiple trains every day.
  - making sure that all the quotations are really precise.

Exam-Style Questions

Now that you've seen an example answer, have a go at these exam-style questions for yourself.

Q1 This question is about **Text A** and **Text B**, where both writers are presenting their views on art.

Text A — 19th-century letter

Dear Miss Tinsham,
I read with concern your recent article on the new wave of art reaching British shores. With all due respect, I see it as nothing short of an abomination. It is created with a flagrant disregard for the conventions and traditions of classical art. These 'artists' seem not to have learnt from their predecessors, but instead insist on violating their canvasses with an assault of colour, which to view, in perfect honesty, is simply excruciating.

Text B — 20th-century newspaper article

The London art scene has rarely been so exciting. We are seeing a real influx of artists who aren't afraid to throw off the iron shackles of 'traditional art' and champion self-expression. They're rule breakers, not intimidated by the giants of the past. They're revolutionaries, constantly looking forward, never back. Only by pushing the boundaries of modern art are we going to see any progression in the medium. When art conforms, it stagnates, and these new experimenters understand that.

Compare how they convey their different attitudes towards art.

You may wish to explore what the writers' attitudes are and what methods they use to convey their attitudes. You should use examples from **both** texts.

Q2 Read the following extract from a novel.

Annie went from room to room, shaking her head at the disarray. The house looked as if it had been burgled. In the living room, a bookcase had been thrown onto the floor, and paperbacks were scattered chaotically across the carpet. In the kitchen, the floor was a treacherous landscape of smashed crockery and broken glass.

Annie frowned and headed cautiously up the stairs, following the crashing sounds into the master bedroom. Lucas stood with his back to her. His hair was a frantic mess, his movements manic as he pulled every item of clothing out of his wardrobe and launched them behind him. He was muttering frenetically under his breath.

"Lucas," Annie said calmly. He span around, surprised by her presence. His wide eyes were wild, beads of sweat had appeared on his forehead and his cheeks were red.

"I can't find it," he said. "I've looked everywhere. It's lost. They'll kill me."

"Don't be ridiculous. They're not going to kick you out just because you've lost your key to the clubhouse," said Annie, her arms folded.

"What would you know about it?" said Lucas, his eyes flashing in annoyance. "They're obsessed with not letting any outsiders in. If they find out I've lost it... I'm doomed. Finished. Condemned."

How far do you agree or disagree with the following statement?

In this extract, Annie and Lucas are realistic and relatable to the reader.

In your answer, make references to the text and consider:

- what impression you get of Annie and Lucas
- what methods are used to create this impression.

Revision Summary Test for Section Three

It's time for another revision summary test. Challenge yourself with these questions.
- These questions are **really tricky**, but they'll help you see **how well you know your stuff**.
- Tackle the **revision summary test** below, or scan the QR code to do it **online**. You can **keep track of your progress** online and see **which areas need more work**.
- There are **sample answers** here: www.cgpbooks.co.uk/blurb-answers

Information, Ideas, Audience and Purpose (p.20-23)

1) What is the difference between explicit and implicit information?
2) Write down three examples of words or phrases you could use to show that you're comparing:
   a) similarities between two texts
   b) differences between two texts
3) a) List three things that can help you identify a target audience.
   b) Briefly explain how each thing you named in part (a) can help you identify a target audience.
4) a) List four common purposes of a piece of writing.
   b) Give one characteristic of each purpose you named in part (a).

Different Types of Text (p.24-27)

5) a) Give two examples of an informative text.
   b) How and why might a writer need to adapt their style when writing to inform?
6) Define bias. How can informative texts sometimes be biased?
7) Briefly explain why a writer may use the following techniques to make a text entertaining:
   a) descriptive language
   b) first-person narrative
   c) different sentence forms
8) List three rhetorical techniques and explain why they are effective in texts that argue or persuade.
9) Why might a writer use a clear and calm tone when writing to advise?
10) When an author is writing to advise, why may they choose to do each of the following?
    a) adapt their language and vocabulary to match their reader's subject knowledge
    b) use second-person pronouns
    c) create a logical structure

The Writer's Viewpoint and Different Texts (p.31-35)

11) What is the difference between the writer's viewpoint and the writer's purpose?
12) How might a writer use language, tone and style to convey their viewpoint?
13) How might a writer make literary fiction more entertaining for the reader?
14) What is literary non-fiction? How is it similar to or different from literary fiction?
15) Briefly explain whether the following texts are literary fiction or literary non-fiction.
    a) the autobiography of a retired professional cricketer
    b) a short story about a trip to the seaside
    c) a piece of travel writing about Rome
    d) an opinion piece in a broadsheet newspaper
16) Describe two ways the writing of a 19th-century text may be different to a modern one.
17) Give one fact about each of the following areas of 19th-century society:
    a) social class
    b) education
    c) women
    d) religion

Tone

Tone can sometimes be difficult to describe, but it comes through in the text's language.

Tone is the General Feeling created by the text

1) A writer's tone is the <u>feeling</u> the words are written with, which creates a particular <u>mood</u> and shows what the writer's <u>attitude</u> is. For example, the tone of a text might be:

   - happy or sad
   - serious or funny
   - sombre or light-hearted
   - emotional and passionate or cool and logical

2) The main way to identify a text's tone is by looking at the <u>language</u>. For example, if a writer has used <u>informal</u> language, the tone might be quite <u>personal</u> or <u>familiar</u>, but <u>formal</u> language would suggest a more <u>serious</u> or <u>distant</u> tone.

3) <u>Punctuation</u> can also give you a clue about tone. For example, if there are lots of exclamation marks, that might suggest that the tone is very <u>emotional</u> or <u>passionate</u>.

4) Tone can reflect the <u>purpose</u> of a text (e.g. informative texts usually have a serious tone) or the <u>audience</u> (e.g. a playful tone might suggest a younger audience).

Think of a writer's tone as being like someone's tone of voice when they're talking.

Look closely at Language to Work Out a text's Tone

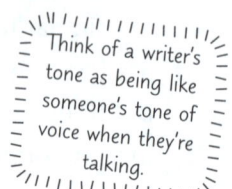

Q4 How far do you agree or disagree with the following statement?
In these lines of the text, the hotel is presented as a creepy place.

> Phillipa stood on the cold, dark street, peering up at the abandoned hotel. Large wooden boards stood impassively across most of the window frames, sentries to the stillness and silence within, guarding the eerie presence of the dilapidated building.
>
> Despite her misgivings, she pushed gently on the front door, and it crept open with an arthritic creak. As she tiptoed over the threshold, small clouds of dust wheezed out of the carpet where she put her feet.

The adjectives used help to create a foreboding tone.

The sinister tone is gripping for the reader, which keeps the text entertaining.

I strongly agree with the statement. The heavily foreboding tone, created by adjectives such as "abandoned", "eerie" and "dilapidated", and reinforced by the personification of the "wooden boards" as silent "sentries", makes the hotel seem creepy and unsettling. It seems as though something frightening could happen at any moment, which strengthens the reader's sense of unease. The onomatopoeia of the words "wheezed" and "creak" creates an even more vivid description and makes the hotel seem like a living being, which heightens the creepy undertone and makes the text unsettling to read.

Don't forget to mention how much you agree or disagree with the statement.

Remember to use technical terms wherever possible.

Mention the combined effect of different features of the text.

You need to make sure you refer back to the statement for questions like this.

Some tones are easier to spot than others...

Sometimes, the tone of a text will be obvious. But watch out for texts that are written with an ironic or sarcastic tone — the words might not mean exactly what they seem to at first (take a look at pages 50-51).

Style and Register

Every text you come across will be written in a particular style, using a particular register...

Style is How the text is Written

1) A text's style is the overall way in which it's written, which includes language choices, sentence forms and structure.

2) There are lots of different styles you might encounter. E.g. cinematic, where the text is written as if the reader is watching a film, or journalistic, which is a balanced way of writing reported news.

3) If the text was written in a factual style, it would include lots of information. An emotive style would try and get an emotional response from the reader.

4) Register is the specific language (choice of words) used to match the writing to the social situation that it's for. Different situations require different registers, for example:

> If you wrote a letter to your local MP to ask them to stop the closure of a local leisure centre, you might use a formal register (e.g. 'the closure will have a detrimental effect'). This is because the audience is an authority figure that you don't know.

> If you wrote a letter to your friend to tell them about the leisure centre closure, you might use an informal register (e.g. 'it'll be rubbish when it shuts'). This is because the audience is someone you're familiar and friendly with.

Register can be thought of as a part of style.

5) Look out for how writers adapt their style and register to suit the purpose and the audience they are writing for.

Write about Style and Register when Analysing Language

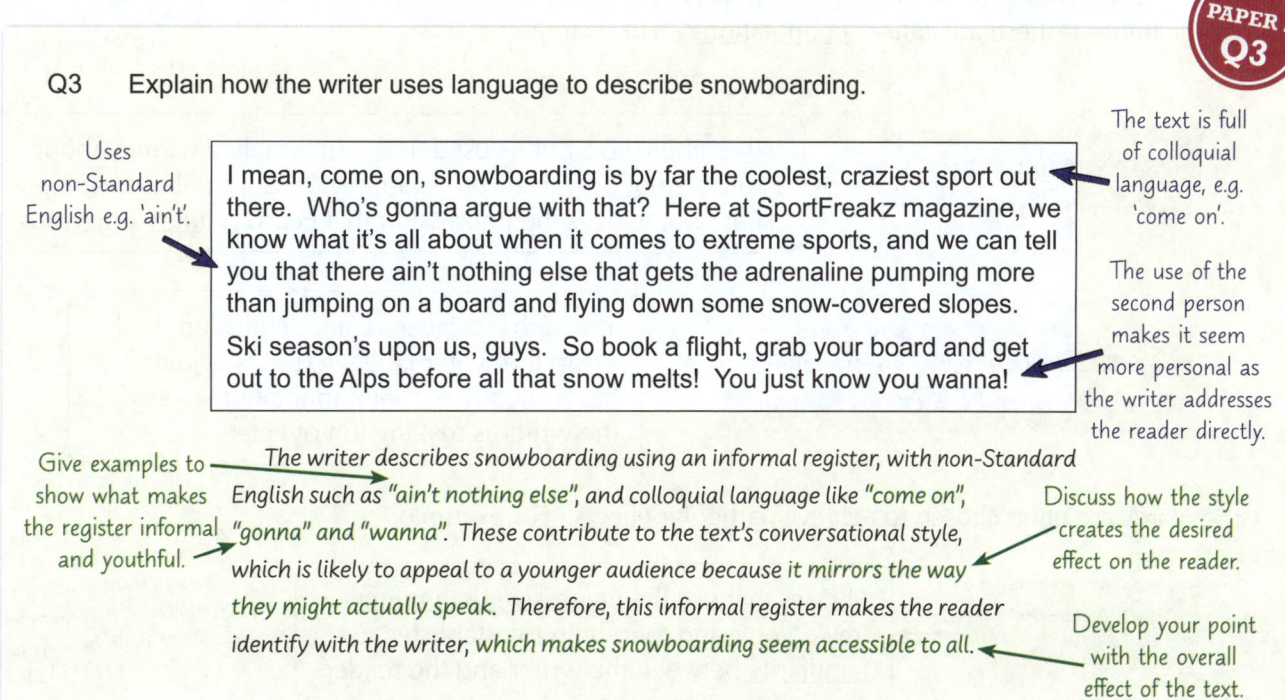

You need to comment on how style and register are created...

Style has to do with language and vocabulary, structure, tone... so think about how the style is built up from all these different features. You also need to think about the text's register and how it's been achieved.

Words and Phrases

Writers choose their words very carefully to produce a desired effect, and you need to comment on this.

Writers use a range of Word Types

It's important to be able to identify the types of words that a writer is using. Have a look at the definitions below to remind you:

Word type	What they are	Examples
Nouns	naming words — they might refer to a person, place, thing or idea	*sister, pen, art*
Pronouns	words that replace a noun	*he, she, it, them*
Possessive pronouns	pronouns that show ownership	*his, hers, ours, theirs*
Verbs	action words	*think, run, swim, shout*
Adjectives	describe a noun or pronoun	*happy, clever, interesting*
Adverbs	give extra information about verbs	*quickly, loudly, accidentally*

Words and Phrases can be used to achieve Different Effects

1) For the reading questions (1-4 on both English Language papers), you need to pay attention to the reasons why a writer has used particular words or phrases.

2) Words can have subtle implications beyond their obvious meaning — these are called 'connotations'. For example:

Analysing the connotations of words is a way of 'reading with insight'. There's more on this on page 6.

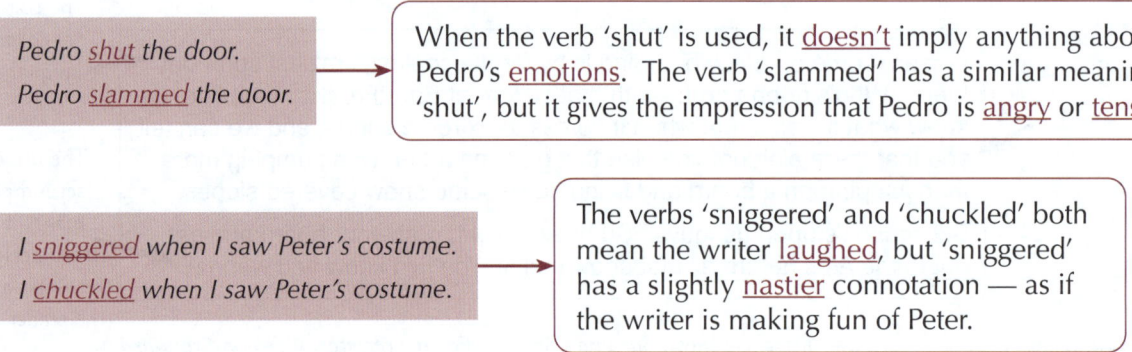

Pedro shut the door.
Pedro slammed the door.
→ When the verb 'shut' is used, it doesn't imply anything about Pedro's emotions. The verb 'slammed' has a similar meaning to 'shut', but it gives the impression that Pedro is angry or tense.

I sniggered when I saw Peter's costume.
I chuckled when I saw Peter's costume.
→ The verbs 'sniggered' and 'chuckled' both mean the writer laughed, but 'sniggered' has a slightly nastier connotation — as if the writer is making fun of Peter.

3) Words are often chosen to achieve particular effects. For example:

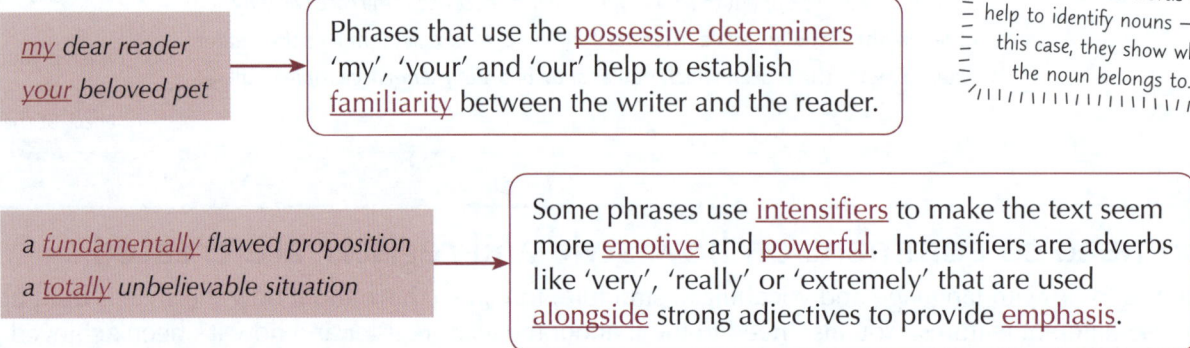

Determiners are words that help to identify nouns — in this case, they show who the noun belongs to.

my dear reader
your beloved pet
→ Phrases that use the possessive determiners 'my', 'your' and 'our' help to establish familiarity between the writer and the reader.

a fundamentally flawed proposition
a totally unbelievable situation
→ Some phrases use intensifiers to make the text seem more emotive and powerful. Intensifiers are adverbs like 'very', 'really' or 'extremely' that are used alongside strong adjectives to provide emphasis.

Section Four — English Language: Language and Structure

Words and Phrases

Words Work Together to create Cumulative Effects

1) Writers can use the words from a specific semantic field (the words associated with a particular theme or topic) to convey an idea to the reader. For example:

Dessert was simply divine; a cloud-like puff of pastry that was lighter than an angel's wing. → Here, the semantic field of heaven is used to make something sound appealing.

2) Keep an eye out for situations where particular types of words are repeated, e.g. sentences with lots of adjectives or paragraphs with lots of verbs.

3) You could comment on the cumulative effect of particular types of words — show you've thought about how the words in the text work together to create tone or affect the reader in some way, e.g.

Adjectives like 'electrifying', 'thrilling', 'tense' and 'intriguing' create a cumulative effect of excitement.

The adverbs 'jovially', 'readily' and 'pleasantly' combine to create an impression of enjoyment.

Try to pick out Significant Words and Phrases

PAPER 2 Q3

Q3 Explain how the writer uses language to describe Bijoux Birthdays' events.

A PICTURE-PERFECT PICNIC

Bijoux Birthdays invite you to celebrate **your special day** in style. Join us for a **magical** evening of entertainment on the **beautiful** banks of the River Fairer. Let us help you to **relax** in the **balmy** atmosphere of a warm summer's evening, **recline** next to the **glistening** waters and **indulge** in the most **sumptuous** of picnics.

We can tailor your evening to suit you. **We can** provide a refreshing feast for your senses. **We can** transport you to another place and time. Just sit back and let us do all the work. All **you** need to do is relax.

We have a large selection of menus for you to choose from, as well as a whole host of different entertainment acts — **maybe** you'd like a string quartet, or **perhaps** you'd be more interested in a circus act? Whatever your tastes, rest assured that we will be able to accommodate you.

If you're planning a celebration, Bijoux Birthdays really is the only choice.

Adjectives like 'magical', 'beautiful', 'balmy', 'glistening' and 'sumptuous' have an alluring cumulative effect — they create a calming atmosphere.

Watch out for repeated grammatical constructions — they give the text emphasis.

The words 'perhaps' and 'maybe' suggest that there is an abundance of choice.

Phrases that use possessive determiners establish familiarity with the reader and make the description more persuasive.

The list of three verbs — 'relax', 'recline' and 'indulge' — makes Bijoux Birthdays sound inviting.

Directly addressing the reader with the pronoun 'you' implies a sense of familiarity between the writer and the reader, giving the description a comforting feel.

Comments like "this is an adjective" aren't quite good enough...

The technical grammar of words and phrases is important, but don't just point it out — you need to analyse its effects. Think about why certain words and phrases have been used and what impression they create.

Figurative Language

Figurative language is the term used to describe words or phrases that are used in a non-literal way. Metaphors, similes and personification are all types of figurative language, and help make writing interesting.

Metaphors and Similes are Comparisons

See pages 32-33 for more on literary fiction and non-fiction.

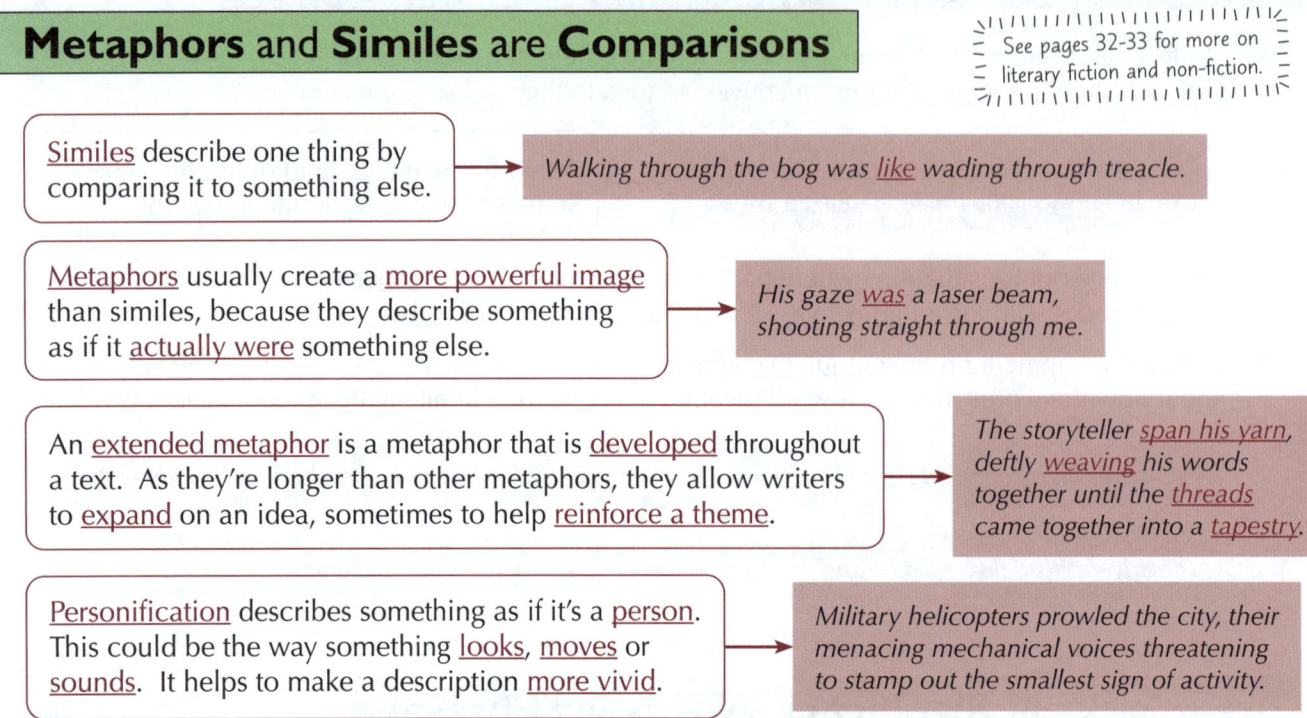

Similes describe one thing by comparing it to something else.
→ *Walking through the bog was like wading through treacle.*

Metaphors usually create a more powerful image than similes, because they describe something as if it actually were something else.
→ *His gaze was a laser beam, shooting straight through me.*

An extended metaphor is a metaphor that is developed throughout a text. As they're longer than other metaphors, they allow writers to expand on an idea, sometimes to help reinforce a theme.
→ *The storyteller span his yarn, deftly weaving his words together until the threads came together into a tapestry.*

Personification describes something as if it's a person. This could be the way something looks, moves or sounds. It helps to make a description more vivid.
→ *Military helicopters prowled the city, their menacing mechanical voices threatening to stamp out the smallest sign of activity.*

Comment on the Effect of figurative language

PAPER 1 Q2

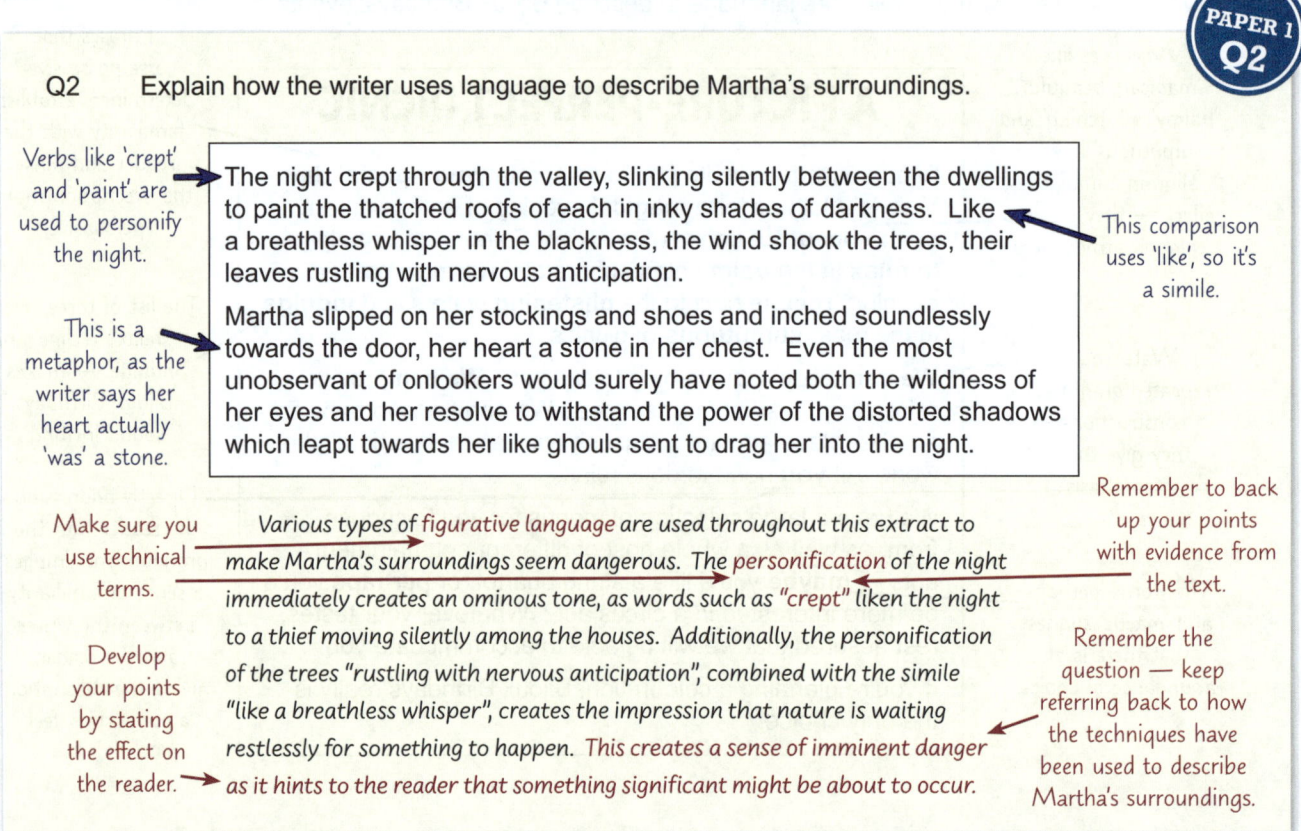

Q2 Explain how the writer uses language to describe Martha's surroundings.

Verbs like 'crept' and 'paint' are used to personify the night.

The night crept through the valley, slinking silently between the dwellings to paint the thatched roofs of each in inky shades of darkness. Like a breathless whisper in the blackness, the wind shook the trees, their leaves rustling with nervous anticipation.

This comparison uses 'like', so it's a simile.

This is a metaphor, as the writer says her heart actually 'was' a stone.

Martha slipped on her stockings and shoes and inched soundlessly towards the door, her heart a stone in her chest. Even the most unobservant of onlookers would surely have noted both the wildness of her eyes and her resolve to withstand the power of the distorted shadows which leapt towards her like ghouls sent to drag her into the night.

Make sure you use technical terms.

Develop your points by stating the effect on the reader.

Various types of figurative language are used throughout this extract to make Martha's surroundings seem dangerous. The personification of the night immediately creates an ominous tone, as words such as "crept" liken the night to a thief moving silently among the houses. Additionally, the personification of the trees "rustling with nervous anticipation", combined with the simile "like a breathless whisper", creates the impression that nature is waiting restlessly for something to happen. This creates a sense of imminent danger as it hints to the reader that something significant might be about to occur.

Remember to back up your points with evidence from the text.

Remember the question — keep referring back to how the techniques have been used to describe Martha's surroundings.

Make sure you focus on the effects of figurative language...

Practise closely analysing figurative language in texts so you can do it in the exam. You might need to write about figurative language in English Language paper 1, questions 2 and 4, and paper 2, questions 3 and 4.

Section Four — English Language: Language and Structure

Warm-Up Questions

There's a couple of exam-style questions on the next page, but before you have a go at those here are some handy warm-up questions for you. Use these to check how much you can remember from the section so far, then go back and review anything you're not sure about.

Warm-Up Questions

1) Is the tone of each of the following sentences sentimental, detached or upbeat?
   a) Investigators have recently confirmed that DNA found at the scene of the burglary matches that of suspect Fergus Maybach.
   b) I had a riot helping out at the birthday party! Who would've guessed that kids were the perfect audience for my magic tricks?
   c) As he stared across the bay where they had first met, he remembered vividly the tinkle of her laughter and the floral scent of her hair.

2) Which of the sentences in question 1 is written in a journalistic style?

3) What is the tone of the following text? Explain your answer.

> At this point I was starting to get a tad — how shall I put it? — cheesed off. It's one thing being patient, accepting the fact that things don't always go to plan and that now and then delays just happen. It's quite another to be told, after paying good money for a ticket to Town A, that for no good reason you're taking a little detour through Village B, River C and Swamp D. I was finding it more and more difficult to follow what I had figured was the local way of dealing with difficulties — smiling and pretending to find the grim industrial scenery interesting. It wasn't.

4) Rewrite each of the following sentences so that they are in a formal register.
   a) Sorry, we don't take credit cards!
   b) Check you've got the proper kit to hand before you go any further.

5) Write down the noun, verb and adverb in this sentence: "Bella approached us excitedly."

6) Explain the different connotations of the underlined verbs in the sentences below.
   "Just go," she <u>whispered</u>.
   "Just go," she <u>spat</u>.

7) a) Is the semantic field of the passage below i) Shakespeare, ii) money or iii) shellfish?
   b) What impression does this create of the narrator?

> I wasn't interested in seeing my sister's school Shakespeare play, but I couldn't afford to miss being at the theatre that night. The owner of DigTech was going to be there watching his daughter, and I was desperate to sell him my latest design idea. I decided to buy myself some extra time by locking him inside the gents toilets with me during the interval. A bit drastic, perhaps, but you have to cash in on this sort of opportunity.

8) What is the cumulative effect of the verbs in this sentence?
   The wind barged across the barren, open moorland and threw itself against the stoic stone walls of the cottage, wrenching the window shutters from their frames.

Exam-Style Questions

It's time to try out what you've learnt, so here are a couple of exam-style questions for you to tackle. Keep in mind the ideas you've just been reading about in this section, and pay close attention to the writer's use of tone, style and register, as well as the words and phrases that they use.

Q1 Read the following extract from an adventure holiday brochure.

> If you're up to your neck in revision, the promise of a long summer holiday might be the only thing keeping you going. For most students, the dream will be of lazy days spent with mates, maybe playing video games, or getting a bit of a tan down the park. There's nothing wrong with wanting a break. You've earned it. But here at Adventure Action, we can give you the chance to do something unforgettable with your summer.
>
> If you're aged 15 to 18, you could spend four weeks on one of our incredible adventure and conservation programmes at breathtaking locations around the world. You could trek through dense rainforest in Peru to help build primary schools in isolated villages. You could take a flight over ancient glaciers to volunteer at a remote bear sanctuary in Alaska. Or you could earn a scuba-diving certificate whilst working in a marine biology lab in The Bahamas. Our programmes are tailored to give you a fantastic experience, where you can bag loads of new skills and be a part of something important.
>
> **Adventure beyond the usual this summer. Apply to Adventure Action today.**

Explain how the writer uses language to describe Adventure Action programmes.

Q2 Read the following extract from a piece of fiction.

> She raised an eyebrow at him icily. Her mouth was a stern, straight line. It did not twitch.
> "Please," he pleaded, "it was a mistake. It won't happen again."
> Her silence was stone cold. He began to wring his hands fretfully. He could feel the sweat prickling like needles on the back of his neck. The seconds crawled by excruciatingly as he waited for her to say something, anything. He briefly considered speaking, but was too fearful of aggravating her further.
> "Evidently," she said at last, "you can no longer be trusted." The only emotion in her voice was disdain.
> His breath caught painfully in his chest; he knew the worst was coming.
> "I have no use for people I cannot trust," she continued. "You are dismissed. Leave now. Resign your post. Never let me see your face again. Understood?"
> Trembling, he managed a clumsy nod.
> "Good. Now get out."
> He turned and, dragging his feet like a condemned man, left the room.

Explain how the writer uses language to describe the two characters.

You may wish to explore how the writer uses particular language techniques, specific words and phrases, or different types of sentence.

Section Four — English Language: Language and Structure

Alliteration and Onomatopoeia

As well as learning about what alliteration and onomatopoeia are, make sure you can spell them.

Alliteration and Onomatopoeia are about how words Sound

1) Alliteration and onomatopoeia use the sounds of words to create an effect:

   Alliteration is when words that are close together begin with the same sound. → *PM's panic! Close call for kids*

   Onomatopoeic words sound like the noises they describe. → *thud, hiss, squish, crackle, smash*

2) Alliteration helps a writer to grab a reader's attention.
3) It's often used for emphasis and to make key points more memorable.
4) Onomatopoeia makes descriptions more powerful — it appeals to the reader's sense of hearing, which helps them imagine what the writer is describing.

Alliteration and onomatopoeia Keep Readers Interested

PAPER 2 Q3

Q3 Explain how the writer uses language to describe the product.

> **MAKE MILKSHAKE MAGIC!**
>
> **Just add our Milkshake Magic to a glass of milk, and listen to the powder fizz and crackle into a delicious drink that you'll be slurping up in no time!**

- The alliteration of 'Milkshake Magic' is repeated for even more emphasis.
- 'fizz', 'crackle' and 'slurping' are all onomatopoeic.

This text is from an advert *aimed at young children*, so the writer uses alliteration in the title "Make Milkshake Magic" to make the product memorable to the reader. It does this by making the advert easy-to-read and emphasising *how* the product transforms regular milk into something special. The onomatopoeic words "fizz" and "crackle" *create a strong impression of how the drink sounds and make the product seem more exciting*. This is especially likely to gain the interest of younger readers as it is a lively and fun description of how the product works. It would *help children to imagine themselves using the product, and therefore make the Milkshake Magic more appealing.*

- Show that you realise who the writing is aimed at.
- Stay focused on 'how' the language interests the reader.
- Explain why the writer has chosen to use the technique.
- Develop the point further if you can.

Think about using these techniques in your own writing...

You need to be able to write about the effects of alliteration and onomatopoeia in the reading sections of both English Language papers, but you could also consider using them in the writing sections too.

Irony

Irony can be important for the tone of a piece of writing, so make sure you're comfortable commenting on it.

Irony is **Saying** the **Opposite** of what you **Mean**

1) Irony is when the literal meaning of a piece of writing is the exact opposite of its intended meaning.
2) The reader can tell the writer is being ironic from the context of the writing.
3) Writers often use irony to express their viewpoint, but it helps to make what they're saying more humorous or light-hearted.

> *It was pouring down with rain — perfect weather for a barbecue.*

The context (the rainy weather) shows that the writer actually means that it was terrible weather for a barbecue.

Irony can sometimes be a **Little Tricky** to **Spot**

PAPER 1 Q4

Q4 How far do you agree or disagree with the following statement?
In these lines, the writer makes the character's feelings explicitly clear.

> Clara sat on her lounger at the edge of the pool, thinking of all the poor souls still trapped in the office. She'd been asked to travel to Spain for work. Stay hunched over her cramped, stuffy desk in London or work in this paradise? A very difficult decision indeed.
>
> As the sun rose higher in the sky and the temperature crept up, she thought of dreary, cloudy London. "It's a tough job," she thought to herself, "but somebody's got to do it."

You can tell she is being ironic because of the context — she describes Spain as a 'paradise' so it can't have been a 'difficult decision'.

Don't forget to mention how much you agree or disagree with the statement.

I agree with the statement, though Clara's feelings are somewhat open to misinterpretation. Her comments about a "difficult decision" and a "tough job" are negative if read literally, but the context makes it clear that they should be taken ironically. She clearly prefers being in Spain — her office in London is "cramped", and the people are "trapped", whereas Spain is a "paradise". The use of irony highlights this contrast and therefore emphasises Clara's happiness.

Moreover, her ironic tone shows that her feelings towards others are perhaps quite unsympathetic. The contrast between her own situation and that of the "poor souls" in London shows that she considers her situation to be much more pleasant. This adds an element of smugness to her feelings about being abroad. The writer therefore not only makes Clara's feelings about her own situation clear, but widens the focus to show her feelings about others' contrasting situations.

Make sure you clearly explain why the language is ironic.

Linking two points together is a good way to develop your answer.

To work out if something is ironic, look at the context...

It might seem confusing that exactly the same words can mean completely opposite things, but the context usually makes it fairly clear when a writer is trying to be ironic — otherwise it wouldn't be very effective.

Sarcasm

There is a subtle difference between sarcasm and irony — have a look at this page.

Sarcasm is Nastier than Irony

1) Sarcasm is language that has a mocking or scornful tone. It's often intended to insult someone or make fun of them, or to show that the writer is angry or annoyed about something.

2) Sarcastic writing usually uses irony — but the tone is more aggressive and unpleasant.

> *The food took 90 minutes to arrive, which was just brilliant. I can think of no better way to spend a Saturday evening than waiting around for a plate of mediocre mush.*

The writer's used irony and a sarcastic tone to show his frustration and anger — it's meant to insult the restaurant that kept him waiting.

3) Satire is a kind of writing that uses sarcasm to make fun of a particular person or thing — it's often used in journalism and reviews.

Explain How you can tell a comment is Sarcastic

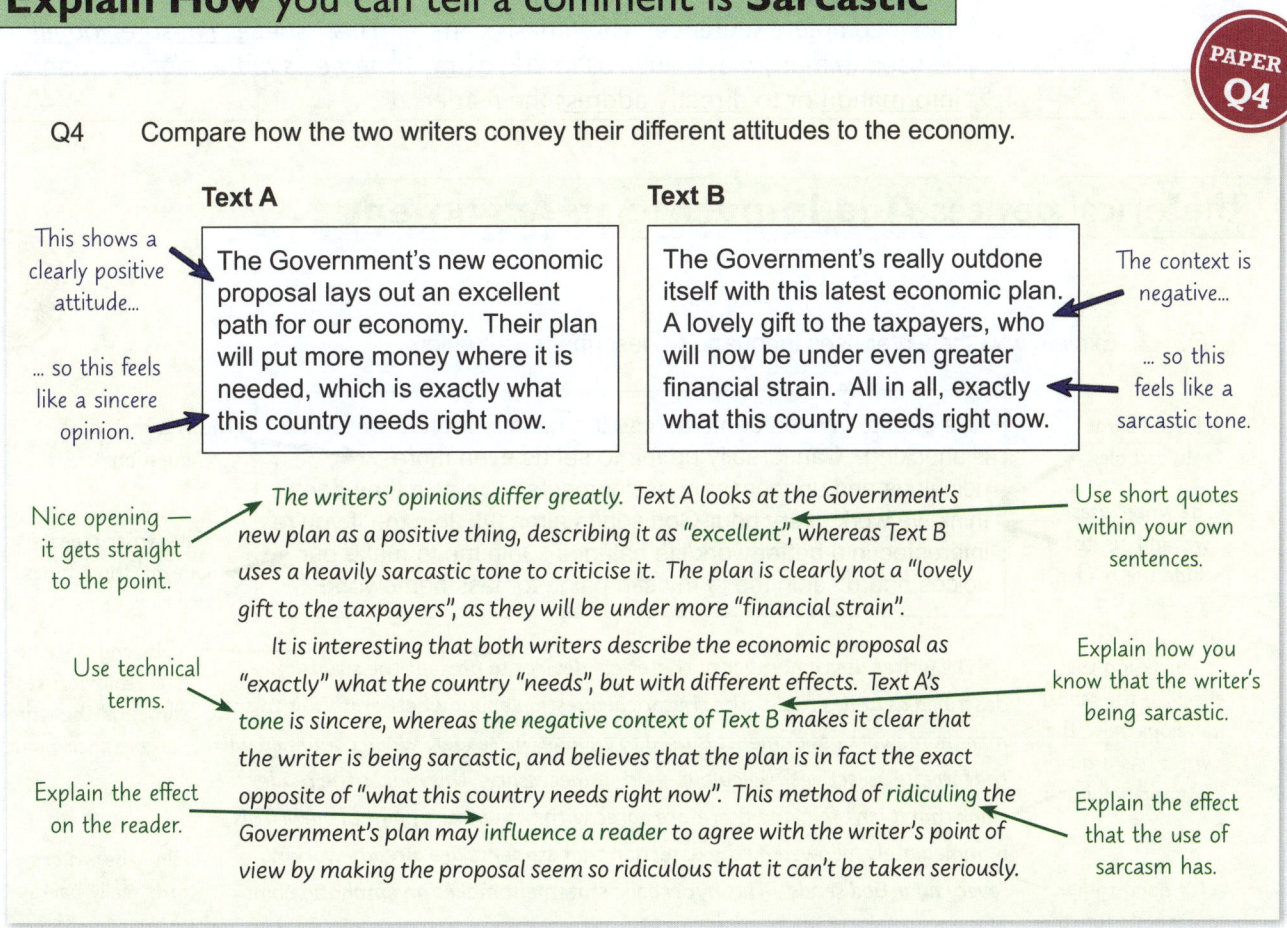

Sarcasm is often used to ridicule someone or something...

Sarcasm can be quite an unpleasant technique to use, but it's also a very effective one. Remember to explain how you know that a piece of writing is sarcastic, and also explain the effect of the sarcasm.

Rhetoric

Rhetorical techniques make language more persuasive. Lots of speeches use rhetoric, for example (see p.86).

There are Lots of Rhetorical Techniques

There are several ways you can be persuaded with rhetoric — make sure you're familiar with the ones below:

Think about how other techniques (e.g. alliteration, sarcasm) could be used as rhetorical devices.

Rhetorical technique	What it is	Example
Rhetorical questions	Questions that require no answer. They make readers engage with the text and realise the answer for themselves. This makes the reader feel like they're making up their own mind.	Is it right that footballers are paid such vast sums of money?
List of three words or phrases	Emphasise the point the writer's making. They often repeat three adjectives.	The cross-country run is painful, pointless and pure evil.
Hyperbole	Intentional exaggeration. It's used to make a point very powerfully.	We had to wait forever for the food to arrive.
Antithesis	Opposing words or ideas are presented together to show a contrast.	Just a small donation from you could have huge consequences for others.
Parenthesis	When an extra clause or phrase is inserted into a complete sentence. Parenthesis can be used in many ways, such as to add extra information or to directly address the reader.	This issue, as I'm sure you all agree, is of the highest importance.

Rhetorical devices Add Impact to an Argument

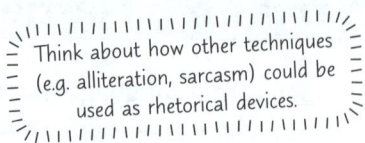

Q3 Explain how the writer uses language to describe the situation.

Here's some hyperbole.

The writer uses 'we' and 'us' to include the reader.

> This plan to give students across the country more homework is shocking. Can it really be fair to set us even more ridiculous and unnecessary assignments? It's as if they don't think we work every hour God sends already! Join me if you're interested in a better work/life balance. Join me to make our voices heard. Join me in my campaign for less homework!

This is a rhetorical question.

The writer repeats 'join me' three times.

Analysing the effect on the reader develops 'how' the writer has argued their point.

It's good to link your points together wherever possible.

The writer *uses a number of rhetorical devices* to present the situation described as undesirable. The rhetorical question about whether it's fair to set more homework assignments is used to engage the reader. When combined with the forceful adjectives "ridiculous" and "unnecessary", this *makes the reader think that it isn't fair*, and therefore agree with the writer's point of view. This is *immediately followed* by the assertion that students are already working "every hour God sends". This hyperbolic statement makes an emphatic point about how hard students work, which generates sympathy from the reader and enhances the argument that more homework would be "shocking".

Opening statement is really focused on 'how' the writer argues their point.

Using the writer's words really backs up your analysis of their viewpoint.

Lots of political speech writers use rhetoric...

Remember, there are lots of different types of rhetorical techniques — this page just tells you about some of the most common ones. Make sure you analyse the effect of a rhetorical technique if you spot one.

Bias

If a text is biased, it doesn't give a balanced view — the writer's opinion affects the writing.

Biased writing is Affected by the Writer's Opinions

1) Biased writers don't usually lie, but they don't give the full picture.
2) Sometimes the writer won't mention something that opposes their viewpoint, or they'll exaggerate something that supports it.
3) Biased writing also often uses generalisations — sweeping statements that aren't necessarily true.
4) Bias isn't always obvious, or even deliberate. Biased writers often seem to be talking in a neutral, factual way — while actually only presenting one point of view.
5) You need to be able to recognise bias, so that you don't mistake opinion for fact.
6) Look out for bias in non-fiction texts like newspaper articles and reviews.

Bias Weakens a writer's Argument

PAPER 2 Q4

Q4 Compare how the two writers convey their different attitudes to *Romeo and Juliet*.

Biased writers may use hyperbole if they are trying to convince you about something.

Text A — 19th century review

Romeo and Juliet, without the slightest shadow of a doubt, is the very greatest work of literature to have ever been penned in the English language. It truly is the pinnacle of Shakespeare's momentous talent and will never be matched by any playwright to come.

They often make opinions sound like facts.

Text B — 20th century biography

Romeo and Juliet is one of the most well-known and widely studied works of literature to have ever been penned in the English language. It was among the most popular of Shakespeare's plays during his lifetime, and it is still performed to this day.

Text A is written in a very biased way. The hyperbolic statements "without the slightest shadow of a doubt" and "never be matched" emphasise the writer's strength of feeling, but the statements are unjustified: the writer gives no evidence other than their own opinion. This bias presents the reader with an emphatic personal argument for how good the play is, but nothing to back it up. This may convince some readers to watch the play, but others may feel the argument is quite weak.

Try to use more interesting vocabulary to get across your exact meaning.

Although Text B is also positive about Romeo and Juliet, the writer bases their viewpoint on factual statements, describing the play as "well-known" and "widely studied". The writer of Text B is also careful to use phrases like "one of the most" and "among the most", which shows that they are aware that there are other successful and popular plays. Overall, Text B presents a more balanced viewpoint towards Romeo and Juliet.

Mention the overall difference between the two texts.

Develop your point by writing about the writer's purpose and how successful they are.

Always ask yourself whether a text is biased...

A good way to spot bias is when the writer presents their opinion as fact (by saying something confidently), but giving no evidence for it. This weakens their argument — they could be saying something ridiculous.

Descriptive Language

You'll find descriptive language in both literary fiction and literary non-fiction texts.

Descriptive Language makes text Interesting

1) Writers use descriptive techniques and vocabulary so that the reader gets a really clear image in their mind of what the writer's describing. It makes the text more interesting, dramatic and convincing.

2) Descriptive techniques include imagery such as metaphors, similes and personification (see p.46).

3) Writers often give descriptions based on their five senses (what they can see, smell, hear, touch or taste).

4) Another sign of descriptive language is when the writer uses lots of adjectives — describing words like 'huge' or 'fiery' that give a specific impression of something. Writers can also use interesting verbs, such as 'saunter' instead of 'walk', to make their descriptions really specific.

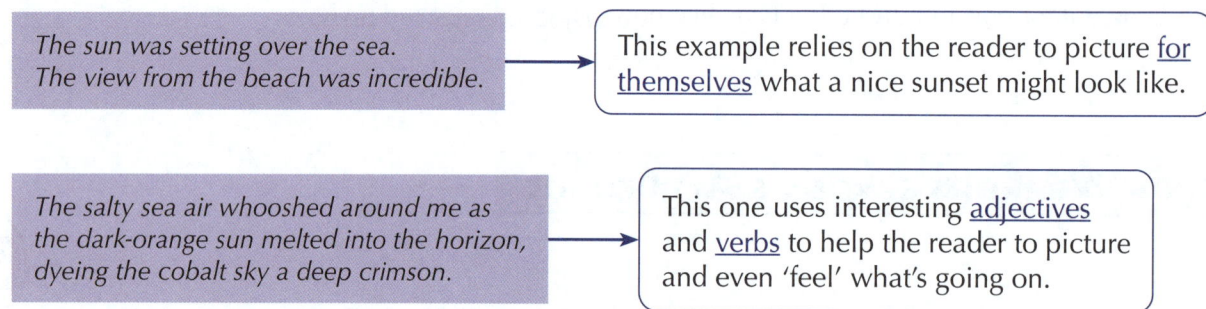

5) Writers can also build up the description of something throughout their work. For example, by writing sentences with contrasting descriptions or descriptions that agree with each other.

Talk about the Effects of Specific Words

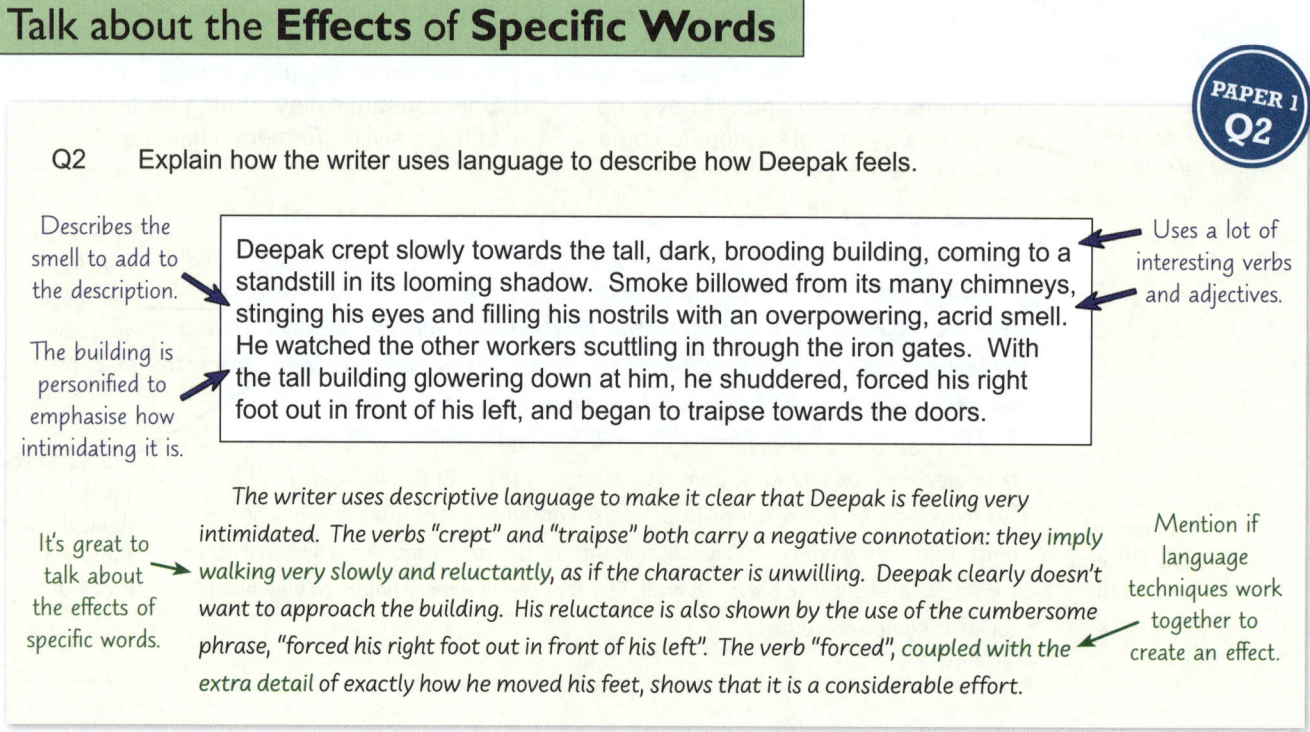

You will find descriptive language in your English Language exams...

Look out for descriptive language in both the literary fiction extract in paper 1 and the literary non-fiction in paper 2. Make sure you write about the effect it has, focusing on the specific words and phrases used.

Section Four — English Language: Language and Structure

Other Language Techniques

This page is helpful for spotting and explaining some higher-level language techniques that might appear in an exam text. It's important to make sure you're confident analysing the effect of language techniques.

Identify and Explain the Effect of language techniques

1) You have to analyse the effect of language for English Language paper 1, question 2 and paper 2, question 3. Make sure you're familiar with the language techniques in the table below so you can really impress the examiner.

Technique	What it is	Example	Effects
Pathetic fallacy	A kind of personification where nature (often weather) is given human feelings and responses.	*The storm raged outside the house, rattling the windows menacingly.*	Often used to reflect characters' emotions and create the mood in a particular scene.
Sibilance	Repeated use of sounds like 's' and 'sh'.	*The ship sailed across the silent sea.*	These sounds create a 'hissing' or 'shushing' effect. This could be comforting or even menacing, depending on where it appears.
Assonance	Use of words that have similar vowel sounds but different consonants.	*I tried to find the pie.*	Can create a sense of rhythm or give a piece of writing a song-like feel.
Superlatives	The most extreme form of an adjective or adverb.	*Frank was the laziest cat that lived on our street.*	Often used for emphasis, or to exaggerate a point. Can also create humour.
Oxymoron	When two opposing ideas are brought together in a word or phrase.	*The ending was bittersweet.*	Can be used for humorous or dramatic effect.
Paradox	A statement that initially appears to contradict itself.	*Sometimes you have to be cruel to be kind.*	Paradoxes can be used to make readers pause and think about a point that the writer might be making.

> For more language devices, look at p.46 for metaphors, p.49 for alliteration and onomatopoeia, and p.52 for rhetorical devices.

2) There's no standard effect that always applies for each technique. Make sure your analysis concentrates on the specific effect of the techniques used in the text you are given.

3) Don't just list all the language techniques you can spot in a text. Only mention the ones that are relevant to the question, and make sure you focus on analysing their effect on the reader.

Always write about the effect of language techniques...

When you comment on a language technique's effect, make sure that your analysis links back to what you were asked about. Even if your analysis is excellent, it won't get top marks if it doesn't answer the question.

Warm-Up Questions

Use these warm-up questions to test your knowledge of language techniques. If there's anything you're not sure about, this is a good chance to read the previous section again. Once you're feeling confident, you can move on to the exam-style questions on the next two pages. Ready, set, write...

Warm-Up Questions

1) Write down whether each of the sentences below use alliteration or onomatopoeia. Then explain one effect that the technique creates.
   a) Without warning, a bunch of brightly coloured bullfinches burst swiftly from the undergrowth.
   b) The buzz and chatter of the students ruined the tranquillity of the scene.
   c) Bag a Bargain at Brigson's — Portsmouth's Premier Pig Farm!

2) Briefly explain the difference between irony and sarcasm.

3) Is the following text sarcastic? Explain your answer using an example from the text.

   > Oh yeah, Kiet is a brilliant secretary — I especially appreciate the way he keeps forgetting to bring a pen and steals mine instead. And he's reorganised our files into a brand new system, which only he can understand — that's really made our lives easier.

4) For each sentence below, name the rhetorical technique and then explain its effect.
   a) Far from the sandwich heaven I'd been hoping for, I found myself in sandwich hell.
   b) I urge you, dear readers, to avoid this new restaurant at all costs.
   c) There's nothing worse than rain during an outdoor theatre performance.

5) Explain why the following text is biased. Use evidence from the text to support your answer.

   > By far the best hobby for young people is the card game "cribbage". All young people from the ages of eight to eighteen adore playing cribbage.

6) Write a paragraph about the effect of some of the descriptive language in the text below.

   > The air smelt of scorched grass. I could feel the blistering sun burning into my skin as I trudged slowly through the prickly, dry vegetation, my heavy load cutting cruel lines into my drooping shoulders. In the distance, the air shimmered in waves with the heat. I felt as if I were underwater, constantly being pulled back by the tidal drag of the temperature, every step an effort, every breath a trial.

7) Write down the technique used in each sentence. Then explain one effect that the technique creates.
   a) It was the toughest conversation he had ever had.
   b) An eagle swiftly swooped and soared through the sky.
   c) The wolf howled loudly and proudly.

Exam-Style Questions

To answer these exam-style questions, you'll need to draw on all of your knowledge about language techniques and how to analyse them. Have a quick glance back at pages 49-55 to refresh your memory, then grab a separate piece of paper to write on and get stuck into this lot.

Q1 Read the following extract from a piece of travel writing.

> The streets of Kuala Lumpur are a labyrinth of lost lanes, back-streets, dead-ends and alleys, which twist and turn and double back on themselves, constantly trying to bewilder the unaccustomed traveller. An apparently infinite series of haphazard side streets break out from the main street of the Chinatown area, like snakes winding across the desert. On every corner hang the pungent but irresistible smells of food stalls offering a cornucopia of exotic cuisines. Heavy trucks rumble past impatiently, whilst thousands of scooters whine and buzz like a swarm of bees, honking horns and hurling out exhaust fumes that stubbornly stagnate in the desperately hot air. The heat is relentless. Even standing still in the shade I can feel the sweat gathering on my forehead.
>
> In search of a bit of peace from the incessant heat and choking fumes, I make my way to the city centre park. Here, neat, well-trodden paths wind their way through lush lime-green lawns. On every side of the park, glimmering steel skyscrapers tower into the sky, peering down at the people walking below. It's like being surrounded by a giant metal rainforest, thronging with life.

Explain how the writer uses language to describe Kuala Lumpur.

Q2 Read the following extracts. Text A is from a letter written in the 19th century, and Text B is from a review posted on a travel website in the 21st century.

Text A
Dear Jane,
  I have arrived at my lodgings in Ware. They are satisfactory, if not impressive — the room must once have been decorated in good taste, but alas, it is the good taste of a bygone age. Nevertheless, the room is clean, tidy and of a good size. As I had expected, the mattress was not of the standard I am accustomed to (nor, for that matter, was the limited refreshment offered by the kitchens), but for a short stay, it will suffice.

Text B
The room smelt like its window hadn't been opened for about a century. The wallpaper was peeling. The carpet was a battlefield between all sorts of suspicious stains. Given the state of the rest of the room, I doubted that the 'fresh' bedding was clean, but it was the mattress that really drew my attention — it was like something from a Victorian prison cell, barely a few inches thick.

Compare how the two writers convey their different attitudes to their rooms.

You may wish to explore what the writers' attitudes are and what methods they use to convey their attitudes. You should use examples from **both** texts.

Exam-Style Questions

Q3 Read the following extract from a short story.

> "Howard, you made it!" Jiang beamed, ushering me through the doors of his mansion. "Come in, come in — you don't want to miss a minute of this party; I promise you, it's my best yet!"
>
> He hastened me through the marble hallway towards the ballroom. I could already hear the thumping of music and the hum of voices. As the golden doors were opened, the noise hit me like a wave. The room was thronged with hundreds of guests, and they were all joking, laughing, making introductions. Their voices wove together into a single, undulating buzz of talk. Beyond their voices was the exuberant playing of the live band; drums and saxophones adding bass and melody to the already throbbing noise. There were other sounds too — the clinking of glasses, the occasional popping of champagne corks followed by cheers.
>
> And the colours! The men were all in tuxedos, cutting sharp lines of white and black, while the women were shimmering in silks of every colour — emerald and scarlet, gold and violet, cobalt and cerise. Lights glittered from the chandeliers, sparkling on the women's jewellery and the martini glasses and the silverware. The ballroom had become a never-ending kaleidoscope of wealth.

How far do you agree or disagree with the following statement?

In these lines of the text, the party seems exciting and lively.

In your answer, make references to the text and consider:
- what impression you get of the party
- what methods are used to create this impression.

Q4 Read the following extract from a letter written in the 19th century.

> Dearest parents,
>
> I write to inform you that I have arrived in the city. Words can scarcely convey the sights, sounds and smells of this place, yet I shall endeavour to describe this world that is so different from the country.
>
> One is immediately struck by the number of people in the metropolis. The streets are rivers of humankind, flowing hither and thither, continuously fed by smaller streams pouring from alleyways and sporadic trickles from dwellings and businesses.
>
> Silence is a stranger to this world. The air is filled with incessant human chatter and the thunderous roar of carts and wagons. Why, I already long for the soothing cacophony of the seabirds squalling on the beach at home.
>
> The bleak streets teem with the most unpleasant odours: noxious gases which ooze out of overflowing sewers. The air is laced with acrid soot that belches from the innumerable chimneys of the factories which provide employment for the less well-to-do of the populace.

Explain how the writer uses language to describe the city.

Narrative Viewpoint

Literary texts will always have a narrator — a voice that is telling the story.

The Narrative Viewpoint is usually quite Easy to spot

1) A first-person narrator tells the story using words like 'I', 'we' and 'me'. A first-person narrator is often one of the characters, telling the reader directly about their feelings and experiences.

   I stood on the fringes of the stage, waiting my turn, fear coursing through my veins. → A first-person narrator establishes a stronger, more personal connection with the reader.

2) A second-person narrator tells the story using words like 'you'. A second-person narrator talks as if the reader ('you') is one of the characters.

   You turn your head to see her walking towards you. Your heart begins to race. → A second-person narrator makes the reader 'feel' what the character is feeling.

3) A third-person narrator is not one of the characters. They tell the story using words like 'he' and 'she' to talk about the characters.

   Jo's elated expression could mean only one thing: she had got a place at medical school. → A third-person narrator has a more detached viewpoint.

   Some third-person narrators are omniscient — they know what all the characters are thinking. Others are limited — they only know what one character is thinking.

4) When writing about a narrator, think about how reliable they are. You might not be able to trust them fully if they don't know something, or if they're trying to affect the reader in some way.

Think about how the Narrator Presents the Characters

PAPER 1 Q4

Q4   How far do you agree or disagree with the following statement?
     In these lines of the text, Faiza thinks Alice is a difficult person to spend time with.

Uses 'she' and is separate to the characters, so it's a third-person narrator. →

> Faiza was walking down the corridor when she noticed that Alice was walking towards her. Faiza sighed, rolled her eyes and braced herself.
> "Hi Faiza!" chirped Alice, with her typically exhausting optimism, "I hope I'll see you at the party later!"
> Faiza's face contorted into an obviously forced smile as she nodded sharply.

Think carefully about how the narrator's perspective is being used to affect the reader. →

I agree with this statement. The writer has used the narrator's perspective to present Alice as unlikeable, despite her actions. Everything she does is positive: she is bright, friendly, optimistic and simply invites Faiza to a party. The narrator presents her optimism as "typically exhausting" though, so her actions come across to the reader as tiresome, rather than positive. This is reinforced by the narrator's heavy focus on Faiza's expressions, which all betray her personal dislike for Alice: she "rolled" her eyes and had a "forced smile".

← *Link your points together to give a really detailed analysis of what the writer has done.*

Get to know these different narrative viewpoints...

It can be quite easy to forget about the narrator, because they're often not one of the characters directly involved in the story. But try to think about how they talk, and whether you can trust what they tell you.

Structure — Whole Texts

Whole text structure is all about the order that writers present events and ideas to the reader.

Structure is important for Fiction and Non-fiction

1) Structure is the way a writer organises their ideas within a text.

2) In non-fiction texts, writers will use structure to help them achieve their purpose. This might be to:

- Build their argument to a powerful conclusion.
- Reinforce the persuasive elements of their text through repetition.
- Set out an informative text in a clear and balanced way.
- Order their advice in a logical and easy-to-follow way.

3) In fiction texts, writers will structure their work in a way they think will entertain the reader. For example, story writing could have a linear or non-linear structure:

Texts with a linear structure are arranged chronologically — events are described in the order in which they happened and the text flows naturally from beginning to middle to end.

Texts with a non-linear structure are ordered in a way that makes the text interesting, rather than in chronological order. They might include things like flashbacks, changes in perspective or time shifts.

4) Linear texts tend to build towards some form of climax, whilst non-linear texts might begin with a dramatic moment and work backwards from there.

5) Whenever you write about structure, you need to show how the writer has used structure to produce a particular effect on the reader.

You could break a text up (e.g. into a 'start', 'middle' and 'end') and look at one part at a time. Consider why the text might have been put together the way it has been.

Writers use structure to Focus the Reader's Attention

1) One of the easiest ways to write about structure is to think about how the writer is directing your attention as you read, as well as why they've chosen to do this at that precise moment in the text. There are lots of ways a writer can do this, for example:

- The writer might draw the reader in by describing something general, then narrow their focus down to something more specific.
- The writer could describe things along a journey and make you feel as if you are travelling with them. This might involve moving from the outside to the inside or just from one place to another.
- A text might start with description and then move on to dialogue. This would shift your focus from setting to characters.
- Often, a writer will use a new paragraph to start a new topic. This could be a smooth transition or it could have a jarring effect that draws the reader's attention to a particular part of the text.
- In non-fiction texts, the writer will usually use paragraphs to lead you from their introduction, through their main points and onto their conclusion.

2) Often, descriptive writing will show rather than tell the reader what to focus on. For example, it might move the reader's attention from one place to another, acting like a camera shot does in a film.

Structure — Whole Texts

Here are some **Structural Features** to look out for

There are lots of structural features you could comment on in the fiction part of your exam. The structural techniques below are popular ones, so make sure you are familiar with them:

Cinematic techniques are features that remind readers of watching a film — zooming in and out, close-ups, etc. → They can highlight the start or end points of a story, as well as direct the reader's focus to important moments. They can create a sense of pace and action.

Flashbacks are when a text's focus briefly jumps back in time, often showing something from the past that is significant in the present. → They can provide more background information to the reader, or build suspense by delaying events in a text's present.

Foreshadowing is when a writer gives hints about what will happen later on in the story. → It highlights important characters, objects or events without revealing their significance.

Structural instability is when a writer frequently jumps from one point (e.g. a place, a time or a perspective) to another. → If the structure is unique or unexpected, it can intrigue readers. Instability might suggest that a narrator is unreliable.

Here are **More Techniques** you can write about

Take a look at the table below for some more devices that you could comment on in fiction texts:

Technique	What it is	Effects
Recurring motifs or imagery	When an idea or image appears multiple times in a narrative.	Links various points in the narrative. Can reinforce an important theme or idea.
Frame narratives	An overarching story that contains other stories within it — e.g. one character might narrate a story to another character.	Can provide a backdrop or context for any embedded narratives.
Embedded narratives	A narrative contained inside a frame narrative, sometimes called a 'story within a story'.	Can provide insight into the frame narrative. May show events from a different perspective, often in a way that changes the reader's opinion.
Juxtaposition	When two contrasting ideas are placed near or next to each other in a text.	Can highlight similarities and differences between ideas that are not often linked. Can also be used to create humour.
Cliffhangers	When a writer ends the story, or a section of the story, in a dramatic and sudden way that introduces a new plot or idea.	At the end of a section it can create suspense over what will happen next. At the end of a story, a cliffhanger might shock the reader or create an impactful ending that is memorable.

For structure questions, you need to make sure you're thinking about the overall structure of a text. It's important to write about specific structural features like these, but try to think about how they contribute to the overall tone, pace or atmosphere of a text.

Structure — Whole Texts

The Narrative Viewpoint will Affect the Structure

1) The narrative viewpoint is not a structural feature itself, so you won't get marks just for identifying that a text is written in the first-person. However, the narrator affects what information the reader receives, so the narrative viewpoint can influence the structure of a text.

2) The narrator might withhold some information, creating tension, or they could skip over certain parts of a story because they are biased.

3) Different narrators will have different effects on the structure of a text:

> - A third-person narrator (see page 59) will often have an overall view of the story, and so the structure might skip around to cover lots of different events.
>
> - For texts with a first-person narrator, the structure will probably follow that character's experiences quite closely.

4) Look out for texts that change their narrative perspective, i.e. they have more than one narrator. This might mean that the structure jumps around or alternates between the different viewpoints.

5) Shifts in perspective can affect the mood of the text or suddenly have the reader focus on something different. They can also give the reader greater insight by revealing what different characters think.

Explain how the writer has Structured the text to create an Effect

PAPER 1 Q3

Q3 Write about how the writer has structured the text to create nostalgia.
In your answer, you could consider how nostalgia increases or decreases throughout the text, and any changes in tone or viewpoint.

> The mountain looked a little mysterious in the half-light of the dusky evening. Its snow-capped peak stood alert, bathing in the dying embers of the setting sun. From there, my eye was drawn to the narrow path that wound its way precariously down past the dark woods and craggy outcrops of the mountain face. I traced the weaving path all the way down, until it vanished behind the spire of a magnificent church that loomed over the town nestled at the foot of the mountain.
>
> This was the town of my youth.
>
> This was the town where I had taken my first steps. This was the town where I had been to school, where I had battled through those tough transition years of teenage angst and, finally, where I had first fallen in love. It was permeated with memories of childhood games and, later in my adolescence, secret late-night trysts.
>
> I crossed the road and entered the alley that would take me deeper into the warren of streets that wound their way around the foot of the imposing church. When I finally emerged into the square, I was assaulted by a barrage of sights and smells that instantly took me all the way back to my youth.

Think about the overall structure of the text as you read. Try to identify any perspective shifts or other obvious structural features.

You can write about individual sentences, but for structure questions you must explain the effect they have on the text's overall structure.

Section Four — English Language: Language and Structure

Structure — Whole Texts

> Immediately, I was back under the oak tree, crouching silently next to my best friend Mirela. We were hiding from James Cotton, and it was matter of grave honour that we preserved our hiding place. Back then, a game of hide and seek was no mere playground triviality, it was a fierce battle of the sexes, a passionately fought war between two equally resolute forces.
>
> Both Mirela and I were fascinated with James: he was old for his age, smart and funny. Obviously, at that age, this fascination manifested itself as bitter hatred. The coyness would come later, along with the feelings of claustrophobia and a yearning for the big city. Mirela hadn't felt the same longing for the metropolis as I had, but she had discovered the coyness that would replace the naive and innocent feud. She had stayed here and built a life for herself; tomorrow morning I was to attend the wedding at which she would become Mrs Cotton.
>
> The tolling of the church bells brought me back to the present with a start. I needed to hurry if I was to get to my parents' house before dinnertime. With a sigh of nostalgia, I began the final leg of my journey back to my former home.

This text contains time shifts — it has a non-linear structure.

The text is structured to create nostalgia through its use of a time-shift. The novel begins with the narrator describing her town as it is in the present, but in the second half of the passage, her focus turns to reflecting on memories of her childhood. This shift is triggered by a "barrage of sights and smells" that transports the narrator "instantly" back to the past. The fact that the narrator's memories of the past merge so seamlessly into her account of the present suggests that the past and present are not so different. This is helped by the fact that the town is used as a link between the passages in the past and those in the present. The fact that the town is the same as it used to be helps to show, by contrast, how much its people have changed, which heightens the sense of nostalgia.

Moreover, the way the paragraphs are structured helps to strengthen this nostalgia. The first paragraph is made up of four sentences, which all go over several lines. By contrast, the second paragraph is just one short line, which makes it stand out to the reader and highlights its importance. The fact that the first paragraph discusses the town and landscape as they currently are, while the short, arresting second paragraph refers to the past and childhood, highlights the greater impact on the narrator of these childhood memories. This alerts the reader to the fact that the rest of the passage will likely be strongly informed by the narrator's nostalgic musings.

Following on from this, the repetition of the phrase "This was the town" in the second and third paragraphs shows how important the town is to the narrator. She uses each utterance of the phrase to mention a new memory, thereby building a sense of nostalgia as she pieces together a picture of her childhood for the reader. The repetition also reflects her mindset, as she temporarily dwells on childhood memories rather than focusing on present events. The structure therefore gives the reader insight into how strongly the past influences the narrator's thought patterns, leaving a stronger impression of the nostalgia she feels.

A perspective shift could involve a shift in time or place or both.

Always use examples to back up your points — you can use short quotes from the text or descriptions of the text.

Recurring themes or ideas (called motifs) can be used to draw together various parts of a text or argument.

You need to talk about the text as a whole, but you can also focus on how the writer has used individual paragraphs.

Make sure you can write about the effects of structural features as well as just identifying them.

Remember to mention how the writer's techniques affect the reader.

Make sure to refer back to the main focus of the question throughout your answer.

Structure is used to create different effects, just like language...

You need to think about how the writer is using structure to create the specific effect in the question. Look out for things like cinematic techniques, perspective shifts, single sentence paragraphs and recurring ideas.

Sentence Forms

Writing about the effects of different sentence forms will earn you marks in questions about language. In structure questions, you need to talk about how individual sentences affect the overall structure of the text.

Sentences are made up of Clauses

1) A clause is a part of a sentence that has a subject and a verb. A clause usually makes sense on its own.

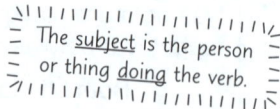
The subject is the person or thing doing the verb.

2) A single clause on its own is called a simple sentence.

The sky was grey and sombre. → This is a single clause that is also a simple sentence. It has a subject ('The sky') and a verb ('was').

3) Simple sentences can be used to explain something clearly and simply. They are also often used to create a sharp or abrupt tone that keeps the reader engaged or creates tension.

4) A compound sentence has two main clauses, linked by a conjunction like 'or', 'but' or 'and'. Both clauses have to be able to make sense on their own. For example:

The sky was grey and sombre, and the rain lashed at our faces. → Writers can use compound sentences to do things like expand on their initial statement, creating more detailed and interesting descriptions.

5) Complex sentences have two or more clauses, but only one of them needs to make sense on its own.

When I arrived, the sky was grey and sombre. → This is a complex sentence — 'When I arrived' wouldn't work as a sentence on its own. This clause could go either before or after the main clause. Writers often create interest by using complex sentences to break up the rhythm of a text.

6) Writers use a variety of sentence forms to achieve different effects and keep the reader interested.

There are Four Main Types of sentence

1) Different types of sentences have different purposes:

- Statements deliver information, e.g. 'The referee made the decision.' They can be found in all texts, but they are particularly common in informative texts like newspaper articles, reports and reviews.
- Questions ask the reader something, e.g. 'What would you do in my situation?' They don't always require an answer — sometimes they are just there to encourage us to think about something.
- Orders, or commands, tell us to do something, e.g. 'Consider the effects of this in the long-term.' They often use imperative verbs (verbs that give an instruction, like 'remember', 'think about' or 'go').
- Exclamations convey strong emotions, e.g. 'How outrageous this is!' They usually end with an exclamation mark, and they're common in persuasive texts.

2) For the reading questions, it's a good idea to think about how and why writers have used particular types of sentence — bear in mind that different sentence types are suited to different purposes.

Section Four — English Language: Language and Structure

Sentence Forms

Writers use Different Sentence Forms to Interest the reader

1) Varying the length of sentences can create different effects. Here are a couple of examples:

   These are just examples — the effects of different sentence lengths will vary from text to text.

   > *The sky was growing darker. I couldn't see where I was going. I stumbled.*

   → Short simple sentences can be used to build tension or to create a worried and confused tone.

   > *I waited excitedly at the foot of the stairs, listening to the footsteps above, thinking about the afternoon ahead, pacing the hall and counting down the minutes until we could set off.*

   → A longer, complex sentence could be used to give the impression of time dragging.

2) The order of words within sentences can also be chosen to create an effect. For example:

   > *I had never seen such chaos before.*
   > *Never before had I seen such chaos.*

   → Writers sometimes use inversion (altering the normal word order) to change the emphasis in a text. Here, inversion helps to emphasise the phrase 'Never before'.

3) If you notice something about the way a writer has used sentences, don't just identify it — you need to analyse the effects to show how they influence the reader.

Comment on the Effects of different Sentence Forms

PAPER 1 Q2

Q2   Explain how the writer uses language to describe their emotions.

This is a long sentence that leaves the reader breathless by the end. It emphasises the feeling of weariness that the narrator is describing.

> It was late evening by the time I returned home from the shops, tired and weary from barging my way past all the desperate Christmas Eve shoppers. It had been a long day, and I was ready for a relaxing bath and a long sleep. It wasn't until I was halfway up the path that I noticed the front door was ajar. My heart began beating wildly inside my chest as I hesitantly advanced towards the door. My hands began to shake. My mind began conjuring apparitions of the unspeakable horrors that could be lurking inside. On reaching the door, I took a deep breath, collected my senses and stepped across the threshold. Everything was quiet and still. I crossed the hall and put down my shopping. Everything looked normal. Nothing was out of place. Suddenly I heard a noise above me. Someone was upstairs. I gasped. But then a change came over me: my fear had turned to resolute anger. Seldom had I experienced such intense fury in all my life. There was an intruder in my house, and they had no right to be there. I made for the stairs.

The repetition in the sentence beginnings 'My heart began', 'My hands began' and 'My mind began' gives emphasis to the physical effects of the narrator's fear.

The use of a colon shows that there is going to be some form of explanation. This highlights the move away from unexplained short simple sentences.

Short, simple sentences are used to reinforce the narrator's feelings of dread.

This inversion disrupts the usual word order and focuses the reader's attention on the narrator's anger.

This longer sentence marks a change in tone from fear to anger.

Make sure you can write confidently about sentences...

It will really help you in the language questions if you're able to talk about the effects of different sentence forms. Try to spend some time learning the technical terms for different forms and types of sentences.

Language & Structure — Knowledge Organiser

Here's a summary of the last section — make sure you're familiar with everything that's covered on these two pages.

Tone

The feeling that words are written with. Tone:

- **Creates a particular mood** — e.g. a happy tone might create a light-hearted mood.

- **Can show writers' attitudes** — e.g. a writer might use a serious tone for a topic they consider important.

- **Can reflect purpose & audience** — e.g. a friendly tone might suggest a familiar audience.

- **Can be conveyed through language & punctuation** — e.g. lots of ellipses and dashes might show that the tone is very uncertain & confused.

Style & Register

Writers adapt style / register to suit purpose & audience.

Style

- The overall way a text is written. Consider:
  1. Language choices 2. Sentence forms 3. Structure
- There are lots of different styles. E.g. cinematic and journalistic.

Register

The specific language used to match writing to its social situation.

Formal register → authority figures or strangers
Informal register → friends

Language Techniques

English Language paper 1, question 2 & paper 2, question 3 specifically test how the writer uses language.

Figurative language
- Similes — Describe one thing by comparing it to something else.
- Metaphors — Describe something as if it actually were something else.
- Extended metaphor — A metaphor that's developed throughout a text.
- Personification — Describes something as if it were a person.

Rhetoric
- Rhetorical questions — engage the reader.
- List of three — used for emphasis.
- Hyperbole — intentional exaggeration.
- Antithesis — highlights contrasts.
- Parenthesis — adds extra information.

Irony
- When the literal meaning is the opposite of the intended meaning.
- Often humorous or light-hearted.
- Can be hard to spot — use context to help.

Sarcasm
- Language with a mocking or insulting tone.
- Often used to make fun of something.
- Uses irony — BUT with extra unpleasantness.

Descriptive language
Makes texts vivid & interesting. Includes:
- Interesting verbs.
- Five senses — see, smell, hear, touch or taste.
- Lots of adjectives to create a clear image.

Bias
- Not presenting the whole picture, e.g. by omitting information, exaggerating or generalising.
- Can be tricky to spot — seems neutral / factual.

Look out for bias in English Language paper 2, e.g. in a non-fiction article.

Other language techniques

Technique	What it is & what it does
Pathetic fallacy	A kind of personification where nature is given human feelings and responses. Reflects character's emotions & sets mood.
Sound effects	• Alliteration — neighbouring words starting with same sound. • Onomatopoeia — words that sound like the noise described. • Sibilance — repeated use of 's' & 'sh' sounds. • Assonance — words with similar vowel sounds. Grabs reader's attention. Makes writing memorable & powerful.
Superlatives	Most extreme form of a describing word. Adds emphasis.
Oxymoron	Two opposing ideas combined in a word or phrase. Used for humorous / dramatic effect.
Paradox	Statement that seems to contradict itself. Makes reader pause & think.

Section Four — English Language: Language and Structure

Words and Phrases

Nouns — Naming words that refer to a person, place or thing.
Pronouns — Words that replace nouns.
Possessive Pronouns — Pronouns that show ownership.
Possessive Determiners — Show who a noun belongs to.

Verbs — Action words.
Adjectives — Describe a noun or pronoun.
Adverbs — Give extra information about verbs.
Intensifiers — Adverbs used for emphasis.

Different words have specific connotations & are chosen to achieve particular effects.
↳ e.g. 'muttered' has a similar meaning to 'said', but implies annoyance.

Groups of words work together to make cumulative effects.
- Semantic field — words associated with a specific theme or topic.
- Repetition of word types — e.g. using lots of verbs can make a text seem exciting.

For both Language papers, you'll need to consider why writers use particular words and phrases and comment on their effect.

Sentence Forms

Different sentence forms achieve different effects:

Simple → single clause sentences
- Can explain something clearly.
- Can create an abrupt tone to build tension.

Compound → 2 main clauses & a conjunction
- Can expand initial statements.
- Can create detailed descriptions.

Complex → main clause & dependent clause
- Can vary the rhythm of a text.

There are four main types of sentence:
1. Statements
2. Questions
3. Commands
4. Exclamations

Narrative Viewpoint

Narrators affect the information a reader receives:

First person
- 'I' / 'we' / 'me'. Often one of the characters.
- Creates a personal connection with reader.

Second person
- 'you'. Addresses reader as if they're a character.
- Reader 'feels' what character is feeling.

Third person
- 'he' / 'she' / 'it'.
- Often detached from a text's action.

The narrative viewpoint affects the structure of a text.

Unusual narrators
- Unreliable narrators — might leave out parts of story deliberately or unknowingly.
- Multiple narrators — can change focus & affect mood.

Structure — Whole Texts

Structure can be used to focus the reader's attention and create an effect.

Non-fiction — structure used to help writers achieve their purpose.

Fiction — structure used to create dramatic effects.

English Language paper 1 question 3 will ask you to analyse the structure of a fictional text.

Cinematic techniques	Direct reader's focus like in a film (e.g. zooms in & out).
Flashbacks	Focus briefly jumps backwards in time.
Foreshadowing	Hints about what will happen later on in narrative.
Recurring motifs	Repetition of images to reinforce key ideas.
Frame narrative	Overarching story containing embedded narrative.
Juxtaposition	Contrasting ideas placed near each other.
Linear structure	Chronological events (i.e. things happen in order).
Cliffhangers	Sudden ending which creates suspense.
Paragraphs	Create logical structure or change focus of narrative.

Be specific when you talk about language and structure...
Remember — when you comment on a text's language or structure, <u>don't</u> give a vague, general explanation of its effect. You need to analyse the specific impact of the technique in its context.

Section Four — English Language: Language and Structure

Worked Answer

Right, it's time for another worked answer. Have a look at the question, extract and sample response on these two pages. Read through the annotations, and make sure you understand the feedback at the end that explains how the answer could be made better. Then write an improved version of the answer.

Q1 Read the following extract from a piece of fiction.

> The shot rang out. Olga powered off the blocks. The sound of the stadium had faded now, and only one thing mattered: putting one foot in front of the other, faster than she had ever done before. This was her race. She was born for this! Her blood pounded in her ears as she sprinted round the track.
>
> In the distance, the finish line was approaching. There were still two runners ahead of her. As she gained on them, she thought back to the first time she had ever stepped onto a race track. Seven years old, nervous, clinging to her mother's hand for comfort. She thought about her first win at a national competition three years later, and remembered the electric feeling that had flooded through her whole body as she stepped onto the podium. She channelled that feeling now.
>
> Faster! Olga urged herself on. Her legs burned. Her lungs screamed. But she was catching up. She overtook one. Still faster! At the last second, she overtook the final competitor and her foot came down first, landing triumphantly over the white line.
>
> Olga slowed to a halt, and doubled over as she gasped for breath. Wiping the sweat from her eyes, she looked up again at the stadium, and nearly cried with joy. She could hardly believe it. She had achieved her lifelong dream: she had won a gold medal at the Olympics.

Write about how the writer has structured this text to create a sense of excitement.

In your answer, you could consider how a sense of excitement increases or decreases throughout the text, and any changes in tone or viewpoint.

structure takes you through Olga's race from start to finish, but is punctuated by flashback moments of close focus on Olga — feel like you're experiencing the race with her strong resolution gives a satisfying ending — excitement peaks in the middle

You <u>don't</u> need to make a <u>detailed plan</u> for this type of question, but <u>quickly</u> jotting down your <u>ideas</u> (like this) can be helpful.

The opening sentence <u>refers back to</u> the question.

The extract is structured to create <u>a sense of excitement</u> by taking the reader on <u>a journey from the starting blocks to the finish line</u>. The majority of the passage takes place in the present and describes the events of the race as it unfolds. <u>This helps to create an overall sense of forward progress in the text, which makes the reader feel as though they are watching the race in real time</u>.

You need to show an awareness of how the text is structured as a <u>whole</u>.

This is a good explanation, but to be even better, it could be <u>developed</u> by referring back to the question — making them feel as though they are there and watching the race helps build <u>excitement</u>.

Section Four — English Language: Language and Structure

Worked Answer

Support your points with short quotations or references to the text. →

However, this sense of forward progress is interrupted by a flashback. The writer uses this <u>non-chronological structure</u> to give the reader context about Olga's life, for example that <u>she started running when she was only seven years old</u>. This gives the race greater emotional importance, as the reader gains an insight into how much Olga has progressed. It makes the reader want her to win even more, which heightens the sense of excitement.

← Good mention of specific **terminology**.

A more **technical term** could be used here e.g. **zoom in** / **focus shift**. →

The text also <u>looks at smaller details</u>, which immerses the reader in Olga's physical experience. For example, the text says "Her legs burned. Her lungs screamed". This gives the reader an insight into how Olga feels as she's running, which makes the race more exciting. <u>Moreover, the fact that the writer uses short sentences here creates an urgent tone, which contributes to the tension and sense of excitement.</u>

← This question type is all about how **structure** is used to create a specific **effect**.

The question wording suggests you could write about how the effect **increases or decreases** throughout the text. →

<u>The text's overall structure results in a decreased sense of excitement in the final paragraph.</u> The first three paragraphs build up to the end of the race, whereas the final paragraph describes Olga's joy that <u>"She had achieved her lifelong dream: she had won a gold medal at the Olympics"</u>. Although a sense of achievement is created through the text's resolution, there is less excitement than in previous paragraphs, as there is no longer any building anticipation. The reader now knows the outcome of the race, so the tension is resolved.

← This quotation is fine, but it could be much **shorter**.

- This answer has explored a variety of structural features — such as the writer's focus and a flashback — and explained how these create a sense of excitement. It also backs up these points with suitable examples.

- To get the top marks, this answer could be improved by:
  - keeping quotations precise
  - using more technical terms, e.g. zoom in
  - making sure all points are fully developed by including a bit more detail.

Exam-Style Questions

You should know the drill by now — use these exam-style questions to help you practise for the real thing.

Q1 This is the ending to a short story. Joan is eighty-six years old, and one of the nurses from her care home has volunteered to take her to the beach.

> They arrived shortly before lunchtime. The seagulls squawked noisily overhead, swooping and circling, bright as doves against the blue sky. The nurse pushed the wheelchair down the boardwalk. Looking out over the sand and the grey-green sea, Joan was transfixed.
> The first time she had been to the beach was as a little girl, shortly before the war broke out. It had been a hot day. The beach was full of people sprawled on multicoloured deck chairs and picnic blankets, lending the scene a carnival feel. She remembered the smell of the water as she raced into the sea for the first time. She remembered the feeling of damp sand between her fingers and toes, and how the sea salt had dried into tiny crystals on her skin. Her mother had packed a picnic of hard-boiled eggs and potato salad. It had been the best day of her life so far, and as her father had bundled her into a towel, tired and sun-soaked, ready to go home, she had already been looking forward to the next visit.
> Now Joan watched the children race delightedly across the sand like she had done. Her nurse bought her fish and chips for lunch. Joan bought sticks of rock for her great-grandchildren. As the sun was going down, and they headed back to the car, Joan looked back over her shoulder. She knew there wouldn't be a next visit — but she didn't mind. She had seen the sea again.

Write about how the writer has structured this text to create a sense of loss.

In your answer, you could consider how a sense of loss increases or decreases throughout the text, and any changes in tone or viewpoint.

Q2 Read the following extract from a piece of fiction.

> The theatre hummed with expectant conversation as the spectators began to fill the stalls. The red velvet seats and gentle golden lighting gave the impression of being caught in the centre of a giant ruby. There was a magical feeling, as if everyone knew they were going to witness something spectacular that night, and eyes kept flickering over to the theatre drapes, wondering when the show would begin.
> Backstage, biting his fingernails down to the nail-bed, was the one they were all waiting for. Mikhail had been told by everyone he met that he was the greatest tenor of all time. Conductors had shed a tear when he sang, audiences had wept openly. But that never stopped him from feeling sick with nerves before a performance. What if his voice faltered? What if he forgot the words? What if he disappointed them all? How catastrophic this performance will be!
> "Sixty seconds to curtain," the stage manager called to him. Mikhail took a deep breath. His palms were damp with sweat. His legs felt like jelly. He didn't know if he was ready for this.

Write about how the writer has structured this text to create tension.

In your answer, you could consider how tension increases or decreases throughout the text, and any changes in tone or viewpoint.

Section Four — English Language: Language and Structure

Revision Summary Test for Section Four

Nice job on reaching the end of Section Four. Now try your hand at these summary questions.
- Yep, these questions are **hard** — they'll really help you see **how well you know your stuff**.
- Tackle the **revision summary test** below, or scan the QR code to do it **online**. Use the CGP RevisionHub to **track your progress** and see **which areas need more work**.
- You can find **sample answers** here: www.cgpbooks.co.uk/blurb-answers

Tone and Style (p.42-43) ☑

1) Briefly explain what is meant by a writer's tone and how you can identify it.
2) Give four examples of a style that a text could be written in. Describe each of these styles.
3) Would you expect the register of these types of writing to be formal or informal? Explain why.
   a) a newspaper article reporting on changes to the tax system
   b) an article about mountain biking on a website aimed at teenagers

Language (p.44-55) ☑

4) Define and give an example of each of these three word types:
   a) pronoun   b) adjective   c) adverb
5) Explain how words can be used to create a cumulative effect.
6) What is the difference between a simile, a metaphor and an extended metaphor?
7) Ella says "the writer uses personification — he describes the young girl as if she were an animal." Why is Ella wrong?
8) Briefly explain what alliteration is and why a writer might use it.
9) Give three examples of onomatopoeic words. Why might a writer use onomatopoeia?
10) What is irony? Why might a writer use it?
11) a) How is sarcasm different to irony?
    b) When might a writer use sarcasm?
12) Name four rhetorical techniques and explain the effect of each one.
13) Explain how you might be able to tell if a text is biased.
14) Define each of these language techniques. Then describe an effect of each technique.
    a) pathetic fallacy   b) oxymoron   c) sibilance   d) superlative

Narrative Viewpoint and Structure (p.59-65) ☑

15) What are the three types of narrative viewpoint? What is the effect of each one on the reader?
16) Briefly explain the difference between a linear and non-linear structure.
17) Give three ways in which a writer might use structure to focus a reader's attention.
18) a) What is a flashback?   b) What is foreshadowing?   c) What is structural instability?
19) Give the definition of each of the following techniques. Describe the effect of each one.
    a) frame narrative   b) embedded narrative   c) juxtaposition
20) Explain how each of the following narrative viewpoints might affect the structure of a text:
    a) a first-person narrator   b) a third-person narrator
21) Briefly define simple, compound and complex sentences. What effect might each one have?
22) What are the four main types of sentence? Explain the purpose of each one.
23) Explain how varying the length of sentences can create different effects.

Section Five — English Language: Writing

Writing with Purpose

All writing has a purpose, so you need to make it clear in both your fiction and non-fiction writing.

Structure your writing to Suit your Purpose

1) The purpose of your writing might be to inform, advise, argue or persuade, or entertain. It could even be more than one of these.

2) For both English Language papers, question 5 will tell you the purpose of your writing.

3) Sometimes it will be obvious, e.g. in paper 2 you might be asked to write a letter to argue or persuade. It can be less obvious though, so sometimes you'll need to work it out, e.g. if you're asked to write a story for paper 1, your purpose would be to entertain.

4) Different purposes will need different structures, so you'll need to think about a structure that will help you achieve your purpose most effectively.

5) You can lay out your structure by writing a plan, so that it stays consistent throughout your answer:

See page 23 for more about writer's purpose.

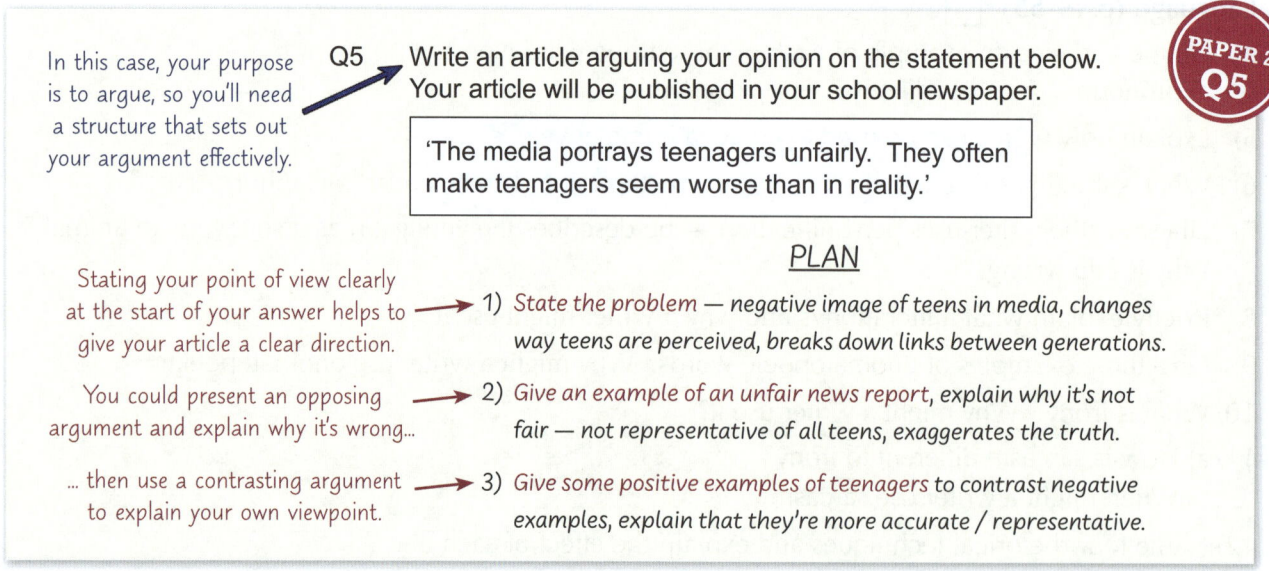

Choose your Tone, Style and Register to match your Purpose

1) In order to get good marks, you also need to show that you can adjust your tone, style and register to suit your purpose.

2) For example, a text written to advise might have an objective, authoritative tone:

Upon consultation with local residents, and in light of their strong opposition, this committee recommends that the proposal be withdrawn immediately.

→ This text uses a formal register and complex language to make its advice seem reliable.

See p.42-43 for more on tone, style and register.

3) A persuasive text needs to be more subjective (based on personal feelings). It might try to create a personal tone that involves the reader in a text:

Like me, you must be weary of the incessant criticism. We're intelligent young citizens who understand the issues threatening our planet. Why are we being ignored?

→ This text uses a rhetorical question and the pronouns 'you' and 'we' to involve and persuade its audience.

See p.52 for some rhetorical techniques that help achieve this.

4) When you adjust your writing to suit your purpose, make sure you're still showing off your ability to use sophisticated vocabulary.

Writing with Purpose

PAPER 1 Q5

Literary Fiction texts are often written to Entertain

Q5 You are entering a writing competition run by an outdoor magazine. Write the beginning of a story based on the prompt 'a visit to the woods'.

The purpose will always be referred to in the question. In this case, you're writing the beginning of a story, so you're writing to intrigue and engage the reader.

The purpose is to entertain, so this story starts in the middle of the action to grab the reader's interest.

I'd never in my life needed a break so badly. My airless writing room had begun to feel suffocating; so had the frustration of my unending writer's block. I gave up, threw down my pen, and went out for a walk.

My *irritation evaporated* almost immediately into the crisp autumn air. Buoyed by the hope of finding inspiration amongst the fiery leaves that crackled and crunched under my boots, I ambled contentedly through the golden wood.

A soft breeze caressed the treetops, whispering its way through the auburn tapestry. All around me on the forest floor, *sunlight and shadow danced in an elegant choreography.*

This was my sanctuary. The perfect haven where my mind could roam freely, without the prison bars of lined paper.

Figurative language helps the reader to imagine the writer's feelings.

This uses complex sentences to keep the writing style varied.

Personification creates a pleasant, tranquil atmosphere.

This short sentence highlights the significance of this place to the narrator.

Non-fiction texts can have a Variety of Purposes

PAPER 2 Q5

Q5 Write an article arguing your opinion on the statement below. Your article will be published in a broadsheet newspaper.

> 'Cosmetic surgery is a psychologically damaging procedure that increases the pressure to achieve an unrealistic level of perfection. It should be banned.'

In this task, your purpose is to explain your point of view and persuade *your readers.*

If you're writing to persuade, you could structure your answer by stating an opposing opinion and then counteracting it.

Public consensus has long seen cosmetic surgery as a mere vanity project, a procedure dreamed up by the wealthy to aid their endless pursuit of perfection. This seems somewhat unfair on the medical establishment.

In truth, cosmetic surgery sits at the height of medical achievement. Far from being a symptom of a shallow society, cosmetic procedures are a solution: they offer the chance of a new life. Plastic surgery has the power to improve lives, something that has always been an important medical objective.

It is time for a sea-change in attitudes to plastic surgery — it is no longer acceptable for the world to view with scorn those who have chosen to specialise in the improvement of the human form.

Emotive phrases like this can help to make the audience sympathise with your viewpoint.

You need to use a confident, assured tone to be persuasive.

There are marks available for adapting your writing to fit a purpose...

Don't forget that writing can often have more than one purpose (see p.23) — make sure you think about all the reasons that you're writing, so that you can adapt your style and produce a high level answer.

Writing for an Audience

For each writing task, you'll need to think about your audience. Your audience is just anyone who's going to hear or read your writing — it doesn't mean you'll have to perform your work.

Work out Who your Audience is

1) For question 5 on both Language papers, you need to think about the audience you're writing for.
2) Sometimes the audience will be specified...

> Q5 You are writing a creative piece that will be published in a teen magazine. Write the beginning of a story based on the prompt 'a person goes travelling'.

PAPER 1 Q5 — Here's the audience — teenagers.

3) ...and sometimes you'll have to work it out — the form and content will give you some clues:

> Q5 Write a broadsheet newspaper article arguing your opinion on the statement below.
>
> 'Students should attend classes virtually. In today's digital society, it's illogical that students still have to leave the house to go to school.'

PAPER 2 Q5 — You're writing a broadsheet newspaper article, so your audience will mostly be well-educated adults.

This statement is about schools, so the audience will be people interested in education, such as parents or teachers.

Choose your Tone, Style and Register to match your Audience

1) Once you know who your audience is, you'll need to adapt your tone, style and register so that they're appropriate to the people who will be reading your writing.
2) For example, you might want to consider the age and level of expertise of your audience, as well as your relationship with them.

See p.42-43 for more on tone, style and register.

Age

- If you're addressing a younger audience, you might use a more light-hearted tone.
- A more formal, serious register might work better for older audiences. You might also use a more complex style than you would for a younger audience.

Relationship with reader

- If you're writing to a familiar audience, you might use a conversational style and a friendly tone.
- If you're writing to an unknown audience, it would be better to use an impersonal tone and a formal register.

Expertise

- Different audiences will have different levels of expertise in the subject you're writing about.
- For example, if you're writing a report for a panel of experts, your register should be more formal, with a style that uses more specialised language than if you were writing for a general audience.

3) Whoever your audience is, avoid using colloquial and overly chatty language in your exam answers.
4) You should always aim to show your writing skills to the examiner by including a range of vocabulary and sentence types.

Section Five — English Language: Writing

Writing for an Audience

Literary Fiction texts need to Engage their Audience

PAPER 1 Q5

Q5 You are entering your school's creative writing competition, which will be judged by your teachers. Write the beginning of a story based on the prompt 'a family reuniting'.

The audience for this question is your teachers.

Amelia's eighteenth birthday had truly been a day like no other. It was the day she first met Jack: a tall, handsome stranger dressed in a naval uniform. Don't be fooled by the intrusion of a charming stranger into this narrative. This is not a romance novel, and Amelia was not Cinderella. Jack was her brother — her long-lost brother, who had left to join the Navy before she had been born, and who returned now with the cowed despondence of a disgraced man.

Amelia could never forget her mother's face as she had opened the door to greet another well-wishing neighbour, only to find her lost son hunched on the doorstep. Her features appeared to melt, losing all definition as they formed themselves into a canvas over which several emotions flashed. At first there was shock, which quickly became anger, then relief, and finally, remorse.

For this task, your immediate audience is a panel of judges — you need to impress them by writing engagingly. Try surprising them with something unexpected, e.g. addressing the reader directly.

To impress teachers, you will need to use a formal, sophisticated register.

Non-fiction texts can use a Personal Tone

PAPER 2 Q5

Q5 Write a speech in response to the statement below. Your speech will be delivered to students at your school, advising them on how to cope with the threat of internet bullying.

> 'Social media has provided a new way for us to interact with our peers. In turn, this has led to the creation of a new forum for bullying — the internet.'

In this task, you're writing for a teenage audience, so you'll need to adjust your tone, style and register accordingly.

We are a generation that has been raised in the era of social media. Every day, most of us use some form of social media to broadcast our identities. We're telling the world, "This is who I am." That's why cyber bullying can be so upsetting — it can feel like your whole identity is being attacked.

There are many different ways to deal with online bullying. The first thing you need to do is report it. You can usually do this on the social media site itself, but if you don't feel comfortable doing this, you should talk to someone in person. Suffering in silence will only make things worse.

If you find you are the victim of persistent bullying, take steps to block the person who is bullying you from contacting you. It's also a good idea to record the bullying in some way — you could take a screenshot, or even just save the messages somewhere. This will make things much easier to report later.

You're writing to advise teenagers. Use words like "we" and "you" to establish a connection and give your advice calmly, without being patronising.

Your tone should be helpful and friendly, but in this case your register should still be quite formal. Don't use any slang or text speak.

Show the examiner that you're aware of your audience...

In question 5 on both English Language papers, the examiner will look carefully at how well-matched your answer is to your audience. Think about your word choices, sentence structures and overall writing style.

Writing Stories

In English Language paper 1, question 5, you might be asked to write the beginning of a story. Your examiner will be looking for a convincing and compelling opening, so make sure you practise writing this type of text.

Grab your Reader's Attention from the Start

1) It's always a good idea to <u>start</u> your stories with an <u>opening sentence</u> that'll make your <u>reader</u> want to <u>carry on</u> reading. For example:

You could start with a <u>direct address</u> to the reader:

> *Everybody has a bad day now and again, don't they? Well, I'm going to tell you about a day that was much, much worse than your worst day ever.*

Or you could try a description of a particularly <u>unusual character</u>:

> *Humphrey Ward was, without a shadow of a doubt, the most brilliant (and most cantankerous) banana thief in the country.*

Try to avoid clichéd openings like 'Once upon a time'.

2) If you start your story in the <u>middle of the action</u>, it'll create a <u>fast-paced</u> atmosphere that makes the reader want to find out <u>what happens next</u>:

> *I couldn't believe it. He was gone. "He must be here," I thought to myself as I went through the shed, desperately throwing aside box after box. It was no use. Tanmay had run away, and it was all my fault.*

3) This example <u>explains</u> some of what's happening after a few sentences, which keeps up the <u>fast pace</u> of the narrative — so the story stays <u>interesting</u>.

4) You could also try <u>prolonging</u> the mystery to create <u>tension</u> in your narrative. Just make sure you <u>reveal</u> what's going on before it gets too <u>confusing</u> for your audience.

5) However you start your writing, you need to make sure it's <u>engaging</u> and <u>entertaining</u> for the reader — so whatever you do, don't <u>waffle</u>.

Try to Build the Tension from the Start

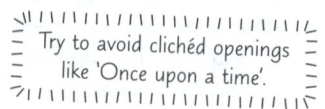

Q5   You are writing a piece for your school's creative writing anthology. Write the beginning of a story based on the prompt 'a trip to the beach'.

> *The waves drowned out my shouts as they crashed against the rocks with thundering force. I had only closed my eyes for a minute, and now I had awoken to find that Amy was nowhere to be seen. I scanned the deserted beach, searching for any sign of my beautiful daughter.*
>
> *Amy had been wearing a blue pinafore dress that made her look like Alice in Wonderland. I remembered joking with her about how funny it would be if the Queen of Hearts had suddenly appeared to chase her along the sands. She had merely giggled and returned to the digging project that was taking up all her attention. But where was she now?*

This story starts in the middle of the action — we don't know who the narrator is or why they're shouting.

This text solves the mystery of what's going on fairly quickly to maintain the pace.

Use key words to show as clearly as possible that you're answering the question.

Try to keep the tension building as you move on from your opening paragraphs.

Section Five — English Language: Writing

Writing Stories

Make your Language and Narrative Viewpoint fit the Task

1) Different word choices will have different effects, so you'll need to pick vocabulary that creates the right tone for your story. For example:

> *The door screeched open and I carefully entered the dingy cellar. Shadows cast by my torch leapt up at me through the gloom.*

Words like 'screeched', 'dingy' and 'gloom' make this writing sound spooky.

> *I burst noisily through the thicket of trees and sprinted towards the shore. The men were still chasing me, bellowing threats.*

Words like 'burst', 'sprinted' and 'chasing' make this writing sound exciting and dramatic.

2) You also need to think about what narrative viewpoint you're going to use (see p.59).

3) A first-person narrator uses the pronouns 'I' and 'we', as they're usually a character in the story.

> *I quickly scanned the book for anything that might help. My heart was racing; I knew I needed to work fast.*

The first-person narrative makes things more dramatic by helping the reader to imagine the story is happening to them.

4) A third-person narrator uses words like 'he' and 'she' to talk about characters from a separate viewpoint.

> *Shamil lit the bonfire carefully, then retreated back a few metres as the feeble fire began to crackle and spit.*

The narrator isn't part of the story. This creates distance, as the narrative voice and the characters are separate from each other.

Use Descriptive Techniques to make your text Engaging

PAPER 1 Q5

Q5 You are entering a competition run by a creative writing website. Write the beginning of a story based on the prompt 'living in the wild'.

> *The sun dipped low beneath the looming, dusky sky. Its daytime glory was reduced to the fading flicker of a tiny ember that only just protruded above the dark horizon.*
> *Down in the valley, the camp hummed with activity: people milled about like ants, erecting tents, cooking meals and lighting fires, the smoke from which crept stealthily up the mound, filling the rider's nostrils with the warming aromas of home.*
> *Beyond the confines of the camp, the open plains bathed in the warmth of the dying light. Come nightfall, the plains would transform from places of refuge into discordant wastelands, answerable only to the laws of nature. Shadows would devour the landscape and wild animals would stalk the grounds, salivating for fresh meat. The remnants of daylight would finally expire, the clouds withering into the blackened sky, and the world would sink into a deep, merciless night.*

This description uses a third-person narrator, so the narrative isn't limited by the rider's perspective.

Use techniques like alliteration and repeating patterns to add rhythm to your text.

Combine visual imagery with other senses to help the reader imagine they are there with the narrator.

Using more sophisticated vocabulary makes the description more interesting.

Using figurative language, like similes and personification, will help to make your text more engaging.

Writing Stories

It's Important to Leave a Good Impression

1) Even though you're asked to write the opening of a story, it's still important that you finish with some impact — you want to leave the examiner with a great impression of your writing abilities.

2) Here are some examples of different ways that you could finish your writing in the exam:

- You could end with an unexpected plot twist to shock the reader.
- You could show the main character coming to some kind of realisation.
- You could create a cliffhanger ending by finishing with a question. This will leave the reader thinking about what will happen next.
- You could foreshadow what might happen later on in the story. This will introduce something new that the story might go on to explore.

3) If you find you're running out of time, think up a quick way to wrap up your answer. Make sure you're ending in a sensible place, and finish with a short, punchy line.

4) Remember — you only have to write the opening to a story. You don't have to resolve everything in your story.

Try to make your Final Paragraphs as Powerful as possible

PAPER 1 Q5

Q5 You have been asked to submit a creative piece to a website for young adults. Write the beginning of a story based on the prompt 'making a bad decision'.

The narrator has had a realisation, which shows that this section is coming to a close.

I knew I should never have stolen the vase. It had been a moment of madness. I had just seen it sitting there, and it looked so beautiful and elegant. All of my problems stemmed from that decision, that single flash of foolishness.

You should aim to build the tension towards a climax.

I spent a long time wondering what to do with the vase. I studied it intently. It was too beautiful to discard, too dazzling to keep concealed any longer. Eventually, I made a decision. I took it to the cliff and threw it over, watching it smash on the rocks below. It was an awful sight, but at least my guilty secret was gone forever.

To make your story's plot more interesting, you could add an unexpected twist that leaves the reader with doubt in their mind.

Late that night, the wind was howling around my tent, and the rain was pelting down on the canvas. Suddenly, there was a huge crash of thunder and a blinding flash of lightning. Terrified, I ran out of the tent, only to be greeted by a strange apparition: there, sitting on top of a tree stump, was the missing vase. It was completely whole. Not a single crack was visible on its smooth, shiny exterior. I whirled around and scoured the field for any sign of an intruder. That was when I saw the old, hunched man walking slowly away.

Wherever you choose to finish, make sure it's exciting and powerful.

Be original and engaging to leave a good impression...

You want to prove to the examiner that you've thought carefully and creatively about your answer, so try to avoid rushing the end of it. Instead, think of ways to make your ending punchy, memorable and impactful.

Section Five — English Language: Writing

Writing Descriptions

For English Language paper 1, question 5 you could be asked to write a description. Your aim is to give your audience a detailed idea about a character or scene, so you'll need to use words to paint a vivid picture.

Descriptions are Detailed

1) Descriptions use strong visual language to create an impression of a person or place for the reader.
2) You don't need to include as much plot or action — focus mostly on describing the subject.
3) Even though there's no plot, you still need to structure your writing — e.g. you could start with a general description, then go on to describe some more specific details.
4) The purpose of a description is normally to entertain the reader, so you need to adapt your writing style accordingly, and keep your language interesting.
5) Appealing to the senses can bring your description to life. Keep your descriptions varied though — if you just list lots of senses, it can feel repetitive.
6) Descriptions need detail. For example, a character description might include:

- A character's physical features, e.g. hair colour, clothing.
- A character's personality, e.g. they could be funny, serious, reserved, extroverted.
- Any other particular features that reveal more about them, e.g. any nervous habits.
- Your personal opinion, e.g. what you like or dislike about them.

Use Language to describe a Character or Scene

Q5 Write a description of a character who is intimidating.

You can use the character's habits to create an impression of their personality.

The woman's fingernails tapped impatiently against the wood of the mantelpiece. She was standing still, but the motion of her perfectly-manicured fingernails, and the impatient huffs of air that were regularly expelled from between her thin lips, made her seem restless and agitated. Somehow she gave off the impression that she never really stopped moving.

Use figurative language to show off your descriptive skills.

She was an angular exclamation mark of a woman, and she stuck out like a sore thumb against our familiar, homely surroundings. She wore her dark hair short; it had been meticulously combed into an unforgiving style that cut into her sharp cheekbones. Her suit was an inky black colour, which only served to emphasise her militantly slender form. When she spoke, her voice was low and commanding, and her expression was set into a permanent frown that was half-angry, half-distracted, and wholly intimidating.

You can write from any narrative viewpoint, as long as it's appropriate to your purpose and audience.

She was the most terrifying person I had ever met.

One way to structure your writing is to start with a tiny detail, then expand outwards.

Use the five senses to create a really detailed description.

Don't lose your focus — remember that your answer needs to be about somebody intimidating.

PAPER 1 Q5

Try to use a good variety of descriptive language...

There are plenty of techniques to choose from here: metaphors, similes, alliteration, personification, the five senses, adjectives, repetition, onomatopoeia, hyperbole — the important thing is to use them engagingly.

Warm-Up Questions

Feeling a bit chilly? Never fear — these questions will get you feeling toasty in no time (when it comes to your English Language skills, that is). Try the questions below as an introduction, and then have a go at the longer exam-style writing tasks on the next page. Write your answers on a separate piece of paper.

Warm-Up Questions

1) Which of the following techniques are common in persuasive writing?
   a) an impersonal tone   b) rhetorical questions
   c) technical terms   d) emotive language

2) Rewrite the informative text below so that it persuades the reader to visit the church.

   > **Lyttlewich Church**
   > Situated in the rural village of Lyttlewich, Howtonshire, Lyttlewich Church is one of the oldest churches in the country: some parts of the church were built in 984 AD. The church receives thousands of visitors a year, and is particularly renowned for its artwork, which has recently been restored.

3) Rewrite each sentence below so that it's appropriate for an audience who have no expertise on the subject.
   a) Fertilisers provide phosphorous and potassium, which are essential for plant growth.
   b) The ossicle bones in the ear (the malleus, incus and stapes) are some of the smallest in the human skeleton.
   c) Roman legionaries used javelins and throwing-darts to defeat their enemies.

4) Write down a good opening sentence for each of the texts below. Make sure it's suitable for the audience given in the question.
   a) An article for a teenage magazine, in which you say that schools should spend more time teaching students how to manage their money.
   b) Instructions for a primary school student to teach them how to bake a cake.

5) Outline how you would start and finish your answer to each of the prompts below:
   a) The opening to a story about a spaceship that crashes on an alien planet.
   b) The opening to a story set on a desert island.

6) Imagine you are going to write a short story about somebody who's lost in a forest.
   a) What narrative viewpoint would you use? Give a reason for your answer.
   b) Write down two descriptive adjectives you could use, and explain their effect.
   c) Write down a simile you could use.

7) Write a descriptive sentence about a busy leisure centre based on each of the following senses.
   a) sight   b) sound   c) touch   d) smell and/or taste

8) You have been asked to write a description of a family member. Draw a spider diagram showing your ideas for things you might include.

Section Five — English Language: Writing

Exam-Style Questions

These fiction-writing questions will help you prepare for English Language paper 1, question 5. You should make a quick plan first, because there are marks for well-organised writing. You'll have roughly 45 minutes in the real exam, so set yourself a timer while you do these to get an idea of how long to spend on it.

Q1 You have been asked to write a piece for a storytelling event at your local library.

Write the beginning of a story based on the prompt 'a camping trip gone wrong'.

Q2 You are contributing to the creative writing column in your local newspaper.

Write the beginning of a story based on the prompt 'conflict at the supermarket'.

Q3 You are entering your school's creative writing competition, which will be judged by your head teacher.

Write a description of a mountainous area. If you wish, you can use the photo below for inspiration.

Writing Newspaper Articles

English Language paper 2, question 5 might ask you to write a newspaper article.

Newspaper articles Report Events and Offer Opinions

1) A newspaper's main purpose is to inform people about current affairs and other topics of interest.

2) Some newspaper articles directly report news. They convey facts about a story or theme, often using an unemotional tone and a sophisticated style to make the information seem accurate and reliable.

3) Other newspaper articles offer the viewpoint of the writer on a news story or theme. These are sometimes called commentaries, columns, editorials or opinion pieces.

4) As well as informing the reader, commentaries try to entertain their audience by making readers engage with the personality of the writer.

You need to make sure that your own viewpoint comes across whichever type of article you write.

Commentaries need to Engage their Audience

1) To grab the audience's interest, a commentary might use a personal tone and a conversational style to help convey the writer's opinions and personality.

> *It seems to me that this lot all need to take a deep breath and stop whinging. Nobody's going to bulldoze our green spaces any time soon — they'll have to spend 25 years making a planning application first.*

This uses colloquial words to create a conversational style and sarcasm to convey the viewpoint of the writer.

2) Rhetorical techniques (see p.52) are commonly used in commentaries to help get the writer's opinions across forcefully and to encourage readers to agree with the writer.

> *What happened to the good old days, when the presence of a heap of spuds on the table at dinnertime brought delight all round? Has all this 'health food' nonsense made us forget our faithful starchy friend?*

This uses rhetorical questions to engage and persuade the reader.

Articles have particular Features

Newspaper articles usually include headlines, straplines and subheadings to engage the reader's attention and convey information clearly.

Headlines tell you, very briefly, what an article is about. Headlines need to capture the audience's interest so that they carry on reading the article.

Subheadings are used to split an article up. Each subheading briefly tells you what the next section of text is about, often in an interesting or humorous way.

SECRET WEDDING FOR DUTTON DUO
Private ceremony for TV's cutest couple

By our showbiz reporter, Joe Snooping

Actors Simon Tremble and Katie Davies, stars of the TV series *Dutton Manor*, married yesterday at a secret ceremony in the Lake District.

LOVE AT FIRST SIGHT
According to insiders, the pair got together just three months ago and their engagement was only announced publicly last week. Thirty close friends and family, including several co-stars, joined them to celebrate, and pop sensation Al Blue performed at the reception.

DIRECTOR IS 'DELIGHTED'
Director of the series, Julian Parker, told The Daily Gossip that he was 'absolutely delighted' for the couple and added that they are 'perfect for each other'. However, he refused to comment on rumours that Simon's character in the show may be killed off when the new series begins in April.

COUPLE TO HONEYMOON IN CARIBBEAN
After their wedding, the couple jetted off on honeymoon to the beautiful island of Antigua. They will stay at a luxury beach resort for two weeks before returning to London to set up their new home.

Straplines are short statements that expand on the headline. They try to hook the reader, after the headline has got their initial interest.

Articles often start with a short paragraph that gives an overview of the story or theme.

Writing Newspaper Articles

Newspapers have Varying Audiences

1) Newspapers are broadly split into two types — tabloids and broadsheets.
2) Tabloids (such as *The Sun* and *The Mirror*) tend to focus on more sensational topics and people, making their news stories accessible and with a wide appeal.
3) Broadsheets (such as *The Telegraph* and *The Guardian*) are thought of as more formal, 'high-brow' journalism — focusing on what are thought to be more sophisticated topics.
4) Question 5 in English Language paper 2 will tell you what form to write in, e.g. 'a broadsheet newspaper article' — make sure you adapt your tone, style and register to the right audience.
5) Most newspapers also publish articles on the internet. If you're asked to write a news article for an online audience, think about how your audience might be different (e.g. younger or with a different level of understanding about the subject), and adapt your writing to suit.

Make sure your Article gives Your Opinion

PAPER 2 Q5

Q5 Write an article explaining your opinion on the statement below. Your article will be published in a broadsheet newspaper.

> 'You will never be able to get the real feel of a place by taking a guided tour. The true heart of any country lies off the beaten track.'

This question is asking you to give your opinion on a topic.

FORGET THE ROAD LESS TRAVELLED

Pay no attention to those who tell you otherwise: guided tours are the best way to experience somewhere new.

At some point or other, we've all been faced with a travel snob: that particular breed of rough-and-tumble traveller who knows all about where to go, what to see and, most importantly, how to see it. The travel snob thinks that guided tours are for the uncultured bores of this planet. The travel snob believes in travel without a destination. And yet, the travel snob will always find time to tell you about a 'hidden gem' that only they can take you to.

You would think someone so educated in the ways of the world would have realised the irony by now — travel snobs are themselves tour guides. The places that they think are 'off the beaten track' are transported, by their own recommendation, right onto 'the beaten track'. They are the one beating the track; they are leading the tourists away from their well-populated honeypot attractions into 'the heart of things'.

In the meantime, guided tours are often run by local people, who will frequently have a real treasure trove of local knowledge. How can a throwaway recommendation from an outsider possibly surpass that? Anybody who wants to see the true heart of a country must be guided by the people who live in it.

Annotations:
- Use a strapline to summarise the article in an interesting way.
- Your headline needs to be short and punchy to engage the reader.
- You're giving an opinion, so your tone should be quite personal.
- Use rhetorical devices like repetition to make your writing entertaining and persuasive.
- Make sure you link your answer to the prompt you're given in the question.
- You can use a sarcastic tone to give your writing a sense of personality.
- Opinion articles often combine a conversational style with complex sentences and vocabulary.

You need to get the style right in a newspaper article...

It's worth having a look at some real newspaper articles as part of your revision. You'll start to spot some patterns in the vocabulary and structure that they use, which will help you write better articles yourself.

Writing Leaflets

Leaflets need to give the reader lots of information in a clear, organised way.

Leaflets can have Varied Audiences and Purposes

1) Leaflets can have any purpose, but they're often used to advise (e.g. a leaflet advising the reader to open a savings account) or persuade an audience (e.g. to vote for a particular political party).

2) They can have a general audience (e.g. a leaflet about the importance of healthy eating) or a more specific audience (e.g. a leaflet advertising a particular museum or exhibition).

3) Leaflets need a clear structure to break up information. This could include:

- a clear title
- subheadings
- bullet points
- boxes around extra bits of information

It's important to break up the information in a leaflet, but don't waste time in the exam trying to make it look pretty or drawing pictures.

4) Leaflets also need to grab the reader's attention, so that they remember all the information they're given. You can use language techniques, such as lists of three or direct address, to achieve this.

Organise your Leaflet in a Clear and Interesting way

PAPER 2 Q5

Q5 Write the text for a leaflet in response to the statement below. The leaflet will be distributed to students, advising them on how they can keep fit.

> 'Keeping fit as a student is too hard. Gym memberships and exercise equipment are too expensive for young people, and students don't have time to exercise.'

KEEPING FIT THE EASY WAY

(Use a title to catch the reader's attention.)

Exercise is important for your health, but as a student your time and budget may be limited. Fortunately, there are many cheap, simple, fun ways to keep fit.

(You're writing for students, but you should still use a formal register and Standard English.)

Walk the walk

Walking costs you nothing, and it doesn't require too much spare time. You could try:

- Walking to a friend's house instead of asking your parents for a lift.
- Planning a longer route to a destination you already walk to.
- Getting off the bus or train a few stops early and walking the rest of the way.

(Use interesting subheadings to organise your answer and hold the reader's interest.)

(Use bullet points to break information up for the reader.)

Pedal power

If you own a bike, cycling is an excellent way to keep fit. Look at your council's website to see if there are cycle routes nearby, or plan a safe route on your local roads.

(Imperatives and direct address create a clear, confident tone.)

Dance the night away

Dancing can help to maintain your fitness and improve your coordination, regardless of your skill level. Try looking for tutorial videos on the internet to help you learn.

Your turn...

These are just a few ideas; there are many more options available. Whether it's skipping, skating or salsa, there will certainly be something for you.

(Alliteration and a list of three emphasise the variety of activities on offer.)

(Short paragraphs can help to break up the information in a text.)

You need to match your writing to the audience in the question...

Leaflets can be written for a wide variety of different audiences. Make sure your leaflet is adapted to the audience you're given in the question — choose a suitable writing style that uses appropriate language.

Section Five — English Language: Writing

Writing Essays

Essays are informative texts that make an argument in support of a particular viewpoint.

Essays present an Argument or Opinion

1) Essays usually demonstrate the writer's point of view. They are often impersonal and objective, so your language usually needs to be quite formal and not too chatty.

2) Essays should follow a logical structure. They need to have:

   - An introduction that sets up the main theme.
   - Well-structured paragraphs that clearly convey your arguments.
   - A conclusion that ties things together.

Essays can sometimes be more personal in tone — make sure yours fits the audience and purpose you're given in the exam.

A good essay will often consider opposing points of view before coming to a conclusion.

3) The purpose of essays is usually to argue, but they can inform, advise or persuade too.

4) You need to make sure you write for the correct audience — essays usually have quite a general audience, but you may have to write for a particular person or group of people.

Essays should Analyse and Conclude

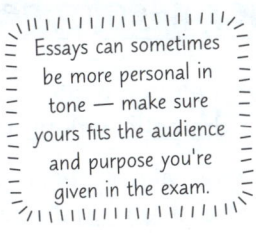

Q5 Write an essay arguing your opinion on the statement below.
Your essay will be published in your school newspaper.

> "Rock-climbing helps build strength, encourages teamwork and, most importantly, is fun. It is therefore the ideal sport for an after-school club."

Why Rock-Climbing is the Perfect Sport for Our School

Rock-climbing would be an ideal after-school activity for several reasons: it increases health and fitness, promotes a sense of adventure and helps to forge friendships. Although it has some critics, largely due to its relatively high cost and risk of injury, this essay will outline why the positives far outweigh the negatives.

Firstly, rock-climbing has benefits for both the minds and bodies of students. Not only does it build strength and aerobic fitness due to the physical exertion needed to successfully reach the top, but rock climbing also builds character. The process of attempting a route, failing, yet trying again until you succeed, is a highly effective way to develop resilience. Participating in rock-climbing would therefore stretch students' physical and mental limits, teaching them invaluable skills which they could apply to many parts of their lives.

Even if you consider both sides of the argument, stick to one clear opinion throughout.

Discourse markers like 'firstly' guide the reader through the text, making the argument easy to follow.

You don't need to create any suspense — you can give your point of view in your title or introduction.

Your language should be formal and impersonal because it is for a school newspaper, but you still need to convey a viewpoint.

In the real answer, you would go on to include several more paragraphs and finish with a conclusion that sums up your opinion.

English Language paper 2 is all about attitudes and viewpoints...

When it comes to writing an essay, just make sure that you're being as objective and analytical as possible. It's still important to share your opinion though, so come to a conclusion that's backed up by evidence.

Writing Speeches

A speech needs to be powerful and moving. You should aim to have an emotional effect on your audience.

Speeches need to be Dramatic and Engaging

1) Speeches are often written to argue or persuade, so they need to have a dramatic, emotional impact on their audience.

2) One way to make a speech persuasive is to give it an effective structure — arrange your points so that they build tension throughout your answer, then end with an emotive or exciting climax.

3) Make sure that your points are linked smoothly, so that the audience can follow your speech easily.

4) You can use lots of language techniques to make your writing engaging and persuasive:

These accusations are hateful, hurtful and humiliating. → Alliteration and the use of a list of three adjectives make this sound strong and angry.

Persuasive language techniques like these are known as rhetorical devices — see page 52.

Do we really have no other option? The current situation is a disgrace! → Rhetorical questions and exclamations engage the reader and make your writing sound more like spoken language.

5) Remember that speeches are spoken, not read. Try to use techniques that are effective when spoken out loud. It's important to end with a clear sign-off, such as 'it's been a pleasure talking to you today'.

Your speech should Make People Think

PAPER 2 Q5

Q5 Write a speech arguing your opinion on the statement below.
Your speech will be delivered at an animal welfare conference.

'The practice of keeping animals in zoos cannot be allowed to continue. It is inhumane and encourages the use of animals as mere entertainment.'

Start off by addressing your listeners directly and announcing the reason for your speech — show that you've understood your purpose and audience.

Try to use lots of personal pronouns like 'I', 'you' and 'we' to engage your audience.

Ladies and gentlemen, I have called you here today to defend the practice of keeping animals in captivity. I believe that zoos represent a positive presence in this country.

The vast majority of modern British zoos are focused on conservation and education. To my mind, these important values are worth preserving. It is essential that we give our youngsters a sense of awareness about the world around them. We must impress upon the youth of today the need to protect endangered species and habitats. Zoos can help us to do this. Modern zoos offer extensive opportunities for these kinds of educational experiences: there are interactive exhibitions, talks from conservationists and live question-and-answer forums that will help to educate our young people.

You could use repetition to increase the dramatic impact of your speech.

Zoos can help us inspire a generation with the importance of conservation. Zoos can help us raise awareness of environmental issues. Zoos can help us by providing a space in which we can work together to build a safer, greener and more ecologically friendly world.

The word 'must' creates a confident tone.

Vary the lengths of your sentences to show pauses and emphasis.

Use rhetorical devices like lists of three to make your argument sound more forceful.

Practise using some rhetorical devices in your writing...

There are plenty of famous speeches throughout history — you could try looking at some of the techniques they use. Your speech doesn't have to impress a crowd of people, but it does have to impress the examiner.

Section Five — English Language: Writing

Writing Letters

Letters are always addressed to a particular person or group of people. This means that they have very specific audiences, so it's very important that you tailor your letter to suit that audience.

Letters need to Start and End correctly

1) If you're asked to write a letter, look at the audience to decide how formal your register should be.

2) If the letter is to someone you don't know well, or to someone in a position of authority, keep it formal with a serious tone. This means you should:

- Use formal greetings (e.g. 'Dear Sir/Madam') and sign-offs (e.g. 'Yours sincerely' if you've used their name, 'Yours faithfully' if you haven't).
- Use Standard English and formal vocabulary, e.g. you could use phrases like 'In my opinion...' or 'I find this state of affairs...'.

Letters often start with the address of the sender, the address of the recipient and the date.

3) If the letter is to someone you know, or someone who isn't in a position of authority, you might use a more conversational style, although it should still be fairly formal. This means you should:

- Start with your reader's name, e.g. 'Dear Jenny', and sign off with 'best wishes' or 'warm regards'.
- Make sure you still write in Standard English (so no text speak or slang) and show the examiner that you can use interesting vocabulary and sentence structures.

State your Viewpoint clearly

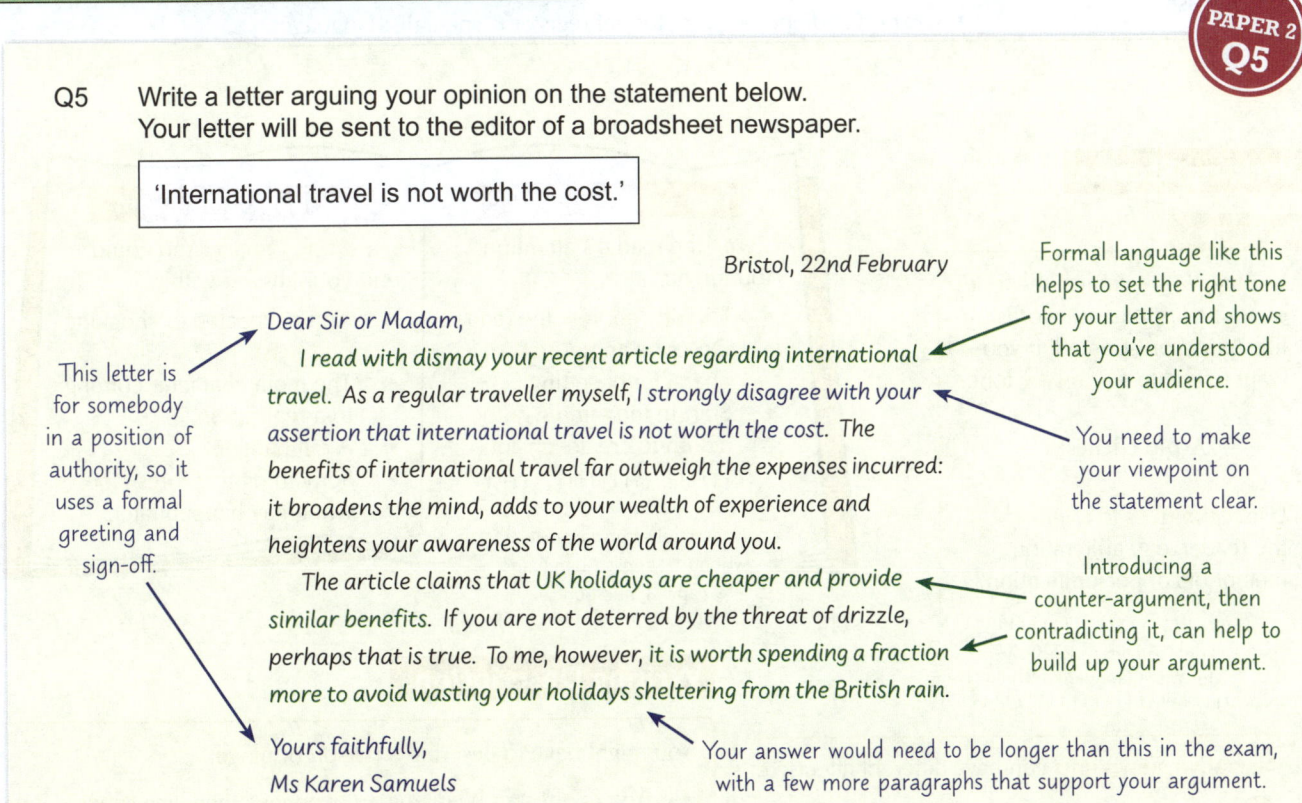

PAPER 2 Q5

Q5 Write a letter arguing your opinion on the statement below.
Your letter will be sent to the editor of a broadsheet newspaper.

'International travel is not worth the cost.'

Bristol, 22nd February

Dear Sir or Madam,
    I read with dismay your recent article regarding international travel. As a regular traveller myself, I strongly disagree with your assertion that international travel is not worth the cost. The benefits of international travel far outweigh the expenses incurred: it broadens the mind, adds to your wealth of experience and heightens your awareness of the world around you.
    The article claims that UK holidays are cheaper and provide similar benefits. If you are not deterred by the threat of drizzle, perhaps that is true. To me, however, it is worth spending a fraction more to avoid wasting your holidays sheltering from the British rain.

Yours faithfully,
Ms Karen Samuels

This letter is for somebody in a position of authority, so it uses a formal greeting and sign-off.

Formal language like this helps to set the right tone for your letter and shows that you've understood your audience.

You need to make your viewpoint on the statement clear.

Introducing a counter-argument, then contradicting it, can help to build up your argument.

Your answer would need to be longer than this in the exam, with a few more paragraphs that support your argument.

You need to write for your audience, but keep your writing high level...

You will need to pay attention to purpose and audience — make sure your letter completes the task in the question and is written in an appropriate style. Whoever your audience is, you always need to write well.

Writing — Knowledge Organiser

These two pages will summarise all of the key knowledge you need from this section. Make sure you know it inside out.

Purpose

Every text has **at least one** purpose.

1. **Informative texts** — are usually clear & accessible with a formal register.
2. **Advisory texts** — often unbiased, with a calm tone & formal register.
3. **Texts that argue** — usually have a clear structure & a serious tone.
4. **Persuasive texts** — often have a conversational tone & emotive language.
5. **Entertaining texts** — usually have a light-hearted tone & an engaging style.

Match your tone, style, register & structure to your purpose.

Audience

Adapt your tone, style & register to suit your audience:

Audience characteristic	How it might affect your writing
Age	• Younger audience — light-hearted tone. • Older audience — formal, serious register & complex style.
Relationship with reader	• Familiar audience — friendly tone & conversational style. • Unknown audience — impersonal tone & formal register.
Expertise	• General audience — accessible language. • Expert audience — very formal register & specialist language.

Some questions will tell you exactly who your audience is, but sometimes you'll have to work out your audience from the question prompt.

Writing Stories

Techniques

Language — establish the tone of your story, e.g. use words like 'burst' or 'sprinted' if you want to create a dramatic tone.

Avoid clichés.

Use techniques to interest the reader, e.g. alliteration, metaphors or personification.

Take a look at pages 42-55 for more language techniques.

Your opening should...

...grab the reader's attention. You might:
- Directly address the reader.
- Describe an unusual character or setting.
- Start in the middle of the action to create tension.

You should finish with...

...a strong impact. You could end your answer with:
- An unexpected or shocking plot twist.
- The main character coming to a realisation.
- A cliffhanger.
- Something that foreshadows what may happen later.

You will be asked to do descriptive or narrative writing in English Language paper 1, question 5.

Narrative viewpoints can have different effects:

1. **First person** — 'I' or 'we'. Creates personal connection with reader.
2. **Third person** — 'He', 'She' or 'They'. More detached viewpoint.

Writing Descriptions

You might have to describe a person or place:
- You could start by giving an overview, then give specific details.
- Don't just focus on physical features — describe a character's personality / a setting's atmosphere.
- Use sensory language — but don't be repetitive.
- You could also give your opinion on what you're describing.

Newspaper Articles

- News articles inform people about current affairs — use facts, an unemotional tone & sophisticated style to seem reliable.
- Commentaries give opinions — use a conversational style to entertain, or rhetorical techniques to persuade.

Articles usually have:

Headlines — a short, snappy summary

Straplines — a short statement that expands on the headline

Subheadings — split article into sections

Two types of newspaper

1. **Tabloids** — focus on more sensational topics. Use accessible language.
2. **Broadsheets** — focus on more sophisticated topics. Use more formal language.

You could be asked to write any of the forms of non-fiction on this page in English Language paper 2, question 5.

Leaflets

- Give lots of information in an organised way.
- Usually advise or persuade.
- Aimed at specific or general audiences.
- Use a clear structure to break up information:
  - ✓ a clear title
  - ✓ subheadings
  - ✓ bullet points
  - ✓ boxes
- Should grab the reader's attention & be memorable.

Speeches

- Written to argue or persuade.
- Have a dramatic, emotional effect on the audience.
- Structured to build tension — end with an emotive or exciting climax.
- Use rhetorical devices, e.g. rule of three, hyperbole.
- Use techniques that are effective when said aloud, e.g. alliteration and rhetorical questions.
- Important to end with a clear sign-off, e.g. "It's been a pleasure".

Essays

- Make an argument / give an opinion & come to a conclusion.
- Purpose is usually to argue, but can also advise, inform or persuade.
- Audience is usually general, but can be specific.
- Often impersonal & objective tone
- Have a logical structure:
  - ✓ introduction — sets up the main theme
  - ✓ paragraphs — cover the pros or cons of argument
  - ✓ conclusion — ties argument together

Whichever type of text you write, you should use interesting vocabulary & sentence structures to pick up marks for AO6. **AO6**

Letters

Should always begin with your address, the address of the recipient and the date.
Directed at a particular person or group of people — level of formality depends on the audience:

Formal letters
- For people you don't know well.
- Formal register & serious tone.
- Formal greetings (e.g. 'Dear Sir/Madam') & sign-offs (e.g. 'Yours sincerely/faithfully').

Informal letters
- For people you know.
- More conversational style.
- Informal greetings (e.g. 'Dear Jenny') & sign-offs (e.g. 'best wishes').

Both types of letters use Standard English — no slang.

EXAM TIP — Plan your essays with a clear conclusion in mind...

In English Language paper 2, question 5, you'll have to argue or explain your view on a topic, so you need to know your opinion before you start. Then, clearly maintain this stance throughout.

Worked Answer

Before you leave this section, have a look at this worked answer for English Language paper 2.

Q1 Write an article arguing your opinion on the statement below. Your article will be published in a broadsheet newspaper.

"In order to prepare young adults for the challenges of raising a family, it should be made compulsory for them to spend time volunteering with young children."

When you're planning, it might help to jot down all your <u>ideas</u> first, and then <u>organise</u> them afterwards.

PLAN

own experience at nursery in Y10 — negative — put off having children. Cover some counter-arguments. My arguments = time pressure on young people; not all want to become parents; natural anyway? Where do you find all the children/parental permission etc.

- Para 1: own experience at nursery in Y10
- Para 2: Counter-arguments: skills (selflessness, communication, imagination), responsibility, prep for parenthood
- Para 3: not all want to become parents (figure?); those who do will be fine (natural process)
- Para 4: time pressure on young people as it is — studying, home life, part-time job already perhaps, already pressured enough into thinking of future
- Para 5: logistical problems (finding the children; those children's parents' views on it; how/who/what)
- Para 6: conclusion — well done to those doing it, sure it's rewarding, but shouldn't be compulsory

Make sure you know what your overall <u>opinion</u> is <u>before</u> you start writing.

DON'T PUSH TEENS INTO PARENTING PRACTICE

When I was fifteen, my school Careers Advisor decided that the best way to teach her Year Tens about the wonderful ways of life was to dump them into the world of work. And so, <u>like a bemused traveller without a map</u>, I found myself, dazed and confused, in my local preschool. I have nothing against this preschool in particular, but the week I spent there was one of the most unpleasant of my life. After the fourth day of being smeared with paint, wet sand and the bodily fluids of various toddlers, I swore I would never work with children again. <u>Which is why I find it remarkable that there are proposals to make this experience compulsory.</u>

It is true that there are several strong arguments in favour of making volunteering with young children compulsory for young adults. It would teach them the patience, selflessness and imaginative thinking necessary for raising a child — important lessons for future parenthood. Furthermore, after first-hand exposure to young children, other young adults may decide that parenthood would not suit them at all, and be able to make more informed choices later in life.

It's great to use interesting language techniques, like <u>similes</u>, to help your reader to <u>empathise</u> with you.

Your <u>opinion</u> on the statement needs to be <u>clear</u> — even if you don't state it explicitly like this.

Show that you're responding to the <u>prompt</u> in the question.

Using an <u>anecdote</u> provides an <u>engaging</u> opening.

The <u>descriptive language</u> in this sentence helps the reader to imagine the scene at the preschool.

The second paragraph is <u>slightly inappropriate</u> for the <u>form</u> — it's become a bit like an essay. It would be better if the <u>style</u> was <u>less formal</u>...

Worked Answer

However, I struggle to comprehend how any young adult could actually finish their compulsory volunteering thinking "yes please". The lessons I was taught at the preschool included "there is no such thing as a clean child" and "home time is the only time worth treasuring". It's also worth remembering that some young people already have no intention of becoming parents. In a recent survey, 10% of them said they had no desire to have children. I would like to see how many of the other 90% flock to join them after an enforced week of torture such as mine.

This is before we even consider that many young people simply wouldn't have the time for volunteering. My own week of work experience meant losing a week of lessons while studying for my GCSEs. Plenty of young people are already ground to the bone, juggling home life, academics and extra-curricular activities in the hope of getting that important first job. Surely this should take priority over spending stressful time with children?

Where these children would come from is another mystery. Personally, I can't imagine my own parents willingly donating me for an unknown teenager to take care of. I also feel sorry for whichever local schools, preschools or councils would become responsible for dealing with the mountains of paperwork involved.

In theory, bringing young people and young children together for voluntary work seems like a lovely idea. I'm sure there are plenty of young people who already volunteer with young children, and I'm sure they benefit from it. This does not mean that we should start forcing all of their peers into it too — a few hours with a messy, crying child isn't going to prepare you for the challenges of raising a family, because you're never going to want to have a family at all.

Annotations:
- Facts and figures are appropriate for a broadsheet newspaper article.
- Broadsheet newspaper articles should have a personal tone.
- This conclusion refers back to the statement in the question, which links the answer together nicely, and shows good organisation.
- ...like this. This kind of informal phrase is better suited to a broadsheet newspaper article.
- Hyperbole can be used to add humour, making your answer entertaining.
- Rhetorical techniques (like rhetorical questions and lists of three) make your answer more persuasive.
- This metaphor adds emphasis to the point about logistical problems.

- This answer is mostly well-matched to its form (a broadsheet newspaper article), and shows a good awareness of purpose (to persuade and entertain) and audience (readers of a broadsheet newspaper).
- It also uses a variety of language techniques effectively (e.g. similes, hyperbole and rhetorical questions).
- The structure is good too. It's written in clear paragraphs, with an engaging introduction and conclusion.
- To get the very top marks, this answer could use some more ambitious vocabulary and punctuation. The second paragraph would also need to be better-matched to the form in the question.

Exam-Style Questions

These questions will help you to prepare for the non-fiction writing question in English Language paper 2. Make sure you quickly plan your answers before you start writing them. This will help you to structure your response — in the real exam there are marks available for a well-organised answer.

Q1 Write an article in response to the statement below. Your article will be published in a broadsheet newspaper, advising readers on the best way to stay fit and healthy.

> "Active hobbies, such as sports, are falling by the wayside because of the popularity of tablets and smartphones. Being constantly glued to screens is bad for our nation's health."

Q2 Write a speech arguing your opinion on the statement below. Your speech will be delivered to your class.

> One of your classmates has said: "I think going to bed early is a waste of time. The later you stay up, the more time you have to play video games."

Q3 Write the text for a leaflet in response to the statement below. The leaflet will be for students who are thinking about taking a gap year before starting work or college.

> "Young people should widen their horizons. It's important that they travel and experience new cultures before they start their adult life."

Q4 Write a letter explaining your opinion on the statement below. Your letter will be sent to the editor of your local newspaper.

> "We should build more houses in rural areas. Having beautiful scenery is not as important as having a plentiful supply of housing for a growing population."

Revision Summary Test for Section Five

This is the final Revision Summary for English Language, so make sure you use it well.
- These questions are **really tricky**, but they'll help you see **how well you know your stuff**.
- Tackle the **revision summary test** below, or scan the QR code to do it **online**. You can **keep track of your progress** online and see **which areas need more work**.
- There are **sample answers** here: www.cgpbooks.co.uk/blurb-answers

Writing with Purpose (p.72-79)

1) Name four different purposes that a piece of writing might have.
2) Explain how you can work out your audience when answering a writing question.
3) Why might an advert for children's breakfast cereal have more than one audience?
4) What three things do you always need to match to your purpose and audience?
5) Give two ways you could start a story that will quickly capture your reader's interest.
6) Rewrite this sentence so it's in the first-person viewpoint. Explain one benefit of doing this.
   Frances skulked down the hallway, delaying her arrival at her Maths classroom.
7) Describe the difference between a first-person and a third-person narrative viewpoint.
8) Why might these be good ways to finish your opening to a story? Give reasons in your answer.
   a) A question that creates a cliffhanger.
   b) An unexpected plot twist.
9) Briefly explain the difference between narrative and descriptive writing.
10) Give three techniques you could use in descriptive writing and write down an example of each.

Writing in Different Styles (p.82-87)

11) Explain the two main ways in which articles inform people.
12) Describe how each of the following features improve the layout of an article:
    a) Headlines   b) Straplines   c) Subheadings
13) Summarise the difference between a broadsheet and a tabloid newspaper.
14) Name three structural features that you could use in a leaflet.
    Explain how each benefits the reader.
15) What would be the form and purpose, and who would be the audience, in an answer to this exam question?
    "Holidays to Europe are overrated — today's European cities are busy, expensive and dull."
    Write an article for a travel magazine giving your views on this subject.
16) Briefly explain the logical structure you should use when writing an essay.
17) How might you adapt a letter when writing to someone you know?
18) What is the main difference between a speech and an essay?
19) What is usually your main purpose when you're writing a speech?
    Suggest two ways a speech can try to achieve this purpose.
20) How might your style of writing be different when writing:
    a) an article for a blog vs. an article for a broadsheet newspaper
    b) an album review for a teen magazine vs. an album review for a broadsheet newspaper
    c) a speech about the impact of social media vs. an essay about social media
21) Write down an example opening and ending for:
    a) a letter to a local councillor, arguing in favour of building a new shopping centre in your area
    b) a letter to a family member, asking if they have any jobs you can do for them.

Sample Exam — Paper 1

These two pages show you some example questions that will help you to prepare for English Language paper 1 — the text to go with questions 1-4 is on page 96. First have a good read through the text and the questions, then have a look at the handy graded answer extracts we've provided on pages 97-105.

Question 1 asks you to Find some Information

Q1 Use lines **12-19** of the text to answer the questions below.
For each question, tick the correct option. There is one correct answer per question.

Q1.1 What was the baby like when it was born?
- Quiet ☐
- Noisy ☐
- Content ☐

[1 mark]

Q1.2 What does Mabel wish she did with the baby's hair?
- Took photos of it ☐
- Put it in a safe ☐
- Put it in a necklace ☐

[1 mark]

Q1.3 What did Mabel **not** know about the baby?
- Its size ☐
- What its face looked like ☐
- Its sex ☐

[1 mark]

Q1.4 What did Mabel do after the baby was born?
- She held its head ☐
- She cried ☐
- She buried it ☐

[1 mark]

Question 2 is about the writer's use of Language

Q2 Explain how the writer uses language to describe Mabel's life in Alaska in **lines 1-11**.
You may wish to explore how the writer uses particular language techniques, specific words and phrases, or different types of sentence.

[8 marks]

Question 3 is about the Structure of the Whole text

Q3 Write about how the writer has structured this text to create a sense of loss.
In your answer, you could consider how a sense of loss increases or decreases throughout the text, and any changes in tone or viewpoint.

[8 marks]

Sample Exam — Paper 1

Question 4 asks for a Personal Response to the text

Q4 How far do you agree or disagree with the following statement?
*In **lines 20-39** of the text, Mabel's feelings are clear, which makes it easy for the reader to feel her emotions.*
In your answer, make references to the text and consider:
- what impression you get of Mabel's feelings
- what methods are used to convey Mabel's feelings.

[20 marks]

You have to do some Creative Writing for Question 5

Q5 You are writing a creative piece for your school magazine.
Choose **one** of the following tasks:

Write a description of a winter cabin in the woods.
If you wish, you can use the photo below for inspiration.

OR

Write the beginning of a story based on the prompt 'facing a problem in winter'.

[40 marks]

The answers to these questions are in the rest of the section...
You don't have to answer these questions yourself. Instead, read on for some sample answers, which will give you an idea of what you need to write in your exam. You can refer back to these pages if you need to.

Exam Text

Here's the text to go with the questions on pages 94-95. It's an extract from the opening of *The Snow Child* by Eowyn Ivey, a novel which was published in 2012, but is set in 1920. In the novel, a woman named Mabel and her husband, Jack, have moved to the cold, remote Alaskan wilderness to start a new life.

> Make sure you always read the contextual information you are given about the text (see above) — it can help you make sense of the text.

Wolverine River, Alaska, 1920

Mabel had known there would be silence. That was the point, after all. No infants cooing or wailing. No neighbor children playfully hollering down the lane. No pad of small feet on wooden stairs worn smooth by generations, or clackety-clack of toys along the kitchen floor. All those sounds of her failure and regret would be left behind, and in their place there would be silence.

5   She had imagined that in the Alaska wilderness silence would be peaceful, like snow falling at night, air filled with promise but no sound, but that was not what she found. Instead, when she swept the plank floor, the broom bristles scritched like some sharp-toothed shrew nibbling at her heart. When she washed the dishes, plates and bowls clattered as if they were breaking to pieces. The only sound not of her making was a sudden 'caw, cawww' from outside. Mabel wrung dishwater from a rag and looked out the kitchen
10 window in time to see a raven flapping its way from one leafless birch tree to another. No children chasing each other through autumn leaves, calling each other's names. Not even a solitary child on a swing.

There had been the one. A tiny thing, born still and silent. Ten years past, but even now she found herself returning to the birth to touch Jack's arm, stop him, reach out. She should have. She should have cupped the baby's head in the palm of her hand and snipped a few of its tiny hairs to keep in a locket at her throat.
15 She should have looked into its small face and known if it was a boy or a girl, and then stood beside Jack as he buried it in the Pennsylvania winter ground. She should have marked its grave. She should have allowed herself that grief.
    It was a child, after all, although it looked more like a fairy changeling. Pinched face, tiny jaw, ears that came to narrow points; that much she had seen and wept over because she knew she could have loved it still.

20 Mabel was too long at the window. The raven had since flown away above the treetops. The sun had slipped behind a mountain, and the light had fallen flat. The branches were bare, the grass yellowed gray. Not a single snowflake. It was as if everything fine and glittering had been ground from the world and swept away as dust.
    November was here, and it frightened her because she knew what it brought — cold upon the valley
25 like a coming death, glacial wind through the cracks between the cabin logs. But most of all, darkness. Darkness so complete even the pale-lit hours would be choked.
    She entered last winter blind, not knowing what to expect in this new, hard land. Now she knew. By December, the sun would rise just before noon and skirt the mountaintops for a few hours of twilight before sinking again. Mabel would move in and out of sleep as she sat in a chair beside the woodstove. She
30 would not pick up any of her favorite books; the pages would be lifeless. She would not draw; what would there be to capture in her sketchbook? Dull skies, shadowy corners. It would become harder and harder to leave the warm bed each morning. She would stumble about in a walking sleep, scrape together meals and drape wet laundry around the cabin. Jack would struggle to keep the animals alive. The days would run together, winter's stranglehold tightening.
35 All her life she had believed in something more, in the mystery that shape-shifted at the edge of her senses. It was the flutter of moth wings on glass and the promise of river nymphs in the dappled creek beds. It was the smell of oak trees on the summer evening she fell in love, and the way dawn threw itself across the cow pond and turned the water to light.
    Mabel could not remember the last time she caught such a flicker.

Graded Answers — Paper 1, Question 1

There are four marks on offer in question 1. Re-read all the question parts on p.94, then look at this page.

Tick the Statements which are Correct

1) Question 1 asks four multiple-choice questions, and there are four marks available. That means you get one mark for each box you tick correctly.
2) Careful though — you need to make sure your information only comes from lines 12-19.
3) It's also important to read the questions carefully — some of the incorrect options might try to trip you up.

This question is a great way to pick up four marks — as long as you read the text and question parts carefully.

Here's the answer to Part 1

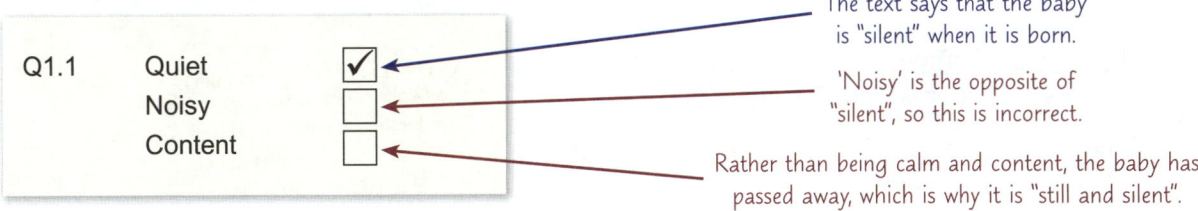

- The text says that the baby is "silent" when it is born.
- 'Noisy' is the opposite of "silent", so this is incorrect.
- Rather than being calm and content, the baby has passed away, which is why it is "still and silent".

This is the answer to Part 2

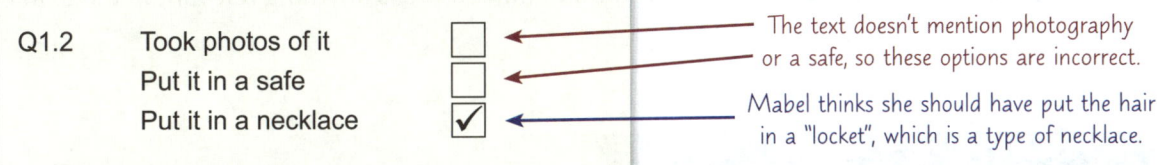

- The text doesn't mention photography or a safe, so these options are incorrect.
- Mabel thinks she should have put the hair in a "locket", which is a type of necklace.

Here's Part 3's answer

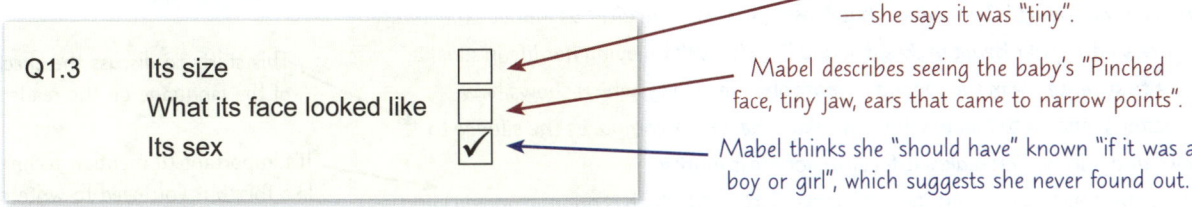

- Mabel knows the baby's size — she says it was "tiny".
- Mabel describes seeing the baby's "Pinched face, tiny jaw, ears that came to narrow points".
- Mabel thinks she "should have" known "if it was a boy or girl", which suggests she never found out.

And this is the answer to Part 4

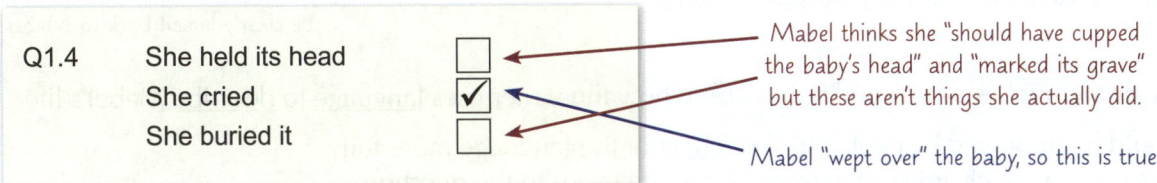

- Mabel thinks she "should have cupped the baby's head" and "marked its grave" but these aren't things she actually did.
- Mabel "wept over" the baby, so this is true.

Read the wording of the text and the questions carefully...

You can easily get full marks for paper 1, question 1, so long as you read the text carefully and make sure you tick the right boxes. For some extra useful pointers, scan the QR code.

Graded Answers — Paper 1, Question 2

Paper 1, question 2 (take a look back at p.94) is a bit more challenging than question 1.

Pick out key Language Features and explain their Effects

1) Question 2 tests how well you can explain the effects of the language used in the extract.

2) The sample question asks you specifically about the language used to describe Mabel's life — so you shouldn't write about the language used to describe anything else.

3) Remember to structure your paragraphs clearly. Each point you make should be supported with evidence from the text. You should then talk about the effect that these examples have on the reader, as well as other reasons why the writer might have included them.

4) You also need to use a range of technical terms to describe the writer's techniques.

5) To get top marks, you should use the information under the question to guide what you write about:

- Language techniques, such as metaphors, similes and onomatopoeia (see p.46 & 49).
- The effect of specific words and phrases, such as how specific verbs are used (see p.44-45).
- The effect of different types of sentence, such as short or long sentences (see p.64-65).

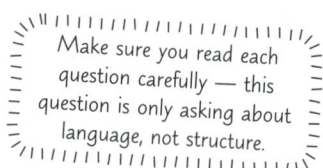
Make sure you read each question carefully — this question is only asking about language, not structure.

6) You don't need to write about every bullet if you don't think there is anything relevant in the extract.

Here's a Grade 4-5 answer extract

> The writer says "the broom bristles scritched like some sharp-toothed shrew nibbling at her heart". This shows that Alaska isn't as "peaceful" as Mabel expected. The shrew eating her heart makes it sound like she isn't enjoying her life in Alaska.
>
> The first sentence in the second paragraph is very long, which shows how significant silence is to Mabel's life in Alaska. The writer compares the silence to "snow" and "air", which makes it feel like her life is empty.
>
> This emptiness is different to the "clackety-clack" (which is onomatopoeia) and "hollering" of the first paragraph, which makes the silence seem even more like it's an important part of Mabel's life.
>
> There is a raven "flapping its way from one leafless birch tree to another" too, which makes you feel like something bad is going to happen.

- It's great to include quotes, but try to keep them short.
- This starts to discuss the effect of the language on the reader.
- It's important to mention techniques like this, but you need to write more about the effect they have, too.
- This last paragraph doesn't seem relevant to the question — it needs to be clearly linked back to Mabel's life.

1) This answer makes some good points about how the writer uses language to describe Mabel's life.

2) It could be improved by explaining the effect of the language more fully, as it's not always clear how the examples are relevant to the question.

3) It could also do with using more technical terms — it only uses one, and it doesn't explain the effect it has very well.

Graded Answers — Paper 1, Question 2

Here's a Grade 6-7 answer extract

> The writer uses a short, direct first sentence to introduce the idea that the most prominent thing about Mabel's life in Alaska is how silent it is: "Mabel had known there would be silence."
>
> The language used in this extract implies that Mabel finds this "silence" threatening and uncomfortable. The verb "scritched" sounds like a small animal clawing the "plank floor", which emphasises Mabel's uneasiness. The word is also onomatopoeic, so it interrupts the "silence", but in a way that's painful and upsetting. The writer is emphasising that the "promise" of peace Mabel hoped to find in Alaska has not been fulfilled; instead, she has been left unhappy.
>
> The image of the solitary raven and the "leafless" trees links Mabel's surroundings with the idea of lifelessness. This increases the overall negative tone of the passage, which leaves the reader with a strong impression that Mabel's life is unhappy.

Referring to the writer shows that you understand they chose to use this language for a reason.

Good use of a brief quote to back up a point.

It's really good to focus on the effects of specific words.

It's important to keep linking the answer back to the question.

1) This answer makes some good points about the <u>effects</u> of the language the writer has chosen, which are <u>backed up</u> with appropriate quotations and <u>linked back</u> to the question.
2) It could be improved by mentioning even more <u>language features</u> or <u>techniques</u>.

This is a Grade 8-9 answer extract

> This extract uses sensory verbs to create images of childhood: verbs such as "wailing" and "hollering" suggest a loud, frenetic atmosphere. This is contrasted sharply with the "silence" of Alaska, which is mentioned twice, at the beginning and end of the first paragraph. This contrast has a jarring effect on the reader, and suggests that Mabel's life in Alaska is characterised by a sense of emptiness and loss.
>
> The writer also uses onomatopoeic verbs such as "scritched" and "clattered" to suggest that the "silence" in Alaska makes any noise seem unnaturally loud and unpleasant, and to bring the reader into the uncomfortable life that Mabel leads. These verbs are used in combination with the vivid simile of a shrew "nibbling" at Mabel's heart, which emphasises her discomfort and suggests that, instead of the peace she had hoped to find, Mabel's life is deeply unhappy.
>
> The writer uses direct speech only once in this extract, when there is "a sudden 'caw, cawww'" from a raven. The intrusiveness of this direct speech is emphasised because of the hard 'C' sound at the beginning of each word. Because the speech feels so out of place, the reader starts to empathise with the intrusion Mabel feels at the noise. This further emphasises the discomfort of her life.

This answer uses a good range of short quotes to back up the points it makes.

It's important to focus on the effect that the language has.

Uses a technical term for a language technique, then fully explains it.

This answer stays focused on the question throughout.

1) This is a <u>really good</u> answer. It makes several points about the writer's <u>choice</u> of language and the <u>effect</u> it has, and then <u>develops</u> each point fully.
2) It also uses complex <u>technical terms</u> correctly and supports each point with relevant <u>quotations</u>.

Talk about the effect of language features on the reader...

If you want to get top marks in the exam, it's not enough to only identify the language features in the text. Make sure you can also explain their effect on the reader. For more tips, scan this code.

Paper 1 Q2 Video

Graded Answers — Paper 1, Question 3

Question 3 is all about the structure of the text. These sample answers will show you what's required.

Think about how the text is Put Together and the Effect this has

1) Paper 1, question 3 is about the structure of the text — you need to talk about how the writer has used structure to create the effect mentioned in the question.

2) This question covers the whole text, so make sure you talk about the overall structure of the extract as you're answering the question.

3) However, you should also comment on the position of specific sentences and the structure of paragraphs — aim to comment on a range of structural features.

4) To get top marks, you'll need to write about everything mentioned in the question:

> - You need to comment on how the writer uses structure to create a sense of loss throughout the text.
> - You need to look at how the sense of loss increases or decreases over the course of the text.
> - Analyse any other structural features that add to this effect — this could include anything else you spot, such as changes in tone or viewpoint.

Structure your paragraphs so that each point is backed up by evidence and fully developed.

Here's a Grade 4-5 answer extract

> In the first paragraph, the writer tells you that there is "failure and regret" in Mabel's past, but it doesn't tell you why straight away. This hints at a sense of loss, which increases throughout the extract and is much greater once we know the reason for it.
> The writer next writes about what Mabel thought Alaska would be like before she arrived there, then compares it to what it's actually like now that she lives there. This creates a sense of loss, as her hopes have not been met and she is disappointed instead.
> It then talks about the past, ten years ago, when she had a baby "born still and silent". Now we understand where Mabel's unexplained grief in the first paragraph comes from, which increases the sense of loss.
> Next the writer writes about the future, as Mabel explains what her life will be like over the coming winter. So it goes from present to past to future, which creates a sense of loss by comparing the different parts of her life and showing what she feels is missing from it.

This answer references the question — it talks about how the sense of loss increases, but it could be more specific in explaining how the writer creates this effect.

A better technical term could be used here, such as 'contrasts'.

This would be better if it went into more depth about Mabel's grief.

This sums up the overall structure, but it needs developing further with specific examples. It also might have been clearer to mention this at the beginning of the answer.

1) This answer describes some structural features of the text and starts to comment on the effect they have.

2) However, it doesn't go into enough detail about how the structure helps to create a sense of loss, or fully develop why the writer's choice of structure is effective.

Section Six — English Language: Sample Exams & Graded Answers

Graded Answers — Paper 1, Question 3

Here's a **Grade 6-7** answer extract

> The writer moves from a description of Mabel's present life to a recollection of her past, then to her fears about the future. By showing how Mabel's life has changed, the writer increases the sense of loss over the course of the text.
>
> The extract begins by focusing on the silence of the present, which emphasises Mabel's sense of loss. The writer lists what Mabel cannot hear — there are "No infants cooing or wailing" and no children "calling each other's names". Listing the missing sounds one after the next emphasises what Mabel is lacking and increases the sense of loss.
>
> The middle of the extract is a flashback, which reveals Mabel's loss: her baby passed away. Through the flashback, the reader can step back in time to Mabel losing her baby. This allows the reader to empathise more with Mabel, which increases the sense of loss.
>
> The focus then shifts to Mabel's thoughts about the future. This shift is emphasised by repetition; in lines 29-34, the repetition of "would" focuses the reader on what Mabel is sure will happen. By contrasting Mabel's current outlook with the hope she once had for her future, the writer shows how much hope Mabel has lost.

Annotations:
- This is a strong opening that sums up the overall structure.
- This explains how the structure helps to create a sense of loss, but it could still go into more detail in its explanation.
- Good focus on answering the question.
- This comments on how the focus changes throughout the extract.
- Good terminology.

This answer could be further developed to explain <u>how</u> each element of structure creates <u>a sense of loss</u>.

This is a **Grade 8-9** answer extract

> This passage has a complex non-chronological structure that seems to follow Mabel's train of thought. This insight into Mabel's mind allows the reader to empathise with her to a greater extent and experience her sense of loss more deeply.
>
> The text starts in the present, where a repetitive sentence structure creates a sense of loss. Three consecutive sentences begin with the negative "No", followed by a mention of absent children. This repetition emphasises what Mabel is missing, creating a sad tone. Although the focus then shifts to the sounds that Mabel can actually hear, the sentences later resume starting with negatives, making the sense of loss seem inescapable.
>
> The second section of the extract is a flashback describing the death of Mabel's baby. Having the past intrude into the present heightens the sense of loss, as it demonstrates that Mabel's past loss remains very present. Furthermore, despite the death of Mabel's baby being a pivotal moment in her life, the flashback is the shortest section in the extract. The lack of detail suggests that the memories are too painful for Mabel to fully revisit and therefore only increases the sense of loss.

Annotations:
- High-level vocabulary makes this answer stand out.
- This makes an interesting point about the smaller-scale structure of the passage.
- This goes into good detail about the effects of the structural technique.
- This answer links its analysis back to the overall structure of the passage.

This is a <u>really good</u> answer — it makes several <u>original</u> points about the structure and its effect. The points are <u>fully developed</u> to explain <u>how</u> the structure helps create a <u>sense of loss</u>.

Show the examiner how the structure creates a specific effect...

The key to an excellent answer for English Language paper 1, question 3, is to show how structural features create a specific effect. Scan here for a video on this question with even more useful tips.

Paper 1 Q3 Video

Graded Answers — Paper 1, Question 4

Question 4 (see p.95) is worth 20 marks, so it's worth spending some time working out how to answer it.

Write about Whether you Agree with the Statement and Why

1) Question 4 is about evaluating how effective the text is.
2) The sample question gives you a statement. You need to give your opinion on it — in this case, how clearly the writer shows Mabel's feelings, and whether it is easy to feel her emotions.
3) You also need to state how much you agree or disagree with the statement.
4) Structure your answer clearly (see page 4) and make sure you include technical terms to get top marks.
5) The bullet points under the question give you guidance about what you need to include in your answer:

> - You could write about the impression you get of Mabel's feelings.
> - You could talk about the techniques the writer uses to show how Mabel feels, i.e. the language or structural devices they use.
> - The question says you need to make references to the text, so you need to include plenty of relevant evidence for every point you make.

Here's a Grade 4-5 answer extract

Overall, I agree with the statement. I mostly feel the same emotions Mabel is feeling, and I think the writer makes it really obvious how she's feeling.

Mabel feels frightened of the winter, and especially of the "darkness". The description of the "few hours of twilight" each day makes you imagine what it would be like not to see daylight for months, so you can start to understand Mabel's feelings of fear and anxiety.

The writer also suggests that Mabel is unhappy. She does this by making the Alaskan winter seem very uncomfortable, with the "glacial wind through the cracks" in the walls and "wet laundry" everywhere.

Some of the words rhyme, which sounds really repetitive, so it makes it seem like Mabel's life is monotonous. The way the words sound makes me feel bored and dull too.

Annotations:
- This is good — it gives an opinion on the statement.
- This starts to address how the text makes the reader feel.
- This could be developed by writing about how these phrases help the reader feel what Mabel is feeling.
- This is a good point about language and its effect, but it needs a clear example from the text and more explanation.

1) This answer starts to comment on how Mabel feels, and how the text makes the reader feel.
2) However, some of the points in this answer need to be developed further by explaining how the writer's choice of language and structure affects the reader.
3) Every point should also be backed up with a good example from the text.

Section Six — English Language: Sample Exams & Graded Answers

Graded Answers — Paper 1, Question 4

Here's a Grade 6-7 answer extract

> I strongly agree with the statement that the writer makes you feel how Mabel feels. She uses descriptive techniques to create a very strong sense of the atmosphere of Mabel's life and emotions.
>
> Mabel is "frightened" by winter, and the writer uses vivid language to show and emphasise this feeling. For example, the writer compares the winter to "a coming death" to show the danger Mabel thinks she is facing, then reinforces this impression using violent words such as "choked" and "stranglehold". This use of powerful descriptive vocabulary helps me to imagine myself in Mabel's position and feel her fear.
>
> The writer also suggests that Mabel feels powerless in the face of her fears. The verbs "would stumble" and "would struggle" indicate her hopeless feelings regarding the winter to come. This description of the winter months helps the reader to empathise with Mabel and the inevitable difficulties that her future will bring.

Annotations:
- "I strongly agree..." — This shows that you've thought about the extent to which you agree with the statement.
- Second paragraph — This paragraph picks out specific language features and comments on their impact.
- "This description... empathise with Mabel" — This shows that you're thinking about the effect of the text on the reader.

1) This answer clearly focuses on how the writer uses language to create a <u>vivid impression</u> of how Mabel is feeling.
2) It uses a good range of relevant <u>quotes</u> as evidence, and <u>develops</u> the points by relating them to the effect on the <u>reader</u>.

This is a Grade 8-9 answer extract

> To an extent I agree with the statement. The focus of the passage shifts from the dismal external landscape to an oppressive interior of "shadowy corners" and "wet laundry". This highlights to the reader how trapped Mabel feels by the "stranglehold" of the encroaching winter. Her home, which should be a place of safety, has become a place of fear, surrounded by "darkness" and vulnerable to "glacial winds". The writer describes common sensations like darkness and cold, which the reader can easily recognise. This makes Mabel's feelings seem very clear, and helps me to empathise with her plight.
>
> However, it also seems that this bleak depiction of winter is a result of Mabel's attitude, which lessens the extent to which I empathise with her feelings. The repetition of "would not" to describe her lack of activity hints at her negative mindset, which is reinforced by the short, blunt sentence on line 39. By contrasting Mabel's lack of hope with Jack's "struggle", the writer implies that there are more proactive responses to the hardships of winter, and suggests that Mabel's dread is at least partly irrational.

Annotations:
- "The focus of the passage shifts..." — This shows an understanding of how the text's structure affects the reader's response.
- "The writer describes common sensations..." — This explains how the language used conveys Mabel's feelings and affects the reader.
- "which lessens the extent to which I empathise with her feelings" — Keep referring back to the statement to make sure your answer is focused.
- Second paragraph — The second paragraph makes a well-developed counter-argument.

1) This is a <u>top grade</u> answer — it gives an answer that clearly responds to the <u>statement</u> in an <u>original</u> way.
2) It has a clear <u>structure</u>, and its points are backed up with relevant <u>quotes</u> and <u>examples</u>.

You always need to support your opinion with evidence...
It doesn't matter if you agree with the statement or not. The important thing is that you back up all your ideas with quotations and evidence. To watch a video with more tips, scan here.

Paper 1 Q4 Video

Graded Answers — Paper 1, Question 5

You'll have a choice of two tasks for question 5, but you only need to do one. See p.95 for the full question.

Include lots of Description in your answer

1) To write a good answer to this question, you need to match your writing to the form, purpose, and audience in the question.

   - The form needs to be either a description or the beginning of a story. Think about the kind of language and writing structures that work well for these forms (see pages 76-79).
   - For both tasks, it's a piece of creative writing for a school magazine, so the purpose is to entertain. You need to use a range of sophisticated vocabulary and language techniques, and a structure that grabs and holds the audience's interest.
   - Your audience isn't mentioned explicitly in the question, but you're writing for a school magazine, so you can guess the audience will be the same age as you. You need to adapt your language, tone and style so that it's appealing to a teenage audience.

2) There are also loads of marks on offer for spelling, punctuation and grammar in this question, so it's really important to write accurately and clearly (see page 8).

Here's a Grade 4-5 answer extract

> The small house stood on its own, surrounded by fir trees and rocks. Snow had gathered against the walls in deep piles. It did not look very inviting, but to Anneka it was the most welcome sight in the world. She had got lost in the woods and she had been worried that she would have to spend the night outside in the forest, which was freezing cold and as scary as a spider's nest.
>
> Anneka walked towards the door and knocked. To her surprise the door swung open and she could see inside the house. She saw a single room with a fire burning in the fireplace and a table set for two, with hot food piled high on the plates. There was only one thing missing from the scene, there were no people inside.
>
> Anneka walked tentatively into the room and began to warm her hands in front of the fire, wondering where the people who lived in the house had gone. The room looked as if someone had just stepped out, but the only path Anneka had seen was the one she had come along, and she had not passed anyone else. Surely they couldn't have just disappeared?

Annotations:
- "The small house stood on its own, surrounded by fir trees and rocks." — This sets the scene, but it could do with some more imaginative description.
- "as scary as a spider's nest" — It's good to use descriptive techniques like similes, but this one isn't very original and it doesn't really create the right tone.
- "There was only one thing missing from the scene, there were no people inside." — The punctuation in this sentence isn't quite right — a colon would fit better.
- "tentatively" — This is a good piece of descriptive vocabulary.
- "Surely they couldn't have just disappeared?" — This sets up a mystery, which makes the reader want to know what has happened.

1) This answer has a fairly clear structure and gets straight into the story.
2) However, it lacks description, and the vocabulary isn't very varied. It could also be made more exciting or complex for its teenage audience.

All these extracts are from answers to the second task in question 5 on page 95 — writing the beginning of a story about facing a problem in winter.

Section Six — English Language: Sample Exams & Graded Answers

Graded Answers — Paper 1, Question 5

Here's a **Grade 6-7** answer extract

> Robin lowered the axe he had been using to chop wood and peered towards the mountains, his eyes squinting in the sharp orange glow of the slowly setting Sun. He was sure he had seen a movement up there, a flash of scarlet against the sparkling white of the snow-capped peaks. But who would be mad enough to venture into the mountains at dusk, in winter, with snow and freezing temperatures forecast that night?
>
> Robin sighed wearily, deciding that it must have been his imagination playing tricks on him, as it so often did out here in the mountains.
>
> A low, ominous rumble echoed down the valley, interrupting his thoughts. Robin froze momentarily, listening intently, then snapped into action, frantically gathering his tools as the sound grew louder and closer.
>
> The avalanche roared destructively and unstoppably towards his isolated home.

This uses the opening sentence of the story to set the scene nicely.

This answer uses interesting language to make the descriptions more vivid and to entertain the audience.

This uses the senses to help the reader to imagine the scene.

The change of pace creates excitement in this story.

1) This has a clear <u>structure</u>, uses good <u>descriptions</u> and builds <u>interest</u> for the reader.
2) It could be improved by using more <u>complex</u> sentence structures and a <u>wider range</u> of punctuation.

This is a **Grade 8-9** answer extract

Scan here for a full-length version of this answer.

> I surfaced suddenly from a fitful sleep, the skin on my forearms tingling with an instinctive awareness that something was wrong. There — that noise again! A skittering, scrabbling, scuffling noise in the far corner of the dimly lit room. I sat up in bed, the quilt clutched to my chest with stone-numb hands, my breath forming foggy billows in the chilly air.
>
> The sun was just rising; its feeble light trickled through the window, fractured into myriad rainbows by the intricate whorls and fingers of ice on the frosty pane. As a brighter beam pierced the gloom, I gasped. There, huddled by the door, a young wolf cub gazed at me with sorrowful, strangely human eyes. His tawny fur was matted with blood, as rich and red as the morning light that now illuminated it fully.
>
> I eased myself out of the wooden bunk, crouched down on the splintered floorboards and held out a trembling hand towards the cub. He gazed at me uncertainly, then slowly, slowly, he stretched forward and snuffled at my fingers, his breath as warm and ticklish as a damp feather duster.

This beginning immediately sets the tone and atmosphere by creating tension.

This uses a first-person narrator to establish a strong connection with the reader.

Vivid description and interesting vocabulary help to set the scene.

Unusual imagery helps to set this answer apart.

1) This has a structure that <u>interests</u> the reader by <u>slowly revealing</u> what's going on.
2) It's also packed with interesting <u>imagery</u> and unusual <u>vocabulary</u> to make it more <u>entertaining</u> to read, which helps it to fit the <u>purpose</u> and <u>audience</u> of the question.

This question is worth 50% of English Language Paper 1...

Paper 1, question 5 is your chance to really show off your creative writing skills. Make sure your writing is entertaining and audience-appropriate to score the top marks. For extra hints, scan here.

Sample Exam — Paper 2

These two pages show you some example questions that will help you prepare for English Language paper 2 — the texts to go with questions 1-4 are on pages 108-109. First have a read through the texts and the questions, then have a look at the graded answer extracts we've provided on pages 110-119.

Question 1 asks you to identify if statements are True or False

Q1   The statements below are about **lines 1-17** of **Text A**.
Tick the boxes next to the **four** statements that are TRUE.

- A   Lisa made her first batches of soup with her parents.
- B   Lisa wasn't initially excited about making and selling soup.
- C   Lisa's parents liked the first sample of soup she made them try.
- D   Lisa's aunt didn't like throwing food away.
- E   Lisa's parents thought the business was a great idea from the start.
- F   People were surprised by Lisa working at such a young age.
- G   Lisa's dad wasn't very good at negotiating with farmers.
- H   Lisa chose working on her business over spending time with friends.

[4 marks]

Question 2 is about Summarising information

Q2   In **Text A** and **Text B**, the writers are describing the parents of the children.
What are the differences between Lisa Goodwin's parents and the parents of the Victorian street sellers?

You need to:
- **infer** information from the text
- talk about **both texts** in your answer.

[8 marks]

Section Six — English Language: Sample Exams & Graded Answers

Sample Exam — Paper 2

Question 3 is about the writer's choice of Language

Q3 Explain how the writer uses language to describe her loneliness in **lines 1-20** of **Text B**.

[12 marks]

Question 4 asks you to Compare writers' Viewpoints

Q4 This question is about **Text A** and **Text B**, where both writers are writing about children who are working.

Compare how they convey their different attitudes to work and childhood.

You may wish to explore what the writers' attitudes are and what methods they use to convey their attitudes. You should use examples from **both** texts.

[16 marks]

You have to Explain your Viewpoint in Question 5

Q5 Write a broadsheet newspaper article arguing your opinion on the statement below.

"More children should get a job before the age of sixteen. Part-time work would teach children valuable skills that they don't learn in school."

[40 marks]

You don't have to actually answer these questions...
On the next two pages, you'll find Text A and Text B — read them carefully. Then use the sample answers on pages 110-119 to build your understanding of how to write great English Language paper 2 answers.

Exam Text A

Here is exam text A, to go with the questions on pages 106-107. It's an autobiographical article written by a young entrepreneur (a person who starts up a business) for a newspaper in the 1990s.

Setting up SouperStar — From Soup Pan to Soup Stand

Lisa Goodwin recalls how she set up her first business at the age of eight.

> Remember to read the contextual information you are given about each text.

When I first told my parents that I wanted to sell soup, I must have been about eight years old — like most sensible parents, they thought I was joking. That weekend, I'd been at my aunt's house helping her harvest vegetables from her garden. It had been a bumper year, and we'd been staggering back and forth, shifting armfuls of all sorts of things into the house. With my aunt, not a single thing could go to waste, so we set about making soup. Gallons of the stuff. We were surrounded by steaming and bubbling pots and pans, and the air was thick with scents of leek and potato, carrot and coriander and spicy butternut squash. Anyway, when my parents didn't take me seriously, I went straight to the fridge to dig out one of the soups my aunt and I had made — it was cream of mushroom, I think — and they absolutely lapped it up. "See!" I said, smiling. So it was then that SouperStar was born.

From day one I couldn't wait to get stuck in. My parents would dutifully help me select produce, whizz up batches of soup and drive me here, there and everywhere so that I could set up shop. I would go to school fairs, farmers' markets — anywhere that would have me. Dad was my champion haggler. He'd barter with local farmers to get crates of carrots or potatoes at rock-bottom prices. If he could get anything for free, well, that was even better! I think a lot of people were bemused by the sight of this young kid, buying produce and selling soup, and my parents put up with it because they thought that I would grow out of it at some stage. While other kids my age were glued to the TV or playing in the park, I was peeling vegetables and frying croutons.

I begged and pleaded with my parents to let me be home-schooled, as I wanted to dedicate more time to the business, but they insisted I should have a "normal" childhood, and fill my head with "necessary" stuff like formulae and equations. A few years later, and I was sitting my O levels* — but instead of panicking over revision, I was, of course, dreaming up new recipes. With all my exams passed and done with, I wanted to press on and really dedicate myself to SouperStar. I think at this point my parents genuinely realised how determined I was, and they began to take it a lot more seriously too.

I struck upon the idea of selling soup at our local train station during the winter months — there was a constant stream of customers all in desperate need of something that would warm up their hands and fill their bellies. Before long, I was hiring extra staff in order to open up soup stands in other nearby train stations and Mum was coming up with advertising slogans and snazzy package designs (her years of marketing experience came in pretty handy here). As the business grew and grew, Mum and Dad couldn't keep up with all the support I needed, so it made sense for them to get even more involved. Mum reduced her hours at work and Dad quit his job entirely. Fast-forward to today, and I'm the managing director of one of the most successful food companies in the area.

Of course, financially, it's worked out well for us (thanks must go to my parents for the initial investment, not to mention being old enough to buy the wine for my French onion soup!), but for me it was never the dream of becoming a millionaire that got me started or even kept me going. It was the passion for building a great business based on great food — and that remains at the heart of SouperStar today.

Glossary

* O levels — the qualifications that preceded GCSEs, with examinations taken at the age of 16.

Exam Text B

This is exam text B, which consists of two interviews from the 1840s conducted with children who work as street sellers. These articles, alongside many others like them, were published in a newspaper to highlight the plight of the poor in London.

The first interview is with a young girl who sells flowers, and is an orphan.

"Mother has been dead just a year this month; she took cold at the washing and it went to her chest; she was only bad a fortnight; she suffered great pain, and, poor thing, she used to fret dreadful, as she lay ill, about me, for she knew she was going to leave me. She used to plan how I was to do when she was gone. She made me promise to try to get a place and keep from the streets if I could, for she seemed to dread them so much. When she was gone I was left in the world without a friend. I am quite alone, I have no relation at all, not a soul belonging to me. For three months I went about looking for a place, as long as my money lasted, for mother told me to sell our furniture to keep me and get me clothes. I could have got a place, but nobody would have me without a character*, and I knew nobody to give me one. I tried very hard to get one, indeed I did; for I thought of all mother had said to me about going into the streets. At last, when my money was just gone, I met a young woman in the street, and I asked her to tell me where I could get a lodging. She told me to come with her, she would show me a respectable lodging-house for women and girls. I went, and I have been there ever since. The women in the house advised me to take to flower-selling, as I could get nothing else to do. One of the young women took me to market with her, and showed me how to bargain with the salesman for my flowers. At first, when I went out to sell, I felt so ashamed I could not ask anybody to buy of me; and many times went back at night with all my stock, without selling one bunch. The woman at the lodging house is very good to me; when I have a bad day she will let my lodging go until I can pay her. She is very kind, indeed, for she knows I am alone. What I shall do in the winter I don't know. In the cold weather last year, when I could get no flowers, I was forced to live on my clothes, I have none left now but what I have on. What I shall do I don't know — I can't bear to think on it."

The second interview is with a young girl who sells nuts.

"It's in the winter, sir, when things are far worst with us. Father can make very little then — but I don't know what he earns exactly at any time — and though mother has more work then, there's fire and candle to pay for. We were very badly off last winter, and worse, I think, the winter before. Father sometimes came home and had made nothing, and if mother had no work in hand we went to bed to save fire and candle, if it was ever so soon. Father would die afore he would let mother take as much as a loaf from the parish. I was sent out to sell nuts first: 'If it's only 1d.** you make,' mother said, 'it's a good piece of bread.' I didn't mind being sent out. I knew children that sold things in the streets. Perhaps I liked it better than staying at home without a fire and with nothing to do, and if I went out I saw other children busy. No, I wasn't a bit frightened when I first started, not a bit. Some children — but they was such little things — said: 'O, Liz, I wish I was you.' I had twelve ha'porths*** and sold them all. I don't know what it made; 2d. most likely. I didn't crack a single nut myself. I was fond of them then, but I don't care for them now. I could do better if I went into public-houses, but I'm only let go to Mr. Smith's, because he knows father, and Mrs. Smith and him recommends me. I have sold nuts and oranges to soldiers. I was once in a great crowd, and was getting crushed, and there was a very tall soldier close by me, and he lifted me, basket and all, right up to his shoulder, and carried me clean out of the crowd. He had stripes on his arm. 'I shouldn't like you to be in such a trade,' says he, 'if you was my child.' He didn't say why he wouldn't like it. Perhaps because it was beginning to rain. Yes, we are far better off now. Father makes money. I don't go out in bad weather in the summer; in the winter, though, I must. I don't know what I shall be when I grow up. I can read a little. I've been to church five or six times in my life. I should go oftener and so would mother, if we had clothes."

Glossary

* a character — a reference

** d. — pence

*** ha'porths — half-pennys' worth

Graded Answers — Paper 2, Question 1

You don't have to write anything for paper 2, question 1 — instead you have to select the correct options. Remind yourself of the question on p.106, then read through these sample answers.

You need to pick out the True Statements

1) Question 1 gives you eight statements about a part of one of the texts — you have to pick out which statements are true.

2) Only four of the statements are true, and there are four marks available — so you need to tick four boxes.

3) Always make sure you've ticked exactly four boxes. If you've ticked the statements that you're sure about and you still haven't ticked four, have a guess at the others — you might get them right.

4) This sample question is about lines 1 to 7 of Text A, so you only need to look at that part of the text to find the answers.

5) Read the statements carefully as they might be about something that is implicit — something that isn't stated outright, but is implied by what the text says.

6) You should aim to get all four marks on this question.

In the actual exam, you may be asked to shade the correct boxes rather than tick them. Make sure you read the instructions carefully.

Here's a Grade 4-5 answer

This answer has spotted two of the true statements — D and F.

A	Lisa made her first batches of soup with her parents.	☐
B	Lisa wasn't initially excited about making and selling soup.	✓
C	Lisa's parents liked the first sample of soup she made them try.	☐
D	Lisa's aunt didn't like throwing food away.	✓
E	Lisa's parents thought the business was a great idea from the start.	☐
F	People were surprised by Lisa working at such a young age.	✓
G	Lisa's dad wasn't very good at negotiating with farmers.	✓
H	Lisa chose working on her business over spending time with friends.	☐

This is false — the text says "From day one I couldn't wait to get stuck in", so she was excited from the very beginning.

This is true — the text says Lisa's aunt believed that "not a single thing could go to waste". This implies that she wouldn't want to throw any food away.

This is false — the text says Lisa's dad was her "champion haggler". This implies he was good at negotiating with farmers.

This is true — the text says "people were bemused" at her working because she was a "young kid". The word "bemused" shows that they were confused and surprised.

Section Six — English Language: Sample Exams & Graded Answers

Graded Answers — Paper 2, Question 1

This is a Grade 6-7 answer

This answer has spotted three of the true statements — D, F and H.

A	Lisa made her first batches of soup with her parents.	☐
B	Lisa wasn't initially excited about making and selling soup.	☐
C	Lisa's parents liked the first sample of soup she made them try.	☐
D	Lisa's aunt didn't like throwing food away.	☑
E	Lisa's parents thought the business was a great idea from the start.	☑
F	People were surprised by Lisa working at such a young age.	☑
G	Lisa's dad wasn't very good at negotiating with farmers.	☐
H	Lisa chose working on her business over spending time with friends.	☑

This is false — the text says that her parents initially thought she was "joking".

This is true — the text says that instead of "playing in the park" as other children did, Lisa was "peeling vegetables". This shows that she was making soup instead of playing with other children.

And here's a Grade 8-9 answer

This answer has spotted all four of the true statements — C, D, F and H.

A	Lisa made her first batches of soup with her parents.	☐
B	Lisa wasn't initially excited about making and selling soup.	☐
C	Lisa's parents liked the first sample of soup she made them try.	☑
D	Lisa's aunt didn't like throwing food away.	☑
E	Lisa's parents thought the business was a great idea from the start.	☐
F	People were surprised by Lisa working at such a young age.	☑
G	Lisa's dad wasn't very good at negotiating with farmers.	☐
H	Lisa chose working on her business over spending time with friends.	☑

This is false — the text says that she made her first batches of soup whilst visiting her aunt's house.

This is true — the text says that Lisa's parents "absolutely lapped it up". This phrase implies they ate it quickly and with enthusiasm.

Remember — only four of the statements are true...

There are an easy four marks available here, so make sure you read each statement carefully before deciding if it's true or false. For a video on how to answer this question, scan this QR code.

Paper 2 Q1 Video

Graded Answers — Paper 2, Question 2

It's time for paper 2, question 2 (take a look back at p.106 for the full question).

Pick out information from **Both** texts

1) Question 2 is testing your ability to pick out information from both texts, then summarise it to show the differences between them.

2) The sample question asks you to pick out information about the parents that feature in the texts — make sure your points focus on the parents, and not anything else.

3) You need to summarise the differences between the parents. First, write down a key point about each of the parents.

4) Then use quotations or paraphrased details to back up your point, and explain how these examples show a difference between the parents.

5) You'll then need to develop your point further, e.g. by offering insights into why the parents are different, or why the writer chose to present them in this way.

6) To get top marks, you need to interpret information from the texts — this means picking out the things that aren't immediately obvious about the parents. Try to make a few inferences that you can explore in depth, rather than listing lots of brief, simple ones.

7) You can use certain phrases to show the examiner when you are making an inference — e.g. 'you can infer from this' or 'this might suggest that'.

Remember to structure your paragraphs clearly (see p.4) and include technical terms to get top marks.

Here's a **Grade 4-5** answer extract

> The nut seller's parents are poor as they are described as "badly off" and sometimes they have to go to bed early to save money. Lisa Goodwin's parents seem to be well off. This difference means that the nut seller's parents expect their daughter to go out to work rather than go to school. On the other hand, Lisa Goodwin's parents don't expect Lisa to go out to work and even "insisted" that she stay in school.
>
> The flower seller's mother is dead and the text doesn't mention her father. Her mother worried about her a lot as it says she used to "fret dreadful". Both Lisa Goodwin's parents are alive and helped her out a lot with her business.
>
> The nut seller doesn't know what she wants to be when she grows up, whereas Lisa Goodwin wants to "dedicate" herself to her business.

- This is a good use of a short quotation to back up the point.
- This needs a quote or an example to back up the point.
- This is good — it shows that a comparison is being made.
- There needs to be an explanation here of how the sets of parents are different.
- This final sentence isn't related to the question, so it wouldn't get any marks.

1) This answer gives some differences between the parents in the two texts.

2) It would be better if all the points were backed up with quotes or examples from the text.

3) The points could also be developed more, e.g. by giving thoughtful insights into the reasons why the parents are different.

Graded Answers — Paper 2, Question 2

Here's a Grade 6-7 answer extract

> The nut seller's parents are a working-class couple living in 19th-century London, who have been "badly off", though the child feels they are "better off now". However, the child is expected to contribute to the household income, even "if it's only 1d.". The nut seller says she was "sent out", which suggests to me that her parents forced her to work.
>
> This contrasts with Lisa Goodwin's parents, who do not seem to have any financial worries as they were able to provide Lisa with "the initial investment" for her business. Unlike the nut seller's parents, Lisa's parents didn't expect their daughter to work at a young age; in fact they thought she was "joking" when she suggested starting her own business.
>
> Before she died, the flower seller's mother was worried about her daughter being on "the streets", which shows she was concerned for her safety. Lisa Goodwin's parents just wanted her to have a "normal childhood" and go to school. This shows the differences between the time periods the two sets of parents were living in, and their levels of wealth.

Annotations:
- Good use of short, relevant quotes to support the points.
- Clear signalling of inference.
- This answer makes inferences about the parents — it comments on the thoughts and actions of the parents that aren't directly stated.
- This is good — it explains the differences by showing awareness of the context in which the texts were written.

This answer makes several **good points**, and uses **relevant quotes** to back **everything** up.

Here's a Grade 8-9 answer extract

> The parents of the nut seller and the parents of Lisa Goodwin have very different attitudes to their own needs and their child's employment. The nut seller's parents are a poor, working-class couple living in 19th-century London. The child recounts how they were "very badly off" in recent winters, but that they are "far better off now". Despite this apparent improvement in their income, the child is still "sent out" to work to contribute to the household income. Lisa Goodwin's parents, by contrast, need no extra support. They dutifully sacrificed their careers in order to support their daughter's ambitions. Lisa's parents prioritise her ambitions over their own, whereas the nut seller's parents prioritise survival over their child's future prospects. The Goodwins' greater wealth lets them give their daughter freedoms the nut seller is denied.
>
> The mother of the flower seller demonstrates a very different attitude to the parents of Lisa Goodwin. She expresses deep concern for her child's safety through her plea that she should "keep from the streets". Lisa Goodwin's parents, however, are concerned at her desire to work so young and perceive her greatest need is to have a "normal childhood". Once again, this demonstrates the very different situations of the sets of parents: the flower seller's mother is destitute and dying, and thinks only of her child's safety. Lisa Goodwin's parents have the luxury of being able to be concerned about the extent of their child's education.

Annotations:
- This is great — a point is made straight away.
- This is an interesting interpretation of the differences between the parents — it makes a perceptive inference about the Goodwins.
- This clearly compares the parents in each text.
- Higher level vocabulary and sentence structures help to make this a top level answer.

This answer makes **well-developed** points, backs them up with **good evidence** and makes an interesting link to the **social** and **historical context** of the texts in order to explore the differences between the parents.

A top-quality answer needs to make inferences...

To get top marks in paper 2, question 2, you need to be able to interpret the texts and make perceptive comparisons between the two texts. For extra help with this question, scan this code.

Paper 2 Q2 Video

Graded Answers — Paper 2, Question 3

Paper 2, question 3 is all about analysing how language is used for effect. Have a look back at page 107 to remind yourself of the question, and then have a read through these sample answers.

Think about the writer's Choice of Words

1) Question 3 is about how the writer has used language to describe something.

2) Make sure you read the question carefully — in this example, you're only supposed to write about lines 1 to 20 from Text B.

3) The sample question is about how the writer uses language to describe her loneliness — so think about the effect of the language used, and how it influences the reader.

4) To analyse language for this question, you should comment on things like:

   - The effect of specific words and phrases, such as how certain verbs are used (see p.44-45).
   - Language features and techniques, such as rhetorical devices (see p.46 and p.49-52).
   - The effect of different sentence forms, such as short or long sentences (see p.64-65).

   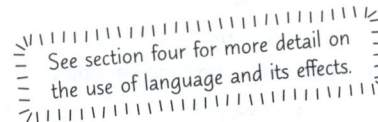
   See section four for more detail on the use of language and its effects.

5) Make sure you use a range of technical terms to describe the writer's techniques, and keep your vocabulary varied and interesting.

Here's a Grade 4-5 answer extract

The flower seller describes her loneliness and all the terrible things that have happened to her in the first person. This helps the reader understand how the girl must be feeling because it is told directly from her point of view.

The flower seller uses strong, emotional language to explain why she is lonely by describing the death of her mother. For example, she says that her mother "suffered great pain" and "knew she was going to leave me". This makes you feel sorry for the mother, as she was in pain, but also for the flower seller as it makes you think about how you would feel knowing you were about to become an orphan.

The flower seller shows how lonely she feels when she says "I was left in the world without a friend." This is a really effective way of making you feel sorry for her and the situation she's in.

Try to avoid repeating yourself in your answer — even if you want to make a similar point, try to phrase it differently.

This paragraph makes a point, then backs it up with quotations and some explanation.

This paragraph refers to a good piece of evidence about loneliness, but it needs to explain how the language affects the reader.

1) This clearly answers the question — all the points are about how the language describes the flower seller's loneliness, and the effect of these language choices.

2) There's room for improvement though — some of the points could do with more examples, and the answer could explain how the language influences the reader more clearly.

Section Six — English Language: Sample Exams & Graded Answers

Graded Answers — Paper 2, Question 3

Here's a **Grade 6-7** answer extract

> The writer immediately shows the flower seller's loneliness through the opening of the interview, which the flower seller begins by stating "Mother has been dead". This blunt phrase instantly creates a sense of loss, which encourages the reader to view the flower seller as lonely.
>
> The repetition in the flower seller's story emphasises how isolated she feels after her mother's death. She uses several similar phrases, such as "left in the world without a friend", "I am quite alone" and "not a soul belonging to me", to reinforce how desolate she is. This makes the reader feel sorry for her, because after the tragedy of her mother's death, the girl has no one to turn to.
>
> The flower seller doesn't say how old she is, but the concern her mother feels for leaving her daughter alone — she "seemed to dread" the thought of her daughter on the streets — suggests that she is too young to look after herself. This makes the flower seller's story seem even more sorrowful.

This is really focused on how the language is used to describe the flower seller's loneliness.

This is good — a language technique has been spotted, then the effect of it has been explained.

Making inferences is great — this demonstrates to the examiner that you've read the text carefully and have really thought about its meaning.

This answer makes some **interesting inferences** about the **effects** of the language on the reader, but it could be improved by using more **technical terms** and higher-level **vocabulary**.

This is a **Grade 8-9** answer extract

> The first-person narrative makes the reader feel they are actually being spoken to by the child, which increases the emotional appeal of her story. Her personal voice allows readers to see the nuances of her feelings; when she emphasises how "alone" she is, without "a soul" to help her, her solitude becomes clear. This humanises her loneliness, so it resonates more with readers.
>
> The flower seller uses language to emphasise that loneliness causes her practical problems as well as being emotionally distressing. In line 8, the girl explains how "nobody" would give her a place to stay, as "nobody" would give her a reference. The repetition of this word highlights her utter isolation, as she lacks the connections to find shelter.
>
> With her final words, the flower seller admits that she "can't bear" to think about the future due to her total isolation and destitution: she has sold all her possessions and has no one to turn to. This uncertain and desperate ending leaves the reader feeling despondent and helpless, allowing them to experience a little of the girl's lonely plight for themselves.

Sophisticated vocabulary makes this answer perceptive and detailed.

It's really good to focus on specific words and the effect they have.

This is great — it analyses the influence of the language on the reader in depth.

This answer makes some interesting and **original points** about the **purpose** of the article. Including details like this will really **impress** the examiner — just make sure that they are **relevant** to the question.

Write a clear answer about the right bit of the text...

It's really important to make sure your answer focuses on the correct part of the text in this question. Structure your writing (see page 4) to help you form a clear answer. For more tips, scan here.

Graded Answers — Paper 2, Question 4

Question 4 is worth 16 marks. Take a look back at page 107, then have a read through these answers.

Compare the writers' different Points of View

1) Question 4 is about what the writers think about work and childhood, as well as how they show what they're thinking.

2) In this question, there's some handy information to guide you. Make sure you read it carefully and cover what it asks for in your answer.

> - You need to identify what the writers' attitudes to work and childhood are, and clearly compare them.
> - You also need to comment on how the writers have shown their attitudes to work and childhood, i.e. the words, phrases and language techniques they've used.
> - You should back up every point you make with relevant evidence from the text — using short quotations is a great way to do this.

3) Make sure you focus on their attitudes to work and childhood, not anything else.

4) The question is also asking you to compare, so make sure you link the two writers' attitudes together using words and phrases such as 'however', 'in contrast' and 'whereas'.

Here's a Grade 4-5 answer extract

> Lisa wanted to work during her childhood, as she says that she "couldn't wait to get stuck in." On the other hand, the nut seller doesn't seem bothered about working and says that "Perhaps" it's "better than staying at home".
>
> Lisa uses chatty language to talk about her childhood and the work she did, for example she calls herself "this young kid". This shows that she was keen to work when she was young, but she thought it was unusual. The nut seller is different. She "didn't mind" working, and she thinks it's normal for children to be working as she says that she "knew children that sold things in the streets."
>
> The nut seller does what she's told to do by her parents when it comes to work. She was "sent out to sell nuts". Lisa Goodwin does the opposite. She tries to tell them what to do as she wanted to stop going to school and start work instead.

This paragraph makes a good, simple comparison, backed up with quotes as evidence.

A better, more technical term to write about informal, conversational language would be "colloquial".

The example doesn't clearly show what the explanation is saying.

This isn't true — she wanted to be home-schooled. Read the text carefully to make sure you understand what it's saying.

1) This answer mentions some different attitudes and starts to comment on how language is used to show the attitudes.

2) However, it could go into more detail by using more examples, and explaining them more clearly and accurately.

Section Six — English Language: Sample Exams & Graded Answers

Graded Answers — Paper 2, Question 4

Here's a Grade 6-7 answer extract

Lisa's enthusiasm for work comes out through her strongly positive, upbeat tone and colloquial language: she describes how even as a child she would work "anywhere that would have" her, and the slang word "whizz" indicates how much she enjoyed making the soup. The attitude she demonstrates to her childhood is that she just wanted to work, rather than have the "normal childhood" that her parents wanted for her. The quotation marks she uses when she talks about "necessary" education show that she is being ironic and doesn't think the education is necessary at all.

The nut seller, however, works because she has to rather than through a personal desire to work, and she seems unenthusiastic about her employment. This is shown by her less positive tone and more reserved style. She says that she "didn't mind" selling nuts and that it is simply "better than staying at home". She shows that, to her, a normal childhood is spent working in the streets like the other children she knew who were all "busy" working.

Using technical terms correctly will get you marks.

The answer makes clear comparisons.

This paragraph consistently covers all the information in the question — what the writers' attitudes are, how they're conveyed and good quotes are used to back up the point.

This answer is good, but to really wow the examiner, try to include some innovative points...

This is a Grade 8-9 answer extract

Lisa's passion and positivity about her work are conveyed through her informal style, and colloquialisms such as "whizz up" and "snazzy". This conversational language portrays Lisa as someone who has a confident and easy-going attitude to work. She also uses humour to engage the reader, ending the piece with a joke about needing her parents to "buy the wine". This humour gives the text warmth, and demonstrates Lisa's zeal for work.

Lisa also shows a proud and arrogant attitude to her work and childhood. The bemusement she describes causing as a "young kid" working shows her pride in having worked amongst adults, and her disdain for "necessary" education shows her arrogance. She seems to believe that a "normal childhood" was not right for her, and that her parents insistence upon it was tiresome.

In sharp contrast to Lisa Goodwin, the nut seller "must" work. Her unenthusiastic attitude regarding work itself comes out through her more resigned tone: she says that it is "better than staying at home". However, she does seem to be motivated by a desire to make more money. Her tone becomes more animated when describing her ideas about how she "could do better".

The nut seller shows her naive attitude to working as a child through the device of a story: she recalls her encounter with a soldier who wouldn't like his own child "to be in such a trade", but she thinks that is because it was "beginning to rain". It seems clear that the soldier is concerned for her safety, but she doesn't comprehend the danger she is in because of her youthful innocence.

This answer picks out some of the more subtle attitudes to work and childhood shown by the writers.

This develops the point further by going into more depth about her attitude to work.

This is a perceptive point — it makes an inference about the situation instead of just taking the writer's words literally.

Plan how you're going to write your answer before you start it...
(1) Look at all of both texts before you answer paper 2, question 4. (2) Make comparisons.
(3) Use linking words to join your ideas up. For a handy video on this question, scan the QR code.

Paper 2 Q4 Video

Graded Answers — Paper 2, Question 5

Make sure you leave plenty of time to write your answer for paper 2, question 5 — it's worth 40 marks. Look back at the question on page 107, then read through these graded pieces of non-fiction writing.

Adapt your Writing Style to the Question

1) For question 5 you need to respond to the statement, by giving your own perspective on the value of part-time work for children under 16.

It doesn't matter whether you agree or disagree with the statement as long as your answer is engaging and well-structured.

2) You need to match your writing to the form, purpose and audience you've been given in the question.

- The form is a broadsheet newspaper article — so you could write in the style of an opinion piece and include a headline, a strapline and subheadings.

- The purpose is to explain your point of view, but as you're responding to a statement you could do this by making an argument for your viewpoint.

- The audience isn't mentioned specifically, but you can work it out. It's a broadsheet newspaper article about work for teenagers, so it's likely to be read by adults with children who are under 16.

See pages 82-83 for more about writing newspaper articles.

3) It's also important to think about the structure of your writing, especially the opening and ending. You need to link your paragraphs together clearly, too.

4) Don't forget there are 16 marks on offer for spelling, punctuation and grammar for this question — it's really important to write accurately and clearly with a good range of vocabulary (see page 8).

Here's a Grade 4-5 answer extract

NO PART-TIME JOBS FOR UNDER-SIXTEENS

I think that children under the age of 16 shouldn't get a part-time job. Although some people might argue that having a job teaches children about the value of money, time management and working as a team, I don't think that this is the case.
    Firstly, most children have good time management skills. Schools start at 9 am, and some even earlier than this, so arriving on time to lessons is already second nature to most children. Why should children have a part-time job when they already know how to manage their time? Secondly, most children have been working as a team since primary school. From sports teams in P.E., to group projects in Science, school teaches children how to work together from a very young age. Why should children give up their weekends for a badly paid job when they already have great teamwork skills?

This opening sentence isn't really appropriate for a broadsheet newspaper.

This answer uses a counter argument to strengthen the point it's making.

A new paragraph should start here.

The repetition of rhetorical questions is a nice language feature — it makes the point of view come across more forcefully.

1) This answer makes some good points that are focused on the question.
2) It could be better matched to the form that the question asks for, though — the tone and style aren't really appropriate for a broadsheet newspaper.
3) The language could also be more varied and interesting — including a bit of humour or using more creative vocabulary would gain more marks.

Section Six — English Language: Sample Exams & Graded Answers

Graded Answers — Paper 2, Question 5

Here's a **Grade 6-7** answer extract

SAVE THE LEARNING FOR THE CLASSROOM

Lots of young people have a part-time job, and I am sure that employment teaches them a whole host of valuable skills: communication, time management and independence to name but a few. However, these skills aren't just learnt in the workplace; many young people develop and refine these skills in the classroom.

Take, for instance, communication. Every day in school, pupils communicate with a wide range of people. Pupils learn to talk respectfully to teachers; they make engaging conversation with their friends; and they communicate their ideas to their peers during group work. School doesn't just allow pupils to practise their verbal communication — it helps them to develop their written communication too. Essays teach students how to summarise their thoughts and present their opinions. What part-time job could develop communication more effectively than this?

The answer uses more sophisticated punctuation confidently and correctly.

The tone of this answer is suitable for the form and purpose. It's a bit more chatty than the previous answer, but it still uses good vocabulary.

The ideas are linked together fluently.

1) This answer uses language techniques, a <u>clear structure</u> and <u>creative vocabulary</u> to get its point across.
2) However, if the author's <u>personality</u> came across more strongly, the text would be more <u>compelling</u>.

Here's a **Grade 8-9** answer extract

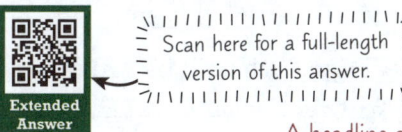
Scan here for a full-length version of this answer.

MINIMUM WAGE, MINIMUM GAIN

Part-time jobs have little value for teenagers under sixteen, argues Charlie Lin.

If someone were to ask me whether I thought under-sixteens should get part-time jobs, my answer, unequivocally, would be "no". As I write this, I can imagine the shocked looks on my readers' faces and the disdainful cries of "but employment teaches children valuable life skills!" To these critics, I say this: there's nothing a part-time job can teach children that they can't learn from other, more rewarding options.

Team 'Work' or Menial Labour?

If you don't believe me, then think about the jobs that are actually available to under-sixteens. Paper rounds, waiting tables, shop assistant — essentially an assortment of mundane, badly-paid Saturday jobs. And what 'valuable life skills' might they learn while toiling away for less than minimum wage? "Teamwork!" you might cry triumphantly, "working in a cafe would teach a young person how to work as part of a team." This may certainly be true if you believe being belittled by the chef and bossed around by the manager counts as 'teamwork'. I, however, do not.

A headline and strapline are used to grab the reader's attention.

The writer shows a clear awareness of their audience.

Really interesting and varied vocabulary makes this answer high level.

Lots of rhetorical techniques are used in this paragraph to make the writer's point of view clear and their argument compelling.

A sarcastic tone makes the argument convincingly, but also gives a sense of the writer's personality.

The writer's <u>opinion</u> and <u>personality</u> is clear in this answer, and it's <u>fluently written</u>. The tone is humorous and chatty, but also subtle, which makes the answer <u>engaging</u> and <u>readable</u>.

The style of your writing will depend on who you're writing for...
If you aren't told who your audience is, think about who's most likely to read your text, then adapt your writing accordingly. For a video with more pointers on this question, scan the QR code.

Introduction to English Literature

It's time to get to grips with English Literature — here's what to expect...

There are Two Exams for AQA English Literature

1) For your English Literature GCSE, you'll have to sit two exams — Paper 1 and Paper 2.
2) Paper 1 lasts 1 hour 45 minutes. It's worth 64 marks (40% of the GCSE).
3) Paper 1 is split into two sections:

- Section A: an essay question about a Shakespeare play (see p.140-144) — e.g. 'Macbeth', 'The Merchant of Venice'.
- Section B: an essay question about a novel from the 19th century (see p.154-156) — e.g. 'A Christmas Carol', 'Jane Eyre'.

4) Paper 2 lasts 2 hours 15 minutes. It's worth 96 marks (60% of the GCSE).
5) Paper 2 is split into three sections:

- Section A: an essay question asking you about a modern text, written after 1914 — e.g. 'Blood Brothers', 'Animal Farm'. This could be a play (see p.138-139) or a novel (see p.151-153).
- Section B: a question about a cluster of poems from the AQA poetry anthology — you'll study either the 'Love and Relationships' cluster, the 'Power and Conflict' cluster or the 'Worlds and Lives' cluster (see p.173-186).
- In Section C, there'll be two unseen poems — you'll have to analyse and compare them (see p.187-196).

Assessment Objectives are the Skills you need for the Exam

The assessment objectives cover all the things you need to do to get a good grade in the exams. They are:

AO1
- Give your own thoughts and opinions on the text.
- Back up your interpretations using evidence from the text (e.g. quotes).

AO2
- Explain how writers use language, structure and form, and what effect this has on the reader.
- Use technical terms to support your analysis.

AO3
- Show that you understand how the text relates to the context in which it was written or set.

AO3 is tested everywhere except the unseen poetry section of Paper 2.

AO4
- Use a range of sentence structures and vocabulary, so that your writing is clear and effective.
- Write accurately, paying particular attention to spelling, punctuation and grammar.

AO4 is only tested in Section A of each paper. It counts for 5% of your overall mark.

You don't need to remember the assessment objectives word for word...

There's no need to memorise these assessment objectives — they're just here to give you an idea of the things you need to think about when you're revising, and when you're writing your answers in the exam.

Section Seven — English Literature: Prose & Drama 121

Writing About Prose and Drama

Prose and drama are similar in lots of ways, so this section covers some of the common features found in the two types of text. Sections Eight (Drama) and Nine (Prose) deal with issues specific to each type of writing.

Think about what the Question is Asking

1) Read the question carefully to make sure you're clear on what it is asking you to focus on. This could be:

- the personality of a character
- a specific mood or atmosphere
- a specific theme or message
- attitudes towards a theme or issue
- relationships between characters

2) Most questions will ask you to comment on how the writer presents something to the reader. This means that you need to focus on language, structure and form.

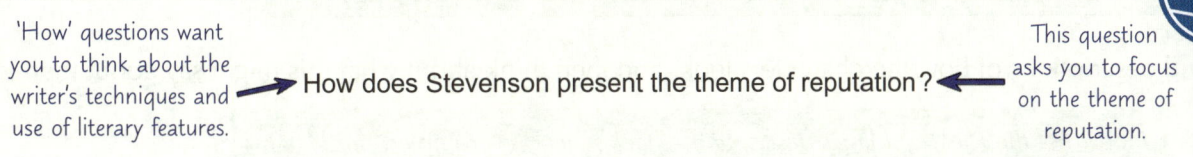

'How' questions want you to think about the writer's techniques and use of literary features. → How does Stevenson present the theme of reputation? ← This question asks you to focus on the theme of reputation.

3) You'll always have to write about a whole text, but some questions will give you an extract to start with.

4) Some questions might give you bullet points of things to consider when writing your essay.

Write about life in a new country and the way it is presented in 'Pigeon English'.

Your answer should cover:
- ideas about life in a new country in the novel ← These bullet points give you some ideas about things you should write about in your answer.
- how these ideas are presented.

5) Everything you write in your essay should answer the question — irrelevant points won't get you marks.

Know the text in Detail

1) You need to show the examiner that you know the text really well, and that you understand what happens and the order it happens in.

2) Make sure you're familiar with all the characters in the text — the examiner will be impressed if you make references to the minor characters as well as the major ones.

See pages 122-123 for more on writing about characters.

Give a Personal Response

1) Write about your personal response to the text. Think about what emotions it evokes and whether you like or empathise with certain characters.

2) To get a top grade, you need to find something original to say about the text. You can make whatever point you like, as long as you can back it up with evidence from the text.

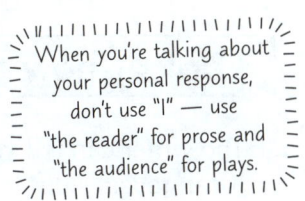

When you're talking about your personal response, don't use "I" — use "the reader" for prose and "the audience" for plays.

The best way to keep focused on the question is to write a plan...
Take a couple of minutes at the start of each question to plan how you're going to write your answer.
It will help you get all of your ideas down before you begin and keep you focused on the question.

Writing About Characters

You need to know about something called 'characterisation' — this means the methods that an author uses to convey information about, or make the reader feel a certain way about, a character in the text.

Characters are always there for a Reason

1) When you're answering a question about a character, bear in mind that characters always have a purpose.
2) This means that you can't talk about them as if they're real people — make it clear that the author has created them to help get a message across.
3) A character's appearance, actions and language all help to get this message across.

Find bits where the writer Describes the characters

Find descriptions of how the characters look, and then think about what this might say about them.

> In 'Lord of the Flies,' Golding's description of Jack's face as "crumpled" and "ugly without silliness" implies that he might have a sinister and unpleasant personality.

Look at the way characters Act and Speak

1) Look at what characters do, and then consider what that says about them.
2) Try to work out why a character does something. Most characters are motivated by a variety of things, but there's usually one main driving force behind what they do.

> In 'Romeo and Juliet', Tybalt's confrontational and violent actions (e.g. stabbing Mercutio) are ultimately driven by his fierce loyalty to the Capulets.

3) The way characters, including the narrator, speak tells you a lot about them.
4) Remember to think about why the author is making their characters speak the way they do. Think about how the author wants you, the reader, to perceive the character.

> In 'An Inspector Calls', Birling repeatedly shouts "Rubbish!" to dismiss what other people have said. But he finishes his own sentences with "of course", to make his own claims seem obvious and matter-of-fact. This means that the audience perceives him to be arrogant and opinionated.

Look at how the characters treat Other People

The writer can tell you a lot about their characters by showing you how they get on with others. It can reveal sides to their character that they keep hidden from the other main characters.

> *My rage was without bounds; I sprang on him, impelled by all the feelings which can arm one being against the existence of another.*

→ In 'Frankenstein', Victor is kind and polite to most of the characters in the novel, but his attack on the monster reveals his concealed anger and violence.

Writing About Characters

Make sure you're Prepared for Character Questions

Characters are key elements of any text, so it's not really a surprise that examiners enjoy asking about them in exams. Here are some important questions to think about when you're studying or revising characters:

Why is the character important?

- How do they affect the plot?
- Do they represent a particular point of view?
- What would happen if they weren't there?

Maureen is a key character in 'My Name is Leon' — she provides a more stable home for Leon and her caring attitude towards Leon and Jake acts as an example of how adults should look after children.

Does the character change over the course of the story?

- Does the character learn anything?
- Does their personality or behaviour change?
- Are the changes positive or negative?
- How do these changes affect the character?

Over the course of 'A Christmas Carol', Ebenezer Scrooge becomes more charitable, generous and empathetic thanks to his experiences with the ghosts. This contrasts with the miserly and selfish character the reader meets at the start of the book.

How does the writer reveal the character's personality?

- How are the character's actions and experiences presented to the reader?
- Is the reader's view of the character the same as other characters' view of them?

The cold-hearted nature of Estella in 'Great Expectations' is revealed by her frequent attempts to "deceive and entrap" men. The reader is able to see her true nature more clearly than Pip, who is blinded by his love for her.

How is the character similar or different to other characters?

- How does the character relate to other characters?
- Do differences between characters impact on the plot?
- What is the writer showing us through these differences?

In some ways, Linda turns into Mrs Johnstone in 'Blood Brothers', becoming a housewife at a young age whilst also having to provide for the family.

Does the reader like or sympathise with the character?

- Why does the reader feel that way about the character?
- How does the writer shape the reader's feelings about the character?
- How does the reader's opinion of the character affect their opinion of the text as a whole?

The reader sympathises with Meena in 'Anita and Me' because her loyalty and trust is betrayed by Anita. Having the narrative in Meena's voice helps create empathy, as it means that Meena's viewpoint is heard throughout.

Get to know the main characters in your texts...

Draw a mind map for each key character in your texts. Add branches for each main aspect of their character — you can use this page to start off. Don't forget to add quotes to back up your ideas.

The Writer's Techniques

There are lots of marks available in English Literature for commenting on the way writers use language.

Analysing the writer's use of Language is key

1) Writers select the language they use carefully — it's up to you to work out why they've chosen a particular word or phrase, and to explain the effect that it has.

2) Look out for any interesting, unusual or specialist vocabulary — think about why it's been used. Take note of any repeated words and phrases too — they will have been repeated for a reason.

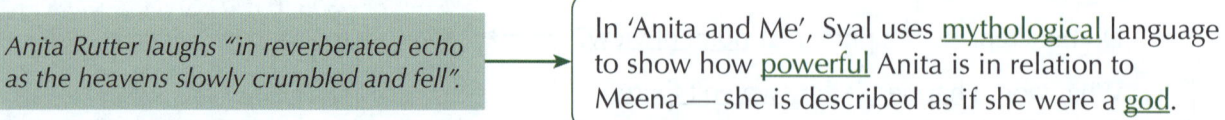

Anita Rutter laughs "in reverberated echo as the heavens slowly crumbled and fell". → In 'Anita and Me', Syal uses mythological language to show how powerful Anita is in relation to Meena — she is described as if she were a god.

3) Examining the language used by characters is really important — think about the way characters speak, why they speak in that way and whether the way they speak is different to other characters.

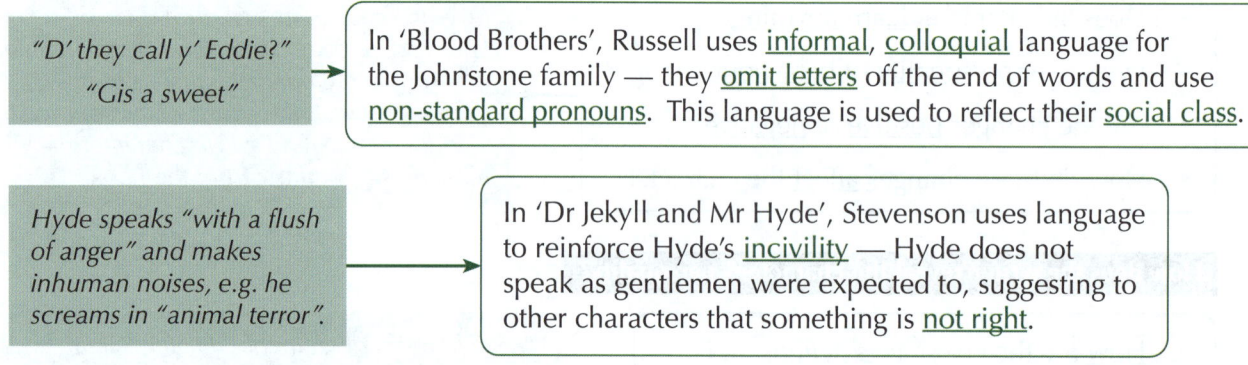

"D' they call y' Eddie?"
"Gis a sweet" → In 'Blood Brothers', Russell uses informal, colloquial language for the Johnstone family — they omit letters off the end of words and use non-standard pronouns. This language is used to reflect their social class.

Hyde speaks "with a flush of anger" and makes inhuman noises, e.g. he screams in "animal terror". → In 'Dr Jekyll and Mr Hyde', Stevenson uses language to reinforce Hyde's incivility — Hyde does not speak as gentlemen were expected to, suggesting to other characters that something is not right.

Look out for Imagery

> Imagery is particularly common in prose texts, but it does crop up in plays too — Shakespeare uses lots of it.

1) Imagery is when an author uses language to create a picture in the reader's mind, or to describe something more vividly. It can add to the reader's or the audience's understanding of the story.

2) Similes describe something by saying that it's like something else:

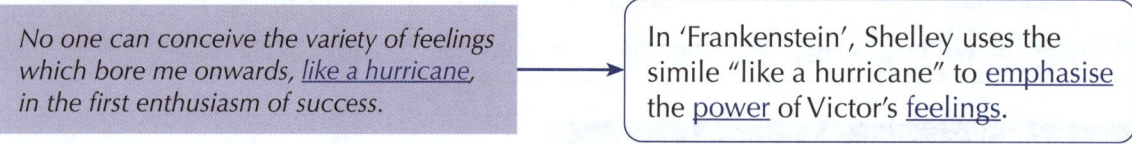

No one can conceive the variety of feelings which bore me onwards, like a hurricane, in the first enthusiasm of success. → In 'Frankenstein', Shelley uses the simile "like a hurricane" to emphasise the power of Victor's feelings.

3) Metaphors describe something by saying it is something else:

The instruments of darkness tell us truths. → In 'Macbeth', Banquo's suspicion of the three Witches is shown by his use of the metaphor "instruments of darkness" to describe them.

4) Personification describes something (e.g. an animal, object or aspect of nature) as if it were human:

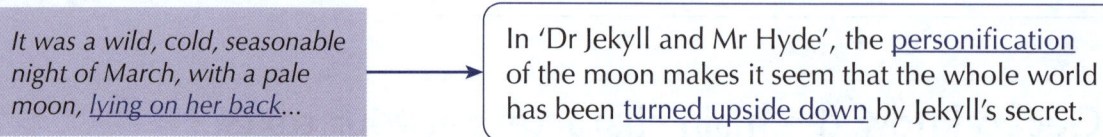

It was a wild, cold, seasonable night of March, with a pale moon, lying on her back... → In 'Dr Jekyll and Mr Hyde', the personification of the moon makes it seem that the whole world has been turned upside down by Jekyll's secret.

The Writer's Techniques

Comment on **Sentence Structure**

1) It's not just particular words and phrases that you can comment on — you should also look at how writers use sentences and paragraphs to reinforce their points.

> *And among us animals let there be perfect unity, perfect comradeship in the struggle. All men are enemies.*

→ In 'Animal Farm', Old Major uses a mix of long and short sentences, as well as rhetoric, to make his speech persuasive.

2) Different sentence lengths create different effects, e.g. a succession of short sentences could build tension or excitement, whereas long sentences might show a character getting carried away with their emotions.

> *"Seen him?" repeated Mr Utterson. "Well?" "That's it!" said Poole. "It was this way."*

→ At the climax of 'Dr Jekyll and Mr Hyde', the characters talk in short bursts. This creates suspense by suggesting that events are happening at a fast pace.

> *There were great round, pot-bellied baskets of chestnuts, shaped like the waistcoats of jolly old gentlemen, lolling at the doors, and tumbling out into the street in their apoplectic opulence.*

→ In 'A Christmas Carol', Dickens uses long sentences to describe the activity on the streets when Scrooge walks through London. This gives the Christmas scenes a sense of endless cheer, emphasising the joy Scrooge has excluded himself from.

Pay attention to **Descriptions** and **Settings**

1) Writers use settings to influence the way you feel about what's happening.

2) In the exam, you could get a passage that describes one of the settings from the text and be asked to talk about how the author has used it to create atmosphere.

3) You need to look at the writer's descriptions and think about why they have been included and what effect they have.

> *Alleys and archways, like so many cesspools, disgorged their offences of smell, and dirt, and life, upon the straggling streets.*

→ In 'A Christmas Carol', Dickens uses descriptive language to present his reader with a realistic, harsh vision of poverty in London.

> *I did not dare return to the apartment which I inhabited, but felt impelled to hurry on, although drenched by the rain which poured from a black and comfortless sky.*

→ In 'Frankenstein', this bleak and dismal setting reflects Victor's hopeless and gloomy mood.

> *When shall we three meet again? In thunder, lightning, or in rain? Hover through the fog and filthy air.*

→ In 'Macbeth', the Witches repeatedly describe the bad weather. This reflects the sinister atmosphere created by the Witches' arrival.

The Writer's Techniques

Writers can present their ideas using **Symbolism**

1) Symbols can be used to reinforce the themes that run through a text. Look out for things that could be a symbol for something else, e.g. a thunderstorm could be a symbol for destruction.

> In 'An Inspector Calls', Priestley uses Eva Smith as a symbol. Her first name sounds like 'Eve', the first woman (in the Biblical account of creation), which suggests she symbolises all women. Her surname is very common and it's also the word for a tradesman, which implies that she represents all ordinary, working-class women.

> In 'Great Expectations', the size and splendour of Satis House symbolises the wealth and grandeur of the upper classes. However, it is crumbling and run-down, which could symbolise their decay.

2) Symbols are often used to create additional meanings. If the literal meaning of a sentence sounds strange, try to work out whether there's another layer of meaning.

> *This boy is Ignorance. This girl is Want. Beware them both...*

→ In 'A Christmas Carol', Dickens uses the characters of Ignorance and Want to symbolise the problems caused by society's neglect of the poor.

Structure is always important

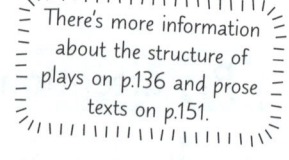
There's more information about the structure of plays on p.136 and prose texts on p.151.

1) Structure is the order that events happen in. Make sure you think about how a writer has put a text together, and what the effect of this is.

2) Structural devices can be used to make a text more interesting. For example:

- Foreshadowing gives hints about what will happen later on in the story.

> In 'My Name is Leon', Leon steals a gun from Mr Devlin's shed, but it's not clear why he takes it. The repeated mentions of the gun hint that Leon will get into some sort of trouble later on. As violence breaks out on the streets of Birmingham, the theft of the gun increases the tension as the reader waits to find out if the gun will be used.

- Flashbacks temporarily shift the story back in time, often showing something from the past that is significant in the present.

> The story of 'Anita & Me' uses flashbacks to reveal significant events that shaped Meena as an individual. Meena recalls overhearing her parents and friends discussing traumatic events they experienced during the Partition, which gives the audience a deeper insight into the way in which Meena learnt about her family's trauma at a very young age.

Remember to write about the effect on the reader...
It's important to refer to the techniques that the writer uses, but if you want the top marks you'll also need to mention how those techniques affect the reader (or the audience if it's a play).

Section Seven — English Literature: Prose & Drama

Context

Texts are influenced by the time and place they're written and set in, as well as by the person who wrote them. You need to consider these influences for each text you study.

Texts are shaped by the **Context** they were written in

1) Think about the setting of the text and what was happening when it was written.
2) Here are a few questions you should ask yourself when thinking about context:

Where is the text set?
- Did the writer base the setting on their own experiences?

When was the text written?
- What was happening at the time the text was written?
- What was society like?

When does the story take place?
- Did the writer base the story in the time in which they lived or a different time?

What do you know about the writer?
- Where is the writer from?
- What is their background?

What genre is the text part of?
- Is the text part of a literary movement?
- Was the writer influenced by other texts?

Show you're aware of the **Issues** the text raises

1) You need to show the examiner that you're aware of the wider issues raised by the text, and comment on how these issues are portrayed in the text.
2) Here are some of the issues that you should look out for:

Social or cultural issues

Authors often comment on the society they're living in, particularly the faults they associate with it.

→ 'Blood Brothers' examines social class, and how it can determine the course of people's lives.

Historical or political issues

Writers may focus on a particular historical situation or political issue.

→ George Orwell wrote 'Animal Farm' in 1945 as an allegory for events which took place around that time in Communist Russia.

Moral issues

Sometimes a text aims to challenge the reader with a moral message.

→ 'Frankenstein' raises the question of whether advances in science are beneficial or dangerous for mankind.

Philosophical issues

Some writers explore a philosophical question through their texts.

→ In 'Romeo and Juliet', Shakespeare questions what romantic love actually is.

Reactions to texts can change over time...

When writing about context, think about whether attitudes toward certain issues have changed over time. The original audience of a text may have viewed a text very differently to how an audience would today.

Themes and the Writer's Message

Texts don't just tell a story — they explore significant issues and questions.

Think about the Themes of the text

1) Texts usually have something to say about the society in which they were written or set.
2) Think carefully about the themes of the text, and what the writer might have been saying about them.

Fate

- Do we control our own lives or are they controlled by fate?

Characters in 'Romeo and Juliet' blame fate for their problems. This makes the audience question whether what is happening is indeed down to fate or whether the characters should take responsibility for their actions.

Gender

- How do the lives of men and women differ?
- What is the impact of gender inequality?

In 'Pride and Prejudice', the Bennet sisters cannot inherit their father's estate because they are female. Their best chance of independence and financial security is to marry well.

Social Class

- What is the impact of social class on characters' lives?
- Is it right that social class is so important?

In 'An Inspector Calls', Priestley contrasts the actions and qualities of the working-class characters with those of the middle classes to highlight the unfairness of the class system.

Ambition

- Is ambition healthy or destructive?
- How can we control our ambition?

By showing Macbeth's downfall, Shakespeare gives the audience a warning about the destructive nature of ambition.

Love

- What is the true nature of love?
- How far will we go to pursue love?

In 'Much Ado About Nothing', Shakespeare contrasts Claudio's shallow, fickle feelings for Hero with the deep love that develops between Beatrice and Benedick.

Work out the writer's Overall Message

1) Think about why the writer might have written the book or play.
2) Look at the issues and questions the text raises.

Dickens' message in 'A Christmas Carol' is that the rich have a duty to help those less fortunate than themselves.

The central message of 'Lord of the Flies' is that all humans have evil inside them and are capable of committing terrible deeds.

You need to study the text carefully to work out the message...

It might take a while to work out the writer's overall message, so make sure you read the text carefully. The fates of characters, significant passages of speech and the ending of the text are all worth examining.

Section Seven — English Literature: Prose & Drama

Using Quotations

You're not allowed to take any of your texts into the exam, so you're going to need to learn some quotations...

Learn **Key Quotations** that are relevant to **Characters** and **Themes**

1) When you're reading a text, make a note of some good quotes to learn. Examiners aren't expecting you to memorise big chunks of text, so the quotes you pick out should be short and snappy.

2) You need to use the quotes to back up the points in your essay, so make sure the quotes you choose are relevant to things you're likely to write about in the exam, e.g. a key character or theme.

3) When you're revising, it's a good idea to make lists of key quotes for each theme or character.

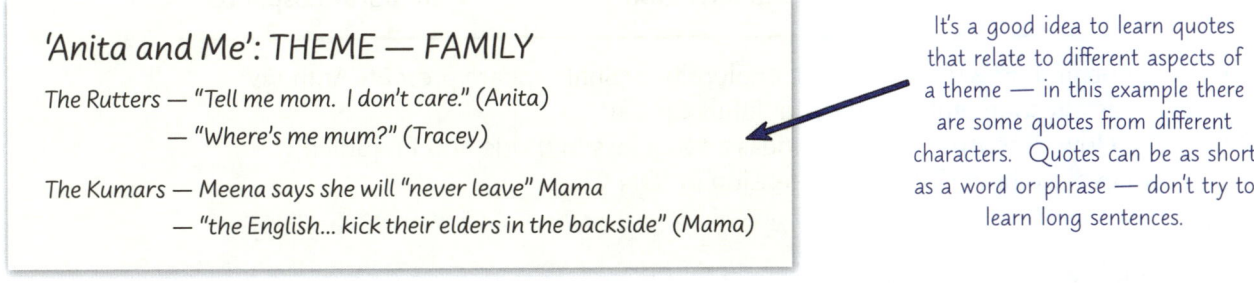

'Anita and Me': THEME — FAMILY

The Rutters — "Tell me mom. I don't care." (Anita)
— "Where's me mum?" (Tracey)

The Kumars — Meena says she will "never leave" Mama
— "the English... kick their elders in the backside" (Mama)

It's a good idea to learn quotes that relate to different aspects of a theme — in this example there are some quotes from different characters. Quotes can be as short as a word or phrase — don't try to learn long sentences.

Embed **Short Quotations** into your sentences

Quoting from Shakespeare is covered on page 143.

1) The best way to use quotes is to embed (insert) them into your sentences. This just means that they should be a natural part of a sentence, allowing you to go on to explain how the quote supports your point.

> In 'An Inspector Calls', the Inspector describes Eva positively, calling her "pretty" and "lively", which makes the audience feel more sympathetic towards her.

2) Using shorter quotations allows you to explain the same point in fewer words.

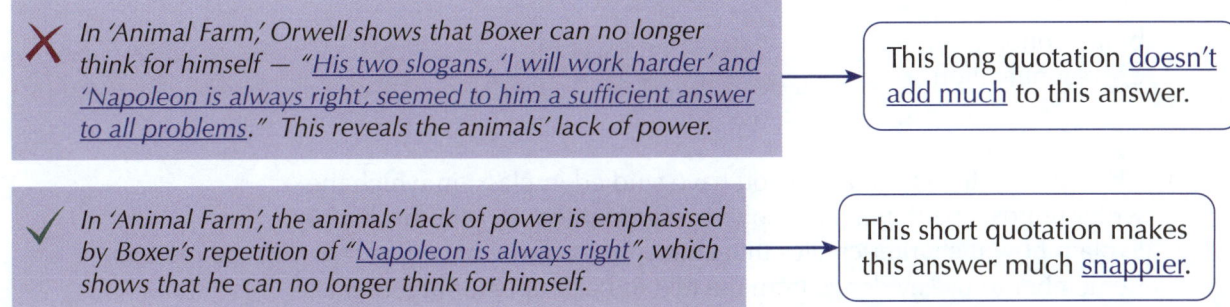

✗ In 'Animal Farm,' Orwell shows that Boxer can no longer think for himself — "His two slogans, 'I will work harder' and 'Napoleon is always right', seemed to him a sufficient answer to all problems." This reveals the animals' lack of power.

This long quotation doesn't add much to this answer.

✓ In 'Animal Farm', the animals' lack of power is emphasised by Boxer's repetition of "Napoleon is always right", which shows that he can no longer think for himself.

This short quotation makes this answer much snappier.

3) If you get an extract question (see page 121) make sure you quote accurately from the text you're given. But don't be tempted to quote huge chunks of text — always be selective with the quotes you use and make sure you explain their significance or effect.

Don't try to learn very long quotes...

When you're revising quotes, don't memorise long chunks of text — short phrases or single words are easier to learn. They'll also help keep your answers concise, which will please the examiners.

Warm-Up Questions

You'll need your set texts to hand when you're answering these questions, but don't worry — you don't need to write any long answers (yet). If you don't know what texts you're studying, now would be a good time to find out from your teacher.

Warm-Up Questions

1) Look at the different types of question in the box and read the sample questions below. For each sample question, write down what type of question you think it is.

   - theme
   - characterisation
   - mood/atmosphere

   a) Beginning with this extract, explore how Shakespeare presents Anthony as a resourceful character in 'Julius Caesar'.
   b) How does Austen present ideas about class in 'Pride and Prejudice'?
   c) Explore how Kelly creates tension in 'DNA'.

2) Choose one of the texts you have studied.
   Write a paragraph describing your personal response to the text.

3) Choose a character from one of the texts you have studied.
   Find five key quotations which illustrate something about their personality.
   Write a sentence explaining what each quotation tells you about them.

4) For the character you chose in question 3, explain how you feel about that character and how the author has made you feel that way.
   Use evidence from the text to back up your argument.

5) Using one of your set texts, find one example of:
   a) simile
   b) metaphor
   c) personification

6) Choose an extract from a text you have studied in class, in which the writer builds a particular atmosphere (e.g. frightening, gloomy, joyful).
   Explain how the writer creates that atmosphere, and what effect it has on the reader.
   Remember to use evidence from the text to back up your argument.

7) Using a text you have studied in class, identify an unusual structural feature (e.g. an instance of foreshadowing, a flashback or a jump in time).
   Write a short paragraph describing the feature and explaining its effect.

Section Seven — English Literature: Prose & Drama

Warm-Up Questions

8) Read the passages below. For each passage, state what you think each object or action in bold symbolises and write a sentence or two explaining your view.

   a) > In 'Lord of the Flies', the boys use the **conch shell** to bring order to their meetings — whoever is holding it is allowed to speak, while everyone else has to keep quiet and listen.

   b) > In 'Jane Eyre', Mr Rochester proposes to Jane underneath the old **chestnut tree** in the grounds of Thornfield. That night, the tree is struck by lightning and split down the middle. Later, Jane discovers that Mr Rochester is already married, so she refuses to marry him and runs away.

   c) > In 'My Name is Leon', Leon, Tufty and Mr Devlin all care about children that, for various reasons, they are no longer able to see regularly. They all find comfort in growing **scarlet emperor runner beans** at the allotments.

9) Choose a text you have studied in class and answer the following questions about it.
   a) When was the text written? Is it set at this time or in a different period?
   b) How does the writer portray the time in which the text is set?
   c) Do the characters encounter any problems related to the text's context, e.g. based on class, race or gender?

10) Choose a text you have studied in class. Write down three of the text's key themes (e.g. social class, gender, power). For each theme, write down an example from the text and explain how it relates to the theme.

   Your examples for this question could be events in the story, characters' reactions to events, or quotes from the text.

11) Think about two of your set texts. What do you think the message of each one is?

12) Which of the following paragraphs shows a better use of quotations? Explain your answer.

   a) > In 'Anita and Me', Meena has unrealistic, childish dreams of what her future holds. She describes winning a talent show and becoming a "major personality" as her "most realistic escape route" from her current life.

   b) > In 'Anita and Me', Meena has unrealistic, childish dreams of what her future holds. She watches a talent show and says "I knew that this could be my most realistic escape route from Tollington, from ordinary girl to major personality in one easy step."

Exam-Style Questions

Writing about texts is an acquired skill — you can only get better at it by practising. The next two sections go into more detail about drama and prose, and you'll find some practice questions at the end of each section. To get you into the swing of it, have a go at answering the ones below.

Q1 Choose a character from a Shakespeare play you have studied. Starting with one scene, explain how Shakespeare presents the character in that scene and in the play as a whole.

Q2 Choose a passage from a prose text you have read which you find particularly tense **or** exciting. Write about the methods the author has used to create tension **or** excitement in the passage and in the text as a whole.

Q3 Choose a modern (post-1914) text that you have studied.
Explore how the author presents **either** power **or** love **or** childhood **or** social class.

Q4 Choose a key theme from a 19th-century text that you have studied. Starting with a short extract from the text, write about how the author explores the theme in that extract and in the text as a whole.

Revision Summary Test for Section Seven

Congratulations — you've reached the end of the section. All in the brain? Have a go at these to check...
- These questions are **hard** — but they'll really help you see **how well you know your stuff**.
- Tackle the **revision summary test** below, or scan the QR code to do it **online**. You can **track your progress** online and see **which areas need more work**.
- There are **sample answers** here: www.cgpbooks.co.uk/blurb-answers

Writing About Prose and Drama (p.121)

1) When a question asks how the writer presents something, you need to focus on three things. The first is language. What are the other two?
2) Give two things you could write about in a personal response to a text.
3) Which of the following sentences is better to include in an essay? Explain why.
   a) The foreshadowing in 'My Name is Leon' meant I felt tense about what would happen — I wanted to keep reading.
   b) The use of foreshadowing in 'My Name is Leon' creates tension and makes the reader want to find out what will happen next.

Writing About Characters (p.122-123)

4) What is characterisation?
5) a) Give three examples of things you could write about when answering a question about a particular character.
   b) For each aspect that you mentioned in part a), write a point about a character you've studied.

The Writer's Techniques (p.124-126)

6) Why might an author choose to use imagery in their writing?
7) Find an example of a simile and a metaphor in a text that you have studied. Explain the effect of each example.
8) What is personification?
9) Why might a writer choose to use a shorter sentence instead of a longer sentence?
10) Write a brief explanation of what authors can use settings for.
11) a) Explain what symbolism is. Give an example of a symbol from a text you have studied.
    b) Explain the effect of the symbol that you chose in part a).
12) What is foreshadowing? Give one possible effect of foreshadowing.
13) What are flashbacks? Why might a writer use a flashback?

Context (p.127)

14) Give five questions you could ask yourself when thinking about the context of a text.
15) Write down three examples of wider issues that might be raised by a text.

Themes and the Writer's Message (p.128)

16) List five examples of themes that are often addressed in texts.
17) Briefly explain how you might work out the overall message of a text.

Using Quotations (p.129)

18) When quoting from a text, why should you try to include short rather than long quotations?
19) Give two examples of things you need to be especially careful of when quoting from the text to answer an extract question.

Reading Plays

Writers use stage directions to show what's happening on stage. Different types of speech give clues about a character's personality, their relationships with other characters and their innermost thoughts.

Stage Directions describe the action on stage

Stage directions are usually written in italics or put in brackets to distinguish them from things that are said.

1) When you're reading a play, look out for the <u>stage directions</u>. These are <u>instructions</u> from the <u>playwright</u> to the director and the actors — they can tell you a lot about <u>how</u> the playwright wants the play to be <u>performed</u>.

2) There are lots of things to look out for in the stage directions. For example, <u>music</u> and <u>sound effects</u> might be used to create a specific <u>mood</u>, or the <u>set</u> may be designed to create a certain <u>atmosphere</u>.

A bass note, repeated as a heartbeat. → In 'Blood Brothers', Russell uses <u>music</u> to build <u>tension</u>. This stage direction emphasises the significance of the moment, and highlights Mrs Johnstone's <u>fear</u>.

3) Stage directions can also describe the characters' <u>actions</u> and the use of <u>props</u>.

PRINCESS bursts into a dance routine with the vegetables → In 'Princess & The Hustler', Odimba uses stage directions to <u>tell</u> the actor playing Princess <u>how to act</u>, and to give the audience an insight into the character's <u>personality</u>.

Stage directions reveal what the writer Wants

You should write about how the stage directions reveal the playwright's <u>intentions</u>.

Action

We see Mickey comb the town, breaking through groups of people, looking, searching, desperate...
('Blood Brothers' — Willy Russell)
→ These stage directions <u>describe</u> what's happening on stage — Mickey's desperate search makes this scene <u>dramatic</u>.

Staging

The dining-room of a fairly large suburban house... It has good solid furniture...
('An Inspector Calls' — J. B. Priestley)
→ In these opening stage directions, Priestley establishes <u>how</u> he would like the <u>set</u> to <u>look</u>. The set reflects the <u>class</u> and <u>status</u> of the Birlings.

Characterisation

Jo dances on dreamily.
('A Taste of Honey' — Shelagh Delaney)
→ This stage direction occurs after Jo has agreed to <u>marry</u> her boyfriend. It hints at her <u>longing to escape</u> and her <u>dreams</u> of a better life.

Dialogue

VIV (shocked) You? Mum!
('Leave Taking' — Winsome Pinnock)
→ The stage direction here tells the actor playing Viv <u>how</u> she should <u>deliver</u> her line.

Reading Plays

Plays contain Different types of Speech

1) <u>Dialogue</u> is when two or more characters are speaking. It shows how characters <u>interact</u> with each other.

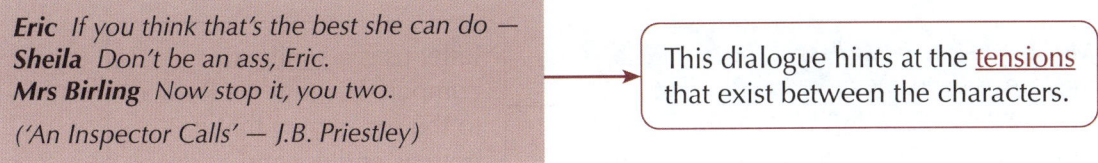

Eric If you think that's the best she can do —
Sheila Don't be an ass, Eric.
Mrs Birling Now stop it, you two.
('An Inspector Calls' — J.B. Priestley)

This dialogue hints at the <u>tensions</u> that exist between the characters.

2) A <u>monologue</u> is when <u>one character</u> speaks for a long time and the other characters on stage <u>listen</u> to them.

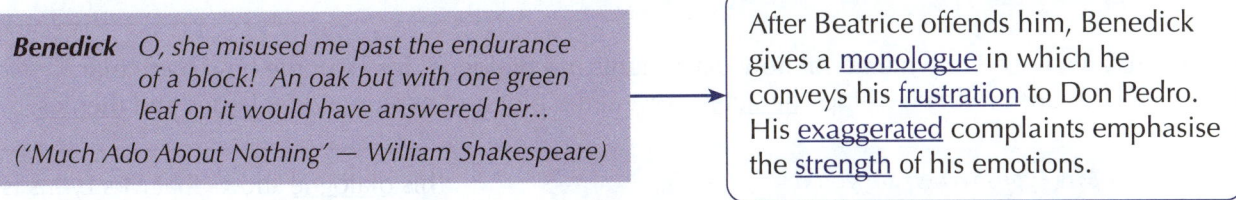

Benedick O, she misused me past the endurance of a block! An oak but with one green leaf on it would have answered her...
('Much Ado About Nothing' — William Shakespeare)

After Beatrice offends him, Benedick gives a <u>monologue</u> in which he conveys his <u>frustration</u> to Don Pedro. His <u>exaggerated</u> complaints emphasise the <u>strength</u> of his emotions.

3) In a <u>soliloquy</u>, a <u>single character</u> speaks their <u>thoughts out loud</u> — other characters can't hear them. This reveals to the audience something of the character's <u>inner thoughts</u> and <u>feelings</u>.

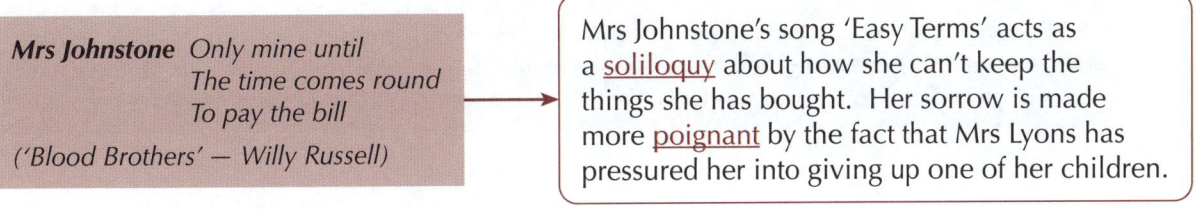

Mrs Johnstone Only mine until
The time comes round
To pay the bill
('Blood Brothers' — Willy Russell)

Mrs Johnstone's song 'Easy Terms' acts as a <u>soliloquy</u> about how she can't keep the things she has bought. Her sorrow is made more <u>poignant</u> by the fact that Mrs Lyons has pressured her into giving up one of her children.

4) An <u>aside</u> is like a soliloquy, but it is usually a <u>shorter comment</u> which is only heard by the <u>audience</u> — other characters don't hear it.

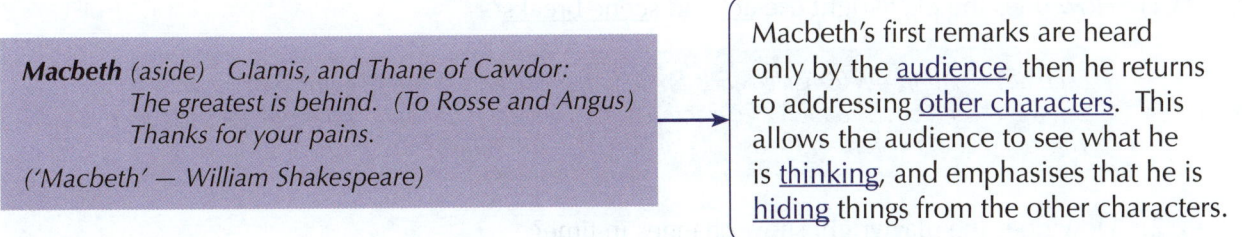

Macbeth (aside) Glamis, and Thane of Cawdor:
The greatest is behind. (To Rosse and Angus)
Thanks for your pains.
('Macbeth' — William Shakespeare)

Macbeth's first remarks are heard only by the <u>audience</u>, then he returns to addressing <u>other characters</u>. This allows the audience to see what he is <u>thinking</u>, and emphasises that he is <u>hiding</u> things from the other characters.

Some playwrights use stage directions more than others...

Different writers use different methods. Shakespeare didn't use many stage directions — he relied instead on characters' speech to tell the story. Modern writers tend to use more stage directions than Shakespeare.

Writing About Plays

When you're writing about a play, keep in mind the fact that it's intended to be watched by an audience.

Write about the Language of the play

1) You need to write in detail about the language used in the play.

2) Writers often use imagery, like similes, metaphors and personification.

> *My bounty is as boundless as the sea,*
> *My love as deep; the more I give to thee*
> *The more I have, for both are infinite.*
> ('Romeo and Juliet' — William Shakespeare)

Juliet uses a simile to compare her love for Romeo to the sea, saying that it is both as endless and as deep.

> *Life's but a walking shadow, a poor player*
> *That struts and frets his hour upon the stage*
> *And then is heard no more.*
> ('Macbeth' — William Shakespeare)

Macbeth personifies life, comparing it to an actor whose influence is limited to his time on stage. This shows that Macbeth thinks life is brief and pointless.

3) You also need to write about how playwrights use dialogue, for example how particular scenes are used to develop characters, reveal the plot and explore wider issues and themes.

> *Mrs Lyons* When are you due?
> *Mrs Johnstone* Erm, well, about... Oh, but Mrs...
> *Mrs Lyons* Quickly, quickly, tell me...
> ('Blood Brothers' — Willy Russell)

This dialogue shows that Mrs Lyons is more powerful than Mrs Johnstone — her interruption and use of imperatives like "tell me" show that she controls the conversation.

4) Think about the effects the language and dialogue have on the audience.

> *In the opening scene of 'DNA' by Dennis Kelly, Jan and Mark constantly speak over and interrupt one another. This increases the pace of the scene and makes it more difficult for the audience to follow, which helps to convey a sense of the stress and confusion that Jan and Mark are experiencing.*

A play's Structure is important too

You need to think about how the play is structured. For example:

1) How does the playwright use act and scene breaks?

> *Each act of 'An Inspector Calls' ends on a cliffhanger, and at the beginning of the next act, the "scene and situation are exactly as they were" at the end of the previous act. This builds the tension and sense of pressure that the Birlings are under.*

2) How does the playwright show changes in time?

> *In 'Blood Brothers', Russell uses a montage (a series of short scenes) to move time forwards four years. The speed at which time passes on stage symbolises the fleetingness of youth, and gives the audience the sense that the play is moving rapidly towards its tragic ending.*

Section Eight — English Literature: Drama

Writing About Plays

Show you know that plays are intended to be Watched not Read

Plays are written to be acted on stage, not read silently from a book. This means that you shouldn't refer to the 'reader' — talk about the 'audience' instead.

At the beginning of 'Princess & The Hustler', Odimba writes that the set should be revealed "as though opening the front of a doll's house". This gives the audience insight into Princess's viewpoint as a child.

→ You should comment on how the play works on stage and how this impacts the audience.

Show you appreciate Stagecraft

1) You also need to show that you appreciate the writer's stagecraft — their skill at writing for the stage. Playwrights use features like silences, actions and sound effects to create a mood, reveal something in a certain way or add drama to a situation — these things are usually mentioned in stage directions (see p.134).

2) Appreciating the stagecraft means asking yourself a few key questions:

- How would this scene look on stage?

- How would the audience react?

- Is it effective?

3) Writers might use stagecraft to vary the pace of the play to keep it interesting for the audience. For example, in Act Two of 'Blood Brothers', Russell uses simultaneous conversations to create a fast-paced scene:

Mickey and Sammy are speaking on one side of the stage whilst Edward and Linda are speaking on the other side. Both conversations have life-changing consequences, and the combination of the two dialogues emphasises the fact that both twins are at a crossroads in their lives.

4) Writers can also use stagecraft to increase the tension, particularly at a climactic moment in the play. In the final act of 'Romeo and Juliet', Shakespeare uses dramatic irony to build up the suspense:

Romeo fights Paris in the tomb while the audience, knowing that Friar Lawrence is on his way, hope he'll arrive and avert the tragedy. He arrives too late: Romeo has already killed Paris and committed suicide. These events happen in a very short space of time, and the tension is incredible. Even though the audience knows from the start of the play that Romeo and Juliet will both die, we still hope that they won't.

Dramatic irony is where the audience knows something that a character on stage doesn't know.

Reading the play aloud will help you understand it...

Try reading bits of the play out loud. Some lines have a particular rhythm to them that is more obvious when they're spoken. Reading aloud can also help you remember quotes from the play.

Writing About Modern Plays

If you're studying a modern play (that's one written after 1914), read on — this is important stuff...

You might have to write about a Modern Play

1) For Paper 2, you'll have to study either a modern play or a modern prose text. Your teacher will be able to tell you which you're doing.

2) The modern plays you might study are:

- An Inspector Calls by J.B. Priestley
- Blood Brothers by Willy Russell
- Leave Taking by Winsome Pinnock
- A Taste of Honey by Shelagh Delaney
- DNA by Dennis Kelly
- Princess & The Hustler by Chinonyerem Odimba

See p.151-153 for information on writing about modern prose texts.

Modern plays are often Realistic

1) Many modern plays try to be realistic, featuring characters who lead ordinary lives. They often include:

- Everyday settings. The setting could be real, e.g. Liverpool in 'Blood Brothers', or made-up but realistic, e.g. Brumley in 'An Inspector Calls'.
- Characters who are ordinary people, rather than kings or heroes.
- Characters who speak in a realistic way — for example, they might use slang or a regional accent.

2) Realistic plays tend to feature issues that affect ordinary people in society, e.g. living in poverty in 'A Taste of Honey'.

3) The writer might use their play to encourage the audience to think about these issues in their own lives — and even change their behaviour as a result.

Modern playwrights often criticise Social Divides

1) Modern British plays often focus on social class divides in Britain.

2) They might write about situations when middle and upper-class people have more opportunities than working-class people. This might be reflected in things like education, job prospects and wealth.

In 'Blood Brothers', one twin is raised in a middle-class family, while the other is raised in a working-class family. The play shows how social class affects the boys' lives. Edward goes to university and becomes a councillor, while Mickey struggles with a low-paid, insecure job from which he is eventually laid off.

3) Some modern writers have used their plays to encourage people to treat everyone equally, regardless of their social class or background.

In 'An Inspector Calls', the working-class character Eva Smith/Daisy Renton is mistreated by all the members of the middle-class Birling family. Priestley uses the play to criticise prejudiced attitudes towards poor or working-class people, and to encourage people to take responsibility for one another in society.

Section Eight — English Literature: Drama

Writing About Modern Plays

Being a **Young Person** is explored in many modern plays

1) Modern plays often present the lives of young people or teenagers, showing a young person growing up and trying to understand the world.

   At the beginning of 'Princess & The Hustler', Princess is very naive, so when she experiences racism at school, her worldview is challenged and her confidence is shaken. As a result, Princess cuts her own hair, representing the loss of her childhood innocence as she comes to realise that the world is not as idyllic as it once seemed.

2) Some writers explore concerns in society about teenagers who commit crime or behave antisocially. E.g. 'DNA' explores how a group of teenagers react after a bullying incident goes wrong and someone is killed.

Some modern plays explore **Gender** and **Race**

1) Modern plays often explore the experiences of different groups in society.

2) Some plays focus on issues that women face, e.g. the expectation that a woman would get married and have children instead of working.

   In 'A Taste of Honey', Jo becomes pregnant without being married and wants to work to support the baby. The play shows some of her efforts to become independent.

3) Other plays explore how some people in society face prejudice or discrimination because of their race or ethnicity.

   In 'Leave Taking', Broderick reveals that Enid's husband suffered racial abuse at work. Pinnock explores the severe effect that this experience had on her husband's temperament.

Think about how the play might be **Staged**

1) Modern writers often use stage directions (see p.134) to show how they want a scene to be performed.

   In 'DNA', Kelly writes that Phil "puts his Coke carefully on the ground" before explaining his plan to cover up Adam's murder. This slow, careful movement shows how undisturbed he is by the incident.

2) The use of lighting, music and special effects can affect the way the play is interpreted.

   Throughout 'Princess & The Hustler', Princess imagines herself winning the Weston-super-Mare pageant. Odimba uses a voice-over and gives stage directions that the room "explodes into a world of pageantry", which sometimes includes music and other special effects. The intensity of these effects changes to match Princess's mood, which gives the audience clues about her emotional state.

Modern plays often address social issues...

Modern plays deal with some pretty tricky themes. Finding out a bit about when and where a play is set can really help to understand the problems the writer is addressing and the messages they want to give out.

Writing About Shakespeare

You'll need to know a bit about Shakespeare for your exam. The next few pages will give you a hand.

Shakespeare's plays can be Serious or Funny

1) You'll have to study a Shakespeare play as part of your course. The plays you might study are:

- Macbeth
- Romeo and Juliet
- The Tempest
- The Merchant of Venice
- Much Ado About Nothing
- Julius Caesar

2) Shakespeare's plays are often split into different genres based on the features they have in common.

Tragedy

- Tragedies (e.g. 'Macbeth' and 'Romeo and Juliet') often focus on big topics — e.g. love, death, war, religion. They can be emotionally powerful and often have a moral message.
- Some of Shakespeare's tragedies are set in an imaginary or historical world. The characters are often kings, queens or other rulers.

Comedy

- Comedies (e.g. 'Much Ado About Nothing' and 'The Merchant of Venice') are written to be funny.
- They feature events and characters that are often exaggerated for humorous effect.
- They can still have a moral message though, and often include serious or emotional elements.

Romance

- Romances are similar to comedies but have darker elements.
- 'The Tempest' is often described as a romance.

History

- Histories are based on real historical events.
- 'Julius Caesar' has sometimes been considered a history play.

3) Some plays might fit into more than one genre, e.g. 'The Tempest' has elements of both romance and comedy, and 'Julius Caesar' has been described as both a tragedy and a history.

Shakespeare's plays share Similar Themes

Shakespeare's plays tend to have similar themes. Some of the most common ones are:

Power & Ambition

'Macbeth' explores the title character's ambition to be king. The play shows his downfall after this desire leads to murder, suggesting that too much ambition can be a bad thing.

Fate & Free Will

The events of 'Romeo and Juliet' suggest that a person's fate is unavoidable. The couple's love is described as "death-marked" in the Prologue, and they are unable to escape their families' conflict.

Love & Relationships

In 'Much Ado About Nothing', Shakespeare contrasts the relationship between Hero and Claudio (shallow and immature) with that between Beatrice and Benedick (deeper and more mature) to explore the real meaning of love.

Justice & Revenge

In 'The Merchant of Venice', two different ideas of justice are shown. Portia believes it would be just for Shylock to show mercy to Antonio, while Shylock thinks he deserves revenge. The play debates whether revenge is ever justified.

Section Eight — English Literature: Drama

Writing About Shakespeare

Show you're aware that Shakespeare was writing 400 Years Ago

1) Shakespeare (1564-1616) wrote his plays about 400 years ago, so it's not surprising that some of the language, themes and ideas can seem a bit strange to us.

2) He lived at the end of a period of European history known as the Renaissance — a time when there were lots of developments in the arts, politics, religion and science. The theatre was very popular at this time.

3) Shakespeare was aware of his audience when writing his plays. A wide range of people went to watch his plays, from the very rich to servants and labourers. Shakespeare tended to include complex imagery and puns for the educated nobles, and slapstick for the uneducated poor.

4) Many people in Shakespeare's Britain believed in the supernatural — people were executed for witchcraft, and superstitious behaviour was common. Several of Shakespeare's plays have supernatural elements, e.g. the Witches in 'Macbeth' and the spirits in 'The Tempest'. The audience would usually have taken these supernatural characters seriously.

5) Shakespeare was keen to keep the British king or queen of the day happy. His plays often had a royal audience — both Elizabeth I and James I enjoyed performances of his plays.

There are many features in 'Macbeth' which could have been included to please King James I. For example, the events following Duncan's murder show the negative consequences for those who try to seize power from the reigning king. James was also obsessed with stamping out witchcraft — Shakespeare's portrayal of the Witches as wholly evil would have pleased the king.

Learn about Theatrical Performances in Shakespeare's time

Knowing a bit about theatrical performances in Shakespeare's time will help you to write top answers about his plays. Here are some of the key features:

1) Only men were allowed to act on stage — all the female roles were played by boys. Shakespeare's comedies include lots of jokes about girls dressing up as boys.

2) Most of the actors wore elaborate costumes that were based on the fashions of when the play was written, and that reflected the status of the character. Plays set overseas, e.g. in ancient Rome or Greece, used costumes appropriate to the location.

3) Musicians helped to create atmosphere in the theatre. They also made sound effects, such as the thunder at the beginning of 'Macbeth'.

4) Plays didn't use much scenery — sets were simple so that they could show different locations in a play, and could be adapted easily to be used for several different plays.

Think about how Shakespeare kept his audience entertained...

When writing about Shakespeare's plays, remember that he meant them to be performed on stage. Mentioning how a particular method could affect the audience is a great way to pick up marks.

Shakespeare's Language

When you're writing about a Shakespeare play, you need to take a close look at the language, and think about the effect it would have on someone watching the play.

Shakespeare uses lots of Imagery

Shakespeare's imagery includes similes, metaphors and personification.

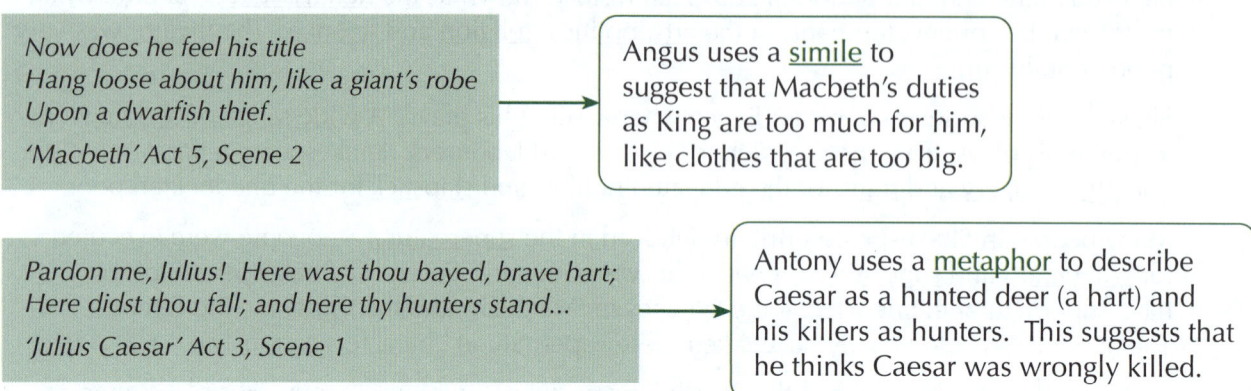

Now does he feel his title
Hang loose about him, like a giant's robe
Upon a dwarfish thief.
'Macbeth' Act 5, Scene 2

Angus uses a simile to suggest that Macbeth's duties as King are too much for him, like clothes that are too big.

Pardon me, Julius! Here wast thou bayed, brave hart;
Here didst thou fall; and here thy hunters stand...
'Julius Caesar' Act 3, Scene 1

Antony uses a metaphor to describe Caesar as a hunted deer (a hart) and his killers as hunters. This suggests that he thinks Caesar was wrongly killed.

Look out for Striking Words and Phrases

When you read through the text, make a note of any words that jump out at you. Think about why they're important, and what effect they have.

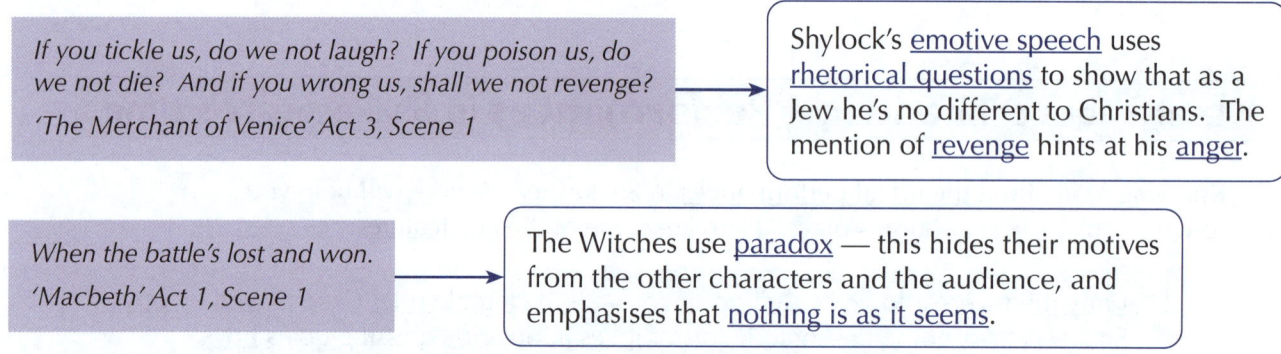

If you tickle us, do we not laugh? If you poison us, do we not die? And if you wrong us, shall we not revenge?
'The Merchant of Venice' Act 3, Scene 1

Shylock's emotive speech uses rhetorical questions to show that as a Jew he's no different to Christians. The mention of revenge hints at his anger.

When the battle's lost and won.
'Macbeth' Act 1, Scene 1

The Witches use paradox — this hides their motives from the other characters and the audience, and emphasises that nothing is as it seems.

Humour is also important in Shakespeare's plays

Shakespeare uses lots of puns and jokes. They can help to relieve tension, lighten the mood and highlight key themes.

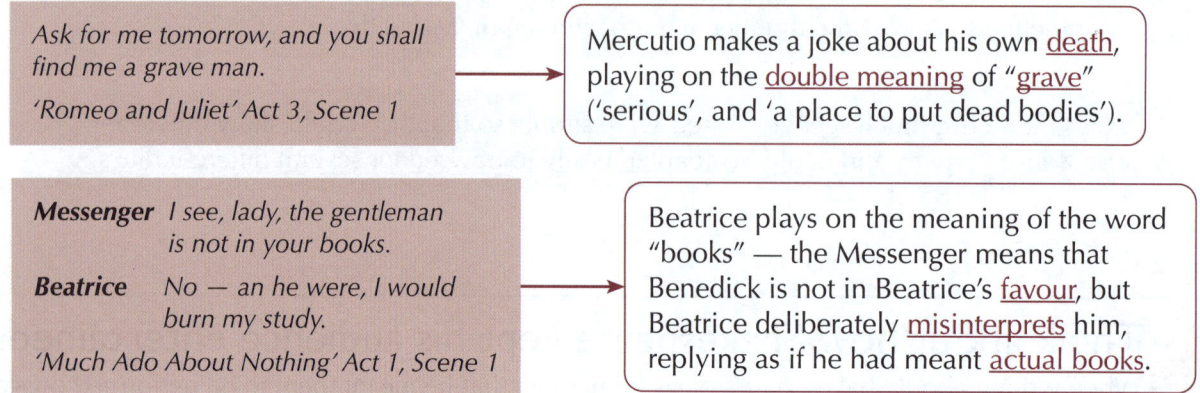

Ask for me tomorrow, and you shall find me a grave man.
'Romeo and Juliet' Act 3, Scene 1

Mercutio makes a joke about his own death, playing on the double meaning of "grave" ('serious', and 'a place to put dead bodies').

Messenger *I see, lady, the gentleman is not in your books.*
Beatrice *No — an he were, I would burn my study.*
'Much Ado About Nothing' Act 1, Scene 1

Beatrice plays on the meaning of the word "books" — the Messenger means that Benedick is not in Beatrice's favour, but Beatrice deliberately misinterprets him, replying as if he had meant actual books.

Section Eight — English Literature: Drama

Shakespeare's Language

Look at Shakespeare's Verse Forms

1) Shakespeare wrote his plays in a mixture of poetry and prose. You can tell a lot about a character by looking at the way they speak.

2) The majority of Shakespeare's lines are written in blank verse (unrhymed iambic pentameter). Blank verse sounds grander than prose and can be used by almost any characters, but lower-class, comic and mad characters generally don't use it.

A line written using iambic pentameter usually has 10 syllables (five unstressed and five stressed).

> *Come I to speak in Caesar's funeral.*
> *He was my friend, faithful and just to me.*
> 'Julius Caesar' Act 3, Scene 2

→ Antony is a powerful Roman, so it is suitable that he speaks in blank verse. It also sounds formal, which is fitting for the funeral speech he is giving at this point.

3) Sometimes Shakespeare uses rhymed iambic pentameter to make speech sound dramatic and impressive, e.g. at the beginning and end of a scene, or when a posh character is speaking.

> *From forth the fatal loins of these two foes*
> *A pair of star-cross'd lovers take their life,*
> *Whose misadventur'd piteous overthrows*
> *Doth with their death bury their parents' strife.*
> 'Romeo and Juliet' Prologue

→ The Prologue acts as an introduction to the play, when the audience are told that Romeo and Juliet are doomed to die. The importance of this message is emphasised by the fact that it is in rhymed iambic pentameter.

4) The rest of Shakespeare's writing is in normal prose. Funny bits and dialogue between more minor or lower-class characters are usually written in prose.

> *Come hither, neighbour Seacole. God hath blest you with a good name: to be a well-favoured man is the gift of fortune, but to write and read comes by nature.*
> 'Much Ado About Nothing' Act 3, Scene 3

→ Dogberry is a lower-class and comical character. He therefore speaks in prose rather than verse. This makes his speech sound natural and informal.

Look out for switches between Poetry and Prose

1) Check for when characters change between verse and prose. You can tell from the lines — if each new line starts with a capital letter, it's verse, but if it carries on from the last line without a capital, it's prose.

2) The switch can give you clues about a character's state of mind, e.g. Lady Macbeth speaks in prose when she is sleep-walking, which shows her loss of control.

3) You need to quote your play correctly. For prose quotes, just quote as you would from a novel. But if it's verse, and the quote goes over more than one line in the original text, show this using a slash — '/'.

> The epilogue to 'The Tempest' is written in rhyming couplets, for example, "Now my charms are all o'erthrown, / And what strength I have's mine own".

→ This answer uses a quote that's in verse and goes over two lines, so it uses a '/' to show where the line break is in the original text.

Get to grips with the Shakespeare play you're studying...

It's important that you know your Shakespeare text really well. If there are any bits of the play that you don't understand, take the time to reread them carefully and work out what they mean before the exam.

The Structure of Shakespeare's Plays

A text's structure has a big impact on how it's understood. Shakespeare's plays are no different...

Shakespeare **Structured** his plays in **Different Ways**

1) You need to think about the overall structure of your Shakespeare play.

2) Most of Shakespeare's tragedies have a tragic structure. In these plays, the first part builds up to a turning point and the second part deals with the consequences of this.

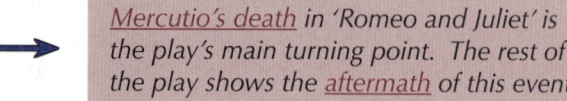

Mercutio's death in 'Romeo and Juliet' is the play's main turning point. The rest of the play shows the aftermath of this event.

3) Some of Shakespeare's plays have a cyclical structure. This means they start and end with the same situation or setting.

'Macbeth' begins and finishes with a battle to defeat a merciless tyrant. This shows that the events have come full circle and order is restored at the end of the play.

4) Some plays feature repetition, with similar images or ideas appearing at different points in the play. This can create suspense or emphasise important themes.

Several omens appear in the early scenes of 'Julius Caesar', which hint at what will happen later in the play and increase the tension.

Look at the **Order** of **Scenes** in a play

1) Shakespeare often uses the order of scenes within a play to create particular effects.

- Some scenes are put near the start of the play to emphasise a key theme — e.g. the fight between the two families at the start of 'Romeo and Juliet' shows how violent the feud is.
- Putting a scene at the start of an act can also set the mood for the rest the act — e.g. Act 2 of 'Macbeth' has a dark atmosphere after Macbeth goes to murder Duncan at the start of the act.

2) Shakespeare's plays have key scenes and minor scenes. Key scenes are usually about the main plot or characters of the play, whereas minor scenes typically feature less important characters or develop a sub-plot of the play.

3) Shakespeare often follows a key scene with a minor scene, or vice versa. This is used to:

- Change the pace — for example, a humorous minor scene coming before or after an emotional key scene can provide light relief for the audience.
- Reflect or contrast different characters, relationships or ideas — e.g. in 'The Tempest', Caliban, Trinculo and Stephano's plot to kill Prospero mirrors Antonio and Sebastian's plot to kill Alonso. Since these characters often have a comedic role and spend a lot of time drinking, their scenes show how silly the arguing between noblemen is.
- Develop important themes — e.g. in 'The Merchant of Venice', Launcelot's jokes about Jews converting to Christianity highlight the split between Jews and Christians, which is part of the main plot of the play.

Work out the structure of your Shakespeare play...

Make a graph of your play's structure. Draw a line that goes up as the tension increases and down as it lessens. Mark any turning points, key and minor scenes and anything else important.

Warm-Up Questions

Plays come in different shapes and sizes, but the way you study them should be pretty much the same — pay close attention to the play's language, structure and stagecraft and you'll be scoring marks all over the place. These questions should get you in the mood for the exam. Take a look at the suggested answers on page 243 when you're done.

Warm-Up Questions

1) In one of the plays you have studied, find an example of how the writer uses stage directions to create a specific mood or atmosphere.

2) Write a brief definition of each of the terms below.
   Then, using a set play you have studied, find an example of each term.

   | Monologue | Aside | Soliloquy |

3) Find one example of each of the following dramatic techniques in a play you have studied:
   a) imagery
   b) repetition
   c) the rhythm of a character's words having a powerful effect.

4) Find an example of humour in a Shakespeare play you have studied. What effect does it have on the scene?

5) Choose a Shakespeare play you have studied in class. Pick a passage you find particularly effective (e.g. frightening, funny or tense) and write two or three paragraphs explaining how Shakespeare makes it so effective. Hint: think about form, structure and language.

6) Read the following extracts, and then complete the tasks below.

   > Don Pedro: My love is thine to teach. Teach it but how,
   > And thou shalt see how apt it is to learn
   > Any hard lesson that may do thee good.
   > *Much Ado About Nothing* Act 1, Scene 1

   > Trinculo:
   > Here's neither bush nor shrub to bear off any weather at all, and another storm brewing. I hear it sing i' th' wind. Yond same black cloud, yond huge one, looks like a foul bombard that would shed his liquor.
   > *The Tempest* Act 2, Scene 2

   > Prince: A glooming peace this morning with it brings,
   > The sun, for sorrow, will not show his head.
   > Go hence, to have more talk of these sad things;
   > Some shall be pardoned, and some punishèd.
   > *Romeo and Juliet* Act 5, Scene 3

   a) For each extract, write down whether it is in verse, blank verse or prose. Write a sentence explaining how you can tell.
   b) What effect do the form and rhyme scheme of the Prince's speech have?

Worked Exam-Style Question

Here's an example of how to write a top-notch essay about one of Shakespeare's plays. Give it a read through, even if you aren't studying 'Macbeth' — it shows you the kinds of things you'll need to include in any exam answer. Remember to read the plan too — knowing what makes a good plan will be really useful.

Q1 Read Act 4, Scene 3 of 'Macbeth', from the beginning of the scene to "Yet grace must still look so." Using this extract as a starting point, discuss how far Shakespeare presents Macbeth as a cruel tyrant.

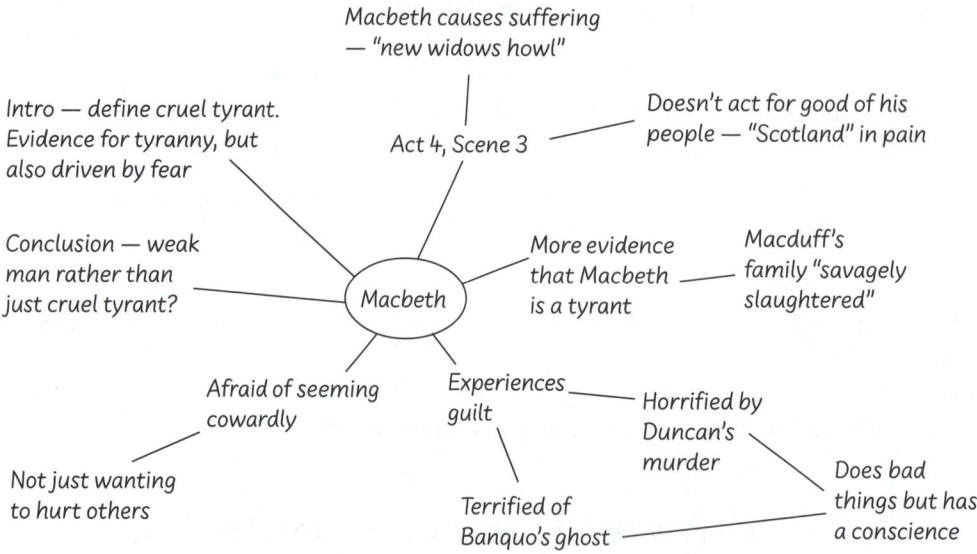

A cruel tyrant could be defined as someone who uses their power to oppress and cause pain to others, has no remorse, and acts for themselves rather than for the good of their people. In 'Macbeth', there is evidence that the main character is a tyrant, including his killing of innocent people to keep his position as king. However he does feel guilt about his bad deeds, and he often acts through fear, suggesting he is not wholly selfish or cruel. <u>He is not simply a cruel tyrant, therefore, but is also a flawed character who is easily controlled by his fears.</u>

⬅ Outline your argument in the <u>introduction</u>.

Don't forget to write about the <u>extract</u> you've been given.

<u>In Act Four, Scene Three</u>, Malcolm and Macduff describe Macbeth as a "tyrant" and discuss his cruelty, saying that <u>"Each new morn, / New widows howl, new orphans cry". This shows that Macbeth is causing misery and suffering to his subjects.</u> The repetition of "new" emphasises that the murders are happening regularly. Macbeth seems prepared to go to any length to hold power and is willing to cause suffering to do so. At this point in the play he is therefore behaving as a cruel tyrant.

Remember to include <u>quotes</u>, and <u>explain</u> how they support your points.

Macduff shows how Scotland as a whole is suffering under Macbeth's rule. He uses <u>personification</u> when describing how heaven "yelled" in pain "As if it felt with Scotland". The word "with" implies that Scotland is also able to feel pain and sadness. This emphasises how the whole country is being oppressed by Macbeth. Macbeth is clearly causing distress rather than acting for the good of the country he rules, reinforcing the reader's impression of him as a tyrannical ruler.

⬅ Naming the <u>technique</u> the writer uses will impress the examiner.

Section Eight — English Literature: Drama

Worked Exam-Style Question

Try to pick out the *examples* that illustrate your point *best*, rather than just listing the events of the play.

The most clear-cut example of Macbeth's tyranny elsewhere in the play is when he hires two murderers to ensure that Macduff's wife and children are "Savagely slaughtered", because the witches' apparition warns him to "beware Macduff". The alliteration of "Savagely slaughtered" gives the phrase a harsh tone that makes the murders seem especially aggressive and cruel, suggesting that Macbeth's decision to have them killed was inhumane. This shows how far he is driven by his selfish desire to be king and by his need to destroy any threat to his power.

Remember to talk about *other parts* of the play as well as the extract.

However, although some of the acts that Macbeth commits are undoubtedly tyrannical, he is deeply troubled by what he has done. After murdering Duncan, it is clear that Macbeth feels very guilty. He says "Methought I heard a voice cry, 'Sleep no more! / Macbeth does murder sleep,' the innocent sleep". His rambling speech, with its repetition of "sleep", shows that he is confused, upset and plagued by guilt. The theme of hallucination and imagination, shown here in the voice Macbeth hears, recurs throughout the play, usually as a sign of his troubled conscience. For example, after having Banquo murdered, Macbeth sees his ghost at the banquet, showing that he is horrified at what he has done. Macbeth's remorse and regret suggest that he is not entirely a cruel tyrant.

Keep referring back to the *question* to make sure you stay *focused*.

Good analysis of how the writer uses *language* to achieve an *effect*.

It's great to show that you've thought about the *broader themes* of the play.

Think carefully about *why* characters act the way they do.

Furthermore, as a brave man, unused to feeling fear, Macbeth is frightened of being thought weak, cowardly or unmanly. It is this fear, at least in part, that drives him to acts of tyranny, rather than just a desire to hurt others. At first, this is because Lady Macbeth questions his bravery and manliness, and later because he questions it himself, and feels the need to prove himself. When Macbeth is killed, the audience feels a mixture of relief, pity and regret. If he was purely a tyrant, his death would come as a relief, so the audience's reaction at this point demonstrates that his character is more complex than this.

This is a good *personal response* to the play.

In summary, Macbeth often behaves in a cruel and tyrannical way. However, his guilt about his acts of tyranny and the fact that he is driven to some of these acts through fear show that he is not a straightforward cruel tyrant. Instead, he is a complicated character, driven by a mixture of motives that are not always cruel or oppressive in their nature. These things together show that, ultimately, Macbeth is merely very human.

Write a strong, memorable *conclusion* to sum up your argument.

Worked Exam-Style Question

This is an example answer to a question about a modern play. The question is about the main character in 'An Inspector Calls', but the answer has got some helpful tips for writing about any modern drama text. So, even if you're not studying 'An Inspector Calls', have a good look through this example answer.

Q1 How does Priestley show the importance of the Inspector to the play as a whole in 'An Inspector Calls'?

Your answer should cover:
- how the Inspector is important to the play as a whole
- how Priestley presents the character of the Inspector.

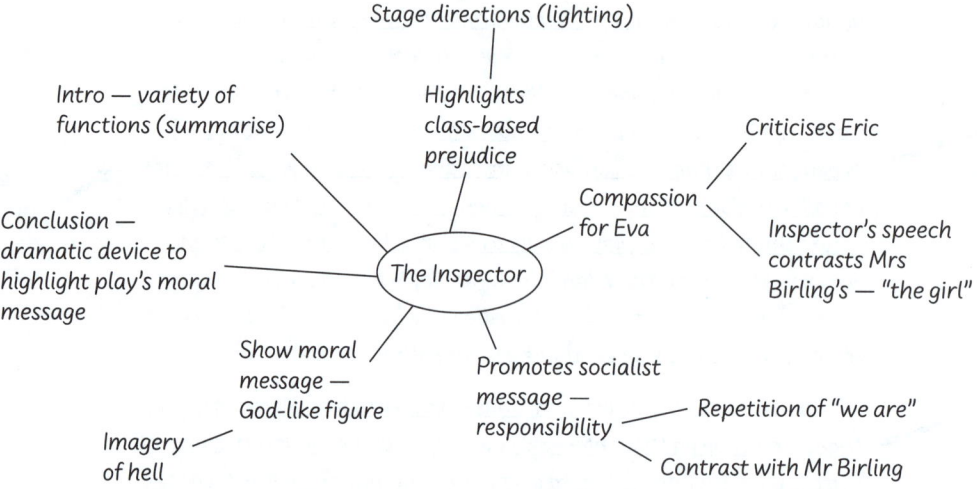

<u>The Inspector in 'An Inspector Calls' serves a variety of important functions within the play.</u> He makes the Birlings recognise their faults and the consequences of their actions; highlights the importance of people taking responsibility for one another; and also serves as an all-seeing, God-like figure, giving the impression that those who do not take responsibility for their crimes will be punished. <u>Priestley presents these aspects of the Inspector's role through the use of stage directions, contrasts, repetition and imagery.</u>

Make sure you address the question in your introduction.

One of the most important functions of the Inspector is to highlight problems within the Birling family and, by extension, within <u>the class-obsessed social system of the early twentieth century. This is illustrated by the stage directions.</u> When the Inspector arrives, the lighting changes from "pink and intimate" to "brighter and harder". This suggests that the Inspector will shine a light on the true nature of the Birling family, shattering their illusion of the 'perfect' family and forcing them to 'see' things more clearly. This includes the reality of how their actions have affected other, less fortunate people.

Show you know about the play's context.

Don't forget to consider the writer's stagecraft.

Section Eight — English Literature: Drama

Worked Exam-Style Question

Priestley also uses the Inspector as a contrasting figure to the Birlings, which helps him to show how wrong class-based prejudice is. The Inspector shows compassion for Eva Smith, criticising Eric for treating her "as if she was an animal, a thing, not a person". *In contrast, most of the other characters do not show any kindness towards Eva because she is of a lower class.* For instance, Mrs Birling repeatedly refers to her as "the girl", as if she cannot bear to mention her name or as if she does not matter as a person. The contrast in the way Mrs Birling and the Inspector talk about Eva, and the Inspector's insistence on treating Eva as a person, makes Mrs Birling appear narrow-minded and shows the audience that it is wrong to look down on the working classes.

← This uses other characters in the play to make a point about the Inspector's character.

Another important function of the Inspector is to promote Priestley's socialist message: that we should all take responsibility for one another. This is shown most clearly at the end of the play, when the Inspector says "We are members of one body. We are responsible for each other". *The repetition of "We are" includes both the other characters and the audience, making it clear that this is how everyone should behave.* This contrasts directly with Birling's belief that a man has to "look after himself and his own". The difference in the two characters' views highlights the selfishness and cruelty of some middle-class attitudes at the time.

It's impressive if you can show you understand the play's overall message.

← This is a good analysis of the writer's technique.

In his final speech, the Inspector's language has an almost God-like quality, suggesting that his main role is as a dramatic device to promote a moral message. He states that if people do not take responsibility for others, then they will learn to do so in "fire and blood and anguish". *This imagery is reminiscent of Hell, implying that the suffering experienced will be particularly painful, and portraying the Inspector as a God-like figure who can judge others.* As *the Inspector's language in this speech is out of keeping with the rest of his language in the play,* it is implied that the audience is supposed to view him as a dramatic device, rather than a convincing character. In this way Priestley uses the Inspector as a vessel for his own views, and to represent the main moral of the play.

Comparing different parts of the play shows you understand it as a whole.

← This shows an awareness of the effects of different techniques.

In conclusion, the character of the Inspector is used by Priestley to show the class-based prejudice of other characters. *Stage directions show his pivotal role in highlighting the Birling family's flaws, and his compassion contrasts their unkindness. His God-like language in his final speech shows that he used by Priestley to express the play's key messages.* His function as a dramatic device therefore makes him the most important character in the play.

← Summarise your main points in your conclusion.

Exam-Style Questions

Now that you've revised drama, here are some practice questions. They're not exactly the same as the ones in the real exam, but they're still great practice. You don't have to answer them all, but try to at least write a plan for any that are relevant to your set plays. There are example answers on pages 146-149 to help you.

Q1 Read **either** the prologue of 'Romeo and Juliet' **or** Act 1 Scene 3 of 'Macbeth', from "Glamis, and Thane of Cawdor" to "Commencing in a truth?", **or** Act 1 Scene 2 of 'Julius Caesar', from the beginning of the scene to "Let us leave him. Pass!".

Using one of these extracts as a starting point, write about how Shakespeare explores fate and free will in the play.

Q2 Read **either** Act 3 Scene 5 of 'The Merchant of Venice', from the beginning of the scene to "on the coals for money.", **or** Act 2 Scene 1 of 'Much Ado About Nothing', from "Come, lady, come" to "his conceit is false."

Using one of these extracts as a starting point, discuss Shakespeare's use of comedy in the play.

Q3 With reference to a post-1914 play you have studied, discuss how the writer presents ideas about gender **or** growing up.

Your answer should cover:
- the ideas about gender or growing up in the play
- how these ideas are presented.

Q4 Read Act 2 Scene 1 of 'The Tempest', from "It was a torment" to "Go, hence with diligence!", **or** Act 1 Scene 1 of 'Macbeth'.

Using one of these extracts as a starting point, explore how Shakespeare presents the supernatural in the play.

Q5 With reference to a post-1914 play you have studied, discuss how the relationship between two central characters changes during the course of the play.

Your answer should cover:
- how the relationship between the two characters changes
- the techniques the writer uses to present the relationship between the two characters.

Section Nine — English Literature: Prose

Writing About Prose

You'll have to study a 19th-century prose text for your course, and you might study a modern prose text too.

You might have to write about two different types of Prose

1) For Paper 1, you'll have to study one of these prose texts from the 19th century:

   - The Strange Case of Dr Jekyll and Mr Hyde by Robert Louis Stevenson
   - A Christmas Carol by Charles Dickens
   - Great Expectations by Charles Dickens
   - Jane Eyre by Charlotte Brontë
   - Frankenstein by Mary Shelley
   - Pride and Prejudice by Jane Austen
   - The Sign of Four by Sir Arthur Conan Doyle

2) For Paper 2, you might have to study some modern prose — the texts you might study are:

   - Lord of the Flies by William Golding
   - Telling Tales — the AQA Anthology of short stories
   - Animal Farm by George Orwell
   - My Name is Leon by Kit de Waal
   - Anita and Me by Meera Syal
   - Pigeon English by Stephen Kelman

> If you're not studying a modern prose text, you'll study a modern play instead — see Section Eight (p.134-150) for more on writing about drama.

Form and Structure both have an impact on a text

1) The form of a prose text affects how the story is told — e.g. short stories might have simple, dramatic plots, whereas novels are longer, so the plot can be more detailed or take place over a longer period of time.

2) The structure of a prose text is also important — different structures can have different effects on the reader.

   - Texts can be split into chapters or sections. This can create cliffhangers or switch the focus of the plot.

   > 'Jane Eyre' is divided into three separate volumes — original readers of the book had to buy each volume separately. Brontë used cliffhangers at the end of the first two volumes, which would have encouraged readers to buy the next volume.

   - Think about how the novel starts and ends, and what the impact of this may be on the reader.

   > 'Animal Farm' has a cyclical structure — elements at the start of the book repeat themselves at the end, but under Napoleon's rule rather than Farmer Jones'. For example, by the end of the book Napoleon has become a drunk, just like Jones. This shows that the new regime is mirroring the old one.

   - Some plots move forwards chronologically (in time order). Others are non-chronological.

   > 'A Christmas Carol' includes three episodes set in different time periods, each of which jumps between different times and places. This gives them a dreamlike quality.

   - The novel may have one main plot, or several plots that link together.

   > 'Pride and Prejudice' has several different stories which interlink. The revelations about Wickham, the romance between Bingley and Jane, and Mr Collins' search for a wife all make the novel more interesting. They also allow Austen to further explore themes such as social class and gender.

Writing About Prose

Writers sometimes use Structural Devices

For more on flashbacks and foreshadowing, see page 126.

1) The author may use structural devices like flashbacks, foreshadowing and different narrative structures.
2) A frame narrative is an overarching story that contains other stories within it.

> 'Frankenstein' uses a frame narrative — Walton's letters frame Frankenstein's story, which in turn acts as a frame for the monster's account. This prompts the reader to question their judgement of events — Walton presents Frankenstein as a "wonderful man", but this is undermined by events in Frankenstein's own narrative.

3) An embedded narrative is a story that is within a frame narrative.

> 'Dr Jekyll and Mr Hyde' has several embedded narratives in the form of written documents (Lanyon's letter, Jekyll's statement) and testimonies from characters. These make the story appear more authentic and make the reader curious — each narrative adds more evidence as the reader starts to form a picture of who Mr Hyde is.

Comment on the writer's choice of Language

1) Authors love using descriptive language, including similes, metaphors and personification.

> "bloodthirsty snarling"
> "the tearing of teeth and claws"
> → In 'Lord of the Flies', Golding uses animal imagery to describe the boys, showing that they are becoming more savage.

2) Particularly keep an eye out for any language or imagery that's repeated — there's usually a reason for it.

> "he locked the note into his safe"
> "he turned to examine the door in the by-street. It was locked"
> → In 'Dr Jekyll and Mr Hyde', there are numerous images of locked doors. These are used to symbolise secrecy, and the way that humans try to hide their dual nature.

3) The language used by characters is also really important. For example:

> "Yow can come with uz, right, but don't say nothin'"
> → In 'Anita and Me', Meena uses Midlands dialect words, slang and non-standard grammar to try to fit in and impress Anita.

Characters' Thoughts are often described

You can find more information about analysing characters on pages 122-123.

1) Novels and short stories give descriptions of characters' thoughts and behaviour.
2) Look out for those bits, quote them, and comment on how they help answer the question.

> The head, he thought, appeared to agree with him. Run away, said the head silently...
> → The narrator of 'Lord of the Flies' describes Simon's thoughts and imagined conversation with the pig's head. This allows the reader to experience Simon's hallucinations.

Don't be afraid to be original...

When it comes to language and structure, there are no wrong points (as long as you have evidence to back them up). If you think of something original about a text, remember it in case you can use it in the exam.

Analysing Narrators

The narrator is the person telling the story — they are the link between the reader and the plot.

There are Different Types of Narrator

1) All prose texts have a narrator — a voice that's telling the story.

2) A first-person narrator is a character who tells the story from their perspective, e.g. Pip narrates 'Great Expectations' and Meena narrates 'Anita and Me'. You get a first-hand description of exactly what the character sees, does and thinks all the way through the story.

> *In what ecstasy of unhappiness I got these broken words out of myself, I don't know. The rhapsody welled up within me, like blood from an inward wound, and gushed out.* → In 'Great Expectations', Pip's narration is very personal and appeals to the reader's emotions. This helps the reader to empathise with him.

3) A third-person narrator is a separate voice, created by the author to tell the story — this type of narrator is used in 'A Christmas Carol' and 'Pride and Prejudice'. They usually describe the thoughts and feelings of several different characters, making them more of a storyteller than a character.

4) Third-person narrators can be omniscient (all-knowing) or limited (only aware of the thoughts and feelings of one character). They may also describe only what can be seen or heard — for example, in 'Animal Farm', the narrator usually just presents the reader with factual information.

> *To Catherine and Lydia, neither the letter nor its writer were in any degree interesting.* → The omniscient, third-person narrator of 'Pride and Prejudice' gives the reader an insight into the thoughts of many of the characters, even though the story follows Elizabeth most closely.

Not all narrators are Reliable

1) Don't automatically trust what a narrator says — they may be unreliable. This is particularly common with first-person narrators, who see things from their own point of view.

> *I have recorded in detail the events of my insignificant existence...* → The first-person narrator of 'Jane Eyre' calls herself "insignificant", but the fact that she's the main character in the book suggests this isn't true.

2) The narrator is not the same person as the author, but watch out for examples of the writer's viewpoint being revealed through the narrator. For example:

> *Scrooge! a squeezing, wrenching, grasping, scraping, clutching, covetous old sinner!* → The third-person narrator of 'A Christmas Carol' has strong opinions on Scrooge, which seem to be Dickens's views.

EXAM TIP — The narrator and the writer are not the same person...

In the exam, keep in mind that what the narrator thinks isn't necessarily the same as what the writer thinks. Refer to how the writer uses the narrator, rather than just what the narrator says.

19th-Century Fiction

You have to study a 19th-century novel, so the next three pages contain some useful background information on life in the period. This will help you understand the texts better, and to write more informed essays.

There was a Big Gap between the Upper and Lower Classes

1) Class was important in the 19th century — your class determined what kind of life you had.

2) Early 19th-century society was divided between the rich upper classes (who owned the land, didn't need to work and so socialised a lot) and the poorer working classes (who relied on the upper classes for work, and were often looked down on because of it).

3) The Industrial Revolution created opportunities for more people to make money, meaning that the middle classes grew in size and influence throughout the century.

4) However, the fact that the middle classes relied on a profession or trade for their wealth meant that they were looked down on by the upper classes.

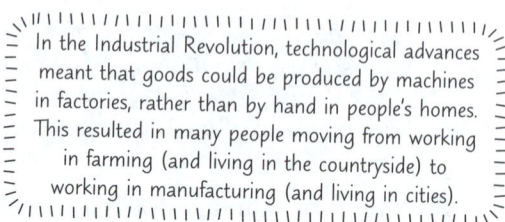
In the Industrial Revolution, technological advances meant that goods could be produced by machines in factories, rather than by hand in people's homes. This resulted in many people moving from working in farming (and living in the countryside) to working in manufacturing (and living in cities).

'Pride and Prejudice' examines and criticises judgements based on social status. Austen mocks 19th-century class prejudices by showing that characters' behaviour is down to personality, not class.

Many cities were Overcrowded and had Terrible Living Conditions

1) In the 19th century, millions of people moved from the countryside to the cities in search of work in the new factories. As a result, the population of cities grew rapidly and uncontrollably.

2) Most of these people ended up living in slums of cheap, overcrowded housing. There was often no proper drainage or sewage system, and many families had to share one tap and toilet. Overcrowding led to hunger, disease and crime.

Dickens uses 'A Christmas Carol' to highlight the problems and poverty of working-class London. He contrasts the wealth of Scrooge with the poverty of the Cratchit family.

Women were often Dependent on men

1) During the 19th century, women were normally dependent on the men in their family, especially in the upper classes. It was usually men who earned a living or owned land which generated income from rent.

2) A woman's best chance of a stable future was a good marriage — there were very few job options available for upper and middle-class women, and women often weren't allowed to inherit land or money.

3) Women didn't have the vote, and generally had to do what their husband told them — they were expected to stay at home and look after children.

'Jane Eyre' was unusual at the time of publication not only because it was written by a woman, but also because its main character is a determined and sometimes outspoken woman. By the end of the novel, Jane is both emotionally and financially independent.

Section Nine — English Literature: Prose

19th-Century Fiction

Education was Not Compulsory until the late 19th century

1) Education was a privilege — only wealthy families could afford to send children away to school, or to hire a governess to live with them and teach the children.

2) Boys' education was more of a priority, and many girls weren't educated at all. An academic education was seen as unnecessary for women — girls from rich families were taught art, music and dance as this would help them to get a husband, and girls from poorer families were expected to go straight into a job that didn't require an education.

3) Many schools were run by the Church and supported by charity donations. The government began funding schools in 1833, but the funding was very limited.

4) School wasn't compulsory until 1880, when an Education Act finally made it compulsory for children between the ages of five and ten to attend school.

In 'Great Expectations', Pip receives hardly any formal education as a child. He is desperate to gain an education, believing this is key to becoming a gentleman, and attempts to improve his education throughout the novel.

Reputation was important

1) In middle and upper-class society, it was important to be respectable.

2) The middle and upper classes were expected to have strong morals and to help others. They were also expected to keep their emotions under strict control and to hide their desire for things like sex and alcohol.

3) If someone was seen doing anything which wasn't considered respectable, their reputation could be ruined. To protect their reputation, people often kept their sinful behaviour and desires secret.

The gentlemen in 'Jekyll and Hyde' are concerned with their reputations. Jekyll creates Hyde in order to hide his sins and preserve his reputation, and Utterson consistently tries to protect Jekyll's reputation. The book explores how this obsession with reputation can actually be destructive.

Many texts were influenced by Romanticism and the Gothic genre

1) 'Romanticism' had a big impact on literature and art in the late 18th century and the early 19th century.

2) The 'Romantics' tried to capture intense emotions and experiences in their work, and were especially influenced by nature. They saw nature as a powerful force that could inspire and restore people.

3) Many 19th-century writers were influenced by the Gothic genre — this generally involved a mysterious location, supernatural elements, troubling secrets and elements of madness.

4) The double (or doppelgänger) is another key feature of Gothic novels — it's where two characters are presented as if they are each a version of the other.

'Frankenstein' includes aspects of the 'Romantic' and the Gothic. Frankenstein travels to the Alps in the hope that the "magnificence" of nature will help him to forget his "sorrows", but it is there that he meets the monster, who is presented as the other side of him.

19th-Century Fiction

Victorian society was very Religious

1) Christianity had a strong influence on life in Victorian Britain. To be good Christians, many people believed they should live by a strict moral code — attending church regularly, avoiding alcohol and exercising sexual restraint.

2) However, others believed that being a good Christian meant being charitable and forgiving.

> At the end of 'A Christmas Carol', Scrooge resolves to "honour Christmas" and to continue his generosity and goodwill "all the year". This appears to be Dickens's view of being a good Christian.

Darwin's theory of Evolution was Controversial

1) In the early 1800s, Christianity taught that God created every species to be perfectly adapted to its environment. The Book of Genesis in the Bible also says that humans were made in God's image, different from all other animals and ruling over them.

2) In contrast, some scientists, including Charles Darwin, claimed that all creatures evolved from common ancestors through a process called 'natural selection'.

3) Darwin also claimed that humans shared a common ancestor with apes. This went against the Christian idea that man's nature was different from that of other animals. People found this unsettling because it meant that there may be an animalistic side to everyone, capable of uncivilised acts and violent crimes.

> In 'Dr Jekyll and Mr Hyde', Hyde is described as the "animal within" Jekyll. Utterson describes him as "hardly human", and Poole says he is "like a monkey". Stevenson may be hinting that Hyde is a less evolved version of Jekyll.

Scientists were Investigating where Life comes from

1) Many 19th-century scientists were fascinated with the origins of life. Some believed that studying electricity might reveal what gives life to people and animals.

2) Scientists experimented with passing electric currents through animal and human bodies. The current made the bodies move, which led some to conclude there was a type of 'animal electricity' (later called 'galvanism') within living things.

> In 'Frankenstein', Shelley implies that Victor uses electricity to animate the monster — he infuses a "spark of being" into a "lifeless thing". This suggests Shelley was influenced by contemporary science.

Make sure you understand the text's context...
Make a list of relevant context points for the 19th-century prose text you've studied (use these pages to get you started). Then jot down a sentence explaining why each point is relevant to the text.

Section Nine — English Literature: Prose

Warm-Up Questions

When you're writing an exam answer about prose texts, always think about the language, the structure and the issues raised in the texts. You also need to remember to focus on the detail and to choose your quotes wisely. Start with the questions on this page, and the practice questions on p.162 should be no problem.

Warm-Up Questions

1) Choose a prose text that you have studied. Open it at the first page and read the opening paragraph. Write down three things that you notice about the way the author has written the paragraph.

2) Using a prose text you have studied in class, find a passage that uses descriptive language to set the scene. Write a short paragraph explaining how the writer makes this description vivid. (Hint: think about their use of imagery, interesting vocabulary and appeals to the senses.)

3) Think about a central character in one of the prose texts you have studied, and write a short paragraph for each of the following questions.
   a) Why is this character important to the novel?
   b) Do you sympathise with this character? Why or why not?
   c) How does this character change over the course of the text?

4) Choose a prose text you have studied. Does the text have a first-person or third-person narrator? Write a short paragraph about the effect this narrator has on the text.

5) Read the passage below.
   a) Make a list of all of the words and phrases that are about reputation.
   b) Using your list from part a), write a short paragraph about the importance of reputation for women in 19th-century Britain.

> "This is a most unfortunate affair, and will probably be much talked of. But we must stem the tide of malice, and pour into the wounded bosoms of each other the balm of sisterly consolation."
>
> Then, perceiving in Elizabeth no inclination of replying, she added, "Unhappy as the event must be for Lydia, we may draw from it this useful lesson: that loss of virtue in a female is irretrievable; that one false step involves her in endless ruin; that her reputation is no less brittle than it is beautiful; and that she cannot be too much guarded in her behaviour towards the undeserving of the other sex."

Worked Exam-Style Question

Take a look at this worked answer for an essay about 'A Christmas Carol'. Even if you haven't studied 'A Christmas Carol', you should still give this answer a good read. It will give you some ideas for how to structure your own answers, as well as the sort of points you could include.

Q1 Read the passage from Chapter 1 of 'A Christmas Carol' which begins "At this festive season of the year, Mr. Scrooge" and ends "Good afternoon, gentlemen!", then answer the question.

Using this extract as a starting point, write about Scrooge and the way he changes throughout the novel.

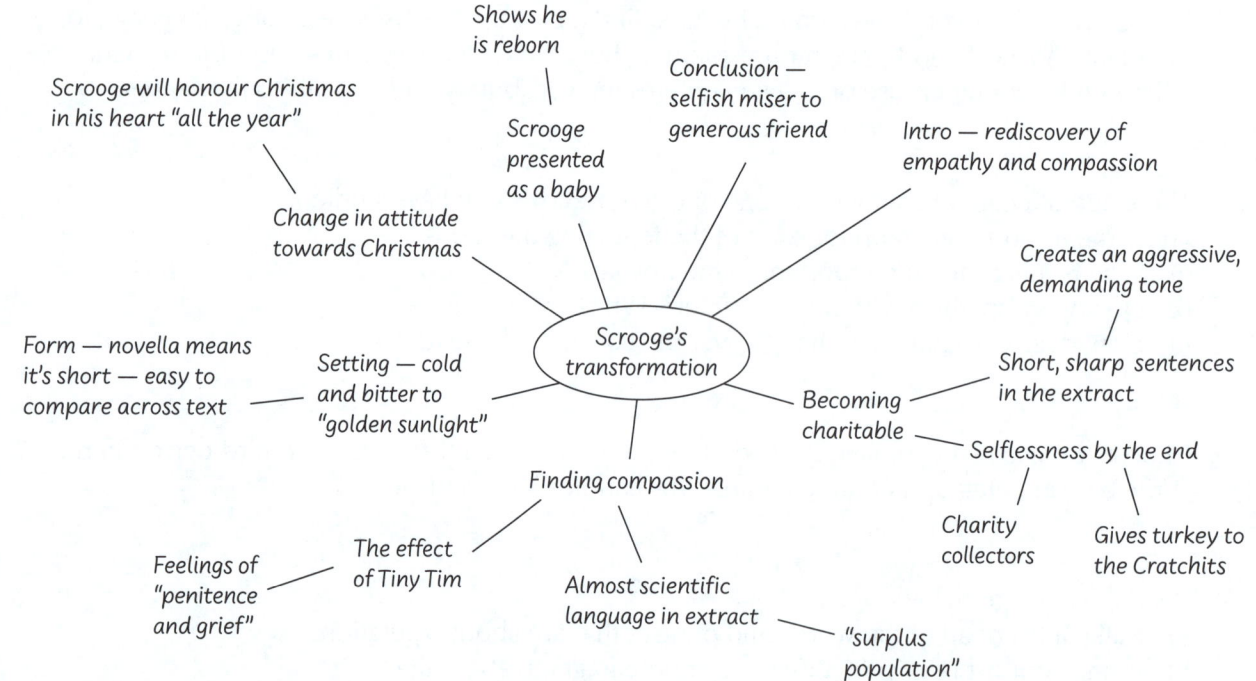

Charles Dickens's 'A Christmas Carol' shows the transformation of Scrooge. The text's structure follows Scrooge as he undergoes a fundamental change of character, rediscovering empathy, compassion and human emotion. He is transformed from a "covetous, old sinner" into someone who keeps the Christmas spirit "all the year". <u>This change is emphasised through Dickens's use of language, setting and structure, as well as how he presents Scrooge's attitude towards Christmas.</u>

One of the most obvious changes in Scrooge is his discovery of charity. <u>His conversation with the charity collectors in the extract highlights his selfishness and greed.</u> When asked to make a "slight provision" to help the poor, he responds with a series of short, sharp questions. These give his speech an aggressive and demanding tone, which highlights his lack of sympathy for other people. <u>However, after the visitation of the three ghosts, Scrooge makes active choices to share his wealth, such as making a generous donation to the charity collectors</u> and buying a "prize Turkey" for Bob and his family. The fact that Scrooge sends the turkey anonymously shows that he doesn't expect anything in return, emphasising his newfound selflessness.

This question is all about <u>how</u> Scrooge changes — refer to the <u>techniques</u> Dickens uses to show this.

It's important to write about the <u>extract</u> given in the question.

<u>Comparing</u> how Scrooge differs in <u>different parts of the novel</u> is key to writing about how he has <u>changed</u>.

Section Nine — English Literature: Prose

Worked Exam-Style Question

Use quotes from the extract in your answer. →

Scrooge is presented as uncompassionate towards the poor in the extract, saying that if the poor would rather die than go to the workhouses then they should "do it" and "decrease the surplus population". Dickens's use of cold, almost scientific language shows how cold-hearted and distanced Scrooge is from the poor. However, this attitude changes over the course of the novel. For example, when the Ghost of Christmas Present tells Scrooge that Tiny Tim may die, he repeats Scrooge's exact words. Hearing his own words applied specifically to Bob's son causes Scrooge to feel "penitence and grief", showing that he regrets his earlier lack of compassion, and contrasting his cold-hearted behaviour at the beginning of the story.

← **This sentence explains the effect that Dickens's language has.**

Dickens uses the setting of the text to reinforce the changes in Scrooge's character. In the first chapter, the narrator describes Scrooge as carrying "his own low temperature always about with him", implying that his heart is as cold as the "biting" weather outside. However, by the end of the text the fog and mist have been replaced with "golden sunlight". This change in the weather reflects the change Scrooge has gone through; from a cold-hearted miser to a man of warmth and generosity. By changing elements of the setting for different effects at the start and end of the text, Dickens invites the reader to make a direct comparison across the story about how Scrooge has changed. The text's form makes it even more likely that readers would draw these comparisons, because as a novella it would often have been read from beginning to end in one sitting.

Don't forget to mention how the form of the text is relevant. →

A further change in Scrooge is his attitude to Christmas. In Chapter 1, Scrooge represents solitude and frugality. His repeated shouts of "Humbug" in response to his nephew's festivity show that he denounces Christmas and therefore the values it represents. However, his attitude in the final chapter is a strong contrast: he says that he will honour Christmas in his heart "all the year". By keeping it in his "heart", an organ that is not only associated with love but that is also crucial for life, it suggests that he will make the positive values of Christmas a vital part of who he is. By the end of the nineteenth century, Christmas had come to represent family and feasting; in showing that Scrooge has embraced Christmas, Dickens further emphasises that Scrooge's solitude and frugality have been overcome.

Use context to support your points where possible. →

At the end of the text, Dickens presents Scrooge as if he has been reborn. He refers to himself as "quite a baby", and this is emphasised by his enthusiastic language, such as his shouts of "Whoop" and "Hallo", which make him sound young and excited. This emphasis on youth and rebirth shows that Scrooge has changed so much that it is as though he has begun a new life.

← **When writing about language, make sure you write about the effect it has.**

In conclusion, the main focus of 'A Christmas Carol' is Scrooge's journey from selfish miser to generous friend. Dickens uses language, setting and the structure of the text to show that Scrooge has learnt to be compassionate to the poor, and has fully embraced the Christmas spirit and the values of kindness, charity and family that it represents.

The conclusion should sum up the main points of the answer. →

Worked Exam-Style Question

For Section A of Paper 2, you need to write about language, structure, form and context. It can be tricky to fit all of these different points into just one answer — luckily, these pages show you how to include everything you need for a brilliant answer about a modern prose text.

Q1   How does Golding present civilisation and savagery in 'Lord of the Flies'?

Your answer should cover:
- ideas about civilisation and savagery in the novel
- how these ideas are presented.

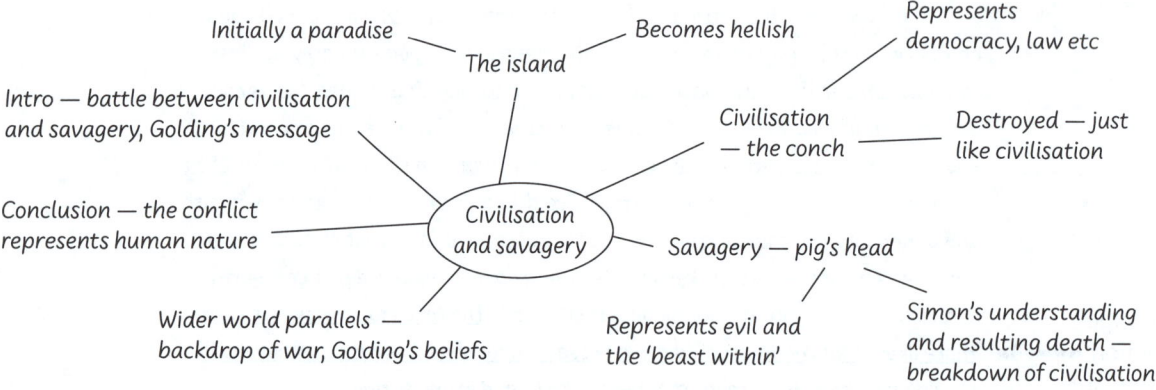

Commenting on the <u>type</u> of novel is a good way to write about <u>form</u> in your answers.

'Lord of the Flies' is an allegorical novel that explores the battle between civilisation and savagery. Throughout the novel, the boys start to lose their sense of civilisation and descend into savagery. The characters, settings, objects and events in the novel act as an allegory for society as a whole, ultimately conveying the author's message that all humans, no matter how civilised, have savagery within them.

It's good to think about how the question relates to the novel's <u>message</u>.

The setting of the island helps to illustrate the conflict between civilisation and savagery throughout the novel. At the beginning it is a paradise, with plenty of fresh water, fruit and firewood, where the boys can "have fun" until they are rescued. By the end, the island is "burning wreckage", with more in common with hell than paradise. This mirrors the boys' loss of innocence and their descent into chaos and savagery. The loss of innocence is particularly evident in Ralph who, at the beginning of the novel, is excited at the prospect of living without adults and "savoured the right of domination", but by the end of the novel has become aware of "the darkness of man's heart" — the evil that exists inside everyone.

This paragraph gives a good introduction to the subject by discussing <u>large-scale</u> points such as setting, before the essay goes into more <u>detail</u>.

This makes it <u>obvious</u> what the paragraph will be about and gives the answer a <u>clear structure</u>.

The conch is a clear symbol of civilisation in the novel. At first, it is used to summon the boys to meetings, and because only the boy holding it is allowed to speak, it comes to represent democracy and the rules of society. It is one of the major reasons for the boys voting for Ralph as leader: "The being that had blown that... was set apart". The description of Ralph's "stillness" and calling him a "being" rather than a boy give him an almost God-like quality, meaning that

You need to think about the <u>language</u> the writer uses and the <u>effect</u> it has.

Section Nine — English Literature: Prose

Worked Exam-Style Question

Think about how objects and characters change through the novel, and what these changes mean.

the conch becomes a powerful sign of authority. As civilisation is eroded and replaced by savagery, so too the conch begins to lose its power for all of the boys except Piggy and Ralph, who continue to use it even when their group consists only of them, Sam and Eric. The other boys do have respect for the conch, but it is easily overwhelmed by their newfound savagery: "Piggy held up the conch and the booing sagged a little, then came up again to strength." This hesitation highlights the conflict between this and their more civilised start on the island. The conch is finally shattered "into a thousand white fragments" by the same rock that kills Piggy. This marks the end of civilisation on the island. From this point forward, Jack's tribe lose any semblance of humanity and even Ralph acts like an animal, obeying "an instinct that he did not know he possessed" to escape, running and hiding from the hunt.

Don't forget to put in quotes to support your points.

The pig's head, the Lord of the Flies, is the opposite of the conch — it represents chaos, savagery and the evil inside each human being. Originally intended as an offering to "the Beast", the pig's head is most powerfully symbolic when it 'talks' to Simon, telling him that the beast is inside them: "You knew, didn't you? I'm part of you?". Its words foreshadow Simon's death because, when he tries to explain what he has learned to the others, they fear that he is the beast, which drives them to kill him with "teeth and claws". This marks a major turning point in the boys' descent from civilisation to savagery. At the end of the novel, the conch is destroyed in Jack's camp, and Ralph uses the stick from the Lord of the Flies as a weapon. This shows that civilisation has been completely overcome by savagery, and that even Ralph has become corrupted by the power of evil.

Details like this show that you know the text really well and have given it a lot of thought.

The naval officer who rescues the boys can be seen as an adult representation of the conflict between civilisation and savagery. Despite his smart uniform and politeness, he is still associated with war, which shows the reader that civilisation and savagery are also in conflict in the adult world. This is in keeping with Golding's beliefs about society. His experiences during World War II led him to realise that even 'civilised' people are capable of committing evil acts.

Shows that you know about the writer's background and beliefs.

Golding explores the conflict between civilisation and savagery throughout the entire novel. He uses the characters, setting and events in the novel to show how civilisation gives way to savagery, and that anybody can become savage and commit evil acts if the rules of civilisation are removed. In this way, Golding draws parallels with historical events and questions the assumption that people can be fully 'good' or that society can be completely 'civilised'.

Remember to write a brief conclusion to sum up your answer.

Exam-Style Questions

Have a go at responding to the questions below — it should give you a good chance to practise what you've learned so you're ready for the exam. Whatever text you've studied, there's at least one question for you. Give yourself around 50 minutes per question — this is roughly how much time you'd have in the exam.

Q1 Discuss how the theme of prejudice is presented in **either** 'Anita and Me' **or** 'Frankenstein' **or** 'Pride and Prejudice'.

Q2 Choose one of the following themes, and explore how it is presented in a prose text you have studied.
  a) marriage and relationships
  b) power
  c) reputation
  d) social class

Q3 What methods does the writer use to create a sense of fear in a prose text you have studied?

Q4 How does the writer present ideas about the nature of evil in **either** 'Lord of the Flies' **or** 'The Strange Case of Dr Jekyll and Mr Hyde'?

Q5 Analyse the extent to which the main character is shown to change or stay the same during the course of a prose text you have studied.

Section Ten — English Literature: Poetry

Poetry — What You Have To Do

Poetry is an important part of your English Literature GCSE. The next three sections will get you up to speed with what you need to do to write cracking poetry essays.

You'll write about poetry in **One** of your Literature exams

The poetry aspect of your GCSE English Literature course is divided into two main sections:

1) Poetry anthology (see Section Eleven) — you'll study a group (or 'cluster') of poems in class. The poems will share common themes.

2) Unseen poetry (see Section Twelve) — in the exam, you have to write about two poems that you've never seen before. You'll get a copy of them in your exam paper and have to analyse them on the spot.

You could be asked about any of the poems from the group you've studied, so you need to know them all well.

Think about **Language**, **Structure** and **Form**

You should always write about language, structure and form in your answers on poetry.

Language

This means looking at what words have been chosen and why. Consider any imagery and poetic techniques that've been used.

For more about form, structure and language, see pages 164-169.

Structure

Structure is about the way a poem is put together. This includes how a poet arranges their feelings and ideas in a poem to convey them most effectively.

Form

A poem's form includes things like the number of lines or the rhyme scheme it uses. Some forms have particular names, e.g. sonnet form (see page 164).

You must show you **Appreciate** what the **Poet** is doing

1) Once you've identified points about language, structure and form, think about the effects that these features create.

2) To get the top marks, you need to consider what these effects suggest about the speaker, or how they make the reader feel.

3) You're the reader, so you should include your personal opinion — you can be as creative as you like, as long as you back up your idea with a relevant quote from the poem.

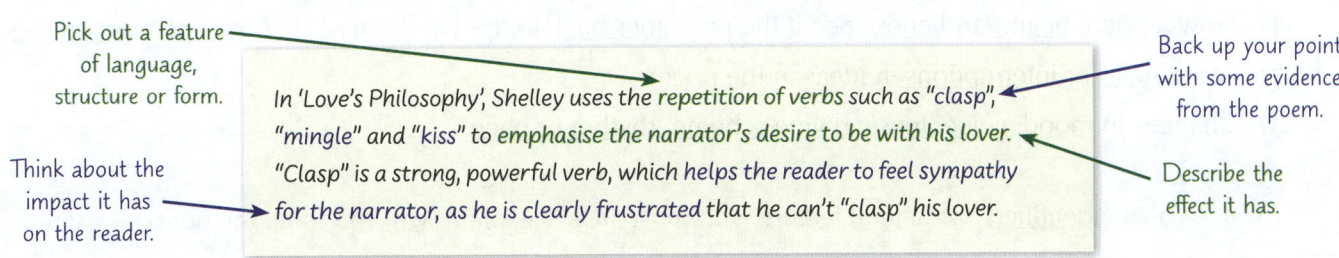

Pick out a feature of language, structure or form.

In 'Love's Philosophy', Shelley uses the repetition of verbs such as "clasp", "mingle" and "kiss" to emphasise the narrator's desire to be with his lover. "Clasp" is a strong, powerful verb, which helps the reader to feel sympathy for the narrator, as he is clearly frustrated that he can't "clasp" his lover.

Back up your point with some evidence from the poem.

Describe the effect it has.

Think about the impact it has on the reader.

Go over the poem several times to properly understand it...

Don't be put off if you feel like you don't understand a poem. Go over it a few more times and start to look at language, structure and form — they often give you a clue about the poem's meaning.

Form and Structure

Form and structure are all about the way a poem is put together. Have a look at this page to find out more.

Poetry comes in Different Forms

Different forms (or types) of poems follow different rules. You need to be able to recognise common forms of poetry for your exam.

Sometimes poets use a certain form but break some of its rules for effect.

Sonnets

Sonnets are usually 14 lines long, with a regular rhyme scheme. They're often about love, e.g. 'Sonnet 29' (Barrett Browning).

Dramatic monologues

A poem narrated by a single persona (a fictional identity who is distinct from the poet) which addresses an implied audience, e.g. 'Porphyria's Lover' (Browning).

Free verse

Free verse has lines of irregular length and no set rhythm. The poem doesn't have to rhyme (although it sometimes does). This means it often sounds like natural speech, e.g. 'A Portable Paradise' (Robinson).

Learn the correct Terms to describe Form

To discuss form properly in the exam, you need to know and use the correct technical terms:

- A stanza (or verse) is a group of lines.
- A tercet is a three-line stanza.
- A quatrain is a four-line stanza.
- A couplet is a pair of lines, usually with the same metre (see p.167).
- A rhyming couplet is a couplet where the final words of each line rhyme.
- A rhyming triplet is where the final words of three successive lines rhyme with each other.

Structure is how a poem is arranged

Structure is how the poet arranges their feelings or ideas in a poem to convey them most effectively. Two poems with the same form can be structured very differently.

Think about:

1) How a poem begins and ends. See if the poet goes back to the same ideas, or if the poem progresses.
2) Any pauses or interruptions in ideas in the poem.
3) Changes in mood, voice, tense, rhyme scheme, rhythm or pace.

Once you've identified a structural feature, you must always explain why you think the poet has used it.

Don't ignore form and structure...

It can be easy to concentrate on language, but you need to write about structure and form as well to get top marks. You can write about any poem's form, even if it's to say that it doesn't have a regular one.

Poetic Techniques

Poets use lots of techniques to get their message across. Here are the ones you need to know.

A poem's Voice is Who's Speaking and How

1) A poem's voice can affect how the poet's message is conveyed.
2) The narrator might speak in the first person ('I') or the third person ('he' or 'she').
3) A first-person voice gives you one person's perspective. It often makes the poem more personal.

> The use of a first-person voice in Rumens's 'The Emigrée' allows the narrator to speak personally about her childhood. Phrases such as "I am branded" show her continued connection with her place of birth.

4) A third-person voice is often more detached from the action. It can give an outside perspective.

> The narrator of Dharker's 'A century later' uses the third person to describe the global struggle for girls' education. This allows the poem to move beyond one girl's experience in order to encompass "A murmur, a swarm" of girls, emphasising their collective power.

Think about who the poem is Addressed To

1) Some poems are written as if the speaker is talking to a specific person — this is called direct address.
2) Direct address can often give the reader hints about the speaker's relationship with another person.

> In Dooley's poem 'Letters from Yorkshire', the narrator directly addresses a man whose lifestyle she admires. The direct address used throughout the poem emphasises the connection between the two characters, and suggests they have a close relationship despite the distance between them.

Some poems include features of Spoken Language

1) Poems can reproduce spoken language, e.g. dialect words or phonetic spellings.

> In 'Remains', Armitage uses contractions such as "he's" and colloquial language like "mates" to represent how the soldier might actually speak. Using an authentic voice makes the war seem more real and frightening by emphasising that the soldier is just like any other person.

2) Some poets use features of spoken language to make the poem more natural and personal.
3) Other poets use spoken language features to convey a speaker's accent.

> Agard's poem 'Checking Out Me History' reflects the speaker's Caribbean accent by using phonetic spellings such as "Dem" and "ole", as well as non-standard grammar, e.g. "she volunteer to go". This implies that the speaker is rebelling against the standard English grammar taught in schools as a way of showing his pride in his Caribbean heritage.

Poetic Techniques

Rhyme can add Power to the poet's message

1) Rhyme helps a poem develop its beat or rhythm. Poets can also use it to reinforce the poem's message.
2) Rhyme can be regular (occurring in a set pattern), irregular (with no pattern) or absent from a poem.
3) This creates different effects — regular rhyme schemes can create a sense of control, whereas an irregular rhyme scheme might show chaos or unpredictability. These effects can link to the poem's themes or message.

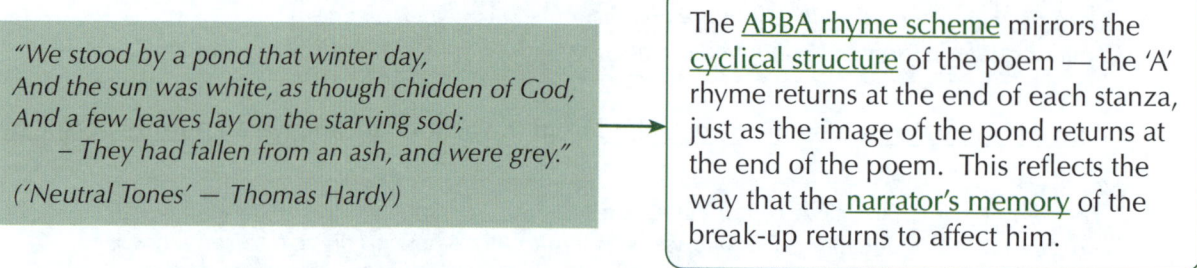

"We stood by a pond that winter day,
And the sun was white, as though chidden of God,
And a few leaves lay on the starving sod;
— They had fallen from an ash, and were grey."
('Neutral Tones' — Thomas Hardy)

The ABBA rhyme scheme mirrors the cyclical structure of the poem — the 'A' rhyme returns at the end of each stanza, just as the image of the pond returns at the end of the poem. This reflects the way that the narrator's memory of the break-up returns to affect him.

4) Sometimes rhymes occur within lines, too. These are called internal rhymes.

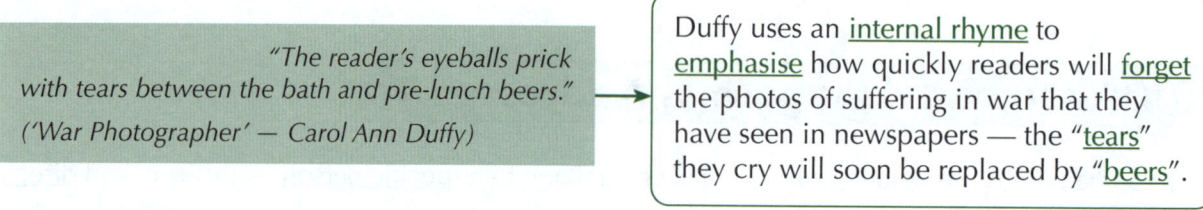

"The reader's eyeballs prick
with tears between the bath and pre-lunch beers."
('War Photographer' — Carol Ann Duffy)

Duffy uses an internal rhyme to emphasise how quickly readers will forget the photos of suffering in war that they have seen in newspapers — the "tears" they cry will soon be replaced by "beers".

Rhythm alters the Pace and Mood of a poem

1) Rhythm is the arrangement of beats within a line. It's easier to feel a rhythm than to see it on the page.
2) Like rhyme, rhythm can be regular or irregular. A strong rhyme scheme often creates a regular rhythm.
3) Rhythm can affect the pace (speed) and mood of a poem — a fast rhythm can make a poem seem rushed and frantic, whereas a slow and regular rhythm can make a poem seem calm.
4) Sometimes poets use rhythm to imitate sounds related to the poem, e.g. a heartbeat or beating drums.

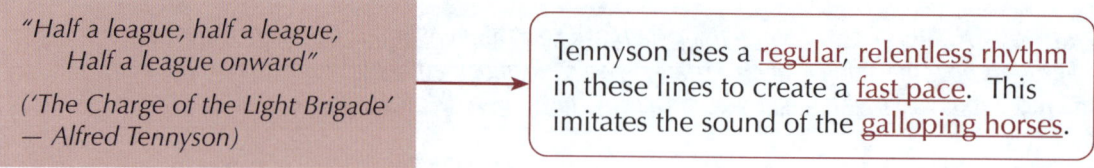

"Half a league, half a league,
   Half a league onward"
('The Charge of the Light Brigade'
— Alfred Tennyson)

Tennyson uses a regular, relentless rhythm in these lines to create a fast pace. This imitates the sound of the galloping horses.

5) The rhythm often reflects the poem's themes, how the narrator is feeling or the overall message.

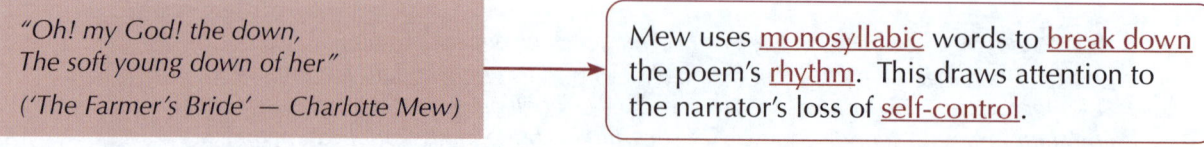

"Oh! my God! the down,
The soft young down of her"
('The Farmer's Bride' — Charlotte Mew)

Mew uses monosyllabic words to break down the poem's rhythm. This draws attention to the narrator's loss of self-control.

Section Ten — English Literature: Poetry

Poetic Techniques

Metre is the Pattern of Syllables in a line

A syllable is a single unit of sound, for example, 'beat' has one syllable and 'sonnet' has two syllables.

1) In poetry, the rhythm of a line is created by patterns of syllables. If the patterns are consistent, then the poem's rhythm is regular.

2) Metre is the technical term for these patterns. There are different types of metre, depending on which syllables are stressed (emphasised) and which are unstressed.

Iambic pentameter is a metre that's commonly used in poetry. It has 10 syllables in a line — an unstressed syllable followed by a stressed syllable, repeated five times over.

|1 |2 |3 |4 |5 |
|But leech|like to|their fain|ting coun|try cling|

('England in 1819', Percy Bysshe Shelley)

Punctuation affects how a poem Flows

Punctuation can affect the pace of a poem, emphasise specific words, or interrupt a poem's rhythm.

1) When punctuation creates a pause during a line of poetry, this is called a caesura.

"Happy and proud; at last I knew Porphyria worshipped me; surprise"
('Porphyria's Lover' — Robert Browning)

The semi-colons create caesurae which make the poem sound fragmented, reflecting the narrator's unstable mind.

2) Enjambment is when a sentence or phrase runs over from one line of poetry into the next one. Often enjambment puts emphasis on the last word of the first line or on the first word of the next line.

"two days of rain and then a break in which we walked,"
('Winter Swans' — Owen Sheers)

The enjambment puts stress on the final word of the first line, emphasising that there is a pause in the weather, and suggesting a pause in the couple's arguing.

"when it blows full Blast"
('Storm on the Island' — Seamus Heaney)

When describing the storm, Heaney uses enjambment to emphasise the word "Blast" by putting it on a new line. This hints at the storm's strength and energy.

3) An end-stopped line is a line of poetry that ends in a definite pause, usually created by punctuation. End-stopped lines can help to maintain a regular rhythm and can also affect the pace of a poem.

"I wander through each chartered street, Near where the chartered Thames does flow,"
('London' — William Blake)

Blake uses repeated end-stopped lines. This helps to give the poem a strong rhythm but also makes his version of London feel restrictive.

Poetic Techniques

Similes and Metaphors add power to Descriptions

1) Similes <u>compare</u> one thing to another — they often contain the words '<u>like</u>' or '<u>as</u>'.
2) Similes are frequently used to <u>exaggerate</u> — the poet usually wants to <u>emphasise</u> something.

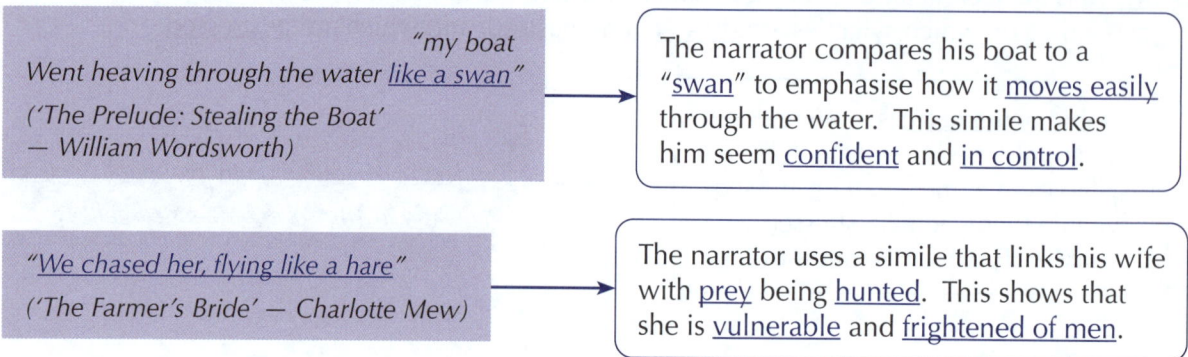

3) Metaphors describe something as though it <u>is</u> something else.
4) They take an object or person and give it the <u>qualities</u> of something else. This means that the poet can put a lot of <u>meaning</u> into a few words.

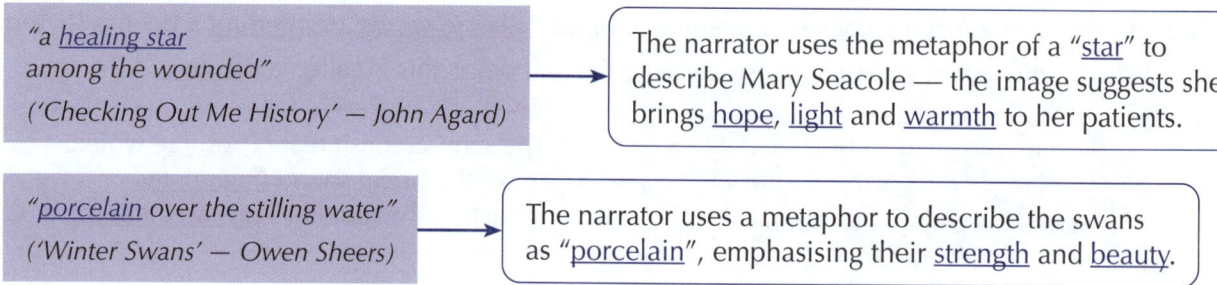

Personification gives an object Human Qualities

1) Personification means describing an <u>object</u> as if it feels or behaves in a <u>human way</u>.
2) It can add <u>emotion</u> or alter the <u>mood</u> of a poem — this can really help the poet convey their <u>message</u>.

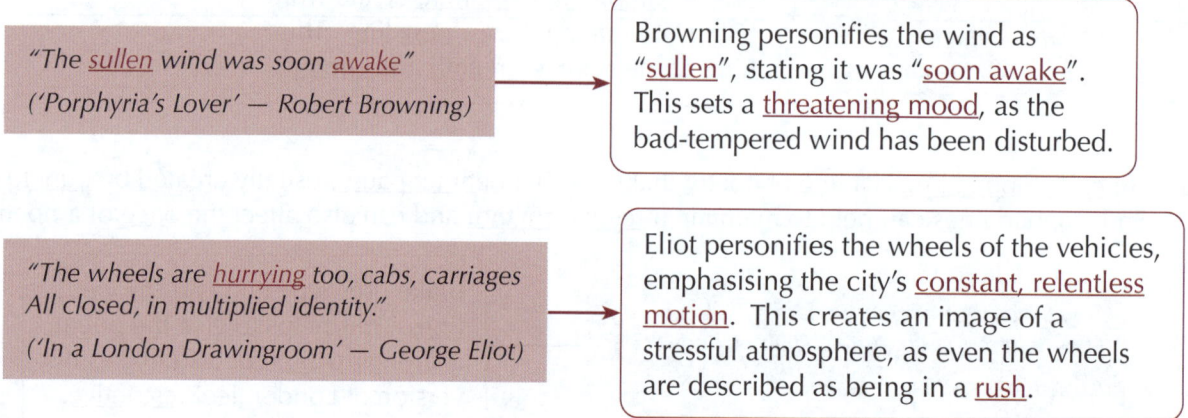

Section Ten — English Literature: Poetry

Poetic Techniques

Imagery isn't just visual

1) Poets often appeal to all the senses (touch, sight, sound, smell and taste) — this is called sensory imagery.
2) Sensory imagery helps to create a vivid image in the reader's mind.

"the skin of his finger is smooth and thick like warm ice."
('Climbing My Grandfather' — Andrew Waterhouse)

→ Waterhouse uses sensory imagery such as "smooth", "thick" and "like warm ice" to show the close bond between the narrator and their grandfather.

"Our brains ache, in the merciless iced east winds that knive us…
Wearied we keep awake because the night is silent…
Low, drooping flares confuse our memory of the salient…"
('Exposure' — Wilfred Owen)

→ The poem uses three senses (touch, sound and sight) to describe how the soldiers feel. The use of so many senses emphasises their pain and confusion.

Poets use the Sounds of words for effect

Mood is the atmosphere of a poem, and tone is the feeling the words are spoken with.

The sounds words create can alter the mood, pace and tone of a poem. Here are some of the most common techniques that use sound for effect:

1) Alliteration is where words that are close together start with the same sound.

"he passed the panelled gates"
('A Wider View' — Seni Seneviratne)

→ The repeated 'p' sound echoes the noise of footsteps as the speaker describes their great-great-grandfather's walk.

2) Assonance is when vowel sounds are repeated.

"How should I greet thee?"
('When We Two Parted' — Lord Byron)

→ The assonant long 'ee' sounds draw out each word — this reflects the long-lasting nature of the narrator's pain.

3) Sibilance is when sounds create a 'hissing' or 'shushing' effect.

"My mother shades her eyes and looks my way"
('Eden Rock' — Charles Causley)

→ The 's' and 'sh' sounds create a hushed tone, reflecting the tranquillity of the scene.

4) Onomatopoeia is when a word mimics the sound it's describing.

"To get out of that blue crackling air"
('Bayonet Charge' — Ted Hughes)

→ The word "crackling" makes the air sound electric, emphasising the danger of the battlefield.

Try to learn some technical terms...

Write down some technical terms on separate pieces of card, and write the meaning on the back of each one. Then, for each card, read the meaning and guess what technical term it is referring to.

Comparing Poems

In the exam you'll have to compare poems — they could be seen or unseen. Here are some general tips.

Compare both poems in Every Paragraph

1) When you're asked to compare poems, you need to find similarities and differences between them.

2) This means you need to discuss both poems in every paragraph. There's a lot to squeeze in, so it's important to structure your paragraphs well.

3) Comparative words help you to do this. They clearly show the examiner if the point you're making is a similarity or difference between the two poems. Here are a few examples:

| similarly | equally | in contrast | however | conversely |

Compare Language, Structure and Form

When you plan your answer, make sure you consider language, structure and form — that way you won't forget to write about them in your essay.

Language

- Think about the language techniques the poets have used, e.g. rhyme, imagery, sound.
- Comment on how the language used in each poem is similar or different, and explain why.

Both 'pot' and 'Homing' use onomatopoeia to emphasise resistance to authority. khan uses the violent-sounding verb "shatter" to reflect the speaker's strong desire to break the glass to free the pot. Similarly, Berry celebrates the "thunking and clanging" of factories, linking them with the distinctive, unrefined regional accent that the speaker prefers over the conformity associated with elocution lessons.

Structure

- Compare the beginnings and endings of the poems, and how the ideas and feelings presented are developed.
- Comment on changes in mood, voice, tense and tone — think about the effect this has.

In 'London', the narrative begins and ends on the dismal streets of London, suggesting that its inhabitants are unable to escape the suffering found there. In contrast, 'War Photographer' ends in a different place to where it begins. However, the fact that the photographer is starting another assignment highlights the unending cycle of war and violence.

Form

- See if the poems have a specific form and explain why you think the poet has made that choice.
- Compare the effects of form in each poem. Think about how they relate to the themes.
- Check if any rules are broken for effect, e.g. a sonnet with 15 lines instead of 14.

"Mother, any distance..." is written loosely in the form of a sonnet. By choosing a form that is normally used for love poems, Armitage emphasises how the speaker still loves his mother. On the other hand, 'Letters from Yorkshire' is written in free verse — the irregular line lengths make the poem flow like natural speech or a letter.

EXAM TIP — Compare the poems in every paragraph...
The examiner wants to see you're comparing both poems. Make it easy for them — write one point of comparison in each paragraph and use comparative words to show your comparisons clearly.

Warm-Up Questions

When it comes to poetry, you need to look at the overall message of the poem — but don't forget to focus on smaller things too, such as line endings, punctuation and even the vowel sounds in the middle of words. They all have a part to play. To see if you've got to grips with this section, have a go at these questions.

Warm-Up Questions

1) Write a brief definition of each of the following poetic techniques:
   a) onomatopoeia   b) caesura   c) enjambment

2) Write out the sentences below. For each sentence, underline the letters or words that are used to create the effect in brackets.
   Write a sentence for each example explaining the effect of the technique used.

   "the fizzy, movie tomorrows / the right walk home could bring." (**onomatopoeia**)
   (*Before You Were Mine*, Carol Ann Duffy)

   "As I switched sound on again, / silence collapsed." (**sibilance**)
   (*With Birds You're Never Lonely*, Raymond Antrobus)

   "the slap of sandalled feet on heat-baked stone" (**assonance**)
   (*The Jewellery Maker*, Louisa Adjoa Parker)

   "a blockade of yellow bias binding around your blazer." (**alliteration**)
   (*Poppies*, Jane Weir)

3) The extract below personifies dawn on a battlefield. Write two paragraphs describing the impression you get of the speaker's feelings and how this impression is created.

   > Dawn massing in the east her melancholy army
   > Attacks once more
   >
   > *Exposure*, Wilfred Owen

4) Read the extract below. Write a sentence explaining the effect of each of the following features of the extract:
   a) the rhyme scheme
   b) the use of direct address
   c) enjambment

   > That's my last Duchess painted on the wall,
   > Looking as if she were alive. I call
   > That piece a wonder, now: Frà Pandolf's hands
   > Worked busily a day, and there she stands.
   > Will't please you sit and look at her? I said
   > 'Frà Pandolf' by design, for never read
   > Strangers like you that pictured countenance,
   > The depth and passion of its earnest glance,
   > But to myself they turned (since none puts by
   > The curtain I have drawn for you, but I)
   >
   > *My Last Duchess*, Robert Browning

Revision Summary Test for Section Ten

Section Ten was full of useful tips and info. When you're ready, test yourself with these revision questions...
- Yep, these questions are **hard** — they'll really help you see **how well you know your stuff**.
- Tackle the **revision summary test** below, or scan the QR code to do it **online**. Use the CGP RevisionHub to **track your progress** and see which **areas need more work**.
- You can find **sample answers** here: www.cgpbooks.co.uk/blurb-answers

Poetry — What You Have To Do (p.163)
1) What are the three main elements of a poem that you have to write about in the exam? Briefly describe what you could write about for each of these elements.
2) List two things that you could write about when thinking about the poem's effects.
3) Once you have made a point, what must you always do to back up your idea?

Form and Structure (p.164)
4) What is the difference between form and structure?
5) Briefly describe each of these forms of poem:
   a) free verse   b) sonnet   c) dramatic monologue
6) Give the definition of the following:
   a) a stanza   b) a tercet   c) a rhyming couplet
   d) a quatrain   e) a couplet
7) Give three things that you could consider when thinking about a poem's structure.

Poetic Techniques (p.165-169)
8) Why might a poet choose to use:
   a) a first-person voice?   b) a third-person voice?
9) What is direct address? What effect might this feature have?
10) Why might a poet include features of spoken language in their poem? Give two reasons.
11) Define each of the following. Then give one possible effect of each.
    a) a regular rhyme scheme   b) an irregular rhyme scheme
12) Choose a poem that you have studied. Describe how the poet has created rhythm.
13) Explain how rhythm can change the pace and mood of a poem.
14) What is metre? How can you work out the metre of a poem?
15) What is the difference between enjambment and end-stopping?
16) Pick a poem that you've studied. Find an example of a simile or metaphor and explain how the poet has used it to explore a theme.
17) In a poem you've studied, find an example of personification. Why might the poet have included it?
18) Find an example of sensory imagery in a poem you've studied and explain its effect.
19) Briefly explain the following terms, then give an example of each from a poem you have studied:
    a) alliteration   b) sibilance   c) assonance   d) onomatopoeia

Comparing Poems (p.170)
20) Give two examples of comparative words or phrases you could use when explaining:
    a) a similarity between two poems.   b) a difference between two poems.
21) In a comparative essay, how often should you be comparing your two chosen poems?
22) Give two things you could comment on when comparing:
    a) language   b) structure   c) form

Section Eleven — English Literature: Poetry Anthology

The Poetry Anthology

You'll have to study a collection of poems in class, which you'll write about in Paper 2, Section B of your exam.

This is what you'll have to do in the Exam

1) You'll be given a copy of <u>one poem</u> from your anthology, and asked to compare it with <u>another</u> poem of your <u>choice</u> from the anthology. You <u>won't</u> have a copy of the anthology in the exam.

2) Your comparison will be based on something the two poems have in common, e.g. a particular <u>theme</u>. Choose your second poem carefully so you'll have lots of <u>comparison points</u> to make in your answer.

3) You'll need to know about <u>all the poems</u> in <u>one</u> of these clusters:

Power and Conflict
- The poems in this cluster explore <u>different types of power and conflict</u> in the world.
- Some poems focus on <u>human power</u> (e.g. 'Ozymandias') or the <u>power of nature</u> (e.g. 'Storm on the Island'). You may also have to write on themes like <u>memory</u>, <u>identity</u> or the <u>effects of conflict</u>.

Love and Relationships
- This cluster is all about <u>different types of relationships</u> between people.
- Some of the poems are about <u>romantic relationships</u> (e.g. 'Winter Swans') or <u>family relationships</u> (e.g. 'Follower'). <u>Desire</u>, <u>distance</u> and <u>memory</u> are also common themes.

Worlds and Lives
- This cluster is about relationships between <u>nature and people</u> and <u>identity and place</u>.
- Some poems explore ideas about <u>race and belonging</u> (e.g. 'On an Afternoon Train from Purley to Victoria, 1955'). Other common themes are <u>home</u>, <u>connection</u> and <u>conflict</u>.

Read the Question carefully and Underline key words

Make sure you're looking at the <u>right poetry cluster</u> (see above if you're unsure which one). Read the question carefully. Underline the <u>theme</u> and any other <u>key words</u> — like so:

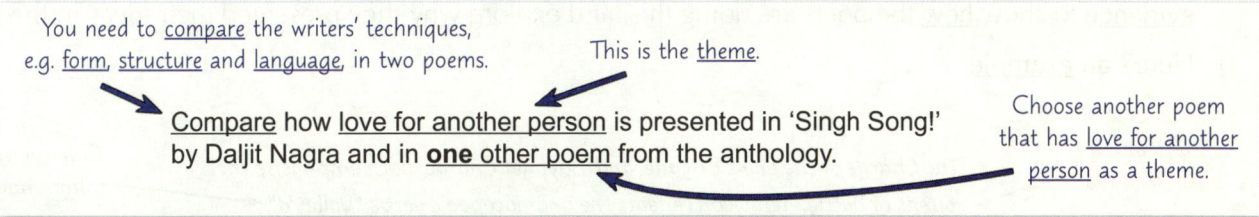

There are Three Main Ways to get marks

1) Give your own <u>thoughts</u> and <u>opinions</u> on the poems and support them with <u>quotes</u> from the text.
2) <u>Explain</u> features like <u>form</u>, <u>structure</u> and <u>language</u>.
3) Describe the <u>similarities</u> and <u>differences</u> between poems and their <u>contexts</u>.

Make sure you have a good knowledge of all your poems...
Draw a mindmap for every poem you've studied — add branches for relevant themes and then add short quotes to each branch. You can then use these quotes to back up your points in the exam.

How to Structure Your Answer

A solid structure is essential — it lets the examiner follow your argument nice and easily.

Start with an Introduction and end with a Conclusion

1) Your introduction should begin by giving a clear answer to the question in a sentence or two. Use the rest of the introduction to briefly develop this idea — try to include some of the main ideas from your plan.

2) The main body of your essay should be three to five paragraphs of analysis.

3) Finish your essay with a conclusion — this should summarise your answer to the question. It's also your last chance to impress the examiner, so try to make your final sentence memorable.

Compare the two poems throughout your answer

1) Don't just write several paragraphs about one poem, followed by several paragraphs about the other.

2) Instead, structure each paragraph of your essay by writing about one poem and then explaining whether the other poem is similar or different.

3) Every paragraph should compare a feature of the poems, such as their form, their structure, the language they use or the feelings they put across.

4) Link your ideas with words like 'similarly', 'likewise' or 'equally' when you're writing about a similarity. Or use phrases such as 'in contrast' and 'on the other hand' if you're explaining a difference.

Remember to start a new paragraph every time you start comparing a new feature of the poems.

Remember to answer What, How and Why in each paragraph

1) You should use a clear paragraph structure to help you develop your points properly. You can use What How Why (see p.4) or any other structure that you've been taught.

2) Each paragraph should have a main idea about what the poets are doing. You should then give evidence to show how the poets are doing this, and explore why they presented their ideas in this way.

3) Here's an example:

Start with a main idea that compares the two poems.

Compare the poems' effects and explain why they've been created.

> 'The Charge of the Light Brigade' and 'Bayonet Charge' both emphasise the sounds of battle. Tennyson repeats the onomatopoeic verbs "Volley'd", "thunder'd" and "Storm'd" to suggest the noise of the cannons that the Light Brigade faced. Similarly, in 'Bayonet Charge', the metaphor "blue crackling air" uses onomatopoeia to vividly depict the noise of machine gun fire. In both poems, this emphasis on sound adds a horrifying dimension to the depictions of conflict, making them vivid and realistic for the reader.

Give evidence from both poems.

Explain how the examples relate to your idea.

Always structure your answers in a clear and logical way...

You should always explain your ideas as fully as you can — don't assume the examiner knows what you're thinking. Instead, try to structure your answer clearly so that your ideas are easy to understand and follow.

How to Answer the Question

Now you're up to speed with how to structure your answer, there are a few other things you should keep in mind when answering an exam question on your anthology poems.

Look closely at **Language**, **Form** and **Structure**

1) To get top marks, you need to pay close attention to the techniques the poets use.
2) Analyse the form and structure of the poems, which includes their rhyme scheme and rhythm.
3) Explore language — think about why the poets have used certain words and language techniques.
4) You also need to comment on the effect that these techniques have on the reader. The examiner wants to hear what you think of a poem and how it makes you feel.
5) This is the kind of thing you could write about language:

> 'Poppies' makes frequent references to the injury and bereavement caused by conflict. The poem opens with a reference to the poppies placed "on individual war graves". By emphasising the personal, individual loss that conflict can cause, Weir highlights the narrator's fear that her own son will be killed in battle. The narrator's anxiety about the violence of conflict is further suggested by the depiction of poppy petals as "spasms of paper red". This metaphor evokes a vivid image of the physical injury that the narrator fears her son may suffer as a soldier, which helps the reader to understand the narrator's fears and to empathise with her. In contrast...

- Analyse the effects of key quotes.
- Always develop your ideas.
- You'd then need to compare this point with another poem.

Always **Support Your Ideas** with **Details** from the **Text**

1) You need to back up your ideas with quotes from or references to the text.
2) Choose your quotes carefully — they have to be relevant to the point you're making.
3) Don't quote large chunks of text — instead, use short quotes and embed them in your sentences.

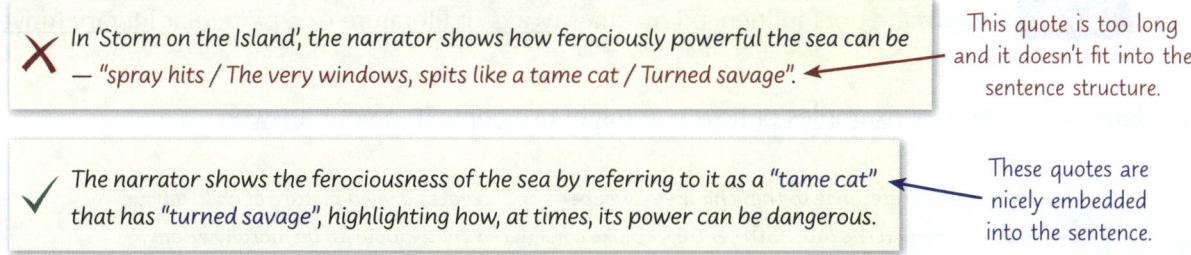

4) Don't forget to explain your quotes — you need to use them as evidence to support your argument.

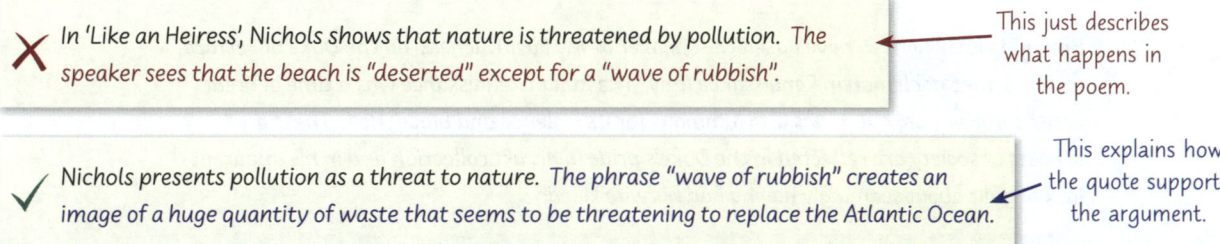

How to Answer the Question

Give Alternative Interpretations

1) You need to show you're aware that poems can be interpreted in more than one way.

2) If a poem is a bit ambiguous, or you think that a particular line or phrase could have several different meanings, then say so.

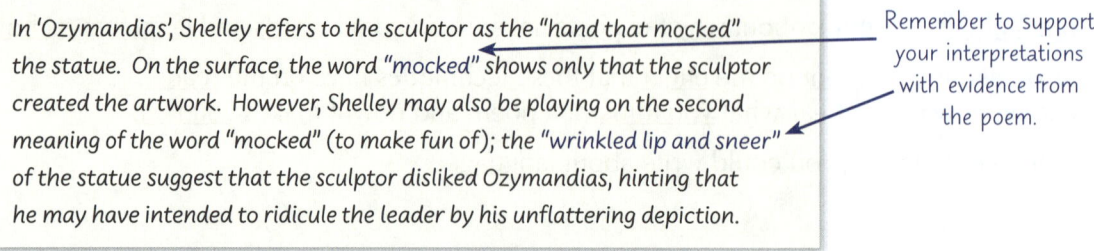

In 'Ozymandias', Shelley refers to the sculptor as the "hand that mocked" the statue. On the surface, the word "mocked" shows only that the sculptor created the artwork. However, Shelley may also be playing on the second meaning of the word "mocked" (to make fun of); the "wrinkled lip and sneer" of the statue suggest that the sculptor disliked Ozymandias, hinting that he may have intended to ridicule the leader by his unflattering depiction.

Remember to support your interpretations with evidence from the poem.

3) Be original with your ideas — just make sure you can back them up with an example from the text.

Show some Wider Knowledge

1) To get a top grade, you need to explain how the ideas in the poems relate to their context.

2) When you're thinking about a particular poem, consider these aspects of context:

Historical — Do the ideas in the poem relate to the time in which it's written or set?

Geographical — How is the poem shaped and influenced by the place in which it's set?

Social — Is the poet criticising or praising the society or community they're writing about?

Cultural — Does the poet draw on a particular aspect of their background or culture?

Literary — Was the poet influenced by other works of literature or a particular literary movement?

3) Here are a couple of examples of how you might use context in your answer:

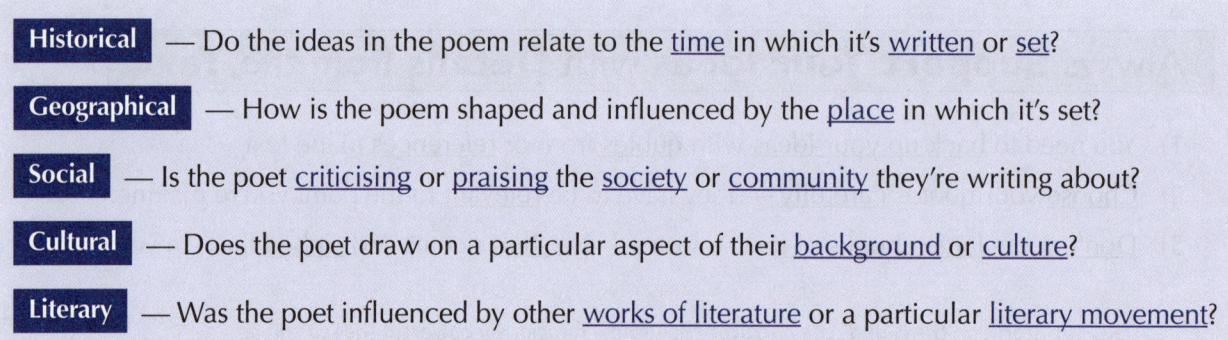

In 'London', Blake's reference to the "chimney-sweeper's cry" creates a vivid picture of child labour, which was common in the late 18th century. Blake considered child labour to be morally wrong, and he may have included this emotive image in order to boost public sympathy for his views.

Browning is thought to have based the speaker in 'My Last Duchess' on the Duke of Ferrara, an important nobleman in Renaissance Italy. The Italian Renaissance was a time of great artistic innovation, but it was also infamous for its violence and bloodshed. These dual aspects of society are reflected in the Duke's pride in his art collection and in his apparent lack of guilt about seemingly having had his wife killed.

Section Eleven — English Literature: Poetry Anthology

How to Answer the Question

Use Sophisticated Language

1) Your writing has to sound <u>sophisticated</u> and <u>precise</u>. — Not very sophisticated.

   ✗ *The narrator of 'Eden Rock' seems to quite like Eden Rock.* — This sounds much better.

   ✓ *Causley's narrator presents a positive view of Eden Rock.*

2) It should be <u>concise</u> and <u>accurate</u>, with no <u>vague words</u> or <u>waffle</u>. — This is too vague.

   ✗ *Hardy uses lots of depressing words and descriptions to express his sorrow.* — Use more specific language.

   ✓ *Hardy uses a range of references to death and winter to express his sorrow.*

3) Your writing should also show an <u>impressive range</u> of <u>vocabulary</u>.

   Don't keep using the same word to describe something.

   ✗ *In 'Name Journeys', the speaker feels cut off from the Punjabi language. The word "dislodged" shows they feel cut off from the language. The idea of feeling cut off is also shown by the fact they "toiled" to speak with a Mancunian accent.*

   Vary how you say things — it sounds much more impressive.

   ✓ *In 'Name Journeys', the speaker feels cut off from the Punjabi language. This sense of separation is emphasised by enjambment in "the Punjabi in my mouth / became dislodged", as the space between the lines emphasises the detachment described.*

4) However, make sure you <u>only</u> use words that you know the <u>meaning</u> of. For example, don't say that a poem has a '<u>volta</u>' if you don't know what it <u>really means</u> — it will be <u>obvious</u> to the examiner.

Use Technical Terms where possible

1) To get top marks, you need to use the <u>correct technical terms</u> when you're writing about poetry.
2) Flick back to Section Ten (p.163-172) for more on these terms, or have a look at the <u>glossary</u> at the back of the book.

Don't write	Write
✗ Simon Armitage uses <u>good images</u>.	✓ Simon Armitage uses <u>effective metaphors</u>.
✗ The poet uses <u>words that are also sounds</u>.	✓ The poet uses <u>onomatopoeia</u>.
✗ The <u>sentences run on from line to line</u>.	✓ The poet uses <u>enjambment</u>.

It's not just what you write...

...it's also how you write it. In the exam, think about your writing style — you should be clear and precise, and you'll need to use the correct terms to show the examiner you know your stuff.

How to Write a Top Grade Answer

If you're aiming for a grade 9, you're going to have to do a little bit extra. Here are a few tips...

Know the Poems inside out

You have to know the poems, their key themes and techniques like the back of your hand. Everyone has their own ways of understanding poetry, but here are a few ideas of how to get to grips with them:

- Read the poems again and again, highlight bits, jot down notes — whatever works for you.
- Make a list of the key themes, and note down plenty of quotes that relate to each one.
- List the major techniques that the poet uses, along with their effect.

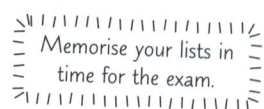

Memorise your lists in time for the exam.

Be as Original as you can

1) There are no wrong interpretations of a poem, so come up with your own ideas.
2) Make sure you can back up your interpretations with evidence from the text. For example:

> In 'Follower' by Seamus Heaney, the narrator describes how his father has become the one who follows and that he "will not go away". As well as describing the physical actions of his father, this statement could also be symbolic of his father's legacy, hinting at the narrator's sadness that he did not learn to plough like his father and suggesting that this feeling "will not go away".

Write about the poems Critically

1) Being critical means giving your own opinions about the poems — e.g. how effective you think the poet's techniques are, and why you think this.
2) You need to phrase your opinions in a sophisticated way. For example:

> In 'Thirteen', the use of the second person in the phrase "fear condenses on your lips" makes the reader experience the scene as Femi's narrator does: as a tangible moment of panic.

Get to grips with Context

It's not enough just to mention a link to context — you need to really explore the effect it has on the poem, or on your understanding of it. For example:

> In common with other Romantic poets, Wordsworth viewed nature as a powerful force that could inspire and transform people. This is evident in the extract from his autobiographical poem 'The Prelude'; the encounter with the "huge peak" leaves him in a "grave / And serious mood", seemingly forcing him to contemplate his own mortality and place in the Universe.

For a top grade, think originally and critically...

When it comes to grade 9, the examiner wants your interpretation and your opinion of the poems. Have a look at the sample answers on pages 180-185 for some ideas of how to write a great poetry essay.

Warm-Up Questions

For a poetry essay, you need to know what to write about and how to write it. When you answer the questions on this page, practise using sophisticated language so it becomes second nature by the time the exam comes round. Remember to use technical terms whenever possible as well.

Warm-Up Questions

1) In your anthology, find a poem that rhymes.
   What effect does the use of rhyme have in this poem?

2) Choose a poem from your anthology that is written in the first person and one that is written in the third person. Do you find it easier to empathise with the first-person narrator or the characters described by the third-person narration? Write a paragraph explaining your answer.

3) For each of the following aspects of form and structure, find an example from any of the poems in your anthology. Write a sentence explaining the effect each example has on the reader.
   a) End-stopping.
   b) Caesurae.
   c) Dramatic monologue.
   d) Enjambment.

4) Using two of your answers to question 3, write a paragraph comparing the form and structure of two of the poems, and explaining how the poets use form and structure to help convey their messages.

5) For each of the following language techniques, find an example from any of the poems in your anthology. Write a sentence explaining the effect each example has on the reader.
   a) Repetition.
   b) Onomatopoeia.
   c) Alliteration.
   d) Assonance.

6) Using two of your answers to question 5, write a paragraph comparing the language of two of the poems, and explaining how the poets use language to help convey their messages.

7) Pick one more poem from your anthology. How does the poet use imagery in the poem? Write a paragraph about your favourite image, explaining what effect it has on you.

Worked Exam-Style Question

Paper 2, Section B will ask you to compare two poems from your poetry anthology. There will be a copy of one of the poems in the exam paper, but you'll have to choose another poem to compare it to. Here's an example of how you might answer a question comparing two poems from 'Love and Relationships'.

Q1 Compare how childhood is presented in Seamus Heaney's 'Follower' and one other poem you have studied.

Mind map:

- Centre: Poem 1: Follower / Poem 2: Before You Were Mine
- **Intro**: Impressions of a parent; How the child-parent relationship changes
- **Conclusion**: The poems tackle similar issues... but they present childhood in different ways.
- **Form**: Highlights its importance. Both poems: regular form — a considered presentation of memory
- **Imagery to show admiration**: Poem 1: use of nautical imagery; Poem 2: Hollywood glamour — Marilyn Monroe
- **Guilt**: Both narrators feel that they've held their parents back. Poem 1: says he was a "nuisance" to his father. Poem 2: feels she took away her mum's freedom
- **Finite childhood**: Poem 1: reversal of the "follower". Poem 2: taking on role of parent — childhood has to end

---

Tell the examiner which poems you've chosen in your first sentence. →

Both Seamus Heaney's 'Follower' and Carol Ann Duffy's 'Before You Were Mine' present ideas about childhood through the narrators' impressions of a parent. The narrator in 'Follower' recalls his childhood memories of his father and reflects on how their relationship has changed over time, whereas in 'Before You Were Mine' the narrator uses memories from her childhood to inform the description of her mother's life before she was born. Both poets use this relationship between child and parent to explore the idea of childhood and how this relationship changes as people get older and leave childhood behind.

Both poems have a regular form; these careful frameworks emphasise how precious the narrators' memories are to them. 'Follower' has six four-line stanzas, and 'Before You Were Mine' consists of four five-line stanzas. In both poems, this creates an unhurried, steady rhythm that reflects the narrators' considered presentation of their memories. This highlights the importance of these childhood memories and implies that both narrators consider the day-to-day activities of their childhoods to have been significant, even if they were just ordinary events at the time.

← *It's important to write about form in your answers.*

Explain why the poets have presented their ideas this way. →

Section Eleven — English Literature: Poetry Anthology

Worked Exam-Style Question

Each paragraph should mark the start of a **new point**.

<u>The imagery used to describe the parents in both poems suggests that the narrators admired them as children.</u> In 'Follower', Heaney uses nautical imagery to emphasise the power and strength of the father, comparing his shoulders to a "full sail strung". <u>Similarly, the narrator in 'Before You Were Mine' describes her mother as "Marilyn", in reference to Marilyn Monroe, a famous actress and model from the 1950s.</u> By using the metaphor of an iconic Hollywood film star to describe her mother, the narrator compares the way that children admire their parents to the way that people admire famous people. In this way, both poets use imagery of strong, powerful and successful people to reflect the way that children often idolise their parents.

Show that you can apply **your own knowledge** to the poem.

Embedding short quotes helps to keep your sentences **clear** and **easy to understand**.

However, as adults, both narrators seem to feel a sense of guilt at holding their parents back. In 'Follower', the narrator describes himself as a <u>"nuisance"</u>, using the onomatopoeic verb "Yapping" to suggest that he was irritating to his father. Similarly, in 'Before You Were Mine' the narrator describes her "loud, possessive yell". <u>The combination of forceful adjectives with the powerful verb "yell" emphasises how demanding the narrator was as a child.</u> Both narrators seem to have been unaware of the negative effect they had on their parents until they were older; this suggests that childhood is a time of innocence and unquestioning acceptance of a parent's love and attention.

It's good to show the examiner that you can analyse the effect of **specific words**.

Both poems also explore the idea that as children grow older they take on the characteristics of their parents. In 'Follower', the father, in whose "wake" the son once followed, is now "stumbling / Behind" the narrator, while the narrator is the one who leads. This happens in the final two lines of the poem, which highlights its significance. <u>This also creates a cyclical structure that reflects the way the roles between the narrator and his father have been reversed since his childhood.</u> The narrator in 'Before You Were Mine' also takes on the role of a parent, asking "whose small bites on your neck, sweetheart?" The word "sweetheart" makes it sound as if the narrator is affectionately mimicking the voice of a parent. <u>In this way, Duffy presents childhood as having an inevitable endpoint, after which the child begins to acquire the traits of their parent.</u>

This paragraph explains each point in a way that **links back to the theme** in the question.

Make sure you include **both similarities and differences** between the poems.

'Follower' and 'Before You Were Mine' both present ideas about childhood through the relationship between a child and their parent. <u>Although the way these relationships are presented differs, they both highlight similar issues: admiring a parent, the guilt that is eventually felt and the inevitable end of childhood.</u> Both poets use structure, vivid imagery and language to present these issues, as well as to convey the complex emotions that arise from them.

Worked Exam-Style Question

Here's another example answer, this time for the 'Power and Conflict' poetry anthology. Have a good read of the question, plan and answer — think about which features make this a good essay. When you're happy with it all, flick over to page 186 and try some practice questions for yourself.

Q1 Compare how the reality of conflict is presented in Ted Hughes's 'Bayonet Charge' and one other poem you have studied.

Plan:

- **Introduction:** Same WW1 context; writers from different times. Different situations and emotions
  - Poem 1: action, terror
  - Poem 2: inactivity, boredom
- **Narrative voice:**
  - Poem 1: third person singular
  - Poem 2: first person plural
- **Structure and form:**
  - Poem 1: enjambment, irregular line length, punctuation show soldier's confusion
  - Poem 2: regular rhyme scheme shows monotony. Half-rhymes & short lines show hopelessness
- **Language:**
  - Poem 1: movement, violent imagery
  - Poem 2: bleak, hopeless language
- **Feelings and attitudes / Reality vs. ideal:**
  - Poem 1: patriotic ideals dropped in heat of battle
  - Poem 2: soldiers ambivalent — question purpose of conflict
- **Conclusion:** Negative views of conflict. Suggest war can't be justified

Central topic: Poem 1: Bayonet Charge / Poem 2: Exposure

Compare the poems in your opening sentence.

Although the action of both 'Bayonet Charge' and 'Exposure' occurs on the battlefields of World War One, the poems offer two very different portrayals of the reality of conflict. While 'Bayonet Charge' depicts the violent action and overwhelming terror experienced by a soldier going into battle, 'Exposure' focuses on the boredom and inactivity of men waiting in the freezing trenches of the Western Front while "nothing happens" on the battlefield. Both poets present war as a profoundly negative experience, in which hope, faith and sense of self are overpowered by pain and fear.

Sum up the main argument of your essay.

Try to explain how the writer has created an effect.

The poems use different narrative voices. 'Bayonet Charge' is written in the third person. The anonymity of the subject, "he", and the fact that he is the only human mentioned in the poem make him seem isolated and alone, even though it is clear that he must be surrounded by other soldiers. This sense of isolation heightens the feeling of terror in the poem by reflecting the soldier's acute focus on his own survival. In contrast, 'Exposure' is written in the first person plural ("our memory", "we hear"), which creates a sense of the shared suffering experienced by the millions of soldiers who fought and died in the First World War. This emphasises the vast scale of misery and loss of life in the war.

Compare the poems' form and structure.

The poets also use other aspects of form and structure to present the reality of conflict. In 'Bayonet Charge', Hughes uses enjambment and uneven line lengths to create an irregular rhythm, echoing the confusion experienced by the soldier. The irregular rhythm is heightened by caesurae in lines 11 and 15. These

Use the correct technical terms.

Worked Exam-Style Question

help to turn the second stanza into a pause in the action, which reflects the soldier's experience of time apparently standing still as he struggles to understand "the reason / Of his still running". In contrast, Owen uses a regular rhyme scheme (ABBAC) to emphasise the monotony experienced by the soldiers. Despite this regularity, half-rhymes such as "wire" / "war" create a sense of jarring discomfort that mirrors the soldiers' suffering.

The different experiences of conflict presented in 'Exposure' and 'Bayonet Charge' are conveyed through the contrasting language the poets use. Owen's language is bleak and hopeless — dawn is personified as a "melancholy army" "massing in the east", a metaphor which has a powerful effect on the reader by subverting their expectations — dawn is usually a symbol of hope, but here it only brings more "poignant misery". The soldiers' sense of hopelessness is also evident in the phrase "love of God seems dying", which suggests that the horrific reality of conflict is causing them to lose their faith in God, or perhaps to believe that a God who can subject them to such suffering has lost faith in them. In contrast to this bleak imagery, 'Bayonet Charge' is filled with frantic movement. Active verbs such as "running" and "stumbling" help to create a vivid image of the soldier's desperate actions as he races into battle. The sense of movement in the poem is also conveyed by the opening phrase, "Suddenly he awoke", which places the reader in the middle of the action from the start. This gives the poem a nightmarish quality, highlighting the feelings of confusion and terror that are driving the soldier.

Both poems suggest that the reality of conflict does not match up to the ideal. In 'Bayonet Charge', Hughes questions the patriotic ideals of "King, honour, human dignity, etcetera", arguing that in the heat of battle they are "Dropped like luxuries" as terror takes over. Information about the horrors of World War One was readily available in the 1950s when Hughes wrote this poem, and there is a sense of pity for the soldiers who fought. Similarly, in 'Exposure', the narrator questions whether anything is achieved by the soldiers' sacrifice. On the surface, the phrase "Since we believe not otherwise can kind fires burn" suggests the soldiers believe their sacrifice is necessary to protect the "kind fires" of home, but the complex, broken syntax reflects their lack of conviction that this is true. This reveals the alienation many soldiers felt: they believed no-one at home appreciated their sacrifice.

'Bayonet Charge' and 'Exposure' both present vividly negative views of the reality of conflict for soldiers on the front line. The experience of the soldiers in the two poems is very different: Hughes focuses on the raw terror and active suffering of a soldier going into battle, whereas Owen concentrates on the hopelessness and passive suffering of men dying from exposure. However, both poets use structure, form and vivid imagery to powerfully convey the soldiers' suffering. Both narrators question the patriotic ideals used to justify war, suggesting instead that there can be no justification for the bleak and dehumanising reality of conflict.

You can give more than one interpretation in your answer.

Use quotes to support your argument.

Bring in some contextual details to your answer.

Compare the language used in the two poems.

Explain the effect of the examples you give.

Your last sentence should sum up your argument, and it needs to be memorable.

Worked Exam-Style Question

On these pages, there's an example answer for the 'Worlds and Lives' poetry anthology. Once you've read the question, plan and answer, you could have a go at answering the question for yourself — perhaps even using a different comparison poem. Then, check out page 186 to try some more practice questions.

Q1 Compare how connection is presented in Seni Seneviratne's 'A Wider View' and one other poem you have studied.

Plan (mind map):
- Poem 1: A Wider View / Poem 2: With Birds You're Never Lonely
- **Context**
  - Poem 1: set in Leeds
  - Poem 2: set in London & New Zealand
  - places often link to family connections
- **Language** — sensory language - sound linked to connection in both
  - Poem 1: sound of echoing footsteps creates connection through time
  - Poem 2: sounds show connection or isolation — speaker's vs woman's reaction to birds
- **Structure and form**
  - Poem 1: five stanzas, most have five lines
  - Poem 2: unrhymed couplets, except for last line
- **Introduction**
  - importance of connection
  - connections can be with people or nature
- **Conclusion**
  - harder for speaker in Poem 2 to establish connection

Explain how the poems you've chosen link to the question.

→ Seni Seneviratne and Raymond Antrobus both explore connection in their poems, but they take differing approaches to the theme. The speaker in 'A Wider View' creates a connection with their great-great-grandfather by imagining his walk home from work, while in 'With Birds You're Never Lonely', the speaker considers the difficulty of connecting with people and nature in London. While both poems present connection as important, the speaker in Seneviratne's poem is more successful in achieving a connection.

Make sure your argument includes comparison.

Mention the context of the poems.

→ Both poems use place to show ideas about connection. 'A Wider View' is set in Leeds, as shown by references to places such as "Marshall's Temple Mill". By naming places their ancestor would have been familiar with, an initial connection is established across the generations between speaker and relative. The connection is deepened later in the poem when the Giotto Tower is described as a shared "axis" between the two of them. In 'With Birds You're Never Lonely', the speaker describes the birds and trees of the forest in Wellington in vivid colour, but then refers to "any grey tree" in London. The difference in the levels of detail shows that the speaker felt more connection to nature in New Zealand and that they feel indifferent to the trees back home. For Antrobus's speaker, more than just familiarity with a place is required for a connection to be achieved.

The poems' forms reflect the extent to which the speakers experience connection. Seneviratne's poem is five stanzas long, matching the number of generations between the speaker and their great-great-grandfather, suggesting connection between them. With the rest of the stanzas being five lines long, the four-line fourth stanza may reflect the speaker's feeling that time is "collapsing",

Consider how a poem's form links to the ideas in the poem.

Worked Exam-Style Question

Use technical terminology in your answer.

as the stanza has a shorter length when the characters finally connect and "meet". On the other hand, the form of 'With Birds You're Never Lonely' emphasises the fragility of connection. On the surface, the fact that Antrobus uses couplets seems to reflect connection, as the lines are in pairs. However, the couplets don't rhyme, which removes one level of potential connection, and the poem as a whole has a disjointed feel, with stanza breaks after every second line. The solitary last line takes this idea further, as by ending the poem with a line by itself, Antrobus gives the impression of total isolation and lack of connection experienced by the speaker in London. The form of the poem leaves the reader with a sense of disconnection and a reminder that connection is difficult, in contrast to how the form of 'A Wider View' shows how the characters connect despite the years between them.

Write about the effect writers' choices have on readers.

Both poems use sound to explore ideas about connection. Seneviratne describes how the speaker's "footsteps echo". This depicts a physical sound in the present day, but, as an echo is a repeated sound, the use of this word also suggests connection between the speaker and their relative. There is the sense that the speaker can almost hear their relative's footsteps as they listen to their own, creating a sense of closeness as the poem moves towards their imagined 'meeting' in the final stanza. In Antrobus's poem, sound is presented as being able to connect but also isolate. The "blaring" of the Tui birds leads the speaker to turn off their hearing aids, which isolates them from their surroundings and prevents connection. This contrasts with the Maori woman who "could tell which bird chirped", suggesting a close connection between her and nature. The word "chirped" has much more positive, pleasant connotations as a sound than "blaring", emphasising the woman's positive connection with her environment.

Think about the connotations of the writers' language choices.

The poems consider the role of knowledge in enabling connection. In 'A Wider View', knowledge is an important part of forming a connection, but it is insufficient in doing so by itself. The speaker in 'A Wider View' seems knowledgeable about their ancestor, giving details such as his work shift being "twelve hours" long, but there is no way to prove he walked the same streets as the speaker. Instead, connection must be created through a leap of the speaker's imagination, thus suggesting that imagination is necessary to connect with others and their experiences. In 'With Birds You're Never Lonely', the speaker also finds that knowledge sometimes isn't enough to build connections. The man in the café is "reading" about trees, but the speaker acknowledges through rhetorical questions that humans don't know what trees might "say about us", suggesting a lack of connection. However, knowledge does play a role in the Maori woman's connection with nature. Her knowledge of birds, taught by her grandfather, means she is "never lonely" around them: she has formed a connection due to her knowledge. Both poems therefore suggest that knowledge can be important for connection, but does not guarantee it.

Integrate quotations into sentences when you can.

Seneviratne and Antrobus both present connection as something that humans long to achieve. Seneviratne's speaker successfully finds connection with their ancestor through shared places and sounds, with the speaker's knowledge and imagination also being important. Although Antrobus's speaker sees the positive example of the woman's connection with the birds, they ultimately find connection more difficult — illustrated most clearly by the poem's form. Achieving connection is therefore presented by Antrobus as something more complex than Seneviratne's poem might suggest.

Refer back to the question in the conclusion.

Exam-Style Questions

Now that you've seen some examples of how to write a brilliant answer for Paper 2, Section B, it's time to put all you've learned into practice. Have a go at these questions under exam conditions. Not all of these questions will be relevant to your cluster, but there should be at least one question you can answer.

Q1 Compare how feelings towards another person are presented in 'Sonnet 29' by Elizabeth Barrett Browning and one other poem from your poetry anthology.

Q2 Compare the ways in which time is presented in two poems from your poetry anthology.

Q3 Compare how war is presented in 'Remains' by Simon Armitage and one other poem from your poetry anthology.

Q4 Compare the way that a sense of place is created in two poems from your poetry anthology.

Q5 Compare how human power is presented in two poems from your poetry anthology.

Section Twelve — English Literature: Unseen Poetry

Five Steps to Analysing a Poem

In the final section of English Literature paper 2, you have to analyse some unseen poetry — here's how...

The examiner is looking for Four Main Things

You'll have to answer <u>two questions</u> in this section — one on an <u>unseen poem</u>, and one where you <u>compare</u> the poem with another unseen poem. To impress the examiner, you need to:

1) Show that you <u>understand</u> what the poems are <u>about</u>.
2) Write about the <u>techniques</u> used in the poems.
3) Use the <u>correct technical terms</u> to describe the techniques in the poems.
4) <u>Support</u> every point you make with <u>quotes</u> or <u>examples</u> from the poems.

Five Steps to analysing an unseen poem

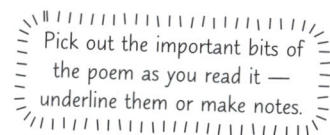
Pick out the important bits of the poem as you read it — underline them or make notes.

1) Work out what the poem's about

- Work out the <u>subject</u> of the poem, e.g. the poem is about the narrator's relationship with his parents.
- Think about <u>who</u> is <u>speaking</u>, and <u>who</u> the poem is <u>addressing</u> — e.g. the narrator's lover, the reader...

2) Identify the purpose, theme or message

- Think about <u>what</u> the poet is saying, <u>why</u> they've written the poem, or what <u>ideas</u> they're using.
- The poem could be an <u>emotional response</u> to something. It might aim to <u>get a response</u> from the <u>reader</u>, or put across a message or an opinion about something.

3) Explore the emotions, moods or feelings

- Consider the <u>different emotions or feelings</u> in the poem and identify its <u>mood</u>.
- Look at how the poet <u>shows</u> these emotions (see step 4).

4) Identify the techniques used in the poem

- Find the <u>different techniques</u> the poet has used and how they create <u>emotions</u>, <u>moods</u> or <u>feelings</u>. Think about <u>why</u> the poet has used them, and what <u>effect</u> they create.
- Techniques can be related to <u>language</u> (<u>alliteration</u>, <u>onomatopoeia</u>, <u>imagery</u> etc.), <u>structure</u> (the order of <u>ideas</u> and any changes in <u>mood</u> or <u>tone</u>) and <u>form</u> (<u>line</u> and <u>stanza</u> length, <u>rhyme schemes</u> etc.).

5) Include your thoughts and feelings about the poem

- Examiners love to hear what <u>you think</u> of a poem and how it makes <u>you feel</u>. Think about how well the poem gets its <u>message</u> across and what <u>impact</u> it has on you.
- Try <u>not</u> to use "<u>I</u>" though — don't say "I felt sad that the narrator's brother died", it's much <u>better</u> to say "It makes the reader feel the narrator's sense of sadness at the death of his brother."
- Think about any <u>other ways</u> that the poem could be <u>interpreted</u>.

Always read the poem with the question in mind...

The first thing to do when you're analysing a poem is to read the question carefully and underline the key words. That'll help you to identify aspects of the poem that are directly relevant to the question.

Worked Exam-Style Question

On the next three pages is a step-by-step guide to answering an unseen poetry question in English Literature paper 2, section C. The first stage is to read the question carefully and annotate the relevant parts of the poem. Keep in mind the five steps to analysing an unseen poem (see page 187).

Q1 a) How are ideas about death and the afterlife _presented_ in 'His Visitor'?

It's asking 'what's the poem's _message_ about death and the afterlife?'

The question wants you to write about what _techniques_ the poet uses, e.g. _form_, _structure_ and _language_.

Subject — a woman revisits her old house.

Mood — dark night, creepy.

His Visitor

I come across from Mellstock while the **moon wastes weaker**
To behold where I lived with you for twenty years and **more**:
I shall go in the grey, at the passing of the mail-train,
And need no setting open of the long familiar door
5   As **before**.

The change I notice in my once own quarters**!**
A formal-fashioned border where the daisies used to be,
The rooms new painted, **and** the pictures altered,
And other cups and saucers, **and** no cosy nook for tea
10   As with me.

I discern the **dim faces** of the sleep-wrapt servants;
They are not those who tended me through feeble hours and strong,
But strangers quite, who never knew my rule here,
Who never saw me painting, never heard my **softling song**
15   **Float along.**

So I don't want to linger in this re-decked dwelling,
I feel too **uneasy** at the contrasts I behold,
And I make again for **Mellstock** to return here never,
And rejoin the roomy silence, and the **mute and manifold**
20   **Souls of old.**

Thomas Hardy

Voice — first-person narrator.

Door doesn't need opening — speaker is ghost.

Repetition of "and" emphasises changes.

Sight is "dim" — barrier between living and dead.

We sympathise with speaker's sense of loss.

Long lines and gentle, regular rhythm give sad tone.

Rhyme scheme: ABCBB. Final line 3 syllables — slows pace and gives ghostly feel.

Exclamation mark shows disbelief.

Another woman?

Alliteration — contrasts with "mute" dead.

Mood — ghostly voice.

Links with line 1 — speaker returning to graveyard.

Surrounded by silent ghosts.

Mellstock — Hardy's name for the place where his first wife was buried
mail-train — a train that carried mail during the night
discern — make out
softling — soft and delicate
manifold — many and varied

Worked Exam-Style Question

Once you've got to grips with the poem and have picked out some short quotes and key ideas which are relevant to the question, spend five minutes planning your answer. Then get writing your answer — just make sure you refer back to your plan as you write.

Plan:

1. Intro
   - Subject — a ghost visits her former home.
   - Sorrow of dead.

Don't spend too long on your plan. It's only rough work, so you don't need to write in full sentences.

2. Death isn't the end
   - Ghost narrator.
   - Ghost is sad, not scary — reader sympathises with her.

3. The dead are powerless
   - She is "uneasy" at the changes, but can't do anything about them.
   - Her only choice is to "rejoin the roomy silence".
   - Sad tone (reinforced by gentle, regular rhythm) — living move on, dead don't.

Focus on three or four key points about the poem.

4. Separation between dead and living
   - She doesn't need the door opened — she's formless.
   - Living are unaware of her.
   - Living are "dim faces" — indistinct.
   - Living are vocal — "softling song". Dead are "mute".

Remember to write about what the poet says and how they say it.

5. Effect of death on the living
   - Poet vs. narrator. He imagines her response.
   - Guilt at the changes/new wife?

6. Conclusion
   - Dead always with us.
   - Living and dead are separate but impact on each other.

Write about the poem's main messages early on in your essay.

The poem 'His Visitor' describes the return of a ghost to the home she shared with her partner for "twenty years and more". In it, the poet imagines her resentment of the changes that have occurred since her death, indirectly revealing his own guilt at allowing these changes to take place. The poem suggests that although the living can affect the dead, and vice versa, ultimately they are separate states with no point of contact.

Clear start, showing that you've understood the poem.

Always use quotes to back up points.

The most obvious point the poet makes about death is that it is not the end. Although the narrator of the poem never explicitly states that she is a ghost, it is made clear when she says, for instance, that she arrives by night and needs "no setting open" of the door. The use of the first person makes the reader empathise with the sadness of the narrator, breaking down the stereotype of ghosts being frightening.

Give a personal response to the poem.

Worked Exam-Style Question

Write about feelings and mood, and use quotes to back up your points.

The feeling of sorrow is emphasised by the powerlessness of the narrator. Although she is "uneasy" at the changes that have been made to her former home, the only way she can ease her discomfort is to leave and "return here never". Death therefore involves giving up a loved home and all that is familiar, and instead accepting the loneliness that comes with joining the "roomy silence". The gentle rhythm of the poem reinforces the narrator's loneliness. The three-syllable lines that end each stanza are separated from the rest of the stanza by the change in rhythm, but they are linked to it by rhyme. They have the effect of making each stanza seem to tail off wistfully, reinforcing the narrator's sorrow, while their content shows her fixation on "before". This suggests that, while the living are able to move forward, the dead are trapped in the past.

Comment on form and the effect it has.

The poet also suggests that death divides the narrator from the living world. The colours of the poem are muted: the "grey" of night and the moon that "wastes weaker" create a feeling of unreality that contrasts with the "cosy nook" of the past. The "dim faces" of the sleeping servants may be shadowy because it is night, or because the narrator exists in the spiritual world, so to her, the material world is vague and unclear. Although the narrator is aware of her surroundings, she cannot interact with them, instead passing through the "long familiar door". The silence of the dead is emphasised by the alliteration of "mute and manifold", which contrasts with the "softling song" of the narrator when she was alive.

Write about any imagery in the poem.

Think about different interpretations to help you get top marks.

Mention and explain any poetic devices that you spot.

Think about any hidden meanings the poem might contain.

The poem also gives clues about the impact of death on the living. By imagining how "uneasy" the narrator feels at the "contrasts" she sees, Hardy gives the reader a hint of the guilt he feels at moving on while she cannot. The changes described are not large, but the use of an exclamation mark and the repetition of "and" in the second stanza shows how significant the poet believes they would have been to the narrator. The mention of "other cups and saucers", traditionally chosen by women, hint that the dead woman's place may have been taken by another woman. This may explain the poet's guilt. However, the fact that he is so concerned with what the ghost would feel suggests, ironically, that he has not really moved on.

Give a good personal response wherever you can.

Mention specific language features and explain why the poet used them.

Sum up the what and how in your final paragraph.

The central message of the poem is that the living and the dead inhabit two separate worlds. Hardy explores this through his use of a ghostly first-person narrator, a gentle regular rhythm which reflects her sad drifting around the house and her eventual return to "roomy silence".

Section Twelve — English Literature: Unseen Poetry

Comparing Two Poems

To do well in the Literature exam, you need to be able to compare two unseen poems. Here are some tips...

You'll have to **Compare Two** unseen poems

1) In the exam, you're going to have to compare two unseen poems.

2) This means that you need to write about the similarities and differences between them.

3) You'll need to discuss the techniques the poets use and their effect on the reader, so focus on the structure, form and language used in the two poems.

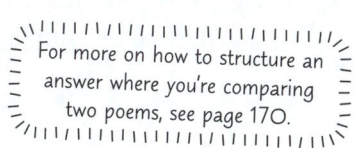
For more on how to structure an answer where you're comparing two poems, see page 170.

Four Steps to answering a comparison question

Don't start writing without thinking about what you're going to say — follow these four steps to organise your ideas:

1) Read the question

- Read the question carefully and underline the key words.
- Check whether the question asks you to write about a specific theme, e.g. 'conflict' or 'family'.

2) Annotate the poems

- Go through and annotate the poems, focusing on the techniques used and the effect they have on the reader.
- As you're annotating the second poem, look for similarities and differences with the techniques you picked out in the first poem.

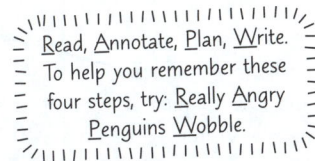
Read, Annotate, Plan, Write. To help you remember these four steps, try: Really Angry Penguins Wobble.

3) Plan your answer

- Identify three or four key similarities and/or differences that you're going to write about.
- Write a short plan that outlines the structure of your answer.

4) Write your answer

- Use your plan to make sure that every paragraph you write discusses one similarity or difference between the two poems. This could be in their themes and ideas, or their form, structure and language.
- Use linking words and phrases, e.g. 'in contrast' or 'similarly', to make it really clear that you're comparing the two poems.

EXAM TIP — **You need to write about both poems in your answer...**
The examiner wants to see that you can discuss the similarities and differences between the two poems — make this easy for them by including at least one clear comparison in every paragraph.

192

Worked Exam-Style Question

Here's another worked example. Use it to get some ideas about how to approach a comparison question.

Q1 b) In both 'His Visitor' and 'Ghosts', the poets write about <u>people's feelings on visiting a former home</u>. What are the <u>similarities</u> and <u>differences</u> between how the poems <u>present these feelings</u>?

You need to compare the poets' <u>techniques</u>, e.g. <u>form</u>, <u>structure</u> and <u>language</u>, in the two poems.

This is the <u>theme</u> you'll be looking at.

Subject — ghosts returning to their former home.

Voice — first person. Similar to 'His Visitor'.

Feelings — not alone. Contrasts with loneliness in 'His Visitor'.

Contrast — emphasises present sorrow. Similar to 'His Visitor'.

Regular metre — driving, upbeat rhythm. Contrasts with 'His Visitor'.

Feelings — sadness and loss. Similar to 'His Visitor'.

Ghosts

I to a crumpled cabin came
Upon a hillside high,
And **with me** was a withered dame
As wearful as I.
5   "**It used to be our home**," said she;
"How I remember well!
Oh that our **happy hearth** should be
Today an **empty shell!**"

The door was flailing in the **storm**
10 That deafed us with its din;
The roof that kept us once so **warm**
Now let the snow-drift in.
The floor sagged to the sod below,
The walls caved crazily;
15 We only heard the **wind of woe**
Where once was **glow and glee**.

So there we stood **disconsolate**
Beneath the Midnight Dome,
And ancient **miner and his mate**,
20 Before our wedded home,
Where we had known such love and cheer**...**
I sighed, then soft she said:
"Do not regret — remember, dear,
    We, too, are dead."

Robert W. Service

deafed — deafened
sod — grass-covered earth
Midnight Dome — a mountain in Yukon Territory, Canada

Feelings — yearning for the past. Similar to 'His Visitor'.

Alliteration — emphasises past happiness and warmth.

Feelings — exclamation mark shows disbelief, as in 'His Visitor'.

Regular ABAB rhyme scheme contributes to the fast, upbeat pace.

Alliteration emphasises contrast between past and present.

Alliteration — shows bond with wife. Contrasts with loneliness in 'His Visitor'.

Ellipsis — suggests speaker is thinking wistfully of the past.

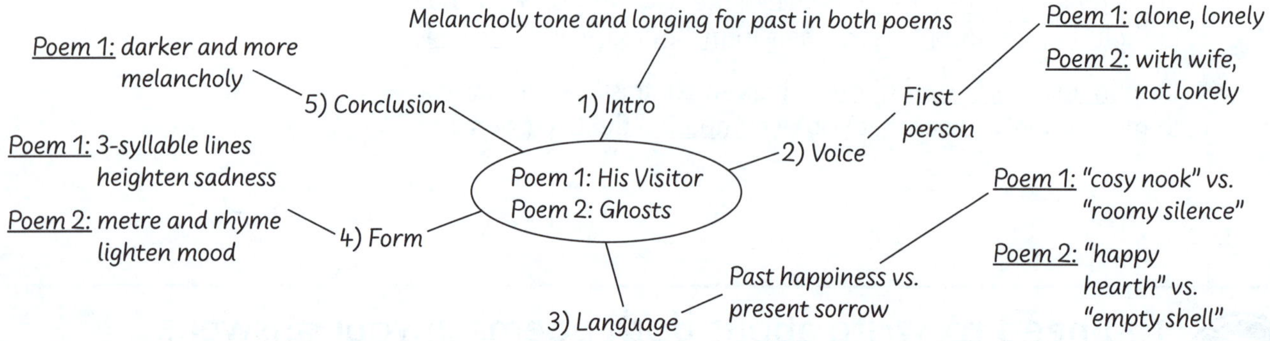

Melancholy tone and longing for past in both poems

- 1) Intro
- 2) Voice — First person
  - Poem 1: alone, lonely
  - Poem 2: with wife, not lonely
- 3) Language — Past happiness vs. present sorrow
  - Poem 1: "cosy nook" vs. "roomy silence"
  - Poem 2: "happy hearth" vs. "empty shell"
- 4) Form
  - Poem 1: 3-syllable lines heighten sadness
  - Poem 2: metre and rhyme lighten mood
- 5) Conclusion
  - Poem 1: darker and more melancholy

Poem 1: His Visitor
Poem 2: Ghosts

Section Twelve — English Literature: Unseen Poetry

Worked Exam-Style Question

Show that you've **understood** the **question**.

'His Visitor' and 'Ghosts' are both melancholy poems in which a ghostly narrator returns to their former home and is distressed to find that it has changed dramatically. Although the poems convey similar feelings about visiting a former home, the poets *use narrative voice, language and form in different ways to put these feelings across*.

Both poems use a first-person narrator. This makes the narrators' feelings seem more real and immediate, and *encourages the reader to empathise with them*. In 'His Visitor', the narrator's isolation is conveyed by her repeated use of the first-person singular pronoun "I", which emphasises her loneliness as she revisits the once-familiar house that's now filled with "*strangers*". In 'Ghosts', however, the narrator is accompanied by his wife. The collective pronouns "we" and "us" highlight their close connection and contrast the loneliness of the narrator in 'His Visitor'.

Explain how the **techniques** in the poems affect the **reader**.

Embed **short quotes** into your writing.

Introduce your paragraphs with a **comparison**.

Both poets use language to emphasise the contrast between past happiness and present sorrow. In 'His Visitor', *the "cosy nook" that symbolises the warmth and comfort the house once offered* is replaced with the afterlife's "roomy silence", and the "happy hearth" in 'Ghosts' contrasts with the now "empty shell" of the cabin. This highlights the narrators' yearning for the past, something that is emphasised by the repeated use of phrases associated with the past, *such as "As before" in 'His Visitor' and "used to be" in 'Ghosts'*, suggesting that both narrators are fixated on the way things were.

Show that you understand the **imagery** in the poems.

Use **quotes** to support your **argument**.

The form of 'His Visitor' helps to convey the narrator's feelings. The three-syllable lines that end each stanza slow the poem's pace and give it an irregular rhythm, with each stanza trailing off wistfully. *This creates a powerful sense of sadness and melancholy.* In contrast, the regular metre and simple ABAB rhyme scheme of 'Ghosts' give the poem a faster pace and a driving, upbeat rhythm which lightens the mood and makes the poem seem *less bleak and melancholy than 'His Visitor'*.

Write about how **form** conveys meaning.

Remember to **compare** the two poems.

Summarise the **similarities** and **differences** in your conclusion.

'His Visitor' and 'Ghosts' both use language to convey similar feelings of sadness, loss and longing for the past, and regret at the changes to their former homes. However, differences in the poets' use of narrative voice and form mean that, overall, the tone of 'His Visitor' is darker and more melancholy than that of 'Ghosts'.

Warm-Up Questions

Before you answer the questions at the bottom of the page, read the poem all the way through and annotate anything you think is important. Once you've got an idea of what the poem's about, the techniques the poet uses and why she uses them, you'll be ready to answer the questions.

Warm-Up Questions

Spring in War-Time

Now the sprinkled blackthorn snow
Lies along the lovers' lane
Where last year we used to go—
Where we shall not go again.

5   In the hedge the buds are new,
By our wood the violets peer—
Just like last year's violets, too,
But they have no scent this year.

Every bird has heart to sing
10 Of its nest, warmed by its breast;
We had heart to sing last spring,
But we never built our nest.

Presently red roses blown
Will make all the garden gay...
15 Not yet have the daisies grown
On your clay.

Edith Nesbit

blackthorn — a bush with white flowers in spring

1) Write down what you think the poem is about, in just one sentence.

2) What do you think the narrator means by "we never built our nest" in the 3rd stanza?

3) How does the poet create a contrast between the signs of spring and the narrator's feelings in the poem?

4) What is the rhyme scheme of this poem and why do you think that the poet chose it?

5) The last line of the poem has a different rhythm. Why do you think that the poet has done this?

Section Twelve — English Literature: Unseen Poetry

Exam-Style Questions

On the next two pages are questions about two poems that you probably won't have read before. They'll test your ability to analyse and compare unseen poetry, just like you'll have to do in the English Literature exam. Remember — read the question, annotate the poems, make a short plan, then write your answer.

Q1 a) Read the poem below.
How does the poet present ideas about what it can feel like to be left alone?

At Sea

With nothing to do now he's gone,
she dusts the house,
sweeps the bleached verandah clear of sand.
The broom leaves a trail of grit on the step,
5   a sprinkling under the hook where it hangs.

A coat for a pillow,
she sleeps downstairs,
dreams the loathed ocean is coming for her,
climbing the cliffs,
10   creeping in through the door.

She wakes to the screaming gulls,
his shirts on the line
and the high tide's breakers'
chill in her arms.

Jennifer Copley

Exam-Style Questions

Q1 b) Both 'At Sea' and 'The Sands of Dee' describe the power of the sea. What are the similarities and differences between how the poems present the sea?

The Sands of Dee

'O Mary, go and call the cattle home,
And call the cattle home,
And call the cattle home
Across the sands of Dee;'
5   The western wind was wild and dank with foam,
And all alone went she.

The western tide crept up along the sand,
And o'er and o'er the sand,
And round and round the sand,
10   As far as eye could see.
The rolling mist came down and hid the land:
And never home came she.

'Oh! is it weed, or fish, or floating hair—
A tress of golden hair,
15   A drowned maiden's hair
Above the nets at sea?
Was never salmon yet that shone so fair
Among the stakes on Dee.'

They rowed her in across the rolling foam,
20   The cruel, crawling foam,
The cruel, hungry foam,
To her grave beside the sea:
But still the boatmen hear her call the cattle home,
Across the sands of Dee.

Charles Kingsley

Sands of Dee — a sandy bay in North Wales
dank — damp and unpleasant
o'er — over
tress — a piece of hair or a plait

Section Thirteen — English Literature: Knowledge Organisers

Blood Brothers — Knowledge Organiser

There's a lot to learn for your GCSE English Literature exam. To help, we've put together this lovely section of Knowledge Organisers — each one has all the key bits about a set text for you to refer to. If one of your set texts isn't covered in this section of the book, scan this QR code — we've included Knowledge Organisers for **all of the AQA set texts** as a handy online extra. Let's kick things off with Willy Russell's *Blood Brothers*.

Characters

Mrs Johnstone	Mickey Johnstone	Linda	Edward Lyons	Mrs Lyons
The twin boys' mother. Loving. Very poor.	Friendly child. Grows up poor. Becomes unstable.	Practical & confident. Torn between twins.	Privileged upbringing. Kind, but naive.	Adopts Edward. Manipulative. Protective.

The Narrator: A mysterious & unsympathetic figure.   **Sammy Johnstone:** Mickey's brother. Naughty child. Turns to crime.
Mr Lyons: Edward's adoptive father. Uncaring boss.   **Chorus:** Group that sings parts of story. Play minor characters too.

Plot — Key Events

Act One
- Mrs Johnstone gives away one of her twin babies to Mrs Lyons.
- The twins (age 7) meet and become "blood brothers".
- The twins & Linda get in trouble with the police.
- The Lyonses move away & the Johnstones are moved too.

Act Two
- Mickey and Edward meet and become friends again.
- Linda gets pregnant and marries Mickey, who is also made redundant by Mr Lyons.
- Edward and Mickey fall out — they live different lives.
- Mickey is jailed for robbery, then becomes depressed.
- Mickey sees Edward and Linda together and goes to confront Edward. The boys find out they're related.

Mickey accidentally shoots Edward, and is killed by the police.

Context & Themes

Money & Social Class
Linked to power. Richer characters have choices in life — "talk of Oxbridge" for Edward.

Childhood & Growing Up
Childhood is a time of innocence & fun — "just a game". Also linked to class — lower-class characters have to grow up faster.

Gender
Husbands / dads absent or lacking. Women have motherly roles, but also act as breadwinners.

Fate & Superstition
Events seem fated, e.g. we know the twins will die. Superstition influences characters (e.g. Mrs J).

Friendship
Presented as carefree and positive for children. More difficult in adulthood.

Identity
The twins show identity is rooted in upbringing / class — they are genetically identical but lead very different lives.

Structure & Form

Two-act structure
Act One is generally more lighthearted. In Act Two, happy events are immediately counteracted by darker ones.

Circular structure — starts & ends with the death of the twins. Creates a sense of doom.

No scene breaks, use of time jumps
Increases pace — sense of the play speeding towards tragedy.

Lyrics and song
The play's songs often act as soliloquies, giving insights into the characters' feelings, e.g. the twins missing each other.

Classical tragedy
The chorus and theme of fate are similar to classical tragedy, so the story seems timeless.

Writer's Techniques

Characters' **speech** emphasises the **class divide**.	"Gis a sweet" (Mickey) "old chap" (Mr Lyons)
Superstitious / bad luck imagery shows the twins are doomed.	"There's a black cat stalking" (Narrator)
Seasonal imagery shows that happiness is **temporary**.	"the lambs in spring" (Narrator)
Dramatic irony — audience knows twins die together.	"I will always defend my brother" (Mickey)
Repeated motifs show how the characters' lives get worse over time.	"And we went dancing" vs. "His mind's gone dancing" (Mrs Johnstone)
Repetition creates a sense of **tension** or **menace**.	"the devil's got your number" (Narrator)

Find the CGP RevisionHub at cgpbooks.co.uk/blurb

A Christmas Carol — Knowledge Organiser

What the Dickens!? Lots of handy information about Charles Dickens' *A Christmas Carol*, you say? Why thank you, kind sir.

Characters

Ebenezer Scrooge
Miserly & friendless. Becomes generous.

Jacob Marley
Scrooge's dead business partner.

Fred
Scrooge's nephew. Cheerful & friendly.

Bob Cratchit
Scrooge's employee. Poor. Loves his family.

Tiny Tim
Bob's sickly son. Selfless & beloved.

Ghost of Christmas Past
Kind & forceful.

Ghost of Christmas Present
Jolly & generous.

Ghost of Christmas Yet to Come
Silent & sinister.

Fan — Scrooge's sister.
Belle — Scrooge's ex-fiancée.
Fezziwig — kind businessman. Scrooge's old boss.

Structure & Form

Divided into 5 chapters:

Circular structure

Chapter 1	Chapters 2-4	Chapter 5
Emphasises Scrooge's flaws.	Ghosts show Scrooge his past, present & future.	Scrooge corrects his flaws.

Non-chronological narrative — jumps back & forth in time.
Omniscient narrator influences reader's view of Scrooge.

Novella is like a carol: Each chapter is called a 'stave' (verse) — suggests the novella should be read aloud to people.

Context & Themes

Christmas Spirit
- Christmas became important & more secular in 19th century.
- Christmas spirit is central to story.
- Involves generosity & kindness — it's personified by the Ghost of Christmas Present.
- Eventually transforms Scrooge.

Family
- Family is important — linked to the idea of happiness.
- Scrooge is isolated & thinks family is a waste of money — but he becomes a "second father" to Tiny Tim at the end.

Poverty & Social Responsibility
- Shines a light on poverty — e.g. the struggles of the Cratchit family.
- Exposes the unfair treatment of poor & argues wealthy must help them — e.g. Tiny Tim only survives because Scrooge helps.

Redemption
- Scrooge's redemption is main focus — whether it will occur or not creates dramatic tension.
- Scrooge is redeemed by choosing to change his mean behaviour.
- Suggests all can be redeemed.

Plot — Key Events

All the events take place between Christmas Eve & Christmas Day.

Chapter One
- Scrooge rudely refuses Fred's invite to Christmas dinner.
- Marley's ghost appears & warns Scrooge to change his ways.

Chapter Two
The Ghost of Christmas Past appears & shows Scrooge moments from his past:
1) A lonely Christmas as a child.
2) Happier Christmases e.g. with his sister / Mr Fezziwig.
3) Belle breaking off her engagement to Scrooge.

Chapter Three
The Ghost of Christmas Present appears to Scrooge and:
- Takes Scrooge to see Cratchits. He learns Tiny Tim will die.
- Shows people enjoying Christmas globally.
- Brings Scrooge to Fred's house, where he is being mocked.

Chapter Four
- The Ghost of Christmas Yet to Come shows Scrooge how people "delight" at his death.
- The Cratchits mourn Tiny Tim.
- Scrooge sees his own grave.
- Scrooge promises to change.

Chapter Five
- Scrooge is back in his bed.
- He has completely changed — he's generous & friendly.
- Scrooge rejoins his family & befriends the Cratchits.

Writer's Techniques

Mood — generally festive & jolly. BUT darker mood used to highlight message of social responsibility.

Tone — chatty language creates lively tone. Lighthearted sarcastic tone becomes darker & more melancholy, but turns joyful at end.

Description — uses descriptive techniques & figurative language throughout to create entertaining descriptions, e.g. describes Scrooge as "solitary as an oyster".

Image	What it represents
Fire & Brightness	Joy & companionship. Scrooge's "very small fire" symbolises lack of joy.
Music	Celebration & happiness — central to festivities.
Weather	Scrooge's character / emotions. Begins foggy & "bleak", but turns "bright" when Scrooge changes.

Section Thirteen — English Literature: Knowledge Organisers

An Inspector Calls — Knowledge Organiser

I like to learn my lessons without any fire or blood or anguish — so here's a painless recap of J.B Priestley's *An Inspector Calls*.

Characters

Inspector Goole — Claims he's a police inspector. Authoritative & moral.

Arthur Birling — Respected businessman. Selfish & ambitious.

Sybil Birling — Arthur's wife. Obsessed with etiquette and social status.

Sheila Birling — Birlings' daughter. Matures during the play.

Eric Birling — Birlings' son. Villain and a victim. Takes responsibility.

Gerald Croft — Businessman & Sheila's fiancé. Doesn't learn from Inspector.

Eva Smith/ Daisy Renton — Never on stage. Represents working class.

Plot — Key Events

Act One
- The Birling family are celebrating Sheila's engagement.
- Inspector Goole arrives & tells them Eva is dead.
- It's revealed Arthur sacked Eva — she campaigned for higher wages.
- Sheila had Eva fired from her next job.
- Inspector reveals Eva changed her name to Daisy Renton. Gerald is shocked. Eric leaves.

Act Two
- Gerald describes his affair with Daisy Renton. Sheila returns her engagement ring and Gerald leaves.
- It's revealed Eva/Daisy was pregnant. Sybil convinced her charity not to help Eva/Daisy and blames the father.
- Sheila guesses Eric is the father. Eric comes back.

Act Three
- Eric says he forced Eva into sex & stole money for her.
- Inspector gives a speech on responsibility. He leaves.
- Gerald returns. He says there is no Inspector Goole. The hospital confirms no-one has died that night.
- Confident it was a hoax, Arthur, Sybil and Gerald relax. Eric and Sheila disagree with them.
- The phone rings — a woman has died and an inspector is on his way…

Context & Themes

The 20th century was a time of big social upheaval.

British Society and Class
British society divided into social classes. Upper & middle class worry about scandal (shown by Arthur / Sybil). Working class (Eva/Daisy) struggle to survive.

Social Responsibility
Priestley was a socialist — play shows importance of social responsibility. Inspector's final speech (Act 3) sums it up: "[We are] members of one body" → "We don't live alone" → "We are responsible for each other"

Family Life
The Birlings seem to be a nice middle-class family, but they're held together by lies.

Young & Old
Young characters agree with Inspector, older ones refuse to change. Gerald caught in middle.

Men & Women
Gender stereotypes start to be overturned. Sheila gains confidence & men's authority is challenged.

Judgement and Learning
- Inspector seems omniscient — adds weight to his judgement.
- Being able to learn and change presented as crucial. Inspector's visit offers a chance to learn. Warns that refusing to change means learning the same lesson "in fire and blood and anguish".

Writer's Techniques

Dramatic irony
Play set in 1912, but first performed 1945. When Arthur says "I say there isn't a chance of war", the audience knows he's wrong — he looks short-sighted.

Imagery
Priestley uses graphic or Biblical imagery to make points strongly. E.g. Inspector describes the disinfectant's effects on Eva/Daisy — "Burnt her inside out".

Euphemism
Birlings don't talk about tricky subjects. Sybil calls Eva/Daisy a "girl of that sort" instead of working class. Inspector speaks directly — at the end, so does Sheila.

Structure & Form

Three acts with no scene breaks	Each act ends on a cliffhanger, and action is frozen between them.
Exits and entrances	Door bangs when characters exit & enter — creates a sense of tension & mystery over who's coming or going.
Takes place in one room	Creates a claustrophobic atmosphere.
Information is released slowly	E.g. photo(s) shown to one character at a time — increases tension.
Morality play	Inspector exposes the characters' sins.

Section Thirteen — English Literature: Knowledge Organisers

Dr Jekyll and Mr Hyde — Knowledge Organiser

Here are the key bits of Robert Louis Stevenson's *Jekyll & Hyde*, all on one page — consider it the novel's friendly alter ego...

Characters

Dr Henry Jekyll
Doctor & scientist. Hides dark desires under respectable appearance.

Mr Edward Hyde
Evil side of Dr Jekyll. Violent, merciless & ugly. Loathed by all.

Jekyll & Hyde are the same person.

Gabriel Utterson
Lawyer & Jeykll's friend. Very rational.

Richard Enfield
Utterson's relative. Typical Victorian.

Poole
Jekyll's loyal butler.

Dr Hastie Lanyon
Doctor. Disagrees with Jekyll's views on science.

Sir Danvers Carew — elderly MP.   **Mr Guest** — Utterson's clerk.

Structure & Form

The story has a main narrative:
- Narrated in 3rd person, but story is limited to Utterson's perspective.
- Chronological — builds tension.

Has embedded narratives (letters / testimonies):
- Act like pieces of evidence in a case.
- Return to the past & explain gaps in the story from other points of view (e.g. Jekyll).

Has many features of the Gothic:
- ✓ mysterious setting
- ✓ disturbing secret
- ✓ the supernatural
- ✓ the double
- ✓ visions

Set in Victorian London, not a traditional Gothic castle — more real & scary.

Plot — Key Events

Chapters 1 & 2
- Enfield tells Utterson that he saw Hyde trample a girl.
- Jekyll leaves everything to Hyde in his will. Utterson is worried. He learns that Jekyll and Lanyon fell out.
- Utterson meets Hyde and is disgusted by him.

Chapter 3
- Jekyll's dinner party.
- Jekyll tries to avoid explaining his connection to Hyde.

Chapters 4 & 5
- Hyde murders Carew.
- Jekyll shows Utterson a letter from Hyde saying that he's leaving forever.
- Utterson suspects Jekyll really wrote the letter.

Chapter 6
- Lanyon grows sick & dies mysteriously.
- He leaves a letter to be opened later.

Chapters 7 & 8
- Jekyll almost transforms in front of his friends.
- Poole visits Utterson, fearing Hyde has murdered Jekyll.
- Utterson breaks down lab door & finds Hyde dead.

Chapter 9
- Dr Lanyon's letter explains why he died — he witnessed Hyde transform into Jekyll.

Chapter 10
- Jekyll's letter explains why he created Hyde — to indulge his secret desires.
- Jekyll lost control as Hyde grew stronger.
- Hyde took over & killed Jekyll & himself.

Writer's Techniques

Setting & Symbolism

London is dark & "foggy" — symbolises mystery & secrecy.

It's like a "city in a nightmare", full of dangerous and scary "labyrinths".

Jekyll's house symbolises his character: main house has an "air of wealth", but back of house is dirty & "distained".

Speech

Gentlemen: polite speech hides anxieties.

Poole: speech reflects lower class — calls Jekyll "master". Doesn't conceal emotions.

Hyde: speech is angry & impolite. Makes inhuman noises, e.g. "hissing".

Language

Main narrative uses formal, controlled language:
- contrast with violent events is shocking.
- reflects Utterson's personality.
- Passages of description make events vivid.

Similes describe Hyde like a "madman", "rat" and "Satan".

Context and Themes

Dual Nature of Man

Jekyll tries to separate his 2 sides:

virtuous / civilised (Jekyll)   vs   sinful / uncivilised (Hyde)

"Man is not truly one, but truly two" (Jekyll)

He shows that even respectable men have dark sides — it's hypocritical to pretend otherwise.

Science & Religion

Christianity was very influential, but science caused conflict by questioning religious ideas, e.g. Darwin's theory of evolution.

Jekyll combines science & religion in "mystic" experiments — could be seen as disrespecting God.

Secrecy

Plot revolves around secret alter ego. Locked doors symbolise secrecy.

Victorian London

Upper class lived in nice houses, working class lived in dirty slums. Gentlemen visit "dismal" parts of city to satisfy hidden desires.

Reputation

A gentleman's reputation was key. Gentlemen were expected to behave politely & have good morals. To stay 'respectable', gentlemen hid desires & repressed emotions.

Macbeth — Knowledge Organiser

Is this a dagger which I see before me? Nope, just a handy, bite-sized summary of Shakespeare's *Macbeth*. You're welcome.

Characters

 **Macbeth** — Scottish nobleman. Ambitious & brave but easily led.

 **Lady Macbeth** — Macbeth's wife. Ruthless, ambitious & persuasive.

 **King Duncan** — Good king. Kind but too trusting.

 **The Macduffs** — Scottish nobles.

 **Banquo** — Macbeth's friend. Noble & kind.

 **Malcolm & Donalbain** — Duncan's sons.

 **Three Witches** — Evil & supernatural. See the future.

Porter — Clown-like character.

Fleance — Banquo's son.

Lennox, **Rosse**, **Menteith**, **Angus** & **Caithness** — Lesser Scottish nobles.

Plot — Key Scenes

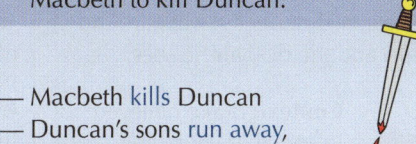

Act One
Scene 3 — Macbeth & Banquo meet three Witches, who predict that Macbeth will be king.
Scene 7 — Lady Macbeth persuades Macbeth to kill Duncan.

Act Two
Scene 2 — Macbeth kills Duncan
Scene 3 — Duncan's sons run away, letting Macbeth take throne.

Act Three
Scene 3 — Banquo killed on Macbeth's orders.
Scene 4 — Macbeth sees Banquo's ghost.
Scene 6 — Uprising against Macbeth plotted.

Act Four
Scene 1 — Witches make more predictions. Macbeth filled with confidence.
Scene 2 — Macduff's family is murdered.
Scene 3 — Macduff grieves & seeks revenge.

Act Five
Scene 1 — Lady Macbeth sleepwalks.
Scene 5 — Lady Macbeth dies offstage.
Scene 8 — Macbeth is killed by Macduff.
Scene 9 — Malcom becomes king — order restored.

Shakespeare's Techniques

Different characters speak in different ways.
- **Nobility**, e.g. Macbeth, talk in blank verse.
- **Lower classes**, e.g. the Porter, talk in prose.
- **Witches** speak in rhyme to show they're unnatural.

Image	What it represents
Light	Goodness & wisdom — loyal Lords are called "stars".
Dark	Evil — witches are "instruments of darkness" and Macbeth describes his evil intentions as "black".
Health/ Disease	The state of Scotland — it "bleeds" under Macbeth's rule and Malcolm is the "med'cine" that will cure it.
Blood	Guilt ("Out, damned spot!") & violence.

Soliloquies show characters' innermost thoughts: E.g. Act 1, S5 — Lady Macbeth's speech to spirits.

Structure & Form

Structured as a typical tragedy:

1st part: Macbeth's rise to power (Acts 1-2)

TURNING POINT: Duncan killed (Act 2, S2)

2nd part: Macbeth's downfall (Acts 3-5)

Circular structure — starts & ends with battle to defeat tyrant. Order restored at end of play.

Foreshadowing & suspense — keeps audience gripped.

Context & Themes

Ambition	Good vs Evil	Loyalty & Betrayal	Kingship	The Supernatural	Reality & Appearances	Fate & Free Will
Ambition is the key theme of the play. Ambition is Macbeth's 'fatal flaw' — it causes his ruin.	The struggle for the throne is a conflict between good & evil — battles at the start & end represent this fight. Macbeth is a "noble" man who is led into evil by ambition.	Loyalty is rewarded & betrayal is punished. Traitors say they're loyal, whereas truly loyal people act loyally.	The Scottish heir didn't have to be the old king's son. People believed that God chose kings, so kings were meant to be holy. There are good kings ("gracious" Duncan) & bad kings ("Devilish" Macbeth).	At the time, many believed in witches. Witches represent evil. They're a supernatural force which drives the play. Visions are supernatural signs of guilt.	Appearances can be deceptive. Some characters are too trusting — e.g. Duncan's trust in Macbeth's "False face" leads to his death. Meanings of words are often unclear — e.g. "Fair is foul".	Could argue Macbeth was doomed from the start, with events destined to happen. Or could argue his free will (trying to fulfil the prophecies) caused his downfall.

Power and Conflict — Knowledge Organiser

There's no need to start counting all the ways in which you love poetry — you'll be here all day. Instead, sit down and soak up this painstakingly condensed Knowledge Organiser for all of the poems in the *Power and Conflict* cluster. You won't need to write about all 15 poems in the exam, but it doesn't hurt to be prepared...

This is the publication year.

London
William Blake — 1794

The speaker describes a walk around London and the despair he sees.

Context: Blake believed in social equality and questioned the Church.

Ozymandias
Percy Bysshe Shelley — 1817

Tells the story of a ruined statue of a once-proud king in the desert.

Context: Shelley was a Romantic — they wrote about intense emotions and were influenced by nature.

My Last Duchess
Robert Browning — 1842

The Duke describes his late wife, whose behaviour he disapproved of. It's hinted that he had her killed.

Context: Likely inspired by the death of the real Duchess of Ferrara.

The Prelude: Stealing the Boat
William Wordsworth — 1850

In the extract, the narrator goes rowing and is awed by the power of nature.

Context: Autobiographical and about childhood. Wordsworth was a Romantic like Shelley (see above).

The Charge of the Light Brigade
Alfred Tennyson — 1854

Many soldiers die after being sent into an ill-advised battle.

Context: A battle in the Crimean War — British soldiers sent with swords to fight Russians, who had guns.

Exposure
Wilfred Owen — 1920

Soldiers endure difficult conditions including terrible weather. They feel disconnected from their lives at home.

Context: Owen wrote this poem while fighting in WWI. He died in action.

Bayonet Charge
Ted Hughes — 1957

A WWI soldier charges enemy lines. His patriotism is replaced with fear.

Context: Hughes's father was a soldier in World War One.

Storm on the Island
Seamus Heaney — 1966

Island-dwellers believe they are prepared for a storm, but still fear it.

Context: Heaney was from rural Northern Ireland. The 'storm' may refer to political violence in Ireland.

War Photographer
Carol Ann Duffy — 1985

A war photographer contemplates the photos he took overseas.

Context: One line seems to reference a famous photo from the Vietnam War, 'Napalm Girl'.

The Emigrée
Carol Rumens — 1993

The narrator explores her feelings towards a city she left as a child.

Context: Rumens is a contemporary poet who also works as a translator.

Tissue
Imtiaz Dharker — 2006

An abstract poem that considers the significance of paper in our lives.

Context: Dharker was born in Pakistan, but raised in Glasgow.

Checking Out Me History
John Agard — 2007

An exploration of identity using heroes from Caribbean history that the narrator wasn't taught about.

Context: John Agard was born in Guyana, then moved to Britain.

Remains
Simon Armitage — 2008

A soldier is haunted by the memory of killing a man who was looting a bank.

Context: Based on the real account of a British soldier who served in Iraq.

Poppies
Jane Weir — 2009

A mother describes her feelings and actions as her son leaves, apparently to join the army.

Context: Commissioned as part of a collection of war poems.

Kamikaze
Beatrice Garland — 2013

Story of a Japanese pilot who returns home after abandoning his mission.

Context: Japanese kamikaze pilots in WWII flew on suicide missions. Failure was seen as dishonourable.

Power and Conflict — Knowledge Organiser

Power

Humans can abuse their power:

- The Duke in 'My Last Duchess', is power-obsessed, which may have led to him ordering the murder of his wife.
- 'Checking Out Me History' shows how the British school system provides limited / one-sided cultural education.

But human power is temporary:

- The statue in 'Ozymandias' has become a ruin over time.
- 'Tissue' uses paper imagery to suggest symbols of human power, like buildings, "drift" away "easily".

Nature is powerful, but dangerous:

- 'The Prelude' & 'Kamikaze' show that nature can influence human actions and emotions.
- 'Storm on the Island' & 'Exposure' show that nature can be threatening.

Conflict

Poem	Link to Theme
'The Charge of the Light Brigade'	Shows the tragic effects of conflict, and suggests those who die in battle are brave and honourable.
'Remains'	Shows that the effects of conflict can last long after the conflict itself.
'Poppies' & 'War Photographer'	These poems show that conflict is difficult even for those who are not directly involved.
'Exposure' & 'Bayonet Charge'	The poems emphasise the harsh reality of conflict — they show it's frightening or bleak, not honourable & noble.

Loss and Absence

- 'Poppies' and 'Kamikaze' show the pain of losing a loved one (in different ways).
- 'The Emigrée' shows the effect of losing a place.
- 'Checking Out Me History' explores a lost cultural heritage.
- 'London' and 'Exposure' feature narrators who have lost hope.
- 'Kamikaze' and 'Exposure' show people who lose their patriotism.

Memory

- 'Remains' and 'War Photographer' show that memories, particularly of conflict, can be very traumatic.
- The narrator of 'The Emigrée' vividly remembers a place that she hasn't seen since she was a child.
- The narrator in 'Kamikaze' implies that memories influenced the pilot & led him to abandon his mission.

You'll need to compare two of the poems in the anthology for Paper 2 of your Literature exam.

Poetic Form

Some of the poems follow strict forms:

'War Photographer'
- Four six-line stanzas, ABBCDD rhyme scheme.
- Reflects the photographer's methodical work.

'Exposure'
- Regular ABBAC rhyme scheme.
- Highlights lack of action and monotony.

'London'
- Strict ABAB rhyme scheme and regular rhythm.
- The city's misery seems relentless and unending.

Others are irregular:

'The Charge of the Light Brigade'
- Varied stanza lengths and rhyme schemes.
- Reflects the chaos of battle.

'Checking Out Me History'
- Stories from British culture use regular quatrains.
- Caribbean stanzas use free verse.
- British education seems restrictive & dull in contrast.

Poetic Techniques

Technique	Poems
Onomatopoeia	• 'The Charge of the Light Brigade' — "thunder'd" / "Shatter'd" • 'Bayonet Charge' — "smacking" / "crackling air"
Repeated sounds	• 'The Prelude' — "struck", "still", "stars" • 'Exposure' — "Slowly our ghosts drag home"
Enjambment	• 'Tissue' — reflects the freedom that the speaker longs for. • 'The Emigrée' — suggests the speaker is absorbed in her memories.
Repetition	• 'Remains' — the speaker replays the shooting in his mind. • 'The Charge of the Light Brigade' — repetition of the "six hundred" highlights the tragic death toll.
Irony	• 'Ozymandias' — the king's proud achievements ultimately become worthless over time. • 'Kamikaze' — the pilot chose not to die, but his family's shame led them to act as if he was dead.
Dramatic irony	• 'My Last Duchess' — the reader sees that the Duke's comments about his wife have a sinister meaning.

Romeo and Juliet — Knowledge Organiser

...*Romeo, Romeo, wherefore art thine play so long?* *Romeo and Juliet* need not be a Shakespearean slog if you're pressed for time — we've squeezed all the juiciest bits out and poured them into the Knowledge Organiser page below. Mm, refreshing...

Characters

The Montagues — Romeo's parents. Hate Capulets.

Romeo Montague — Passionate, romantic & impulsive.

Juliet Capulet — Beautiful, intelligent & increasingly independent.

The Capulets — Juliet's parents. Hate Montagues.

The Friar — Father figure to Romeo. Herbalist.

Benvolio — Romeo's peaceful cousin.

Mercutio — Romeo's fun-loving friend.

Tybalt — Juliet's violent cousin.

The Nurse — Raised Juliet — they are very close.

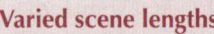
Paris — Juliet's wealthy suitor.

Rosaline — Romeo's early love interest.
Prince — rules Verona.

Structure & Form

Main genre of play is a **tragedy**.

Order of Scenes:
- Start — comedy / romance
- ↓
- **TURNING POINT** — Mercutio's death (Act 3, S1)
- ↓
- End — tragedy

Varied scene lengths
- **Short** scenes change mood: e.g. In Act 5, S1 & S2, action hurtles out of control.
- **Long** scenes develop events & characters: e.g. Act 2, S2 develops the love between Romeo & Juliet.

Plot — Key Scenes

Act One
- Prologue — Reveals outcome of the play.
- Scene 1 — Montagues fight Capulets. Romeo is lovesick.
- Scene 5 — Romeo & Juliet meet at the Capulets' ball.

Act Two
- Scene 2 — The famous balcony scene. Romeo hears Juliet talk about her love for him & they agree to marry.
- Scene 6 — The Friar marries Romeo & Juliet in secret.

Act Three
- Scene 1 — Tybalt kills Mercutio, then Romeo kills Tybalt. The Prince banishes Romeo.
- Scene 4 — The Capulets decide Juliet will marry Paris.
- Scene 5 — Romeo & Juliet's farewell. She refuses to marry Paris, angering her father.

Act Four
- Scene 1 — Friar forms a plan — Juliet will fake her death & Romeo will be told to get her from tomb.
- Scene 5 — Juliet found 'dead'.

Act Five
- Scene 1 — Romeo hears Juliet is dead.
- Scene 2 — Friar's letter not delivered.
- Scene 3 — Romeo & Juliet kill themselves. Families go to tomb & reconcile.

Context & Themes

Religion
- The Church had a big influence in the 16th century — e.g. Romeo & Juliet respect the Friar's "wisdom".
- But love is more important than religion to Romeo & Juliet. They kill themselves even though suicide was considered a sin.

Marriage
- Marriage was sacred — the Friar tries to stop Juliet's marriage to Paris because she has already married Romeo.
- Marriage was sometimes for money — the Capulets tell Juliet to marry Paris because he's rich.

Family
- Family honour was important — Juliet has to choose between personal happiness or family duty.
- Men lead families — Lord Capulet says Juliet is "ruled" by him.

Love
- Different types of love — true, courtly, sexual & young.
- Love is destructive — Romeo & Juliet die for love.

Conflict
- Feud is inescapable — even peaceful characters forced to fight.
- Feud conflicts with love — Romeo is Juliet's "loathèd enemy".
- Death finally stops feud — Romeo & Juliet's deaths end it.

Fate
- Romeo & Juliet are "star-cross'd lovers" who were doomed to die from the start — Romeo calls himself "fortune's fool".
- But other characters contribute to tragedy — e.g. Friar, Nurse.

Shakespeare's Techniques

Dramatic irony creates suspense for the audience. E.g. Everyone thinks Juliet is dead after she drinks the Friar's mixture, but the audience know she's alive.

Different characters speak in different ways.

 The upper class, e.g. the Prince, use blank verse.

 The lower class, e.g. Nurse, talk without much rhythm.

Rhythm shows emotions — e.g. In Act 2, S3, Romeo speaks in a steady rhythm when he tries to be calm.

Puns offer humour & layers of meaning. 'Grave' means 'serious', but it also refers to Mercutio thinking he'll be dead tomorrow. → 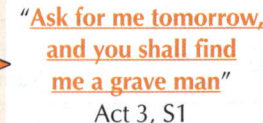 "Ask for me tomorrow, and you shall find me a grave man" Act 3, S1

Practice Papers — English Language

205

As final preparation, here are some practice papers to test how well-prepared you are for the real thing.
- There are two practice papers:
  Paper 1: pages 205-208
  Paper 2: pages 209-213
- Before you start each paper, read through all the instructions, information and advice on the front.
- You'll need some paper to write your answers on.
- When you've finished, have a look at the answers starting on page 251 — they'll give you some ideas of the kind of things you should have included in your answers.
- Don't try to do both of the papers in one sitting.

General Certificate of Secondary Education

GCSE
English Language
Paper 1

Time allowed: 1 hour 45 minutes

Centre name				
Centre number				
Candidate number				

Surname	
Other names	
Candidate signature	

Instructions to candidates
- Answer **all** the questions.
- Write your answers in **black** ink or ball-point pen.
- Write your name and other details in the boxes above.
- Cross out any rough work that you do not want to be marked.
- You should **not** use a dictionary.

Information for candidates
- The marks available are given in brackets at the end of each question.
- There are 80 marks available for this exam paper.
- You must use good English and clear presentation in your answers.

Advice for candidates
- You should spend about 15 minutes reading through the text and all five questions.

This extract is the opening of a short story set in New Zealand, written in 1922 by Katherine Mansfield.

At the Bay

Very early morning. The sun was not yet risen, and the whole of Crescent Bay was hidden under a white sea-mist. The big bush-covered hills at the back were smothered. You could not see where they ended and the paddocks and bungalows began. The sandy road was gone and the paddocks and bungalows the other side of it; there were no white dunes covered with reddish grass beyond them; there was nothing to mark which was beach and where was the sea. A heavy dew had fallen. The grass was blue. Big drops hung on the bushes and just did not fall; the silvery, fluffy toi-toi* was limp on its long stalks, and all the marigolds and the pinks in the bungalow gardens were bowed to the earth with wetness. Drenched were the cold fuchsias, round pearls of dew lay on the flat nasturtium leaves. It looked as though the sea had beaten up softly in the darkness, as though one immense wave had come rippling, rippling — how far? Perhaps if you had waked up in the middle of the night you might have seen a big fish flicking in at the window and gone again...

Ah-Aah! sounded the sleepy sea. And from the bush there came the sound of little streams flowing, quickly, lightly, slipping between the smooth stones, gushing into ferny basins and out again; and there was the splashing of big drops on large leaves, and something else — what was it? — a faint stirring and shaking, the snapping of a twig and then such silence that it seemed some one was listening.

Round the corner of Crescent Bay, between the piled-up masses of broken rock, a flock of sheep came pattering. They were huddled together, a small, tossing, woolly mass, and their thin, stick-like legs trotted along quickly as if the cold and the quiet had frightened them. Behind them an old sheep-dog, his soaking paws covered with sand, ran along with his nose to the ground, but carelessly, as if thinking of something else. And then in the rocky gateway the shepherd himself appeared. He was a lean, upright old man, in a frieze* coat that was covered with a web of tiny drops, velvet trousers tied under the knee, and a wide-awake* with a folded blue handkerchief round the brim.

One hand was crammed into his belt, the other grasped a beautifully smooth yellow stick. And as he walked, taking his time, he kept up a very soft light whistling, an airy, far-away fluting that sounded mournful and tender. The old dog cut an ancient caper or two and then drew up sharp, ashamed of his levity, and walked a few dignified paces by his master's side. The sheep ran forward in little pattering rushes; they began to bleat, and ghostly flocks and herds answered them from under the sea. "Baa! Baaa!" For a time they seemed to be always on the same piece of ground. There ahead was stretched the sandy road with shallow puddles; the same soaking bushes showed on either side and the same shadowy palings*. Then something immense came into view; an enormous shock-haired giant with his arms stretched out. It was the big gum-tree outside Mrs. Stubbs' shop, and as they passed by there was a strong whiff of eucalyptus. And now big spots of light gleamed in the mist. The shepherd stopped whistling; he rubbed his red nose and wet beard on his wet sleeve and, screwing up his eyes, glanced in the direction of the sea. The sun was rising. It was marvellous how quickly the mist thinned, sped away, dissolved from the shallow plain, rolled up from the bush and was gone as if in a hurry to escape; big twists and curls jostled and shouldered each other as the silvery beams broadened. The far-away sky — a bright, pure blue — was reflected in the puddles, and the drops, swimming along the telegraph poles, flashed into points of light. Now the leaping, glittering sea was so bright it made one's eyes ache to look at it. The shepherd drew a pipe, the bowl as small as an acorn, out of his breast pocket, fumbled for a chunk of speckled tobacco, pared off a few shavings and stuffed the bowl. He was a grave, fine-looking old man. As he lit up and the blue smoke wreathed his head, the dog, watching, looked proud of him.

Glossary
*toi-toi — a type of tall grass
*frieze — coarse woollen cloth
*wide-awake — a type of wide-brimmed hat
*palings — pointed fence-posts

Section A: Reading

*You should spend about 45 minutes answering **all** the questions in this section.*

1. Use **lines 1-11** of the text to answer the questions below.
   For each question, tick the correct option. There is one correct answer per question.

   1.1   Why is it hard to see the landmarks near the bay?
         It is too misty ☐
         It is too dark ☐
         They are underwater ☐
   (1 mark)

   1.2   Which of the following is not found near the bay?
         Houses ☐
         Fields ☐
         A lighthouse ☐
   (1 mark)

   1.3   Why are the plants drooping?
         They haven't been watered enough ☐
         They are covered in dew ☐
         They don't get enough sunlight ☐
   (1 mark)

   1.4   What does the narrator imagine happened overnight?
         A giant fish washed up on the beach ☐
         The sea came far inland ☐
         A boat was damaged in a storm ☐
   (1 mark)

2. Explain how the writer uses language to describe the shepherd and his animals in **lines 16-22**.
   You may wish to explore how the writer uses particular language techniques, specific words and phrases, or different types of sentence.
   (8 marks)

3. Write about how the writer has structured this text to create a sense of mystery.
   In your answer, you could consider how a sense of mystery increases or decreases throughout the text, and any changes in tone or viewpoint.
   (8 marks)

4   How far do you agree or disagree with the following statement?

*In **lines 23-42** of the text, the setting is presented as a beautiful place.*

In your answer, make references to the text and consider:
- what impression you get of the setting
- what methods are used to describe the setting.

(20 marks)

Section B: Writing

You should spend about 45 minutes answering the question in this section.
You are advised to plan your answer.

5   You are entering a creative writing competition run by a young adult book publisher. Choose **one** of the following tasks:

Write a description of a lake. If you wish, you can use the photo below for inspiration.

OR

Write the beginning of a story based on the prompt 'going on a boat'.

(40 marks)

General Certificate of Secondary Education

GCSE
English Language
Paper 2

Time allowed: 1 hour 45 minutes

Centre name	
Centre number	
Candidate number	

Surname	
Other names	
Candidate signature	

Instructions to candidates
- Answer **all** the questions.
- Write your answers in **black** ink or ball-point pen.
- Write your name and other details in the boxes above.
- Cross out any rough work that you do not want to be marked.
- You should **not** use a dictionary.

Information for candidates
- The marks available are given in brackets at the end of each question.
- There are 80 marks available for this exam paper.
- You must use good English and clear presentation in your answers.

Advice for candidates
- You should spend about 15 minutes reading through the texts and all five questions.

Text A

The following text is an extract from an article written by a nanny, Monica Albelli.
It was published in a broadsheet newspaper in 2013.

Confessions of a Nanny

Being a nanny — whether you're a Mary Poppins, a Nanny McPhee or a Mrs Doubtfire — is a very tricky job. You have to be liked by two opposing "teams" to which a "perfect" nanny means completely different things. "You must be kind, you must be witty, very sweet and fairly pretty… If you don't scold and dominate us, we will never give you cause to hate us" — this is how the
5 children in Mary Poppins, Michael and Jane, want the newspaper ad for their nanny to read. Their father, Mr Banks, is keener on discipline. Mrs Banks seems to believe perfection lies somewhere in between that and the children's ideal.

I have always loved children and had a natural ability to connect with them with ease, no matter their gender, nationality or character. But when you're a nanny, kids come with parents.
10 And parents come with problems, opinions and expectations of their own, often in conflict between themselves.

Lesley, a successful publisher, and Brian, a dentist, were Scots in their mid-40s. They worked long hours but seemed to love Therese, seven, Tom, nine, and William, 11. Their approach when it came to the kids' upbringing though was completely different from each other. Confident
15 and motivated, Lesley believed her children's time should be spent doing homework, reading books or playing educational games. Brian, cheerful and laid back, wanted us to "just have fun". He asked me not to be strict with the kids, while Lesley kept pressuring me to turn them into responsible and hard-working individuals. I would arrive at their house to find a note from Brian, asking me to take them to the park, and then receive a text from Lesley with a to-do list.
20 Lesley would often come home late to find the kids already asleep. "I'm not a good mum," she once confessed. "I'm actually a bit jealous. I think they are starting to like you more than they like me."

I reassured her that this was not true and that she was doing her best.

The kids and I had bonded. Once, as I was getting ready to leave, Tom curled around my
25 leg, while Lesley tried to persuade him he had to let me go. They liked having me around so much that they started asking Brian if I could sleep over. Had we bonded too much?

Then things changed. Lesley seemed upset about something, and Brian was more and more absent. One day they told me they wouldn't be needing me any more as they had decided to get an au pair, who could also help with the house. I knew that wasn't the real reason. They had, I
30 realised, been asking me to become everything they weren't and, as soon as I started to achieve that, they felt threatened.

I tried to see it from their point of view. Being a nanny is difficult, but being a parent is even harder. Having a nanny is also hard.

I remembered what a friend used to say whenever I shared my frustrations with her: "You
35 care too much. It's just a job."

Should a nanny be indifferent, see herself as a doctor and treat all family members as her patients, being impartial and never getting emotionally involved? How can Mary Poppins be indifferent? She is cool and funny, strict at times, but always caring — the perfect nanny. But she is a fictional character, and so are Mr and Mrs Banks, and Michael and Jane.
40 Many dysfunctional families later, I have learned to care at the same time as keeping a distance, and that there is no such thing as the perfect family — or the perfect nanny.

Text B

The following text was written by Charlotte Brontë, a famous 19th-century author. Charlotte was working as a governess — a woman employed to teach and care for the children in a household. This is an extract from a letter written to her sister in 1839.

Dearest Lavinia,*

I am most exceedingly obliged to you for the trouble you have taken in seeking up my things and sending them all right. The box and its contents were most acceptable.

I have striven hard to be pleased with my new situation. The country, the house, and the grounds are, as I have said, divine. But, alack-a-day! there is such a thing as seeing all beautiful around you — pleasant woods, winding white paths, green lawns, and blue sunshiny sky — and not having a free moment or a free thought left to enjoy them in. The children are constantly with me, and more riotous, perverse, unmanageable cubs never grew. As for correcting them, I soon quickly found that was entirely out of the question: they are to do as they like. A complaint to Mrs. Sidgwick brings only black looks upon oneself, and unjust, partial excuses to screen the children. I have tried that plan once. It succeeded so notably that I shall try it no more. I said in my last letter that Mrs. Sidgwick did not know me. I now begin to find that she does not intend to know me, that she cares nothing in the world about me except to contrive how the greatest possible quantity of labour may be squeezed out of me, and to that end she overwhelms me with oceans of needlework, yards of cambric to hem, muslin night-caps to make, and, above all things, dolls to dress. I do not think she likes me at all, because I can't help being shy in such an entirely novel scene, surrounded as I have hitherto been by strange and constantly changing faces. I see now more clearly than I have ever done before that a private governess has no existence, is not considered as a living and rational being except as connected with the wearisome duties she has to fulfil. While she is teaching the children, working for them, amusing them, it is all right. If she steals a moment for herself she is a nuisance. Nevertheless, Mrs. Sidgwick is universally considered an amiable woman. Her manners are fussily affable. She talks a great deal, but as it seems to me not much to the purpose. Perhaps I may like her better after a while. At present I have no call to her. Mr. Sidgwick is in my opinion a hundred times better — less profession, less bustling condescension, but a far kinder heart.

As to Mrs. Collins' report that Mrs. Sidgwick intended to keep me permanently, I do not think that such was ever her design. Moreover, I would not stay without some alterations. For instance, this burden of sewing would have to be removed. It is too bad for anything. I never in my whole life had my time so fully taken up.

Don't show this letter to papa or aunt, only to Branwell.* They will think I am never satisfied wherever I am. I complain to you because it is a relief, and really I have had some unexpected mortifications to put up with. However, things may mend, but Mrs. Sidgwick expects me to do things that I cannot do — to love her children and be entirely devoted to them. I am really very well. I am so sleepy that I can write no more. I must leave off. Love to all. — Good-bye.

C. BRONTË.

Glossary
* A nickname for Charlotte's sister, Emily.
* Branwell — their brother.

Section A: Reading

*You should spend about 45 minutes answering **all** the questions in this section.*

1   The statements below are about **lines 1-19** of **Text A**.
    Tick the boxes next to the **four** statements that are TRUE.

    A   Monica Albelli thinks being a nanny is a difficult job. ☐
    B   Parents and children usually look for the same things in a nanny. ☐
    C   Parents almost always agree on the duties of a nanny. ☐
    D   Lesley and Brian are both professionals of a similar age. ☐
    E   Lesley and Brian care about their children. ☐
    F   Brian likes his children to play educational games. ☐
    G   Both parents think discipline is important. ☐
    H   Lesley and Brian sometimes gave Monica conflicting instructions. ☐

    (4 marks)

2   In **Text A** and **Text B**, the writers are employed by people who are very different from each other.
    What are the differences between Lesley and Mrs Sidgwick?
    You need to:
    •   **infer** information from the text
    •   talk about **both texts** in your answer.

    (8 marks)

3   Explain how the writer uses language to describe her role as a governess in **lines 1-15** of **Text B**.

    (12 marks)

4   This question is about **Text A** and **Text B**, where both writers work with children.
    Compare how they convey their different attitudes to looking after other people's children.
    You may wish to explore what the writers' attitudes are and what methods they use to convey their attitudes. You should use examples from **both** texts.

    (16 marks)

Section B: Writing

You should spend about 45 minutes answering the question in this section.
You are advised to plan your answer.

5   Write an article for a broadsheet newspaper arguing your opinion on the statement below.

"Parents are often too strict with their children. They expect them to work far too hard, at school and at home. Young people should be allowed to have fun while they still can."

(40 marks)

Practice Papers — English Literature

> Here are some practice papers to test how well-prepared you are for your GCSE English Literature exams.
> - There are two practice papers in this section:
>   Paper 1: pages 214-227
>   Paper 2: pages 228-237
> - Before you start each exam, read through all the instructions and information on the front.
> - You'll need some paper to write your answers on.
> - When you've finished, have a look at the answers starting on page 252 — they'll give you some ideas of the kind of things you should have included in your answers.
> - Don't try to do both of the exams in one sitting.

General Certificate of Secondary Education

GCSE English Literature

Paper 1: Shakespeare and the 19th-Century Novel

Surname
Other names
Candidate signature

Centre name
Centre number
Candidate number

Time allowed: 1 hour 45 minutes

Instructions to candidates
- You should answer **one** question from **Section A** (p.215-220) and **one** question from **Section B** (p.221-227).
- Write your answers in **black** ink or ball-point pen.
- Write your name and other details in the boxes above.

Information for candidates
- The marks available are given in brackets at the end of each question.
- There are 64 marks available for this exam paper.
- There are 34 marks available for Section A. This includes 30 marks for answering the question, plus 4 marks for accuracy in spelling, punctuation and the use of vocabulary and sentence structures.
- There are 30 marks available for Section B.

Section A: Shakespeare

Answer **one** question from this section.

Macbeth

1 Read the extract below, then answer the question.

Using this extract as a starting point, write about how Shakespeare explores masculinity in *Macbeth*.

Your answer should cover:
- the ways that Shakespeare presents masculinity in this extract
- the ways that Shakespeare presents masculinity in the play as a whole.

(30 marks)
(+4 marks for spelling, punctuation and the use of vocabulary and sentence structures)

From Act 1, Scene 7. *At this point in the play, Lady Macbeth is chastising Macbeth for his unwillingness to kill Duncan.*

	Lady Macbeth:	Art thou afeard
		To be the same in thine own act and valour
		As thou art in desire? Wouldst thou have that
		Which thou esteem'st the ornament of life,
5		And live a coward in thine own esteem,
		Letting 'I dare not' wait upon 'I would,'
		Like the poor cat i' the adage?
	Macbeth:	Prithee, peace:
		I dare do all that may become a man;
10		Who dares do more is none.
	Lady Macbeth:	What beast was't, then,
		That made you break this enterprise to me?
		When you durst do it, then you were a man;
		And, to be more than what you were, you would
15		Be so much more the man. Nor time nor place
		Did then adhere, and yet you would make both:
		They have made themselves, and that their fitness now
		Does unmake you. I have given suck, and know
		How tender 'tis to love the babe that milks me:
20		I would, while it was smiling in my face,
		Have pluck'd my nipple from his boneless gums,
		And dash'd the brains out, had I so sworn as you
		Have done to this.

Romeo and Juliet

2   Read the extract below, then answer the question.

Using this extract as a starting point, write about how Shakespeare presents Romeo as a romantic lover in *Romeo and Juliet*.

Your answer should cover:
- the ways that Shakespeare presents Romeo in this speech
- the ways that Shakespeare presents Romeo in the play as a whole.

(30 marks)
(+4 marks for spelling, punctuation and the use of vocabulary and sentence structures)

From Act 2, Scene 2. *At this point in the play, Romeo has gone to see Juliet at her house and is watching her at her window.*

[*enter Juliet above*]

Romeo: But soft, what light through yonder window breaks?
It is the east and Juliet is the sun!
Arise fair sun and kill the envious moon
Who is already sick and pale with grief
5 That thou her maid art far more fair than she.
Be not her maid since she is envious,
Her vestal livery is but sick and green
And none but fools do wear it. Cast it off.
It is my lady, O it is my love!
10 O that she knew she were!
She speaks, yet she says nothing. What of that?
Her eye discourses, I will answer it.
I am too bold. 'Tis not to me she speaks.
Two of the fairest stars in all the heaven,
15 Having some business, do entreat her eyes
To twinkle in their spheres till they return.
What if her eyes were there, they in her head?
The brightness of her cheek would shame those stars
As daylight doth a lamp. Her eyes in heaven
20 Would through the airy region stream so bright
That birds would sing and think it were not night
See how she leans her cheek upon her hand.
O that I were a glove upon that hand,
That I might touch that cheek.

The Tempest

3 Read the extract below, then answer the question.

Using this extract as a starting point, explore how far Shakespeare presents Caliban as deserving of sympathy in *The Tempest*.

Your answer should cover:
- the ways that Shakespeare presents Caliban in this extract
- the ways that Shakespeare presents Caliban in the play as a whole.

(30 marks)
(+4 marks for spelling, punctuation and the use of vocabulary and sentence structures)

From Act 1, Scene 2. *In this passage, Prospero and Miranda have gone to visit Caliban, Prospero's slave.*

Caliban: I must eat my dinner.
This island's mine, by Sycorax my mother,
Which thou tak'st from me. When thou cam'st first,
Thou strok'st me and made much of me, wouldst give me
5 Water with berries in't, and teach me how
To name the bigger light, and how the less,
That burn by day and night, and then I loved thee,
And showed thee all the qualities o' th' isle,
The fresh springs, brine-pits, barren place and fertile.
10 Cursed be I that did so! All the charms
Of Sycorax, toads, beetles, bats, light on you!
For I am all the subjects that you have,
Which first was mine own king, and here you sty me
In this hard rock, whiles you do keep from me
15 The rest o' th' island.

Prospero: Thou most lying slave,
Whom stripes may move, not kindness! I have used thee,
Filth as thou art, with human care, and lodged thee
In mine own cell, till thou didst seek to violate
The honour of my child.

The Merchant of Venice

4 Read the extract below, then answer the question.

Using this extract as a starting point, explore how Shakespeare presents ideas of justice and mercy in *The Merchant of Venice*.

Your answer should cover:
- the ways that Shakespeare presents justice and mercy in this speech
- the ways that Shakespeare presents justice and mercy in the play as a whole.

(30 marks)
(+4 marks for spelling, punctuation and the use of vocabulary and sentence structures)

From Act 4, Scene 1. *At this point in the play, Portia, disguised as a lawyer, is presiding over Antonio's trial.*

	Portia:	The quality of mercy is not strained;
		It droppeth as the gentle rain from heaven
		Upon the place beneath. It is twice blest;
		It blesseth him that gives and him that takes.
5		'Tis mightiest in the mightiest; it becomes
		The thronèd monarch better than his crown.
		His sceptre shows the force of temporal power,
		The attribute to awe and majesty,
		Wherein doth sit the dread and fear of kings;
10		But mercy is above this sceptred sway;
		It is enthronèd in the hearts of kings;
		It is an attribute to God himself,
		And earthly power doth then show likest God's
		When mercy seasons justice. Therefore, Jew,
15		Though justice be thy plea, consider this:
		That, in the course of justice, none of us
		Should see salvation: we do pray for mercy,
		And that same prayer doth teach us all to render
		The deeds of mercy. I have spoke thus much
20		To mitigate the justice of thy plea,
		Which if thou follow, this strict court of Venice
		Must needs give sentence 'gainst the merchant there.

Much Ado About Nothing

5 Read the extract below, then answer the question.

Using this extract as a starting point, explore how Shakespeare presents the changing relationship between Benedick and Beatrice in *Much Ado About Nothing*.

Your answer should cover:
- the ways that Shakespeare presents Benedick and Beatrice's relationship in this conversation
- the ways that Shakespeare presents Benedick and Beatrice's relationship in the play as a whole.

(30 marks)
(+4 marks for spelling, punctuation and the use of vocabulary and sentence structures)

From Act 1, Scene 1. *In this passage, Don Pedro, Benedick and Beatrice are talking.*

	Don Pedro:	... Be happy, lady, for you are like an honourable father.
	Benedick:	If Signior Leonato be her father, she would not have his head on her shoulders for all Messina, as like him as she is.
	Beatrice:	I wonder that you will still be talking, Signior Benedick: nobody marks you.
5	**Benedick:**	What, my dear Lady Disdain! Are you yet living?
	Beatrice:	Is it possible disdain should die, while she hath such meet food to feed it as Signior Benedick? Courtesy itself must convert to disdain, if you come in her presence.
	Benedick:	Then is courtesy a turncoat. But it is certain I am loved of all ladies, only
10		you excepted; and I would I could find in my heart that I had not a hard heart, for truly I love none.
	Beatrice:	A dear happiness to women, they would else have been troubled with a pernicious suitor. I thank God and my cold blood, I am of your humour for that; I had rather hear my dog bark at a crow than a man swear he loves me.
15	**Benedick:**	God keep your ladyship still in that mind, so some gentleman or other shall scape a predestinate scratched face.
	Beatrice:	Scratching could not make it worse, and 'twere such a face as yours were.
	Benedick:	Well, you are a rare parrot-teacher.
	Beatrice:	A bird of my tongue is better than a beast of yours.
20	**Benedick:**	I would my horse had the speed of your tongue, and so good a continuer. But keep your way, a God's name, I have done.
	Beatrice:	You always end with a jade's trick, I know you of old.

Julius Caesar

6 Read the extract below, then answer the question.

Using this extract as a starting point, examine the ways Shakespeare presents Caesar as an arrogant character in *Julius Caesar*.

Your answer should cover:
- the ways that Shakespeare presents Caesar in this extract
- the ways that Shakespeare presents Caesar in the play as a whole.

(30 marks)
(+4 marks for spelling, punctuation and the use of vocabulary and sentence structures)

From Act 3, Scene 1. *At this point in the play, Caesar has just been asked to pardon Metellus Cimber's brother, Publius Cimber.*

	Caesar:	I could be well moved, if I were as you;
		If I could pray to move, prayers would move me;
		But I am constant as the northern star,
		Of whose true-fix'd and resting quality
5		There is no fellow in the firmament.
		The skies are painted with unnumber'd sparks,
		They are all fire and every one doth shine,
		But there's but one in all doth hold his place:
		So in the world; 'tis furnish'd well with men,
10		And men are flesh and blood, and apprehensive;
		Yet in the number I do know but one
		That unassailable holds on his rank,
		Unshaked of motion; and that I am he,
		Let me a little show it, even in this:
15		That I was constant Cimber should be banish'd,
		And constant do remain to keep him so.
	Cinna:	O Caesar —
	Caesar:	Hence! wilt thou lift up Olympus?
	Decius:	Great Caesar —
20	**Caesar:**	Doth not Brutus bootless kneel?
	Casca:	Speak, hands for me!
		[*CASCA first, then the other Conspirators and BRUTUS stab CAESAR*]
	Caesar:	Et tu, Brute! Then fall, Caesar.
		[*Dies*]

Section B: The 19th-Century Novel

Answer **one** question from this section.

Robert Louis Stevenson: *The Strange Case of Dr Jekyll and Mr Hyde*

7   Read the extract below from 'Henry Jekyll's Full Statement of the Case', then answer the question.

Using this extract as a starting point, write about how Stevenson explores morality in the novel.

(30 marks)

In this extract, Jekyll questions whether he is to blame for the crimes that Hyde has committed.

I was the first that could thus plod in the public eye with a load of genial respectability, and in a moment, like a schoolboy, strip off these lendings and spring headlong into the sea of liberty. But for me, in my impenetrable mantle, the safety was complete. Think of it — I did not even exist! Let me but escape into my laboratory door, give me but a second or two to mix
5   and swallow the draught that I had always standing ready; and whatever he had done, Edward Hyde would pass away like the stain of breath upon a mirror; and there in his stead, quietly at home, trimming the midnight lamp in his study, a man who could afford to laugh at suspicion, would be Henry Jekyll.

The pleasures which I made haste to seek in my disguise were, as I have said, undignified;
10   I would scarce use a harder term. But in the hands of Edward Hyde, they soon began to turn towards the monstrous. When I would come back from these excursions, I was often plunged into a kind of wonder at my vicarious depravity. This familiar that I called out of my own soul, and sent forth alone to do his good pleasure, was a being inherently malign and villainous; his every act and thought centred on self; drinking pleasure with bestial avidity from any degree of
15   torture to another; relentless like a man of stone. Henry Jekyll stood at times aghast before the acts of Edward Hyde; but the situation was apart from ordinary laws, and insidiously relaxed the grasp of conscience. It was Hyde, after all, and Hyde alone, that was guilty. Jekyll was no worse; he woke again to his good qualities seemingly unimpaired; he would even make haste, where it was possible, to undo the evil done by Hyde. And thus his conscience slumbered.

Charles Dickens: *A Christmas Carol*

8 Read the extract below from Chapter 3, then answer the question.

Using this extract as a starting point, write about how poverty is presented in *A Christmas Carol*.

(30 marks)

_____

In this extract, the Ghost of Christmas Present reveals Ignorance and Want to Scrooge.

From the foldings of its robe, it brought two children; wretched, abject, frightful, hideous, miserable. They knelt down at its feet, and clung upon the outside of its garment.

"Oh, Man! look here. Look, look, down here!" exclaimed the Ghost.

They were a boy and girl. Yellow, meagre, ragged, scowling, wolfish; but prostrate, too, in
5 their humility. Where graceful youth should have filled their features out, and touched them with its freshest tints, a stale and shrivelled hand, like that of age, had pinched, and twisted them, and pulled them into shreds. Where angels might have sat enthroned, devils lurked, and glared out menacing. No change, no degradation, no perversion of humanity, in any grade, through all the mysteries of wonderful creation, has monsters half so horrible and dread.

10 Scrooge started back, appalled. Having them shown to him in this way, he tried to say they were fine children, but the words choked themselves, rather than be parties to a lie of such enormous magnitude.

"Spirit! are they yours?" Scrooge could say no more.

"They are Man's," said the Spirit, looking down upon them. "And they cling to me, appealing
15 from their fathers. This boy is Ignorance. This girl is Want. Beware them both, and all of their degree, but most of all beware this boy, for on his brow I see that written which is Doom, unless the writing be erased. Deny it!" cried the Spirit, stretching out its hand towards the city. "Slander those who tell it ye! Admit it for your factious purposes, and make it worse. And bide the end!"

"Have they no refuge or resource?" cried Scrooge.

20 "Are there no prisons?" said the Spirit, turning on him for the last time with his own words. "Are there no workhouses?"

The bell struck twelve.

Charles Dickens: *Great Expectations*

9 Read the extract below from Chapter 8, then answer the question.

Using this extract as a starting point, write about how Dickens presents Miss Havisham as a frightening character.

(30 marks)

In this extract, Pip meets Miss Havisham for the first time.

She was dressed in rich materials — satins, and lace, and silks — all of white. Her shoes were white. And she had a long white veil dependent from her hair, and she had bridal flowers in her hair, but her hair was white. Some bright jewels sparkled on her neck and on her hands, and some other jewels lay sparkling on the table. Dresses, less splendid than the
5   dress she wore, and half-packed trunks, were scattered about. She had not quite finished dressing, for she had but one shoe on — the other was on the table near her hand — her veil was but half arranged, her watch and chain were not put on, and some lace for her bosom lay with those trinkets, and with her handkerchief, and gloves, and some flowers, and a prayer-book, all confusedly heaped about the looking-glass.
10   It was not in the first moments that I saw all these things, though I saw more of them in the first moments than might be supposed. But, I saw that everything within my view which ought to be white, had been white long ago, and had lost its lustre, and was faded and yellow. I saw that the bride within the bridal dress had withered like the dress, and like the flowers, and had no brightness left but the brightness of her sunken eyes. I saw that the dress had been
15   put upon the rounded figure of a young woman, and that the figure upon which it now hung loose, had shrunk to skin and bone. Once, I had been taken to see some ghastly waxwork at the Fair, representing I know not what impossible personage lying in state. Once, I had been taken to one of our old marsh churches to see a skeleton in the ashes of a rich dress, that had been dug out of a vault under the church pavement. Now, waxwork and skeleton seemed to
20   have dark eyes that moved and looked at me. I should have cried out, if I could.

Charlotte Brontë: *Jane Eyre*

10 Read the extract below from Chapter 37 (Volume 3, Chapter 11), then answer the question.

Using this extract as a starting point, write about Mr Rochester and the way he changes throughout the novel.

(30 marks)

In this extract, Jane has returned to find Rochester at Ferndean.

"Jane! you think me, I daresay, an irreligious dog: but my heart swells with gratitude to the beneficent God of this earth just now. He sees not as man sees, but far clearer: judges not as man judges, but far more wisely. I did wrong: I would have sullied my innocent flower — breathed guilt on its purity: the Omnipotent snatched it from me. I, in my stiff-necked rebellion, almost
5 cursed the dispensation: instead of bending to the decree, I defied it. Divine justice pursued its course; disasters came thick on me: I was forced to pass through the valley of the shadow of death. His chastisements are mighty; and one smote me which has humbled me for ever. You know I was proud of my strength: but what is it now, when I must give it over to foreign guidance, as a child does its weakness? Of late, Jane — only — only of late — I began to see
10 and acknowledge the hand of God in my doom. I began to experience remorse, repentance, the wish for reconcilement to my Maker. I began sometimes to pray: very brief prayers they were, but very sincere.

"Some days since: nay, I can number them — four; it was last Monday night, a singular mood came over me: one in which grief replaced frenzy — sorrow, sullenness. I had long had the
15 impression that since I could nowhere find you, you must be dead. Late that night — perhaps it might be between eleven and twelve o'clock — ere I retired to my dreary rest, I supplicated God, that, if it seemed good to Him, I might soon be taken from this life, and admitted to that world to come, where there was still hope of rejoining Jane.

"I was in my own room, and sitting by the window, which was open: it soothed me to feel
20 the balmy night-air; though I could see no stars, and only by a vague, luminous haze, knew the presence of a moon. I longed for thee, Janet! Oh, I longed for thee both with soul and flesh! I asked of God, at once in anguish and humility, if I had not been long enough desolate, afflicted, tormented; and might not soon taste bliss and peace once more. That I merited all I endured, I acknowledged — that I could scarcely endure more, I pleaded; and the alpha and omega of my
25 heart's wishes broke involuntarily from my lips in the words, 'Jane! Jane! Jane!'"

Mary Shelley: *Frankenstein*

11 Read the extract below from Chapter 24 (Volume 3, Chapter 7), then answer the question.

Using this extract as a starting point, write about how Shelley explores revenge in *Frankenstein*.

(30 marks)

In this extract, Frankenstein describes his desire for revenge on the monster.

... How I have lived I hardly know; many times have I stretched my failing limbs upon the sandy plain and prayed for death. But revenge kept me alive; I dared not die and leave my adversary in being.

When I quitted Geneva my first labour was to gain some clue by which I might trace the steps of my fiendish enemy. But my plan was unsettled; and I wandered many hours round the confines of the town, uncertain what path I should pursue. As night approached, I found myself at the entrance of the cemetery where William, Elizabeth, and my father reposed. I entered it and approached the tomb which marked their graves. Everything was silent, except the leaves of the trees, which were gently agitated by the wind; the night was nearly dark; and the scene would have been solemn and affecting even to an uninterested observer. The spirits of the departed seemed to flit around and to cast a shadow, which was felt but not seen, around the head of the mourner.

The deep grief which this scene had at first excited quickly gave way to rage and despair. They were dead, and I lived; their murderer also lived, and to destroy him I must drag out my weary existence. I knelt on the grass and kissed the earth, and with quivering lips exclaimed, "By the sacred earth on which I kneel, by the shades that wander near me, by the deep and eternal grief that I feel, I swear; and by thee, O Night, and the spirits that preside over thee, to pursue the daemon who caused this misery, until he or I shall perish in mortal conflict. For this purpose I will preserve my life: to execute this dear revenge will I again behold the sun and tread the green herbage of earth, which otherwise should vanish from my eyes for ever. And I call on you, spirits of the dead; and on you, wandering ministers of vengeance, to aid and conduct me in my work. Let the cursed and hellish monster drink deep of agony; let him feel the despair that now torments me."

Jane Austen: *Pride and Prejudice*

12 Read the extract below from Chapter 1, then answer the question.

Using this extract as a starting point, explore how Austen portrays the relationship between Mr and Mrs Bennet.

(30 marks)

In this extract, Mrs Bennet is trying to persuade Mr Bennet to visit Mr Bingley, who has just moved in to nearby Netherfield Park.

"I see no occasion for that. You and the girls may go, or you may send them by themselves, which perhaps will be still better, for as you are as handsome as any of them, Mr. Bingley may like you the best of the party."

"My dear, you flatter me. I certainly have had my share of beauty, but I do not pretend to be anything extraordinary now. When a woman has five grown-up daughters, she ought to give over thinking of her own beauty."

"In such cases, a woman has not often much beauty to think of."

"But, my dear, you must indeed go and see Mr. Bingley when he comes into the neighbourhood."

"It is more than I engage for, I assure you."

"But consider your daughters. Only think what an establishment it would be for one of them. Sir William and Lady Lucas are determined to go, merely on that account, for in general, you know, they visit no newcomers. Indeed you must go, for it will be impossible for us to visit him if you do not."

"You are over-scrupulous, surely. I dare say Mr. Bingley will be very glad to see you; and I will send a few lines by you to assure him of my hearty consent to his marrying whichever he chooses of the girls; though I must throw in a good word for my little Lizzy."

"I desire you will do no such thing. Lizzy is not a bit better than the others; and I am sure she is not half so handsome as Jane, nor half so good-humoured as Lydia. But you are always giving her the preference."

"They have none of them much to recommend them," replied he; "they are all silly and ignorant like other girls; but Lizzy has something more of quickness than her sisters."

"Mr. Bennet, how can you abuse your own children in such a way? You take delight in vexing me. You have no compassion for my poor nerves."

"You mistake me, my dear. I have a high respect for your nerves. They are my old friends. I have heard you mention them with consideration these last twenty years at least."

Sir Arthur Conan Doyle: *The Sign of Four*

13 Read the extract below from Chapter 11, then answer the question.

Using this extract as a starting point, explore how Conan Doyle presents the loving relationship between John Watson and Mary Morstan.

(30 marks)

In this extract, Watson and Mary reveal the contents of the treasure-box.

"What a pretty box!" she said, stooping over it. "This is Indian work, I suppose?"

"Yes; it is Benares metal-work."

"And so heavy!" she exclaimed, trying to raise it. "The box alone must be of some value. Where is the key?"

5   "Small threw it into the Thames," I answered. "I must borrow Mrs. Forrester's poker." There was in the front a thick and broad hasp, wrought in the image of a sitting Buddha. Under this I thrust the end of the poker and twisted it outward as a lever. The hasp sprang open with a loud snap. With trembling fingers I flung back the lid. We both stood gazing in astonishment. The box was empty!

10   No wonder that it was heavy. The iron-work was two-thirds of an inch thick all round. It was massive, well made, and solid, like a chest constructed to carry things of great price, but not one shred or crumb of metal or jewellery lay within it. It was absolutely and completely empty.

"The treasure is lost," said Miss Morstan, calmly.

As I listened to the words and realized what they meant, a great shadow seemed to pass from 15 my soul. I did not know how this Agra treasure had weighed me down, until now that it was finally removed. It was selfish, no doubt, disloyal, wrong, but I could realize nothing save that the golden barrier was gone from between us. "Thank God!" I ejaculated from my very heart.

She looked at me with a quick, questioning smile. "Why do you say that?" she asked.

"Because you are within my reach again," I said, taking her hand. She did not withdraw it. 20 "Because I love you, Mary, as truly as ever a man loved a woman. Because this treasure, these riches, sealed my lips. Now that they are gone I can tell you how I love you. That is why I said, 'Thank God.'"

"Then I say, 'Thank God,' too," she whispered, as I drew her to my side. Whoever had lost a treasure, I knew that night that I had gained one.

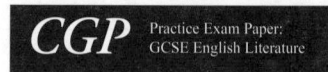

General Certificate of Secondary Education

GCSE
English Literature

Surname
Other names
Candidate signature

Centre name
Centre number
Candidate number

Paper 2: Modern Texts and Poetry

Time allowed: 2 hours 15 minutes

Instructions to candidates
- You should answer **one** question from **Section A** (p.229-231), **one** question from **Section B** (p.232-235) and **both** questions in **Section C** (p.236-237).
- Write your answers in **black** ink or ball-point pen.
- Write your name and other details in the boxes above.

Information for candidates
- The marks available are given in brackets at the end of each question.
- There are 96 marks available for this exam paper.
- There are 34 marks available for Section A. This includes 30 marks for answering the question, plus 4 marks for accuracy in spelling, punctuation and the use of vocabulary and sentence structures.
- There are 30 marks available for Section B and 32 marks available for Section C.

Section A: Modern Prose or Drama

Answer **one** question from this section.

JB Priestley: *An Inspector Calls*

1   Write about how Priestley presents Arthur Birling as a selfish character in *An Inspector Calls*.
    Your answer should cover:
    - the techniques that Priestley uses to present Arthur Birling
    - how Priestley uses the character to explore ideas about selfishness.

    (30 marks)
    (+4 marks for spelling, punctuation and grammar)

Willy Russell: *Blood Brothers*

2   Write about the character of Mickey and the way he changes during the course of *Blood Brothers*.
    Your answer should cover:
    - how Mickey changes as the play develops
    - the techniques that Russell uses to present Mickey.

    (30 marks)
    (+4 marks for spelling, punctuation and grammar)

Winsome Pinnock: *Leave Taking*

3   Write about cultural identity and the way it is presented in *Leave Taking*.
    Your answer should cover:
    - ideas about cultural identity in the play
    - how these ideas are presented.

    (30 marks)
    (+4 marks for spelling, punctuation and grammar)

Dennis Kelly: *DNA*

4   Write about how Kelly uses the character of Leah to explore ideas about morality in *DNA*.
    Your answer should cover:
    - how Kelly presents the character of Leah
    - how Kelly uses the character to explore ideas about morality.

    (30 marks)
    (+4 marks for spelling, punctuation and grammar)

Chinonyerem Odimba: *Princess & The Hustler*

5   Write about hopes and dreams and the way they are presented in *Princess & The Hustler*.
    Your answer should cover:
    - ideas about hopes and dreams in the play
    - how these ideas are presented.

(30 marks)
(+4 marks for spelling, punctuation and grammar)

Shelagh Delaney: *A Taste of Honey*

6   Write about how Delaney uses the character of Jo to explore the lives of women in *A Taste of Honey*.
    Your answer should cover:
    - how Delaney presents the character of Jo
    - how Delaney uses the character to explore the lives of women.

(30 marks)
(+4 marks for spelling, punctuation and grammar)

William Golding: *Lord of the Flies*

7   Write about fear and the way it is presented in *Lord of the Flies*.
    Your answer should cover:
    - ideas about fear in the novel
    - how these ideas are presented.

(30 marks)
(+4 marks for spelling, punctuation and grammar)

AQA Anthology: *Telling Tales*

8   Write about death and the way it is presented in 'Chemistry' and one other story from *Telling Tales*.
    Your answer should cover:
    - ideas about death in the two stories
    - how these ideas are presented by each writer.

(30 marks)
(+4 marks for spelling, punctuation and grammar)

George Orwell: *Animal Farm*

9 Write about education and learning and the way they are presented in *Animal Farm*.
Your answer should cover:
- ideas about education and learning in the novel
- how these ideas are presented.

(30 marks)
(+4 marks for spelling, punctuation and grammar)

Kit de Waal: *My Name is Leon*

10 Write about family and the way it is presented in *My Name is Leon*.
Your answer should cover:
- ideas about family in the novel
- how these ideas are presented.

(30 marks)
(+4 marks for spelling, punctuation and grammar)

Meera Syal: *Anita and Me*

11 Write about friendship and the way it is presented in *Anita and Me*.
Your answer should cover:
- ideas about friendship in the novel
- how these ideas are presented.

(30 marks)
(+4 marks for spelling, punctuation and grammar)

Stephen Kelman: *Pigeon English*

12 Write about violence and the way it is presented in *Pigeon English*.
Your answer should cover:
- ideas about violence in the novel
- how these ideas are presented.

(30 marks)
(+4 marks for spelling, punctuation and grammar)

Section B: Poetry

Answer **one** question from this section.

Love and Relationships

> The poems in this cluster are:
> - *When We Two Parted* by Lord Byron
> - *Love's Philosophy* by Percy Bysshe Shelley
> - *Porphyria's Lover* by Robert Browning
> - *Sonnet 29* by Elizabeth Barrett Browning
> - *Neutral Tones* by Thomas Hardy
> - *The Farmer's Bride* by Charlotte Mew
> - *Walking Away* by C. Day-Lewis
> - *Letters From Yorkshire* by Maura Dooley
> - *Eden Rock* by Charles Causley
> - *Follower* by Seamus Heaney
> - *"Mother, any distance..."* by Simon Armitage
> - *Before You Were Mine* by Carol Ann Duffy
> - *Winter Swans* by Owen Sheers
> - *Singh Song!* by Daljit Nagra
> - *Climbing My Grandfather* by Andrew Waterhouse

13 Compare how the breakdown of a relationship is presented in Thomas Hardy's 'Neutral Tones' and one other poem you have studied.

(30 marks)

Neutral Tones

We stood by a pond that winter day,
And the sun was white, as though chidden of God,
And a few leaves lay on the starving sod;
    — They had fallen from an ash, and were grey.

5   Your eyes on me were as eyes that rove
Over tedious riddles of years ago;
And some words played between us to and fro
    On which lost the more by our love.

The smile on your mouth was the deadest thing
10   Alive enough to have strength to die;
And a grin of bitterness swept thereby
    Like an ominous bird a-wing...

Since then, keen lessons that love deceives,
And wrings with wrong, have shaped to me
15   Your face, and the God-curst sun, and a tree,
    And a pond edged with greyish leaves.

Thomas Hardy

Power and Conflict

The poems in this cluster are:

- *Ozymandias* by Percy Bysshe Shelley
- *London* by William Blake
- *The Prelude: Stealing the Boat* by William Wordsworth
- *My Last Duchess* by Robert Browning
- *The Charge of the Light Brigade* by Alfred Tennyson
- *Exposure* by Wilfred Owen
- *Storm on the Island* by Seamus Heaney
- *Bayonet Charge* by Ted Hughes
- *Remains* by Simon Armitage
- *Poppies* by Jane Weir
- *War Photographer* by Carol Ann Duffy
- *Tissue* by Imtiaz Dharker
- *The Emigrée* by Carol Rumens
- *Kamikaze* by Beatrice Garland
- *Checking Out Me History* by John Agard

14 Compare how nature is presented in William Wordsworth's 'The Prelude: Stealing the Boat' and one other poem you have studied.

(30 marks)

The Prelude: Stealing the Boat

One summer evening (led by her) I found
A little boat tied to a willow tree
Within a rocky cave, its usual home.
Straight I unloosed her chain, and stepping in
5   Pushed from the shore. It was an act of stealth
And troubled pleasure, nor without the voice
Of mountain-echoes did my boat move on;
Leaving behind her still, on either side,
Small circles glittering idly in the moon,
10   Until they melted all into one track
Of sparkling light. But now, like one who rows,
Proud of his skill, to reach a chosen point
With an unswerving line, I fixed my view
Upon the summit of a craggy ridge,
15   The horizon's utmost boundary; far above
Was nothing but the stars and the grey sky.

Poem continues on the next page

Poem continued from the previous page

            She was an elfin pinnace; lustily
            I dipped my oars into the silent lake,
            And, as I rose upon the stroke, my boat
20   Went heaving through the water like a swan;
            When, from behind that craggy steep till then
            The horizon's bound, a huge peak, black and huge,
            As if with voluntary power instinct,
            Upreared its head. I struck and struck again,
25   And growing still in stature the grim shape
            Towered up between me and the stars, and still,
            For so it seemed, with purpose of its own
            And measured motion like a living thing,
            Strode after me. With trembling oars I turned,
30   And through the silent water stole my way
            Back to the covert of the willow tree;
            There in her mooring-place I left my bark, –
            And through the meadows homeward went, in grave
            And serious mood; but after I had seen
35   That spectacle, for many days, my brain
            Worked with a dim and undetermined sense
            Of unknown modes of being; o'er my thoughts
            There hung a darkness, call it solitude
            Or blank desertion. No familiar shapes
40   Remained, no pleasant images of trees,
            Of sea or sky, no colours of green fields;
            But huge and mighty forms, that do not live
            Like living men, moved slowly through the mind
            By day, and were a trouble to my dreams.

William Wordsworth

Worlds and Lives

The poems in this cluster are:
- *Lines Written in Early Spring* by William Wordsworth
- *England in 1819* by Percy Bysshe Shelley
- *Shall earth no more inspire thee* by Emily Brontë
- *In a London Drawingroom* by George Eliot
- *On an Afternoon Train from Purley to Victoria, 1955* by James Berry
- *Name Journeys* by Raman Mundair
- *pot* by shamshad khan
- *A Wider View* by Seni Seneviratne
- *Homing* by Liz Berry
- *A century later* by Imtiaz Dharker
- *The Jewellery Maker* by Louisa Adjoa Parker
- *With Birds You're Never Lonely* by Raymond Antrobus
- *A Portable Paradise* by Roger Robinson
- *Like an Heiress* by Grace Nichols
- *Thirteen* by Caleb Femi

15 Compare how feelings towards places are presented in George Eliot's 'In a London Drawingroom' and one other poem you have studied.

(30 marks)

In a London Drawingroom

The sky is cloudy, yellowed by the smoke.
For view there are the houses opposite
Cutting the sky with one long line of wall
Like solid fog: far as the eye can stretch
5   Monotony of surface & of form
Without a break to hang a guess upon.
No bird can make a shadow as it flies,
For all is shadow, as in ways o'erhung
By thickest canvass, where the golden rays
10   Are clothed in hemp. No figure lingering
Pauses to feed the hunger of the eye
Or rest a little on the lap of life.
All hurry on & look upon the ground,
Or glance unmarking at the passers by
15   The wheels are hurrying too, cabs, carriages
All closed, in multiplied identity.
The world seems one huge prison-house & court
Where men are punished at the slightest cost,
With lowest rate of colour, warmth & joy.

George Eliot

Section C: Unseen Poetry

Answer **both** questions from this section.

For a Five-Year-Old

A snail is climbing up the window-sill
into your room, after a night of rain.
You call me in to see, and I explain
that it would be unkind to leave it there:
5   it might crawl to the floor; we must take care
that no one squashes it. You understand,
and carry it outside, with careful hand,
to eat a daffodil.

I see, then, that a kind of faith prevails:
10   your gentleness is moulded still by words
from me, who have trapped mice and shot wild birds,
from me, who drowned your kittens, who betrayed
your closest relatives, and who purveyed
the harshest kind of truth to many another.
15   But that is how things are: I am your mother,
and we are kind to snails.

Fleur Adcock

16a How does Adcock present the narrator's attitude to parenthood in 'For a Five-Year-Old'?

(24 marks)

The Beautiful Lie

He was about four, I think… it was so long ago.
In a garden; he'd done some damage
behind a bright screen of sweet-peas
– snapped a stalk, a stake, I don't recall,
5   but the grandmother came and saw, and asked him
"Did you do that?"

Now, if she'd said *why* did you do that,
he'd never have denied it. She showed him
he had a choice. I could see in his face
10 the new sense, the possible. That word and deed
need not match, that you could say the world
different, to suit you.

When he said "No", I swear it was as moving
as the first time a baby's fist clenches
15 on a finger, as momentous as the first
taste of fruit. I could feel his eyes looking
through a new window, at a world whose form
and colour weren't fixed

but fluid, that poured like a snake, trembled
20 around the edges like northern lights, shape-shifted
at the spell of a voice. I could sense him filling
like a glass, hear the unreal sea in his ears.
*This is how to make songs, create men, paint pictures,
tell a story.*

25 I think I made up the screen of sweet-peas.
Maybe they were beans, maybe there was no screen:
it just felt as if there should be, somehow.
And he was my – no, I don't need to tell that.
I know I made up the screen. And I recall very well
30 what he had done.

Sheenagh Pugh

16b In 'For a Five-Year-Old' and 'The Beautiful Lie', both poets write about relationships between adults and children. What are the similarities and differences in the way these poems present those relationships?

(8 marks)

Answers

Section Three — English Language: Understanding Texts

Page 28 — Warm-Up Questions

1) a) True
   b) False
2) a) Rita
   b) Rita
   c) Rakesh
   d) E.g. "bad enough that we have to go to this reunion at all"
   E.g. "Rita glared pointedly at her watch"
   E.g. "admiring his reflection"
3) a) To advise. E.g. 'because the writer uses simple language that the reader will understand to suggest what the reader should do'.
   b) To entertain. E.g. 'because the writer uses descriptive verbs such as "crawling" and "gallop" to engage the reader'.
   c) To persuade. E.g. 'because the writer uses a rhetorical question to encourage the reader to agree with their argument'.
4) E.g. 'Writer A dislikes mixed schools, and believes that all schools should be single-sex. In contrast, Writer B likes mixed schools. Writer B also differs from Writer A because Writer B thinks that parents should be the ones to choose.

Pages 29-30 — Exam-Style Questions

1) 1.1) Loudly
   1.2) It looks too bright
   1.3) In a friendly way
   1.4) A handshake
2) Answers should analyse both texts, using relevant quotes from both texts to infer several differences between the behaviour of the wives. Here are some things you could mention:
- The wife in Text B is to an extent independent of her husband and "works full time", but the wife in Text A lives only to be "amenable to [her husband's] needs".
- The wife in Text A is "sweet and charming" by doing all the tasks for her husband, whereas the wife in Text B behaves "sweetly" when giving her husband housework to do.
- The writer in Text B says that his wife "spurns the idea" that she should do all the housework, whereas the writer in Text A says that his wife is solely responsible for this task ("the home is her sphere").
3) The following four statements should be ticked:
- On the second day, the writer got up early.
- The writer enjoyed the pony trek.
- You can abseil at Lowbridge Park.
- The writer liked the archery instructor.
4) All your points should use relevant examples and terminology, and comment on the effects of the language used. Here are some things you could mention:
- Casual style to make voting seem less daunting, e.g. "political lingo".
- Use of alliteration in the subheadings to grab the reader's attention and make the point memorable.
- Use of the imperative form ("don't panic", "have a look") to describe the decision-making process clearly.
- Use of technical language to make the description seem informed.
- Writer uses direct address ("you'll probably have noticed") to create a sense of familiarity that encourages the reader to trust their advice on voting.

Page 40 — Exam-Style Questions

1) Answers should clearly compare the different ideas and techniques in each text, using quotations to support points. Here are some things you could mention:
- In Text A, the writer illustrates their dislike of a new art style using hyperbole ("nothing short of an abomination"). In Text B, the writer expresses their admiration for a new art style, also using hyperbole ("They're revolutionaries").
- Both texts use formal language, e.g. "I read with concern" in Text A, "progression in the medium" in Text B. This makes their opinion seem more important / authoritative.
- Text B makes the restrictions of traditional art seem negative using a metaphor, "the iron shackles of 'traditional art'", whereas Text A thinks that the rules of traditional art are good: new artists should have "learnt from" older examples.
2) Your answer should offer an opinion on the statement. It should comment on the techniques used to describe both characters, using relevant examples and terminology to support each point. Here are some things you could mention:
- I agree that both characters feel realistic and relatable, because dialogue is used to give an insight into each character's mindset, such as Annie: "Don't be ridiculous." and Lucas: "They'll kill me." This indicates that Annie is calmer and less prone to being overdramatic in comparison to Lucas.
- The cumulative use of short sentences in Lucas's speech also emphasises his stress and panic which make his problem and his reaction to it feel realistic and relatable, e.g. "I've looked everywhere. It's lost. They'll kill me."
- The contrast between the two characters makes each character's personality stand out more and their individual perspective seem clearer. E.g. the adjectives used to describe Lucas's actions ("frantic", "manic") contrast with the adverbs used to describe Annie's actions, which are carried out "cautiously" or "calmly".

Section Four — English Language: Language and Structure

Page 47 — Warm-Up Questions

1) a) Detached   b) Upbeat   c) Sentimental
2) Sentence a)
3) E.g. 'The tone is conversational. The writer uses slang phrases such as "cheesed off", and contractions like "it's", as well as humour when describing the trip to "River C and Swamp D".'
4) a) E.g. 'Customers are advised that we do not accept credit cards.'
   b) E.g. 'It is essential to ensure you have the correct tools before proceeding.'
5) Noun: Bella   Verb: approached   Adverb: excitedly
6) E.g. 'The verb "whispered" suggests that the speaker and listener are working together, whilst "spat" suggests that the speaker doesn't like the listener.'
7) a) ii) money
   b) E.g. 'It suggests that the narrator is very motivated by money. They see their sibling's theatre show as an opportunity to "cash in" and talk about time as something you can "buy".'
8) E.g. 'The verbs are very violent, which creates the impression that the wind is powerful and destructive.'

Page 48 — Exam-Style Questions

1) All your points should use relevant examples and terminology, and comment on the effects of the language used. Here are some things you could mention:
   - Contrast between "lazy days" with "something unforgettable" emphasises how extraordinary the trips are.
   - Use of an informal style (e.g. "bag loads of new skills") makes Adventure Action seem fun and appealing.
   - The short, punchy sentences in the last paragraph create an energetic tone, making the programmes seem exciting.
   - Descriptive but simple adjectives ("incredible", "fantastic") to illustrate how fun the activities are.

2) All your points should use relevant examples and terminology, and comment on the effects of the language used. Here are some things you could mention:
   - Words and phrases associated with cold to emphasise the woman's detached personality ("icily", "stone cold").
   - The phrases "breath caught painfully" and "sweat prickling like needles" suggest that the man's fear is physically painful.
   - The simile "like a condemned man", which emphasises that the man feels resigned to his fate, and indicates that the woman is in a position of great power.

Page 56 — Warm-Up Questions

1) a) Alliteration. E.g. 'It creates a sense of the speaker's surprise by repeating the harsh "b" sound.'
   b) Onomatopoeia. E.g. 'It helps the reader to imagine the noise created by the students.'
   c) Alliteration. E.g. 'It makes the text more memorable, so that consumers are more likely to recognise the brand.'

2) E.g. 'Sarcasm is nastier than irony, because it has a mocking tone that's often meant to insult someone.'

3) Yes. E.g. 'The text is sarcastic because the positive phrase "Kiet is a brilliant secretary" contrasts with the negative context "he keeps forgetting to bring a pen".'

4) a) Antithesis. E.g. 'It highlights the contrast between the writer's expectations and reality, which makes the reality seem more disappointing.'
   b) Parenthesis. E.g. 'It creates familiarity between the writer and the readers, so they are more likely to be persuaded.'
   c) Hyperbole. E.g. 'It emphasises how terrible the writer feels the rain would be.'

5) E.g. 'It gives the writer's opinion as fact ("By far the best hobby") and makes generalisations, such as claiming that all young people "adore" playing cribbage.'

6) E.g. 'The descriptive adjectives "blistering" and "prickly" suggest that the weather is physically uncomfortable. The imagery "as if I were underwater" helps the reader to imagine the physical strain on the narrator, which is furthered by the descriptive verb "trudged".'

7) a) Superlative. E.g. 'The use of the most extreme form of the adjective 'tough' highlights that the conversation described was a very challenging one.'
   b) Sibilance. E.g. 'The repeated use of the 's' sound creates a sense of pace and reflects the smooth motion of flight.'
   c) Assonance. E.g. 'The assonance of "ow" and "ou" mirrors the wolf's howl, helping the reader to imagine the sound.'

Pages 57-58 — Exam-Style Questions

1) All your points should use relevant examples and terminology, and comment on the effects of the language used. Here are some things you could mention:
   - Alliterative phrases such as "labyrinth of lost lanes" to emphasise how confusing the writer finds Kuala Lumpur.
   - The use of alliteration in "lush lime-green lawns" creates a sense of the neatness and uniformity of the park.
   - Onomatopoeic verbs such as "whine" and "buzz" help the reader to understand the writer's attitude to Kuala Lumpur as a loud and confusing place.

2) Answers should clearly compare the different ideas and comment on the techniques in each text, using quotations to support points. Here are some things you could mention:
   - The writer of Text A has a fairly balanced viewpoint: they acknowledge positive aspects, like the room's size, as well as negative aspects, such as the "limited refreshment". This makes the writer seem more reasonable.
   - The writer of Text B has a more negative viewpoint than the writer of Text A — they instantly "doubted" that the bedding was clean, which, combined with a complete absence of positive points about the room, shows that the writer is quite biased.
   - Hyperbole is used in Text B to emphasise the writer's dislike of the hotel room — "hadn't been opened for about a century". The writer of Text A, however, uses discourse markers such as "Nevertheless" and "but" to show their more balanced viewpoint.

3) Your answer should offer an opinion on the statement. It should comment on the techniques used to describe the party, using relevant examples and terminology to support each point. Here are some things you could mention:
   - The cumulative effect of using several descriptive verbs together in "joking, laughing, making introductions" emphasises how much is going on at the party and creates an exciting atmosphere.
   - Onomatopoeic verbs such as "thumping" and "clinking" help the reader to imagine what the party sounds like, which makes the scene seem livelier.
   - The description of colours in the third paragraph appeals to the reader's senses and helps them to visualise the scene, making the party seem even more like an interesting and exciting place to be.

4) All your points should use relevant examples and terminology, and comment on the effects of the language used. Here are some things you could mention:
   - The use of sibilance ("sights, sounds and smells") to draw the reader's attention to the overwhelming nature of senses that are experienced in the city.
   - The use of superlative ("the most unpleasant odours") to emphasise the foul smell of the city.
   - The use of assonance in the phrase "bleak streets teem" as the repeated vowel sounds make it feel like the smell is everywhere.

Page 70 — Exam-Style Questions

1) All your points should use relevant examples and terminology, and comment on how the structural features used create a sense of loss. Here are some things you could mention:
   - The shift in time that the extract uses — it starts in the present day, goes back to the past, then returns to the present. This allows the reader to become emotionally invested in Joan, so the reader feels her sense of loss more deeply.
   - The progression from "she had already been looking forward to the next visit", to "there wouldn't be a next visit", which emphasises the sadness of the fact that Joan's life is drawing to a close.
   - The motif of Joan looking at the sea, which is revisited in the first and last paragraph, and is contrasted by the way she "raced into the sea" in the second paragraph. This structure creates a sense of loss, as this comparison highlights the difference between what Joan's life used to be like and what it is like now.

2) All your points should use relevant examples and terminology, and comment on how the structural features used create tension. Here are some things you could mention:
- The perspective shift from the people in the stalls to their focus on the drapes of the stage. This creates tension as the reader sees the audience's excitement and then is shown what it is that they are excited about; this builds anticipation as the reader also waits with them for the performance to begin.
- The change of focus onto the character of Mikhail backstage in the second paragraph. This gives the reader information about what is going on behind the scenes, building on the tension introduced in the first paragraph by showing Mikhail's nerves. By adding a personal element to the text, the reader is more invested in the outcome of the show, which increases the tension.
- The switch from Mikhail's thoughts to the stage manager's dialogue in the third paragraph, interrupting Mikhail's thought process from the previous paragraph. This reminds the reader that time is still passing and that Mikhail's performance is rapidly approaching. This makes the reader feel nervous for him, which creates a heightened sense of tension.

Section Five — English Language: Writing

Page 80 — Warm-Up Questions

1) b) rhetorical questions and d) emotive language
2) E.g. 'Hiding away in the sleepy village of Lyttlewich, Howtonshire, is a true gem of English architecture that you can't afford to miss. Thousands of visitors flock to the ancient Lyttlewich Church every year to marvel at its truly stunning artwork. Isn't it about time you joined the crowd?'
3) a) E.g. 'Fertilisers provide nutrients that are essential for plant growth.'
   b) E.g. 'The ear bones are some of the smallest in the body.'
   c) E.g. 'Roman soldiers used weapons to defeat their enemies.'
4) a) E.g. 'Money can be tricky to get your head around, so why aren't schools teaching us how to deal with it?'
   b) E.g. 'Before you start making your yummy cake, ask an adult to help you get everything you'll need.'
5) a) E.g. Start: Middle of the action, inside the spaceship. Chaotic, fast pace, lots of description, sensory language. Introduce the crew members working.
       E.g. Finish: First encounter with an alien. Both the humans and aliens are behaving quite aggressively. Cliffhanger as alien pounces forward.
   b) E.g. Start: Joyful, sunny day as a bird is migrating with his family. Pastoral imagery, peaceful and dreamlike, sense of wonder and excitement.
       E.g. Finish: He gets separated from his family and lands on a desert island. Some animals comfort him and offer help.
6) a) E.g. 'First person, to give an insight into the character's thoughts and feelings.'
   b) E.g. '"Eerie", to make the forest seem scary and sinister. "Timid", to make the character seem afraid.'
   c) E.g. 'The moon was shining as brightly as a new penny.'
7) a) E.g. 'From the diving board, the swimmers below look like a shoal of brightly coloured fish.'
   b) E.g. 'The noises in the pool echo like whalesong.'
   c) E.g. 'I feel the roughness of the tiles under my bare feet.'
   d) E.g. 'The bitter chlorine catches in the back of my throat.'
8) Answers should include ideas for descriptive techniques and devices that could be used to describe a family member.

Page 81 — Exam-Style Questions

1) Answers need to be entertaining for an audience of adult regular readers. They need to use interesting language techniques to create a suitable tone and style. Writing needs to be structured and clear. Here are some techniques you could include:
- The five senses: The air smelt of damp vegetation.
- Personification: The leaves whispered in the night.
- A first-person narrator: I shivered with cold as a brisk winter breeze crept into our tent.

2) Answers need to be entertaining for adults who will read the local newspaper. They need to use interesting language techniques to create a suitable tone and style. Writing needs to be structured and clear. Here are some techniques you could include:
- Direct address: You might think that nothing exciting could ever happen in a small supermarket in the sleepy town of Drizzleford. You'd be wrong.
- Personification: Rows and rows of cleaning products stood by on the shelves, saluting ambling passersby.
- An unusual character: The town's oldest resident, Agatha Hart, was a tiny lady who, despite being well past retirement age, loved her job in customer services. Although her sweet pastel blouses and pleasant smile may have suggested otherwise, one thing was certain: she loved a good squabble.

3) Answers need to be entertaining for an adult. They need to use interesting language techniques to create a suitable tone and style. Writing should be structured and clear. Here are some techniques you could include:
- The five senses: Crisp air carried the scent of fir and pine, and gritty dust crunched beneath his feet.
- Similes: As far as the eye could see, rugged peaks stood proudly like an assembly of wise druids.
- Alliteration: The sky was a bright and brilliant blue.

Page 92 — Exam-Style Questions

1) Answers need to create an appropriate tone and style using suitable vocabulary and language techniques. They need to include a headline and may include other layout features, such as a strapline or subheadings. Writing needs to be well-organised, clear and technically accurate. Here are some techniques you could include:
- Direct address: "You shouldn't spend too long staring at the screen of your tablet or smartphone."
- Imperative verbs: "Start doing something active today."
- Reassuring language: "It's okay if you haven't tried a sport before — most sports clubs welcome beginners."

2) Answers need to reflect purpose and audience using suitable vocabulary and language techniques. They should include an opening and closing address to the audience. Writing needs to be well-organised, clear and technically accurate. Here are some techniques you could include:
- Rhetorical questions: Do you really care about video games more than your health and wellbeing?
- Lists of three: The more sleep you get, the happier, healthier and brainier you'll be.
- Emotive language: It's absolutely vital that you get enough sleep: your health and happiness depend on it.

3) Answers need to create an appropriate tone and style using suitable vocabulary and language techniques. They should have a title, and should be broken into clear sections using e.g. subheadings or boxes. Writing needs to be well-organised, clear and technically accurate. Here are some techniques you could include:
- Direct address: You should leap at the chance to swap humdrum, drizzly British life for something new.

- Lists of three and alliteration: Travel will give you the confidence, compassion and courage you'll need in your adult life.
- Analogy: Trying to understand different cultures without going out and experiencing them is like trying to bake a cake without flour: dense and disappointing.

4) Answers need to create an appropriate tone and style using suitable vocabulary and language techniques. They should include an address and date, address the recipient directly and use a formal sign-off. Writing needs to be well-organised, clear and technically accurate. Here are some techniques you could include:
- Formal language: Dear madam, I write to express my concern over the state of the nation's housing supply.
- Anecdotal evidence: I have witnessed dozens of young people struggle to find appropriate, affordable housing.
- Linking phrases: Moreover, as a country, our population is crammed disproportionately into cities and towns.

Section Seven — English Literature: Prose & Drama

Pages 130-131 — Warm-Up Questions

1) a) characterisation
   b) theme
   c) mood/atmosphere

2) Answer depends on chosen text.
   Here are some points you could consider:
- What did you think about the characters?
- How did you feel at different points in the text?
- Did you agree with the writer's message?

3) Answer depends on chosen text.

4) Answers should focus on what the character is like, how the writer presents them and how this makes you feel about them. Here are some points you could consider:
- Actions: What does the character do in the text? How does he or she treat other people? How do their actions make you feel about them?
- Structure: Does the character change over the course of the text? Do they learn anything?
- Language: How is the character described? How does the character speak? Does this make them likeable or not to you?

5) Answer depends on chosen text.

6) Answers should focus on what atmosphere the writer creates, how they create it and the effect it has on the reader. Here are some points you could consider:
- Structure: Does the writer reveal what's happening gradually or suddenly?
- Language: What words does the writer use? How do they make you feel? Does the writer use any techniques to create or add to the atmosphere (e.g. imagery)?
- Form: Are the sentences long or short? Do they vary in length? What effect does this have?

7) Answers should focus on what the structural feature is and the effect it creates. Here are some points you could consider:
- What is the feature? Why do you think the writer chose to use it at this point in the story?
- Does it add to your enjoyment of the text? If so, how?
- How would the text be different if the writer had not used this feature or had used a different structure?

8) a) E.g. "The conch shell represents democracy — it enables the boys to impose a fair system on their meetings that allows them all a chance to put their views across."
   b) E.g. "The old chestnut tree symbolises Jane's relationship with Mr Rochester. Just as the tree is split in two by lightning, Jane and Mr Rochester are separated by the revelation that he is already married."
   c) E.g. "Driving is a symbol for freedom. The students have little control over their lives, but they believe that driving would give them some freedom and a sense of being able to escape from their lives."

9) a) Answer depends on chosen text.
   b) Answer depends on chosen text. Here are some points you could consider:
   - How does the writer describe the setting?
   - Does it seem like a generally pleasant time in which to live or not? Why or why not?
   - Do you think it's a realistic description of life during this time? Why or why not?

   c) Answer depends on chosen text. Here are some points you could consider:
   - Are men and women treated differently? Do they have different opportunities?
   - How does social class affect people's lives?
   - Are some characters treated differently on the basis of their race, beliefs or background?

10) Answer depends on chosen text. E.g. for 'A Christmas Carol', you could have picked out the following themes:
- Social responsibility
  It is implied that Scrooge helping the Cratchits at the end of the novel saves Tiny Tim's life. This shows how important social responsibility is — it can save lives.
- Redemption
  The contrast between Scrooge's behaviour at the beginning and at the end of the novel. This emphasises that anyone, even someone as miserly and mean as Scrooge, has the potential to be redeemed.
- Family
  The Cratchits are "happy, grateful, pleased with one another, and contented with the time", despite their poverty. This shows that family can bring comfort and joy to life, regardless of the hardships that people have to endure.

11) Answer depends on chosen text. E.g.
- You might write that the message of 'Macbeth' is: 'Ambition and lust for power can drive the humanity out of a person.'
- You might write that the message of 'Pride and Prejudice' is: 'Don't judge people on first impressions or superficial qualities.'

12) Paragraph a) shows better use of quotations, because it uses short quotations that are embedded into the text.

Page 132 — Exam-Style Questions

1) For this question, you have to focus on a single scene from a Shakespeare text you're studying and then write about the rest of the play. Make sure you pick a scene that you think shows your chosen character in an interesting light, so you'll have plenty of things to write about. This answer is for the character of Beatrice in 'Much Ado About Nothing', starting with Act 2, Scene 1, but it's worth reading even if you're studying a different play. Here are some things you could mention:
- Act 2, Scene 1 of 'Much Ado About Nothing' starts with Beatrice criticising Don John because he is "too like an image and says nothing". This shows her to be judgemental and somewhat cruel in her assessment of others.
- Despite this, however, she appears to be well-liked. Rather than telling her off for her cruelty, Leonato just reminds her that she will never find a husband if she continues to be so "shrewd of tongue". This shows that he is more concerned about the consequences of her behaviour than how rude she is being, which implies that he cares about her future and wellbeing.

- Beatrice's conversation with Leonato also highlights her wit. For example, she answers Leonato's hope that she will be "fitted with a husband" by arguing that "Adam's sons are my brethren, and truly I hold it a sin to match in my kindred." In this line, she plays on the biblical idea that all men are descended from Adam in order to emphasise her point. This shows her intelligence and ability to think quickly. Jokes about incest would have been considered shocking in Shakespeare's day, so this also shows the extent to which Beatrice flouts convention and ignores the rules of society.
- Beatrice shows that she is unafraid to speak directly when she asks Benedick to "Kill Claudio" in Act 4, Scene 1. Her blunt request seems shocking because it comes directly after several lines in which she and Benedick confess their love for each other. This contrast emphasises that she is willing to speak her mind and does not feel the need to be polite to Benedick. It also hints at her vulnerability: she is fearful of love, having been hurt before, and so needs proof of Benedick's commitment to her in order to trust him. This shows that her character is a mixture of toughness and vulnerability.
- Beatrice's anger towards Claudio shows that she can be very loyal. She states that Claudio has "slandered, scorned, dishonoured" Hero. The use of three strong verbs implies the strength of her feeling against him. Beatrice's loyalty to Hero — whose story she never doubts — softens her character and shows how, although she often speaks harshly, she shows loyalty to the people that she cares about.

2) For this question, you have to focus on a single passage from a prose text you're studying and then write about the rest of the book. You should focus on the ways that the author has created a feeling of tension or excitement. This answer is for tension in 'Frankenstein', starting with Chapter 23 (or Volume 3, Chapter 6), from "It was eight o'clock..." to "I rushed into the room.", but it's worth reading even if you're studying a different novel. Here are some things you could mention:

- Imagery is used to create tension in the passage, as Frankenstein awaits the monster's revenge. For example, Frankenstein's anxiety is reflected in the personification of the "restless waves" and the simile of the clouds, which move "swifter than the flight of the vulture". This constant movement creates a feeling of unease in the reader, increased by the presence of the "vulture", which is often seen as an omen of death.
- In the passage, Shelley uses the weather to reinforce this atmosphere of unease and build the sense of tension further. There is a "heavy storm of rain" and the moon's rays have been "dimmed". This creates an atmosphere of restlessness and threat, which echoes the turmoil and danger that Frankenstein faces. The wind has also risen with "great violence", which foreshadows the violence that the monster will presently unleash on Elizabeth.
- Shelley uses the structure of Frankenstein's narration in the novel to create tension. Frankenstein is writing with hindsight about things that have already happened to him, so he is able to make references to events that will occur later in the story. This includes explaining in Chapter 8 that his brother and servant were the "first hapless victims" of the monster, implying that there will be others. This makes the reader nervous about the fates of the other characters. He also says that the times during and just after his marriage to Elizabeth in Chapter 22 (Volume 3, Chapter 5) were "the last moments" of his life when he felt "happiness". This suggests that the events to come in the rest of the novel will be unhappy, creating anticipation about what will happen and increasing the sense of tension in the novel.
- The novel's settings, which include the Alps and the Arctic seas, are intimidating. In Chapter 9 (or Volume 2, Chapter 1), Frankenstein describes the "immense mountains and precipices that overhung" him in the Alps. The adjective "immense" indicates the huge size of the mountains, and the verb "overhung" suggests that they seemed threatening and powerful. The novel's extreme settings appear strange and dangerous to the reader, which makes them feel like anything could happen there. This emphasises the feeling of tension in the novel.

3) This question asks you to focus on a particular theme. Make sure you choose a theme that is relevant to the text you have studied. Focus on how the writer uses language, structure and form to present the theme. This answer is for the theme of social class in 'An Inspector Calls', but it's worth reading whatever play you're studying, because it'll give you an idea of the kind of things you should be writing about. Here are some things you could mention:

- The play emphasises the power that social class can give — Sheila uses her "power" as the daughter of the well-known, well-off Mr Birling to have Eva/Daisy fired, and it's heavily implied that as a result Eva/Daisy is forced to turn to a life of prostitution. Although this event had a huge effect on Eva/Daisy's life, Sheila says that, to her, it "didn't seem to be anything very terrible at the time". Priestley shows that a relatively unimportant decision by a middle-class woman like Sheila can prove catastrophic for a working-class woman such as Eva/Daisy.
- Eva Smith is presented as a symbol of the suffering that the working classes are forced to undergo as a result of middle-class families — there are "millions of Eva Smiths and John Smiths", which suggests that her story symbolises the difficulties of the working classes as a whole.
- The Birling family believe the working classes to be inferior, which is reflected in the way Sybil refers to Eva/Daisy dismissively as a "girl of that sort". However, Eva/Daisy is shown to be morally superior to some of the middle-class characters, turning down Eric's stolen money even though she needs it. This suggests that Priestley thought that social class didn't define a person's character or moral values.
- The Inspector, who reflects Priestley's own socialist views and acts as his 'mouthpiece', presents an alternative to the Birlings' class-obsessed perspective. He disagrees with Arthur Birling's selfish, characteristically middle-class beliefs — the Inspector says that all people "are members of one body" who shouldn't ignore each other's needs, regardless of social class.

4) This question asks you to focus on a particular theme. Make sure you choose a theme that is relevant to the text you have studied. Focus on how the writer uses language, structure and form to present the theme. This answer is about the lives of women in 'Pride and Prejudice', starting with Chapter 13, from the start of the chapter to "do something or other about it.", but it's worth reading whichever text you're studying, because it'll give you an idea of the kind of things you should be writing about. Here are some things you could mention:

- In the extract, Austen emphasises how important it is that the novel's young female characters find husbands. She describes how Mrs Bennet's eyes "sparkled" at the hope that Mr Bingley may be visiting; the verb shows how excited she is, because she hopes that he will marry Jane. Mrs Bennet's reaction is typical of her excitable and emotional character, but it also shows how important marriage was for women at the time Austen was writing — it wasn't socially acceptable for upper and middle-class women to have jobs, which meant they were unable to earn money for themselves, and so were reliant upon marrying a wealthy husband to ensure their financial security.

- Mr and Mrs Bennet's discussion in the extract of the entailment of the Bennet estate shows how the law treated women unfairly. It means that only a male heir can inherit the property, who in this case is Mr Collins. Mr Bennet explains that Mr Collins could turn the female family members out of the house "as soon as he pleases" when he is the owner. This phrase emphasises how little control the female family members will have when the entailment comes into effect. This highlights the unequal position of women in Regency England, because the law is not set up in their favour.
- Austen also explores some of the unfair expectations of women in Regency society. In Chapter 8, Miss Bingley describes how an "accomplished" woman is expected to have several abilities including "singing" and "drawing", as well as other features including a certain "tone of voice". The large number and specific nature of these requirements makes them seem unachievable, and therefore suggests that they were unfair towards women.
- Austen portrays a strong female character in Elizabeth. She is confident about breaking some social conventions. For example, in Chapter 7, she is not worried about getting "dirty stockings" when walking to see Jane, despite Mrs Bennet saying that she would "not be fit to be seen" in that state. Mrs Bennet's disapproval suggests that Elizabeth's independence and lack of social propriety are unusual, emphasising that women typically had to conform to strict expectations of appearance and behaviour to maintain their reputations.
- Austen also demonstrates how women could suffer harshly for breaking social conventions. Regency society's beliefs about social propriety for women meant that Lydia's elopement with Wickham is viewed as a very serious problem. It destroys her reputation: Mary says that Lydia's virtue is now "irretrievable", and Mr Collins claims that Lydia's death would have been a "blessing" in comparison. This highlights how breaking social conventions regarding marriage could have serious consequences for the woman involved.

Section Eight — English Literature: Drama

Page 145 — Warm-Up Questions

1) E.g. In 'An Inspector Calls', Priestley uses stage directions to help create an atmosphere of stately formality. For example, the furniture is described as "solid" and the room as a whole appears "substantial" but "not cosy and homelike".

2) Monologue — e.g. one person speaking alone for a long period of time. Example depends on chosen text.
Aside — e.g. a short comment that reveals a character's thoughts to the audience, but not to the other characters. Example depends on chosen text.
Soliloquy — e.g. when one character speaks their thoughts aloud for a long time, but no other character can hear them. Example depends on chosen text.

3) Answers depend on chosen text.

4) E.g. In Act 2, Scene 4 of 'Romeo and Juliet', Mercutio mocks people who swordfight for being pretentious, calling them "lisping" and "fashion-mongers". This gives the scene a light-hearted tone that reflects the events of the play at this point — Romeo is in love with Juliet and they are due to be married. The humour here suggests to the audience that all is well and things will have a happy ending. This makes the following scenes even more tragic because the audience has been misdirected into thinking the play could end happily.

5) Answers should focus on how the passage makes you feel and how Shakespeare achieves this. Here are some points you could consider:
- How do you feel when you read the passage? E.g. Is it funny, sad, exciting or frightening?
- How does Shakespeare convey the characters' feelings? Look at what they say and how they speak.
- What has happened directly before the passage and what happens next? Does the position of the passage in the text enhance its effect or affect your reading of it?

6) a) Don Pedro's speech — blank verse
The lines are written in iambic pentameter but they don't rhyme.
Prince's speech — verse
The lines are written in rhymed iambic pentameter.
Trinculo's speech — prose
The start of each line doesn't begin with a capital letter.
b) The Prince's speech is written in verse form with rhymed iambic pentameter, and it has an ABAB rhyme scheme. These combine to make it sound serious and important.

Page 150 — Exam-Style Questions

1) For this question, you'll need to write about fate and free will in the extract you've been given, and then pick out specific examples from elsewhere in the play to illustrate how Shakespeare explores fate and free will. This answer is for 'Romeo and Juliet', but it's worth reading whichever of Shakespeare's plays you're studying. Here are some things you could mention:
- A conflict between fate and free will is evident in the play's prologue. Romeo and Juliet are referred to as "star-cross'd lovers", implying that their lives are controlled by fate, not by their own choices. The prologue also states that their death is the only thing that can "bury their parents' strife", or end the feud between the Montagues and the Capulets, suggesting that there is a purpose to their deaths. In this way, Shakespeare introduces the audience to the idea that Romeo and Juliet's deaths are unavoidably fated.
- The form of the prologue echoes this theme of fate: it is written in iambic pentameter, the steady rhythm of which gives the feeling of a pattern long established, which cannot be changed. The prologue is also written in rhyming verse, ending with a rhyming couplet — "attend" and "mend". This makes the declaration of Romeo and Juliet's fate seemed fixed and final, which suggests they have no free will to change their destiny.
- Having established that Romeo and Juliet are destined to die, Shakespeare gives the audience several reminders throughout the play, which strengthens the sense that their lives are controlled by fate. For example, Lady Capulet wishes that Juliet "were married to her grave" and Juliet sees Romeo "As one dead in the bottom of a tomb", foreshadowing their eventual suicides.
- However, although there is strong evidence that fate plays a significant part in the events of 'Romeo and Juliet', the importance of free will should not be underestimated. For example, it could be argued that because the characters often seem to know in advance what consequences their actions will have, they could simply act differently. This is illustrated when Romeo kills Tybalt — before he fights him he realises that killing Tybalt "begins the woe others must end." In other words, he knows that Tybalt's death will have repercussions, yet he still chooses to fight. When he kills Tybalt, he calls himself "fortune's fool", suggesting that he wants to blame fate for what he has done, and that he is simply pretending to have had no other choice.

2) For this question, you'll need to explain Shakespeare's use of comedy in your extract, and then pick out specific examples from elsewhere in the play to illustrate Shakespeare's use of comedy. This answer is for 'The Merchant of Venice', but it's worth reading whichever of Shakespeare's plays you're studying. Here are some things you could mention:

- Shakespeare's use of comedy in the extract provides light relief for the audience before a long, emotional courtroom scene. However, it also highlights themes that are important to the courtroom scene, such as the conflict between Jews and Christians that forms the backdrop of the play. This shows how Shakespeare uses the placement of comedic scenes within the structure of the play to add to its overall impact.
- In the extract, Shakespeare uses puns to create humour. For example, Jessica and Launcelot use the word "bastard" to mean both 'illegitimate' and 'pointless' when discussing the "bastard hope" that Shylock might not really be Jessica's father and therefore that she might not be Jewish herself. Since her mother is also Jewish, the word "bastard" also suggests that it is a 'pointless' hope. Shakespeare's audience would likely have been aware of the dual meaning of the word, and so may have been entertained by the cleverness of the characters. However, the pun also shows the prejudice against Jews that existed in Shakespeare's time, because it demonstrates how it was considered better to be a Christian, providing a serious undertone to the humour in the extract.
- Further comedy in the extract comes from Launcelot's complaint that Jews converting to Christianity will raise the "price of hogs" in Venice. Launcelot is making a joke about the fact that Christians eat pork and Jews do not, so more Christians will make pork more expensive as there will be greater demand for it. In this remark, Launcelot deliberately trivialises the serious issue of Jewish-Christian relations by focusing on something as unimportant as the price of pork. Although his comment may appear insensitive to modern-day audiences, an audience during Shakespeare's time would likely have been amused by Launcelot's flippant attitude and deliberate ignorance of the issues at hand.
- In Act 1, Scene 2, Shakespeare uses mockery and exaggeration to create humour. Portia and Nerissa discuss the suitors who have tried to win Portia's hand in marriage, and the use of exaggeration makes each sound ridiculous, such as Monsieur le Bon, who is so keen to show off his fencing skills that he would "fence with his own shadow". The portrayal of each man as an over-the-top cliché of a bad suitor would be amusing for the audience, as it emphasises Portia's continuing bad luck in finding an appropriate husband.
- Shakespeare's use of disguise and mistaken identity is also humorous. In Act 2, Scene 2, Launcelot's father, Old Gobbo, is blind and so cannot recognise his son. Launcelot tricks him into thinking that his son has "gone to heaven", before eventually revealing his true identity. This interaction is an example of dramatic irony, as Launcelot's identity would always be clear to the audience, which makes this interaction especially funny on stage. Launcelot's disguise also highlights one of the play's key ideas, that appearances do not always match reality. This is perhaps shown most clearly by the phrase "All that glitters is not gold", which is found inside the gold casket in Act 2, Scene 7, suggesting that something being visually impressive does not make it a good thing. Shakespeare's use of comedic disguise therefore emphasises this serious message that appearances cannot always be trusted.

3) This question requires you to think carefully about ideas about gender or growing up, so all your points need to be clearly about one of those themes. This answer is about gender in 'An Inspector Calls', but it's worth reading whatever play you're studying, because it'll give you an idea of the kind of things you should be writing about. Here are some things you could mention:

- Both Birling and Gerald have a stereotypical, often patronising, view of women, which Priestley seeks to highlight and condemn. This is most strongly seen in their treatment of Sheila. For example, Gerald tries to shut Sheila out, stating that she has "obviously had about as much as she can stand" after the questions from the Inspector. He does not make the same comment about himself or the other men, suggesting that he does not consider women capable of coping with difficult issues and that he sees them as mentally weaker than men.
- Men in the play are held to different moral standards than women. Birling appears to defend Gerald by implying that a lot of young men have affairs and telling Sheila that she "must understand" this, indicating that he thinks it is acceptable or at least should be quietly ignored. This suggests that infidelity is tolerated for men in a way that it would not be for women. Through this, Priestley reveals the unequal positions of men and women in early 20th-century Britain.
- Priestley uses the character of the Inspector to challenge the characters' prejudiced views about women. For instance, he questions whether women should really be protected from "unpleasant things". This repeats the words of Birling from earlier in the play, who wanted to protect Sheila from "unpleasant business". The repetition highlights how the Inspector is presenting a different viewpoint, one which suggests that women are capable of dealing with upsetting things as well as men. The contrast of views makes the attitudes of some of the Birlings seem overprotective and prejudiced.
- Priestley also shows female characters who challenge stereotypes about women. For instance, Sheila changes throughout the play and becomes more assertive, insisting that she has "a right to know" about Gerald's behaviour. She takes on a similar role to the Inspector, asking questions of the other characters and trying to get them to see how they have not learn their lesson — "You're just beginning to pretend all over again". By presenting Sheila as strong and independent, Priestley shows how stereotypes about women can be wrong.

4) For this question, you need to talk about your extract and then pick out specific examples of the supernatural elsewhere in the play, and explain them in detail. This answer is for 'Macbeth', but it's worth reading whatever play you're studying, because it'll give you an idea of the kind of things you should be writing about. Here are some things you could mention:

- The Witches are the first characters to appear on stage in Act 1 Scene 1, which highlights their importance. They are accompanied by "thunder and lightning", which makes them seem more threatening, increasing the audience's perception of the supernatural as something powerful and dangerous.
- The focus on the Witches in the first scene reflects how they are the most notable supernatural presence in the play. Shakespeare presents their supernatural powers of prediction as a very powerful force, which drives the play forwards and influences Macbeth to commit terrible crimes, such as murdering Duncan.
- The Witches also speak in rhyming couplets in this scene, including "done" and "won". This emphasises the fact that they are different to the other characters — they exist outside the natural order of the world, so they speak unnaturally. The rhyme and rhythm they use makes their speech sound like a chant, which gives it a magical, spell-like quality.
- Elsewhere, the three Witches are portrayed as unattractive and unnatural — they are "so withered and so wild" that they look scarcely human, and they curse a sailor to sleep "neither night nor day", which emphasises their cruelty. This hints at the negative way that society in Shakespeare's time, and especially the reigning monarch, King James I, viewed witchcraft.
- Lady Macbeth uses supernatural imagery — she calls on "spirits" to help her, which links her with the Witches and the supernatural. This helps the audience to recognise how far she will go to gain power and understand that she is a morally corrupt character.

- The supernatural elements in the play are often ambiguous — the appearance of Banquo's ghost, the dagger and the blood on Lady Macbeth's hands could all be figments of the characters' imaginations, or they could be genuine supernatural occurrences. This ambiguity adds to the complexity of the characters of Macbeth and Lady Macbeth — the reader is left wondering whether they are truly seeing supernatural visions, or if they have been driven mad by their guilty consciences. It also reinforces the fear that the supernatural causes in the play, as the visions inspire very strong feelings of horror in Macbeth and Lady Macbeth.

5) For this question, you need to write about the relationship between two characters over the course of a whole play. This means you need to pay particular attention to the changes that occur between the two characters as the play progresses. This answer is for 'Blood Brothers', but it's worth a read even if you haven't studied the play. Here are some things you could mention:
- Mickey and Edward become best friends and "blood brothers" almost as soon as they meet. This highlights their youthful innocence at that point in the play, as well as the immediate, instinctive bond between them. In contrast, at the end of the play Mickey uses the recurring motif of "Blood brothers" to express his sense of betrayal and anger. This emphasises how much the characters' relationship has changed since their first meeting as children.
- Just before Edward departs for university, Russell uses a montage to illustrate the continuing happiness of the relationship between Mickey and Edward as teenagers. The stage directions say that both characters "smile" frequently, which emphasises the joy and freedom of youth and their pleasure in each other's company. This contrasts with the characters' actions and emotions immediately after Edward returns from university: the stage directions say that Edward "laughs" and jokes, but Mickey is "unamused" and denounces their blood brother bond as "kids' stuff". This contrast highlights the turning point in their relationship — Mickey has come to view Edward as "still a kid", and resents that he himself has had to grow up too quickly. Their relationship continues to deteriorate until the end of the play.
- The balance of power in the relationship between Mickey and Edward changes as time goes on. As children, Mickey has the power in the friendship. He has knowledge that Edward wants, and behaves in a way that Edward admires. When Edward shouts at Mrs Lyons, "you're a fuckoff!", it is clear that he's already strongly influenced by what Mickey says, even when he doesn't know what it means. As adults, Edward holds the influence in Mickey's life — he gets Mickey a house and a job. Mickey resents this, feeling that he "didn't sort anythin' out" for himself, and this contributes to the final confrontation between the brothers.
- The changing relationship between the two boys as they enter adulthood, and their eventual deaths, could be interpreted as a comment on the divisions between social classes in 20th-century Britain — even a bond as strong as the one between Mickey and Edward can be destroyed. In his final speech, the narrator asks whether "class" was to blame for the deaths of the two brothers, suggesting that this is part of Russell's message in the play.

Section Nine — English Literature: Prose

Page 157 — Warm-Up Questions

1) Answer depends on chosen text. Here are some points you could consider:
- The writer's choice of language — is it formal and written in Standard English, or more informal and written using slang or dialect words?
- The sentence structures the writer uses — does the writer use long sentences to describe something in detail, or short, punchy sentences to create an exciting beginning for the reader?
- The writer's tone — what is the overall feeling of the text in the first paragraph? Does it seem particularly cheerful, conversational or melancholy? How is this achieved?

2) Answers should focus on how the writer sets the scene and what effect the description has. Here are some points you could consider:
- Where is the passage set? What is the place like?
- How does the passage make you feel? Can you pick out any words or phrases that contribute to this effect?
- Does the writer use techniques such as imagery to make the description more vivid? If so, what effect does it have on the reader?

3) For example:
   a) Elizabeth Bennet is the central character in Jane Austen's 'Pride and Prejudice'. She is important because she is involved in much of the action, and is portrayed as one of the wisest characters, so we trust her judgement. She has the strongest will of any of the Bennet sisters and she follows her own mind. Because of this, she is responsible for many of the novel's turning points.
   b) Elizabeth is a presented as sympathetic character, which helps the reader to identify with her feelings and decisions. She is presented as a caring, witty character, but her mistakes (e.g. misjudging Darcy and Wickham) make her seem like a real person.
   c) Elizabeth's opinion of Darcy and her sister's suitor, Wickham, changes as she recognises that she has misjudged them. By the end of the novel she has realised that appearances can be deceptive, and that it is wrong to judge people on first impressions.

4) E.g. In 'Anita and Me', the narrator writes in the first person, as an adult looking back on the events of her childhood. This allows the reader to follow her thought processes and empathise with her. The use of a grown-up narrator gives an adult perspective on the events and emotions of childhood, which adds humour and pathos to the narrative.

5) a) For example: "most unfortunate affair", "much talked of", "useful lesson", "loss of virtue in a female is irretrievable", "one false step involves her in endless ruin", "reputation is no less brittle than it is beautiful", "she cannot be too much guarded in her behaviour".
   b) For example: "Reputation was extremely important for women in nineteenth-century Britain. Women who damaged their reputation by behaving in an 'improper' way were regarded as having lost their "virtue", a situation that was judged "irretrievable". This shows that, once a woman's good reputation was lost, there was no way of getting it back — she would have been affected for life. Such women were used as a "useful lesson" to prevent other women from behaving in the same way."

Page 162 — Exam-Style Questions

1) For this question, don't try to pick out every point in the novel where prejudice occurs. Instead, you should pick a few key scenes and explain how the writer uses language, structure and events to portray prejudice. You should also consider other characters' reactions to it, and what effect the theme of prejudice has on the novel as a whole. This answer is for 'Anita and Me', but it should come in handy whichever novel you're studying. Here are some things you could mention:
- In 'Anita and Me', racial prejudice is often casual, such as Deirdre calling her dog "Nigger" because it's black, without realising it's offensive. This casual racism shows the ignorance of some of the residents of Tollington, who often don't realise the impact of their racism. This is reinforced later in the novel, when Sam says that he "never meant" Meena when he made racist comments.

- The novel highlights the role of education and the media in inadvertently encouraging racism — Meena says that all she learned at school about India was from "tatty textbooks" showing Indians as servants, or from "television clips" showing "machete-wielding thugs". This means that neither she nor her classmates are given a fair picture of the country on which to base their assumptions. It also makes Meena feel ashamed of her Indian heritage.
- The racist attitudes of characters in the novel reflect the views of many British people in late 1960s and early 1970s, when the novel is set. For example, Sam Lowbridge makes his racist views public by shouting "If You Want a Nigger for a Neighbour, Vote Labour!" on television — this was the slogan used by supporters of a real Conservative MP who was elected in Smethwick (a town in the West Midlands) in 1964.
- Characters in the novel react differently to racial prejudice. Mama's reaction to racism is to try to disprove racial stereotypes — for example, she purposely speaks English "without an accent". In contrast, Papa tells Meena that she shouldn't accept racist abuse: "first you say something back, and then you come and tell me." The Kumars' mild, non-violent reaction to racism paints them in a much better light than the racist characters in the novel, and emphasises how unfair and illogical racial prejudice is.

2) This question asks you to talk about your chosen text in relation to a particular theme, so make sure the examples you choose are relevant to that theme. Remember to discuss how language, form and structure are used to present the theme. This answer is about social class in 'Pride and Prejudice', but it should come in handy whichever novel you're studying. Here are some things you could mention:
- 'Pride and Prejudice' was written during the late eighteenth century, when class distinctions based on wealth and family connections were fairly rigid, and people were expected to marry within their own class. This expectation, and the struggle to overcome it, is one of the main themes of the novel.
- Most of the characters in the novel are aware of the restrictions of class. For example, Elizabeth recognises that because of her mother's family background, she and Jane are not necessarily 'good enough' to marry Darcy or Bingley, and Darcy himself describes Elizabeth's family as "decidedly beneath" his own.
- Although Elizabeth is aware of the barrier that class creates between herself and upper-class characters like Darcy and Lady Catherine, she is never intimidated by them. For example, whilst Mr Collins is "employed in agreeing to every thing her Ladyship said", Elizabeth is not afraid to speak her mind and criticise Lady Catherine's behaviour, for example telling Lady Catherine that she has "no right" to interfere in her business. Austen uses Elizabeth to criticise the restrictions of the class system, suggesting that they don't need to be as strictly adhered to as some in Regency society might think.
- Austen satirises attitudes to social class using the character of Lady Catherine. Lady Catherine is so convinced that her upper-class status makes her superior that it does not occur to her that the other characters might not agree with her views. For example, she is "shocked and astonished" that Elizabeth won't promise not to marry Darcy.
- Lady Catherine is determined that Darcy will marry her daughter because they are "descended… from the same noble line", despite the fact that Anne is "pale and sickly" and "spoke very little", making it clear that she would not be a good wife for Darcy. This contains an implicit judgement of those who see social class as the most important factor in a happy marriage.

3) This question asks you about the writer's methods, so you need to pay close attention to things like structure and language in your answer. Remember to pick out key events and quotations to illustrate your points, and make sure you relate your points to the historical context of the novel. This answer is for 'Animal Farm', but it's worth reading whatever your set text is, because it gives you an idea of the kind of things a good answer should mention. Here are some points you could include:
- The feeling that all is not well on Manor Farm is present from the beginning of the novel. In the first sentence we are told that Mr Jones is "too drunk" to do his job, showing that he does not have control over the farm. This impression is furthered by the fact that the meeting takes place at night and in secret, and involves Major's "strange dream", which makes it seem almost supernatural.
- Major talks about the "hideous cruelty" of slaughter, uses emotive language such as "slavery" and repeatedly refers to humans as the "enemy". This builds the sense that something is about to happen, so the reader feels the same suspense as the animals, because they know that they are plotting a rebellion that could lead to failure and death. The feeling of fear increases once we realise what Napoleon is capable of. The clearest example of this is when he violently expels Snowball from the farm, and it becomes clear that he has been planning this takeover for some time. We find out that Napoleon took the puppies that he uses to terrorise the other animals from their mother and "reared them privately", implying that he has been planning to seize power since the beginning.
- Following Snowball's expulsion, the mood of fear and uncertainty grows. The scene in which Napoleon slaughters animals he believes are "in touch" with Snowball is terrifying because it shows his power over the other animals. This reminds the reader of Stalin's secret police in the Soviet Union, who tortured and executed politicians who were not loyal to Stalin.
- Perhaps the most horrifying image in the novel occurs right at the end, when the animals realise that they cannot distinguish between man and pig. The line "The creatures outside looked from pig to man, and from man to pig… but already it was impossible to say which was which" creates a real sense of fear, because it is a macabre and disturbing image which reminds the reader of fairytales where men are turned into the beasts that they resemble. The reader realises that the utopian society described by Major can never be achieved, and that the animals will never be free of tyranny and oppression. Again, this echoes events in the Soviet Union, where Stalin's expulsion and subsequent assassination of Trotsky effectively wiped out the possibility of a utopian communist society and resulted instead in fear and oppression.

4) For this question, you need to work out what the author's ideas about the nature of evil are, then explain how these ideas are presented. This answer is for 'Lord of the Flies', but it's worth reading if you're studying a different set text. These points give you some ideas of the kind of things you could include:
- The main message of 'Lord of the Flies' is that evil is present in everyone, that it is only the constraints of society that prevent people from committing evil acts, and that evil can be easily brought to the surface by fear. Golding served in the navy during World War II, and was shocked by the fact that civilians were bombed and by the way that prisoners in concentration camps were treated. It was this experience that made him believe that humans are essentially savage, and that outside of the boundaries of civilisation people are capable of great evil.

- In the novel, the boys don't realise that the evil is inside them, so they make it into a real being — "the beast" — which gives them something to "hunt and kill". This allows them to think of themselves as good, backing up Jack's statement that they are inherently capable: "We're English; and the English are best at everything", and building their belief that by hunting they are ridding themselves of evil. However, the more savagely they act and the more they hunt the beast, the stronger the evil inside of them grows and the more real the beast seems. The beast continually changes shape, from a "snake-thing", to something that "comes out of the sea" to "something like a great ape". In this way, Golding shows the reader that the beast is not real, and also demonstrates how evil continually changes shape depending on what the boys are most scared of.
- When Simon says of the beast that "maybe it's only us", the others laugh at him — they are unable to accept the idea that there could be evil in each of them. Simon's death therefore symbolises the end of reason and goodness. In the scene in which Simon is killed, the boys are nameless and act as a "single organism" which kills with "teeth and claws". This animal imagery shows how savage the boys have become, and how they are losing the final traces of civilisation. Even Ralph feels "a kind of feverish excitement" when he talks about Simon's murder, which shows how strong evil is and how it is present even in the characters that are usually considered 'good' and 'civilised'.
- The novel is set against the backdrop of a nuclear war: Piggy talks about the "atom bomb" and says "They're all dead." This, together with the appearance of the naval officer at the end, reminds the reader that the boys' evil is minor on the wider scale of human evil, and reinforces Golding's message that savage behaviour is man's natural state.

5) For this question, you can write about any prose text that you've studied, so make sure you pick one that you can think of plenty to write about. You need to write about the ways in which the main character has changed, and the ways in which they've stayed the same through the course of the novel. This answer is for 'Great Expectations', but it'll give you an idea of the sort of points you need to make whatever text you're studying. Here are some things you could mention:
- The novel is a Bildungsroman, which means that it follows the progress of one character, in this case Pip, as he grows up. At the start of the novel, Pip is a young, naive boy. His main aspiration is to be Joe's apprentice, and he has no ambition to better himself. This changes when he first sees Satis House and meets Estella, and begins to feel that his own home is "coarse and common". In much the same way, his home becomes a metaphor for his character and he starts trying to improve himself. It is this struggle for education, social class and wealth that causes the first big change in Pip's character.
- This change is demonstrated by the way that Pip acts towards Joe. At the start of the novel, Pip says that he "was looking up to Joe in my heart." However, following his move to London, and once he feels that he has become a gentleman, Pip treats Joe coldly because Estella "would be contemptuous" of Joe. This shows how Pip is blinded by wealth and status, and how his 'rise' in society has made him a harder, more selfish person, who judges people by their social standing and is prepared to hurt his oldest friend in order to impress Estella.
- Pip eventually starts to understand that wealth and status do not bring happiness. This realisation is foreshadowed by Dickens' description of London, a place that in the 19th century was associated with wealth and status, as having "the most dismal trees in it, and the most dismal sparrows, and the most dismal cats, and the most dismal houses". Repetition of the word "dismal" shows how disappointed Pip is with London, and later with his own social advancement.
- A second great change in Pip's character occurs when he meets Magwitch for the second time. Pip's realisation that his wealth, education and social standing are the result of a convict's generosity, rather than a favour from Miss Havisham, challenges his views about the social hierarchy he believes in, and makes him recognise his own "worthless conduct" towards Joe. This is a major turning point in Pip's character, as it makes him realise that social class and status are very different from generosity and goodness of heart, and that the latter qualities are more important in a person.
- Dickens uses the character of Pip to represent the failings of a society that believed happiness could be attained through social climbing and wealth. By having Pip recognise the error of his ways, Dickens showed that he believed people were capable of altering their views and placing greater importance on decency, loyalty and hard work than on money and status.

Section Ten — English Literature: Poetry

Page 171 — Warm-Up Questions

1) a) A word that sounds like the noise it's describing, e.g. splash, creak.
   b) A pause or break in a line, often marked by punctuation.
   c) A sentence that runs over from one line to the next.

2) "the fizzy, movie tomorrows / the right walk home could bring."
   E.g. "The onomatopoeic word "fizzy" sounds lively and bubbly, emphasising the feeling of excitement about the future."

   "They accuse me of absence, they circle me."
   E.g. "Sibilance creates a hissing sound, which highlights the menacing tone."

   "Slowly our ghosts drag home"
   E.g. "The assonance of the long 'o' sounds makes the journey sound difficult and lengthy."

   "a blockade of yellow bias binding around your blazer."
   E.g. "The alliteration causes hard 'b' sounds to dominate the line, creating a harsh tone which suggests the narrator is distressed."

3) Your answer should consider how dawn is personified in the extract and what this tells the reader about the speaker's feelings (e.g. lonely, scared, depressed). Here are some things you could mention:
- Dawn is personified as an "army". This reminds the reader of soldiers preparing to attack, and suggests that the speaker dreads the coming day.
- Dawn is normally a positive symbol, associated with light and new beginnings. The speaker views it negatively, suggesting that he has lost hope.
- Dawn is described as "melancholy" — this reflects the feelings of the soldiers in the trenches. They are weary and depressed rather than energised and ready to fight.
- The words "once more" show that the attack continues with no respite, and creates a sense that there will be no end to the war or to the soldiers' suffering.

4) a) E.g. "The strict rhyme scheme uses rhyming couplets (AABB etc.) to emphasise the Duke's obsessive need for order and control."
   b) E.g. "The direct address brings the narrator to life, making his presence a dominant feature of the narrative."
   c) E.g. "The Duke's speech often runs on from one line to the next, which creates the impression that he doesn't give his visitor a chance to speak, and shows his desire to dominate the conversation."

Section Eleven — English Literature: Poetry Anthology

Page 179 — Warm-Up Questions

1) E.g. 'War Photographer' by Carol Ann Duffy has a regular rhyme scheme — it is "set out in ordered rows" like the photographer's spools. This helps to emphasise the care that the photographer takes over his work.

2) E.g. In 'The Charge of the Light Brigade', the narrator uses the third person to describe a battle between British cavalry and Russian forces during the Crimean War. This makes it more difficult to empathise with the soldiers because there is no insight into their individual thoughts or feelings, which creates distance between them and the reader. In contrast, in 'Poppies', Jane Weir uses the first person to explore the experience of a mother whose son has gone off to war. The first-person perspective allows for an intensely personal description of her emotions and reaction to her son leaving, which makes it easier for the reader to empathise with the speaker.

3) a) E.g. "'Forward, the Light Brigade!' / Was there a man dismay'd?"
   (Charge of the Light Brigade, Alfred Tennyson)
   Effect: End-stopping imposes order on the poem, reflecting the way that the soldiers' actions are controlled by the officers.
   b) E.g. "My father spins / A stone along the water. Leisurely"
   (Eden Rock, Charles Causley)
   Effect: This caesura slows the pace of the poem, which emphasises the feeling of peace.
   c) E.g. Porphyria's Lover, Robert Browning
   Effect: It emphasises the sense of the narrator's control over Porphyria, because his is the only perspective the reader hears.
   d) E.g. "spits like a tame cat / Turned savage."
   (Storm on the Island, Seamus Heaney)
   Effect: Enjambment places emphasis on the word "Turned", which highlights how suddenly the storm arrives.

4) E.g. Tennyson uses form to convey a sense of order in 'Charge of the Light Brigade'. For example, end-stopping in the lines "'Forward, the Light Brigade!' / Was there a man dismay'd?" creates a controlled rhythm that reflects the way that the soldiers' actions are controlled by the officers. In contrast, in 'Storm on the Island' Heaney uses enjambment to describe the storm: for example, he says that it "spits like a tame cat / Turned savage." Here, enjambment is used to emphasise the word "Turned", which highlights how suddenly the storm arrives, and how little power the islanders have against nature.

5) a) E.g. "I struck and struck again"
   (The Prelude: Stealing the Boat, William Wordsworth)
   Effect: The repetition of "struck" emphasises the narrator's fear and desperation to get away.
   b) E.g. "the waterlogged earth / gulping for breath"
   (Winter Swans, Owen Sheers)
   Effect: The word "gulping" helps the reader to imagine the sound made by the walkers as they walk across the muddy ground.
   c) E.g. "With sidelong flowing flakes that flock"
   (Exposure, Wilfred Owen)
   Effect: Alliteration emphasises the relentlessness of the snow.
   d) E.g. "a green-blue translucent sea"
   (Kamikaze, Beatrice Garland)
   Effect: The smooth, long 'u' sound makes the sea seem appealing.

6) E.g. 'Kamikaze' uses assonance to emphasise the beauty of nature. For example, the repeated long 'u' sound in the phrase "green-blue translucent sea" creates a smooth sound that emphasises the beauty of the sea. This highlights the pilot's appreciation of the natural world and hints that it influenced his decision to return home. In contrast, 'Exposure' uses alliteration to emphasise the terrible conditions the soldiers are experiencing: the snow is described as "flowing flakes that flock", which makes it sound relentless and overwhelming. This contributes to the cumulative sense of threat in the stanza, which reflects Owen's negative depiction of war overall in the poem.

7) E.g. In 'Follower', Seamus Heaney uses nautical imagery to emphasise the father's strength and skill. One effective image in the poem is the description of the father's shoulders as "globed like a full sail strung". This simile likens the father to a ship, which creates an image of strength and power for the reader.

Page 186 — Exam-Style Questions

1) For this question, you have to think about the way that the poets use form, structure and language to describe feelings towards another person, so make sure you choose a second poem that has plenty to write about on the subject. Comparing them means writing about the similarities and differences, so make some links between the poems in your answer. This answer is for 'Sonnet 29' by Elizabeth Barrett Browning and 'Love's Philosophy' by Percy Bysshe Shelley, but it gives you an idea of the kind of things you need to write whichever poems you're analysing. Here are some points you could make:

- Both poets use form to help convey a sense of longing for another person. In 'Love's Philosophy', the final line of each stanza is shorter than the other lines, which makes it stand out. This adds weight to the rhetorical question in each stanza, which emphasises the narrator's desire to be with his lover. The short lines also slow the pace of the poem — this creates a sense of wistfulness, which emphasises the narrator's yearning for his lover. In contrast, 'Sonnet 29' uses the sonnet form to link the narrator's feelings to a tradition of love poetry. However, whereas in a standard sonnet the solution often arrives in line 9, in 'Sonnet 29' it arrives early: "Rather, instantly / Renew thy presence" appears in line 7, hinting that the narrator cannot wait for her lover's arrival. The enjambment of these lines emphasises the words "instantly" and "Renew", which further underscores the narrator's eagerness to see her lover.

- 'Love's Philosophy' has a regular ABAB rhyme scheme, reflecting the constancy of the narrator's feelings towards his lover. However, half-rhymes such as "river" / "ever" create a note of discord, emphasising the narrator's sorrow at the fact that he and his lover are not together. This half-rhyme also emphasises the words "for ever", which underscores the narrator's desire for an eternal connection with his loved one. 'Sonnet 29' also has a strong rhyme scheme, with half the lines ending with the same sound, for example "tree" / "see". This helps to drive the poem forward, reflecting the narrator's impatience to be reunited with her lover. The end-rhyme "thee" is repeated four times, which emphasises the narrator's obsession with her lover and longing for him to return.

- 'Love's Philosophy' and 'Sonnet 29' both use natural imagery to emphasise feelings of longing for another person. In 'Love's Philosophy', Shelley personifies nature, for example "the mountains kiss high heaven", to suggest that all of nature craves intimacy. This adds weight to the narrator's argument that he and his lover should be together. Similarly, Barrett Browning's narrator compares her thoughts to "wild vines" to show that her longing for her lover is uncontrollable. The natural metaphor extends to her lover, who she likens to a "strong tree" about which she grows. This suggests that she yearns for his support.

2) For this question, you have to think about the way that the poets use form, structure and language to present time, so make sure you choose poems that have plenty to write about on the subject. Remember, you're comparing the two poems, so you need to think about similarities and differences between them. This answer is for 'The Emigrée' by Carol Rumens and 'War Photographer' by Carol Ann Duffy, but it gives you an idea of the kind of things you need to write whichever poems you're analysing. Here are some points you could make:

- Both 'The Emigrée' and 'War Photographer' use form to emphasise the changes in the main characters' circumstances that have occurred over time. 'War Photographer' is made up of four equal-length stanzas, and it has a regular rhyme scheme, which reflects the safety and security of the photographer's present situation. This contrasts with phrases such as "running children in a nightmare heat", which describe the chaos the photographer has witnessed in the past. This contrast between the poem's form and language emphasises how the photographer's past is very different from the life he currently leads. 'The Emigrée' also uses form to emphasise the differences between the narrator's past and present. The first two stanzas use lots of enjambment, but the final stanza includes more end-stopped lines. This underscores the contrast between the freedom of the narrator's past and the confined "city of walls" that characterises her present life.
- In 'The Emigrée', time is presented as a destructive force using a war metaphor: "time rolls its tanks / and the frontiers rise between us". By comparing time to an army, and suggesting that it has created the "frontiers" between herself and the past, the narrator suggests that time is responsible for the fact that she is unable to return. Similarly, in 'War Photographer' the influence of the past is presented as something that is personally destructive to the photographer. This is shown by the "tremble" of his hands as he develops the photographs, which is linked to the events of the past by the references to both "then" and "now" in the stanza.
- The main characters in both poems are symbolically taken back through time at the end of their narratives. In 'The Emigrée' this is presented positively: although the narrator says that there's "no way" for her to physically return to the old city, a personified version of her old home appears to her and takes her "dancing". This hints that her memories of the past are strong enough to overcome her present unhappiness. 'War Photographer' ends with the suggestion that the photographer is flying to another war zone, showing that the past is repeating itself. The final rhyming couplet makes his return seem unavoidable; because of his job, the photographer has no choice except to return to another version of the past that haunts him.

3) For this question, you have to think about the way that the poets use form, structure and language to present ideas about war, so make sure you choose a second poem that has plenty to write about on the subject. Comparing them means writing about the similarities and differences, so make some links between the poems in your answer. This answer is for 'Remains' by Simon Armitage and 'Exposure' by Wilfred Owen, but it gives you an idea of the kind of things you need to write whichever poems you're analysing. Here are some points you could make:

- 'Remains' has no regular rhyme scheme; this contributes to the conversational tone of the poem, which highlights the involvement of ordinary individuals in war and helps the reader to relate to the narrator of the poem. In contrast, in 'Exposure', Owen uses a regular rhyme scheme (ABBAC), which reflects the monotonous nature of the men's experience of war, but the rhymes are often half-rhymes (for example "snow" and "renew"). The rhyme scheme offers no comfort or satisfaction — the jagged rhymes reflect the confusion and fading energy of the soldiers.
- Both poets use the experience of soldiers in war to convey a message about how violent, but often monotonous, conflict can be. This is partly conveyed in both poems through the use of structure. 'Remains' has a repetitive structure: the events recounted in the first half of the poem are repeatedly mentioned in the second half. This highlights the traumatic impact of war on those who fight in it, as it shows that the narrator has flashbacks to the death of the looter even when he is "on leave". 'Exposure', on the other hand, has a repetitive structure that emphasises the static, hopeless nature of war. All of the stanzas end with half-lines, and in four of them the phrase "But nothing happens" is used. This simple half-line highlights the lack of change or hope for the men in the trenches, and makes clear that for them the war seems endless and inescapable.
- Both poets use alliterative techniques to emphasise the danger that soldiers are exposed to as part of war. In 'Remains', Armitage uses sibilance to create a sense of the difficult conditions the soldiers must live in. The phrase "sun-stunned, sand-smothered land" emphasises how hot and dusty the desert is, and places emphasis on the violent verbs "stunned" and "smothered", which indicate the violent nature of the conflict. In line 4 of 'Exposure', meanwhile, sibilance is used to mimic the sound of the sentries' "whisper", which creates a sense of ominous quiet that helps the reader to understand the tense atmosphere. Then, in the fourth stanza, alliteration is used to create a sense of chaos and danger in the phrases "sudden successive flights of bullets" and "flowing flakes that flock". This emphasises the danger that the soldiers face, not just from "bullets" but from the "deathly" winter weather.
- Both poets explore war in relation to the soldiers' lives at home. In 'Remains', the writer focuses on how the trauma of war disrupts the narrator's home life. All the narrator has to do is "blink" for the memories to return to haunt him; this emphasises the long-term psychological impact that the realities of war can cause for a person. In 'Exposure', on the other hand, Owen makes the soldiers' homes seem pleasant and appealing, using personification to describe the "kind fires" of home and the "smile" of the sun. This contrasts with the poor conditions, such as the "merciless" winds, that the soldiers experience whilst at war, and helps to emphasise the harshness of conflict.

4) For this question, you have to think about the way that the poets use form, structure and language to describe a particular place. You could choose to analyse poems that use different language to describe a similar place, or poems that describe very different places — just make sure you can think of plenty to say about the similarities and differences between the poems. This answer is for 'London' by William Blake and 'The Prelude: Stealing the Boat' by William Wordsworth, but it gives you an idea of the kind of things you need to write whichever poems you're analysing. Here are some points you could make:

- Both poems use form to help create a sense of place. 'London' uses an unbroken ABAB rhyme scheme, which echoes the relentless misery of the city, and contributes to the sense that London is a place full of pain and sorrow. In contrast, the extract from 'The Prelude' uses blank verse. The regular, unrhymed iambic pentameter of the poem makes it sound serious and important, which emphasises the power of the looming mountains.

- The places described in both poems are presented as confining and inescapable. In 'London', Blake repeats the word "chartered", meaning 'legally defined' or 'mapped out', even using it to describe the River Thames. This makes it seem like natural features are controlled by human rules, which emphasises the power that authorities such as the monarch and the ruling classes have over the physical place and make the city seem oppressive. In contrast, Wordsworth uses repetition to make nature seem powerful and uncontrollable: in the phrase "a huge peak, black and huge", the word "huge" is repeated, which emphasises the sheer size of the mountain. This highlights that it dominates the narrator's view and makes it seem like he can't escape from it.
- Blake uses sensory imagery to present London as a place that is full of sadness and pain. For example, the emotive image of the "chimney-sweeper's cry" appeals to the reader's sense of hearing, which helps them to imagine the chimney sweeper's misery at the dangerous work he has to do. Wordsworth also uses sensory imagery to appeal to the reader's sense of hearing: he twice uses the word "silent" to describe the waters of the lake, which helps the reader to imagine the sense of quiet in the narrator's surroundings.

5) For this question, you have to think about the way that the poets use form, structure and language to present the power of humans in the poems you choose. Remember, you're comparing the two poems, so you need to think about similarities and differences between them. This answer is for 'Ozymandias' by Percy Bysshe Shelley and 'Checking Out Me History' by John Agard, but it gives you an idea of the kind of things you need to write whichever poems you're analysing. Here are some points you could make:
- Both poems examine the power of an individual. In 'Ozymandias', the individual (Ozymandias) was extremely powerful during his lifetime — he was a "king of kings" — but now he is reduced to the "colossal wreck" of a statue in the middle of a desert, showing that he is completely powerless. Conversely, in 'Checking Out Me History', the narrator had little power in the past: he repeats the phrase "Dem tell me" to highlight how little control he had over his own education and therefore his "identity". However, by the end of the poem he has taken power from the authorities: he says that he is "carving out" his own identity. 'Ozymandias' hints that striving for power is ultimately pointless because power doesn't last; in contrast, 'Checking Out Me History' suggests that it is vital in order to overcome injustice.
- The poets both use form to emphasise their message about striving for power. Agard uses a mixture of stanza forms, non-standard English, and no regular rhyme scheme. This indicates a rebellion against the formal structures of poetry and spelling that he would have been taught in school and shows that he is in control of his own education now. On the other hand, 'Ozymandias' is written in sonnet form, but it doesn't follow a regular sonnet rhyme scheme. This reflects the way that human power and structures can be destroyed by time and nature.
- Both poets use strong, aggressive language to show that those in power can be brutal. For example, in 'Ozymandias' the statue's "wrinkled lip" and "sneer" hint at his cruelty and lack of care for his subjects. There is no mention of Ozymandias's subjects rebelling against him, but by emphasising the ruler's brutality, Shelley may be hinting that such an attempt to gain power may be justified. In 'Checking Out Me History', violent verbs such as "Blind me" show the damage the narrator feels the authorities have done to him, emphasising their lack of concern for his wellbeing. In both poems, the use of strong, violent language may hint that striving for power over oppressive regimes is justified.

Section Twelve — English Literature: Unseen Poetry

Page 194 — Warm-Up Questions

1) E.g. It's about the narrator's sense of loss after someone she loves dies.
2) E.g. The narrator means that she and her lover never got the chance to live together and make a home, because he died.
3) E.g. The descriptions of spring are vivid and life-like, which contrasts with the narrator's dead lover. Phrases like "the violets peer" and "Every bird has heart to sing" describe the beauty and joy of spring and rebirth. At the same time, the final line of each stanza describes the narrator's feelings — she is unable to appreciate the beauty around her, and feels only loss and regret, rather than joy.
4) E.g. The rhyme scheme is ABAB. This gives the poem a simple rhythm, which emphasises the sadness of what the narrator is saying.
5) The final line is missing four syllables compared to the other lines. This emphasises the last line and makes it feel like it finishes too soon, which reflects the relationship between the narrator and her lover — it ended too soon, and now something is missing.

Pages 195-196 — Exam-Style Questions

1a) For this question, you have to think about what the poet is saying about loneliness and solitude, and how she says it. Make sure you comment on how form, structure and language are used to present feelings and ideas in the poem. Here are some points you could make:
- The poem has a nightmarish quality — the woman is alone, waiting nervously for her husband's safe return. The atmosphere is tense, as if something bad may be about to happen. The second stanza deals with the woman's actual nightmare, and the alliterative words "coming", "climbing" and "creeping" make the sea feel very menacing and hostile. It's like someone creeping in and stealing her lover. She wakes up, but with the "screaming gulls" and the sea "chill in her arms" it still feels as if she's in a nightmare.
- The main feeling of the first stanza is boredom — she has "nothing to do now he's gone". She needs to keep busy, so she cleans the house. But the cleaning is futile; the broom "leaves a trail of grit". This could show that the act of cleaning can't cleanse her mind of her fear and anxiety.
- The second stanza describes the woman going to bed. She "sleeps downstairs", perhaps because she can't bear to be alone in their shared bed. This shows how even small things can be a painful reminder of the person you're missing. She also uses a "coat for a pillow" — the coat could well be her partner's, and by sleeping with it she may feel closer to him.
- In the third stanza, the onomatopoeic "screaming gulls" creates a vivid image that contrasts with the silence of the rest of the poem, where the only sounds are the sweeping of the broom and the sibilance of the sea creeping closer. The screaming gulls might also be reminiscent of the screams of drowning sailors, highlighting the woman's fear that her partner will die at sea.
- His shirts are hanging on the washing line, which is a reminder that he's coming back, and feels homely and hopeful for a moment. But the final two lines, "and the high tide's breakers' / chill in her arms", immediately recall the sea and the woman's constant fear that her partner will never return. The "chill" of the waves in the woman's arms seems like a forewarning of death — as if she's holding her partner's cold, drowned body in her arms.

- The structure of the poem, broken into three stanzas, mimics the structure of the woman's life whilst her partner is away — it's divided into day, night, day. There's no rhyme, which reflects her slightly panicky state of mind. The final stanza is heavily enjambed, which creates a feeling of time moving faster, of disorder and confusion. The final stanza is also a line shorter, possibly reflecting her partner's early death.

1b) For this question, you have to think about how the power of the sea is presented in the two poems. Make sure you comment on how form, structure and language are used to present feelings and ideas in the poem. You're comparing the two poems, so you need to think about similarities and differences between them. Here are some points you could make:
- Both poems present the sea as something dangerous and powerful. The subject of 'At Sea' fears that her partner will die at sea, while 'The Sands of Dee' describes the death of a girl who is drowned by 'The western tide'.
- Both poets use language to convey the sounds of the sea. In 'The Sands of Dee', the use of repetition (e.g. "o'er and o'er", "round and round") mirrors the sound of the waves and creates a sense of the relentless, unstoppable power of the sea. Similarly, in 'At Sea', the sibilance in the first stanza (e.g. "she dusts the house, / sweeps") echoes the sound of the sea and suggests its inescapable presence.
- The poets both create a tense, frightening atmosphere through the imagery they use. For example, the onomatopoeic image of "screaming gulls" in 'At Sea' creates tension and anxiety by suddenly breaking the silence of the poem with a sound that suggests fear and suffering. In 'The Sands of Dee', the imagery of the "rolling mist" and the alliterative description of the "wild" "western wind" creates a sense of danger and of the power of nature.
- The two poets personify the sea in similar ways. Kingsley describes it as "cruel, crawling" and "hungry", while Copley depicts it "coming", "climbing" and "creeping". In both cases, the imagery the poets use and the harsh alliterative 'c' sounds make the sea sound menacing and unstoppable.
- The form of the two poems is very different, and is used to create different effects. 'At Sea' is written in free verse, with variable line lengths and no rhyme, which makes it seem unstructured and chaotic. This reflects the way the sea affects the woman, mirroring the lack of structure in her life when her partner is away at sea. In contrast, the form of 'The Sands of Dee' reflects the movement of the sea. Unlike 'At Sea', Kingsley's poem has a regular rhyme scheme, AAABAB, which creates a strong rhythm, mirroring the relentless movement of the waves.

Practice Papers — English Language

Pages 207-208 — English Language: Paper 1

1) 1 mark for each correct answer, up to a maximum of four marks.
   1.1) It is too misty
   1.2) A lighthouse
   1.3) They are covered in dew
   1.4) The sea came far inland

2) All your points should use relevant examples and terminology, and comment on the effects of the language used. Here are some things you could mention:
- Descriptive verbs such as "huddled" are used to suggest that the sheep are fearful. This is reinforced by the words used to describe their movements: the sheep "trotted along quickly" as if in fear.
- In contrast, the writer presents the dog as unafraid and even nonchalant. It runs along "carelessly" suggesting that it is "thinking of something else". This makes the roles of the animals clear: the dog is a working pet, whilst the sheep are animals in captivity.

- The writer uses imagery to give really fine details of how the shepherd looks: his coat is "covered with a web of tiny drops". This detail helps to give the reader a clear picture of the shepherd, but also to help them feel the cold, wet conditions.
- The entrance of the shepherd is described using a shorter, less detailed sentence than the ones that surround it ("And then in the rocky gateway the shepherd himself appeared."). This helps to make his entrance seem dramatic, which emphasises his character's importance.

3) All your points should use relevant examples and terminology, and comment how the structural features used help to create a sense of mystery. Here are some things you could mention:
- The writer builds a sense of mystery towards the beginning of the extract by posing unanswered questions. The questions "how far?" and "what was it?" at the end of the first and second paragraphs create an atmosphere of suspense, leaving the reader wondering about the answers to these mysteries. Having the focus shift away from answering these questions in the paragraphs following them suggests that the landscape does not give up its secrets easily, making it seem all the more like a mysterious place.
- The repeated imagery of the mist creates a sense of mystery in relation to the setting. At the beginning of the extract, the bay is "hidden under a white sea mist". This creates a sense of intrigue, as the fact that the landscape is not fully visible makes it seemingly full of secrecy. However, in the last paragraph, the mist "dissolved" and more of the landscape is revealed. This cyclical structure, with the mist being mentioned at the beginning and the end, gives the final paragraph a sense of resolution, as the mist finally clearing decreases the sense of mystery.
- The writer's use of cinematic zooming-in techniques decreases the sense of mystery throughout the extract. The writer first describes "the whole of Crescent Bay", which was "hidden under a white sea-mist", giving the reader a broad but vague view of the landscape. The writer then moves on to describe a few larger landscape features, such as the "bush-covered hills" and the "paddocks and bungalows", before zooming in on much smaller details, such as the "pearls of dew" on the flowers. As more features are described and the detail becomes increasingly minute, the reader is able to piece together a picture of the bay and get to know it more intimately, which results in the setting becoming less mysterious.

4) Your answer should offer an opinion on the statement. It should comment on the techniques the writer uses to describe the setting, using relevant examples and terminology to support each point. Here are some things you could mention:
- I mostly agree that the setting is presented as a beautiful place. The writer repeatedly uses imagery related to light, such as "big spots of light gleamed" and "the leaping, glittering sea" to emphasise how dazzling the scenery is once the mist has lifted. This repeated imagery also creates feelings of hope and excitement, and associating these positive emotions with the landscape makes it seem even more beautiful.
- However, the writer doesn't always present the setting as beautiful. In line 30, the tree is described as a "shock-haired giant" with "his arms stretched out". This use of personification creates a sense of unease, as the reference to a giant suggests that the setting could pose an unusual threat to the shepherd.

5) Answers to either question need to use an appropriate tone, style and register to match the purpose, form and audience. Writing needs to be well-organised, clear and technically accurate. Here are some techniques you could include:

In a description:
- Figurative language: A faint curtain of mist rose off the lake, swathing everything in a sheet of fine white cloud.

- Similes: Just past the end of the jetty, waiting like a promise, was the little red boat.
- Descriptive words and phrases: Tendrils of gelatinous pond weed emerged from the water's edge.

In the opening of a story:
- An interesting, dramatic opening sentence: "The boat appeared too suddenly for them to avoid it."
- Direct address: "If you'd seen what I saw on that misty October evening, you'd have done the same thing."
- Descriptive words and phrases: "As we stepped onto the boat, the water was so still it looked like a mirror, perfectly reflecting the amber-tinged clouds hanging lazily in the summer sky."

Pages 212-213 — English Language: Paper 2

1) 1 mark for ticking each of the following statements:
   A Monica Albelli thinks being a nanny is a difficult job.
   D Lesley and Brian are both professionals of a similar age.
   E Lesley and Brian care about their children.
   H Lesley and Brian sometimes gave Monica conflicting instructions.

2) Answers should use relevant quotes from both texts to summarise several differences between the two people. Here are some things you could mention:
- Mrs Sidgwick and Lesley are very different people, particularly in their attitude towards the people they employ. Mrs Sidgwick does not treat her governess as if she's a person; it is thanks to Mrs Sidgwick that Charlotte feels as if she is "not considered as a living and rational being". In contrast, Monica hints that, to an extent, Lesley treated her as a friend: for example, she "confessed" to Monica about her insecurities regarding her children.
- Lesley seems to care more about other people's feelings than Mrs Sidgwick. Lesley doesn't tell Monica the "real reason" that she was fired, suggesting that she might be trying to save Monica's feelings. In contrast, Charlotte writes as if Mrs Sidgwick does not consider Charlotte's wellbeing; Charlotte has "never" been so "fully" occupied before, which makes her so tired that she "can write no more".
- Mrs Sidgwick does not seem to take an interest in her children's education. Charlotte maintains that Mrs Sidgwick "does not intend to know me", even though the children are with her "constantly". This implies that she is distanced from her children and their well-being. Lesley, however, has strong views concerning Albelli's role, wanting her to create "responsible and hard-working individuals". Although Lesley also becomes distanced from her children, she views this development negatively; she feels "jealous" and "threatened" by Albelli, and replaces her.

3) All your points should use relevant examples and terminology, and comment on the effects of the language used, focusing on how it is used to describe Brontë's role as a governess. Here are some things you could mention:
- Brontë uses an informal exclamation, "But, alack-a-day!" to express the overwhelming nature of her job as a governess. The exclamation contrasts with the generally formal nature of the letter, which features phrases like "exceedingly obliged". This emphasises the extent of her frustration at her job, as her negative feelings about being a governess can barely be concealed.
- Brontë uses descriptive language to express her viewpoint in a strong and compelling way. For example, she uses a list of adjectives, describing the children she takes care of as "riotous, perverse, unmanageable". The cumulative effect of these negative adjectives helps to emphasise Brontë's displeasure with her current situation.
- Brontë uses hyperbole to emphasise the hardships she is facing. For example, she says that she doesn't have "a free moment or a free thought left" because all her time is spent looking after children. This makes Brontë seem exasperated and suggests that she does not enjoy the amount of time she spends with the children.

4) Answers should clearly compare the different attitudes in each text and comment on the techniques used to convey these attitudes, using quotations to support points. Here are some things you could mention:
- Brontë's letter suggests that she feels limited and confined by the duties involved in looking after other people's children. She refers to her wards as being "constantly" with her. Brontë's choice of adverb suggests that she gets no respite from the children; it also indicates that she resents this constant imposition.
- Albelli indicates a similarly close proximity to her wards: the image of the young boy "curled" around her leg is a symbol of the closeness between them. However, she uses rhetorical questions to suggest that this closeness is desirable, which challenges negative attitudes such as Brontë's. She questions "How can Mary Poppins be indifferent?", to suggest that nannies should aim to be close to children in their care, even whilst maintaining some degree of professional detachment.
- Brontë suggests that the expectations of her role as a nanny are unattainable. She states that she cannot do what Mrs Sidgwick demands; "to love her children and be entirely devoted to them". Emotive language used throughout the extract supports this, with verbs such as "overwhelms" and "squeezed" implying that she is over-exerted. In contrast, Albelli highlights the danger of nannies surpassing expectations and fulfilling the role of a mother, as Lesley feels "threatened" by her success with the children. This implies that Albelli feels the problems faced by parents over childcare are greater than the problems experienced by nannies.

5) Answers need to use an appropriate tone, style and register to match the purpose, form and audience. They need to include a headline and may include other layout features, such as a strapline or subheadings. Writing needs to be well-organised, clear and technically accurate. Here are some techniques you could include:
- Direct address: Our parents are trying their best to help us succeed, but they need to understand that putting us under so much pressure will ultimately be counterproductive.
- Repetition: Working hard isn't always a negative thing: it creates a sense of achievement, a sense of ambition and a vital sense of purpose.
- Facts and statistics: Some of the most academically successful education systems have the highest rate of student dissatisfaction.
- Satirical language: Draining the joy from a young person's life with constant chores and homework is, of course, one of the hallmarks of good parenting.
- Rhetorical questions: Should children look back on their childhood and struggle to remember anything but homework and chores?

Practice Papers — English Literature

Pages 215-220 — English Literature — Paper 1: Section A (Shakespeare)

1) For this question, you have to write about masculinity, so you need to pick out important bits of the play where Shakespeare addresses this theme, and explain how each bit you write about relates to the question. Don't forget to write about the extract in detail as well as the rest of the play. Here are some points you could make:

- In Act 1, Scene 7, Lady Macbeth links the idea of masculinity to bravery and violence. She bullies her husband into killing Duncan by questioning his masculinity: "When you durst do it, then you were a man". From Lady Macbeth's perspective, the ability to commit violent acts is a key element of masculinity.
- Macbeth's view of masculinity in the extract contrasts with that of Lady Macbeth. He explains that to kill his king would not "become" a man, and that if he commits the murder he is "none": not a man at all. Macbeth incorporates concepts of honour and loyalty into his ideas about masculinity, which shows that he is morally more principled than Lady Macbeth.
- However, as the scene progresses, Lady Macbeth persuades Macbeth to change his mind, and he decides once again that he will kill the king. It is clear that Lady Macbeth's attacks on his masculinity have influenced him, as he tells Lady Macbeth that due to her "undaunted mettle" (bravery) she deserves to "Bring forth men-children only". This shows that, like Lady Macbeth, he has come to associate masculinity with the desire to commit violent acts, regardless of whether or not it is the moral thing for someone to do.
- Shakespeare challenges this view of masculinity by presenting Macbeth and Lady Macbeth's actions as cowardly. They kill Duncan in his sleep, and they pin his murder on his innocent servants. Audiences at the time would have considered Macbeth's actions to be unmanly and dishonourable. His lack of honour and unmasculine behaviour sets the scene for his eventual downfall.
- As the play progresses, Macbeth becomes less willing to commit 'masculine' acts of violence; instead he acts like Lady Macbeth, manipulating other people to achieve his own ends. This suggests that he is moving away from the "brave" warrior of Act 1, which was the masculine ideal of the Middle Ages, when the play is set.

2) For this question, you have to write about Romeo as a romantic lover, so you need to pick out important bits of the play where Shakespeare addresses this idea, and explain how each bit you write about relates to the question. Don't forget to write about the extract in detail as well as the rest of the play. Here are some points you could make:

- In Act 2, Scene 2, there is a strong sense of Romeo's physical attraction for Juliet, as he enjoys looking at her and imagining being with her: "See how she leans her cheek upon her hand. / O that I were a glove upon that hand". Shakespeare shows that Romeo physically desires Juliet, but also hints that his romantic feelings for her at this stage in the play are relatively shallow and rooted in lust rather than true affection.
- However, we also see how strongly Romeo admires Juliet. For example, he compares her to the sun: "what light through yonder window breaks?". This makes it seem as though he feels that the world is lit up by Juliet's presence. He goes on to say that the moon is jealous of her, "pale with grief / That thou… art far more fair than she." This metaphor suggests the power of Romeo's romantic feelings and his sense of awe at her beauty. The comparison is particularly dramatic given that the two have just met; this emphasises Romeo's ability to fall in love very quickly, but also suggests the depth of his new love for Juliet.
- At the start of the play, Romeo's romantic feelings for Rosaline appear juvenile. Mercutio mocks him for crying "Ay me!", and Friar Lawrence criticises him for "doting" on her rather than "loving" her. This shows that the other characters think Romeo is being silly about his romantic feelings for Rosaline. By portraying Romeo's romantic feelings for Rosaline as childish and unrealistic, Shakespeare makes the audience doubt whether his love for Juliet is any more authentic.
- Romeo's devastation at Juliet's apparent death suggests that his love for her is deeper than it was for Rosaline. He uses aggressive language, including grotesque verbs such as "Gorged", to portray death as greedy, showing that he is disgusted by the way Juliet has been taken and considers it unfair. This extreme emotional reaction implies that he had a true affection for Juliet. This is further emphasised by his subsequent suicide in order to be with her, which suggests to the audience that his feelings of love were so strong that he felt he could not live without her. By the end of the play, the audience is therefore encouraged to view Romeo as a character who is capable of feeling romantic love to an extreme extent.

3) For this question, you have to write about Caliban as deserving of sympathy, so you need to pick out important bits of the play where Shakespeare addresses this idea, and explain how each bit you write about relates to the question. Don't forget to write about the extract in detail as well as the rest of the play. Here are some points you could make:

- In the extract, Caliban claims to have been betrayed by Prospero. Commenting on how he initially trusted him, he cries "Cursed be I that did so!". The strong exclamation shows that Caliban feels very upset, and his distress invites the audience to feel sympathy for him. Furthermore, his belief that he should be "Cursed" implies that he feels trusting Prospero was a mistake that he regrets. This hints that Prospero has betrayed his trust. The idea that Caliban has been betrayed incites further sympathy for him from the audience.
- Caliban believes the island was stolen from him, claiming that Prospero "tak'st" it from him. His knowledge of the area is shown in his description of its "fresh springs, brine-pits, barren place and fertile". The detailed list suggests that he has a deep understanding of the island, giving support to his claim that it belongs to him. This encourages the audience to agree with his claim that Prospero is a thief who has stolen his land. Caliban's treatment may represent how, during the time that Shakespeare was writing, European colonists were taking over lands in other parts of the world, often oppressing the people living there, in the same way that Caliban's lands are taken from him before he is enslaved. The moral issues around colonisation and how people were being mistreated were often debated at the time; Shakespeare may be encouraging the audience to similarly consider whether Caliban has been mistreated and may therefore deserve sympathy.
- However, Caliban's immoral behaviour makes him less deserving of sympathy. In Act 1, Scene 2, Prospero claims that Caliban "didst seek to violate / The honour of my child", suggesting that he tried to rape Miranda. Later in the play, in Act 3, Scene 2, Caliban encourages Stephano to use Miranda to have a "brood" of children. This callous attitude towards Miranda, seeing her only as a possession to be taken or as a means for having children, portrays Caliban as crude and violent, especially towards women. This makes the audience doubt whether the earlier sympathy they felt for Caliban was rightly placed, and question whether Caliban or Prospero's version of events about what happened when Prospero came to the island is closer to the truth.
- Moreover, in Act 3, Scene 2, Caliban initiates the plot to take revenge on Prospero. This shows he is inclined to vengeance and violence. He suggests to Stephano various ways to kill Prospero, including that he should "Batter" him with a log, "paunch" him with a stake or "cut" his wind-pipe. The detail of the description and the violence of the verbs Caliban uses suggests that he relishes the idea of killing Prospero. Caliban's enjoyment of violence implies that he is an immoral character, and therefore someone who Shakespeare intends the audience to have only limited amounts of sympathy for.

4) For this question, you have to write about justice and mercy, so you need to pick out important bits of the play where Shakespeare addresses these themes, and explain how each bit you write about relates to the question. Don't forget to write about the extract in detail as well as the rest of the play. Here are some points you could make:
- Portia's speech in the extract explores in detail the two related themes of mercy and justice. The speech is written in blank verse, which makes it seem more important than if it were written in prose. This emphasises that these are key themes in the play.
- The speech presents the concepts of mercy and justice as two very different things. Portia links justice with the laws of Venice: if Shylock follows his "plea" for "justice", then the "strict court" of Venice will be forced to sentence Antonio. Mercy, on the other hand, is presented as a human quality that can be used to "mitigate" the law; in this speech, Portia asks Shylock to consider abandoning his case against Antonio in the name of "mercy", even though "justice" would convict him.
- Portia's speech hints at a negative portrayal of justice that is reinforced throughout the play. Many of the characters associate justice with the character of Shylock, who is obsessed with "justice and his bond." His cruel quest for revenge on Antonio relies on the justice of the court, which shows that Venetian justice is unreliable and can lead to unfair consequences.
- In contrast, the portrayal of mercy in Portia's speech is strongly positive. She calls mercy an "attribute to God" that comes from "heaven", and says that if justice alone were followed then nobody would "see salvation". This suggests that mercy is a divine attribute, which is required in order to reach heaven. This would have resonated strongly with the predominantly Christian audiences of the Elizabethan era, who would have understood mercy as an important quality that a good Christian person should have.
- The idea that showing mercy is the right thing to do under any circumstances is reinforced throughout the play. Despite Portia's speech, and Bassanio's offer of money, Shylock refuses to show mercy to Antonio, insisting that "no power in the tongue of man" can persuade him to change his mind. His insistence on justice and refusal to be merciful condemns him: Portia twists the rules of the court so that justice no longer works in his favour, and he can no longer harm Antonio; furthermore, Shylock's own life and fortune are forfeit.
- Antonio's final request as part of Shylock's punishment is to insist that he "become a Christian". Audiences in Shakespeare's time would have associated Christianity with mercy, so it is appropriate that Shylock's final punishment is to be forced to embrace the ideals of mercy and forgiveness that he previously rejected.

5) For this question, you have to write about the changing relationship between Benedick and Beatrice, so you need to pick out important bits of the play where this is shown, and explain how each bit you write about relates to the question. Don't forget to write about the extract in detail as well as the rest of the play. Here are some points you could make:
- At the start of the play, Benedick and Beatrice have a combative but playful relationship. Both characters use wordplay, which emphasises their wit and suggests that they enjoy arguing with each other. Between them, they cleverly develop the same extended metaphor using animal imagery: Benedick calls Beatrice a "parrot-teacher", and in return, Beatrice replies, "A bird of my tongue is better than a beast of yours." She also suggests that she is cleverer than Benedick by linking his intelligence to that of a "beast" that cannot speak. This interplay is likely to persuade the audience that, although their relationship appears antagonistic, they are perfectly matched in character and intelligence and may well fall in love by the end of the play. This is reinforced by the audience's prior expectations of the play: based on Shakespeare's other comedies, they'll be expecting a happy ending.
- However, on an underlying level, Beatrice seems to have a poor opinion of Benedick at this point in the play. For example, she uses a metaphor to describe how "disdain" cannot die as long as Benedick is there to "feed" it, implying that she will always feel disdain for him. She also comments that he "always" ends with "a jade's trick", hinting that he has treated her badly in the past. Shakespeare makes it clear that she has some negative feelings towards Benedick, and that their relationship is not wholly positive at this stage.
- Later in the play, Benedick and Beatrice's relationship changes as they fall in love. They confess how they feel about each other in Act 4, Scene 1, when Benedick says "I do love nothing in the world so well as you", and Beatrice says "I love you with so much of my heart that none is left to protest". The use of exaggeration shows their strong feelings for each other, and the openness and honesty of these declarations contrasts with their usual witty language, highlighting how their relationship has changed to the point where they now openly express love for each other.
- Towards the end of the play, in Act 5, Scene 2, Benedick and Beatrice continue to argue playfully. For instance, Benedick asks Beatrice which of his "bad parts" she first fell in love with; Beatrice replies by claiming that he has no space for "any good part" to fit. These teasing insults show that their witty and playful relationship will continue even though they are now in love, suggesting that this aspect of their relationship has not changed.
- Furthermore, the pair acknowledge that their playful conversation may have always been a way of expressing their affection for each other. Benedick claims that they are "too wise to woo peaceably". This suggests that their playful banter is an important part of their courtship. It also implies that they may have had feelings for each other even in the first scene, when they used similar language. This makes it clear that, while their relationship has changed in the sense that they now know and accept how they feel about each other, their affection for each other may well have been present all along.

6) For this question, you have to write about Caesar as an arrogant character, so you need to pick out important bits of the play where Shakespeare addresses this idea, and explain how each bit you write about relates to the question. Don't forget to write about the extract in detail as well as the rest of the play. Here are some points you could make:
- In the extract, Caesar describes himself as superior to other people. He uses a simile to compare himself to the "northern star", to show how his mind cannot be changed, because the northern star does not appear to move in the sky. His statement that the northern star has "no fellow" in the sky to match it also implies that he believes he is superior to all other people, because of his refusal to change his mind. Since he is the leader of Rome, this is partly true, however the extreme extent to which he stresses his uniqueness and superiority makes him appear vain and arrogant.
- Caesar's arrogance proves to be flawed when, immediately after this speech, he is murdered by the assassins. Dramatic irony is used in this scene, for the audience is aware of the assassins' plan. This is partly because the structure of the play means it has been discussed in previous scenes, and partly because an audience of the time would likely have known about Caesar's murder from their knowledge of Roman history. This dramatic irony means that Caesar appears especially foolish to the audience. Shakespeare suggests that Caesar's high view of himself is misplaced, and that his position is not as "unassailable" as he believes it to be.

- Throughout the play, Caesar shows arrogance in ignoring omens about him. For example, in Act 1, Scene 2, a soothsayer tells him to "beware the ides of March", but Caesar calls him "a dreamer". He also ignores other warnings, such as the advice of priests in Act 2, Scene 2, and Calphurnia's dream in the same scene of people washing their hands in his blood. The repeated motif of Caesar's failure to heed the advice he is given shows that he only values his own opinion, which emphasises his arrogance. His refusal to listen ultimately leads to his death, which suggests that Shakespeare intended the audience to view arrogance as a fatal flaw in Caesar's personality.
- Brutus's motivations for killing Caesar include a fear of his arrogance. He describes his fear that Caesar, as a future ruler, will look only "in the clouds, scorning the base degrees" — those who helped him gain power. The metaphor of clouds suggests that Brutus believes Caesar wants to be higher up than others, while believing that his supporters are "base", indicating that they are still on Earth and therefore inferior. One of Brutus's stated motivations for killing Caesar is the desire to "prevent" this from happening, which implies that Caesar's arrogance, or Brutus's fear of it, contributed in part to his death.

Pages 221-227 — English Literature — Paper 1: Section B (The 19th-Century Novel)

7) For this question, you have to write about morality, so you need to pick out important bits of the novel where the writer addresses this theme, and explain how each bit you write about relates to the question. Don't forget to write about the extract in detail as well as the rest of the novel. Here are some points you could make:
- The novel emphasises the internal conflict that can be caused by immoral desires. This can be seen in the extract, as Jekyll says that he has "called" Hyde from his "own soul". This highlights the link between them, and reinforces the idea that Hyde's "depravity" represents the dark side of Jekyll's personality. Elsewhere in the novel, Stevenson uses the language of battle to show how Jekyll struggles to suppress this dark side: there is a "war" within Jekyll, and the "two natures that contended in the field" of his mind sound like two forces meeting on a battlefield. Jekyll claims that this struggle applies to all of mankind: he says that "man is not truly one, but truly two". This reflects Stevenson's message that all humans have an immoral side.
- Jekyll's language in the extract hints at his ambiguous morality: he describes Hyde's behaviour using some positive language, suggesting that he cannot bring himself to entirely condemn Hyde's actions. Whilst he claims to be "aghast" at Hyde's behaviour, he also describes the "sea of liberty" that Hyde brings him, and he reacts to Hyde's "depravity" with "a kind of wonder". This hints at the conflict between how Victorian ideas of morality dictate that Jekyll should feel and how he actually feels: whilst he feels forced to condemn Hyde's actions in writing, there is a sense that underneath he envies and almost admires him.
- Stevenson also uses other characters in the novel to illustrate the flaws in Victorian views of morality. Victorian society had a rigid set of moral values, so to maintain a good reputation, people had to repress many of their true feelings and desires in public. For the characters in the novel, preserving a good reputation appears to be more important than actually acting morally. For example, Utterson is more concerned about preserving Jekyll's reputation than bringing Hyde to trial: after Carew's murder, he says to Jekyll, "If it came to a trial, your name might appear." This shows his concern for Jekyll's reputation, and emphasises that he prioritises it over the pursuit of justice.
- The novel suggests that evil is ultimately more powerful than moral behaviour. Hyde grows stronger as the novel progresses, and eventually he overpowers Jekyll, and causes his death. This highlights Stevenson's message that trying to hide immoral desires beneath a civilised, moral exterior is very dangerous.

8) For this question, you have to write about poverty, so you need to pick out important bits of the novel where the writer addresses this theme, and explain how each bit you write about relates to the question. Don't forget to write about the extract in detail as well as the rest of the novel. Here are some points you could make:
- Scrooge's encounter with Ignorance and Want in this extract represents a turning point for his character, as he has a strong reaction to the way they look and begins to understand the effects of his attitude towards the poor. Ignorance and Want look like starving children: they are "ragged" and "wretched", which causes Scrooge to feel "appalled". By presenting Ignorance and Want as children, Dickens reinforces the message that the poor are not to blame for their situation, and that they should be helped rather than punished.
- Scrooge's emotional reaction to Ignorance and Want in the extract contrasts with the portrayal of him as unfeeling at the beginning of the novel, where he asks "Are there no prisons?" for the poor to go to. This suggests that he regards poverty as a crime, which is in keeping with the attitudes of many people in Victorian society: people in debt could be thrown into 'debtor's jail', and they were not released until they had repaid their debts.
- Dickens also uses the characters of Ignorance and Want to convey a wider message to his audience. The Ghost of Christmas Present explains that the children are a result of "Man's" neglect, which reflects Dickens's belief that Victorian society was to blame for the lack of education (Ignorance) and basic amenities such as food (Want) among poor children. The spirit explains that ignoring the problems of poverty will lead to "Doom", which suggests that Dickens thought upper- and middle-class attitudes to poverty would have negative repercussions for the whole of society.
- Dickens uses Scrooge's character to attack the mentality that Victorian society had towards the poor. Scrooge initially represents selfish members of the middle and upper classes in Victorian society. He refuses to give to charity, and he calls poor people "surplus population", saying it would be better if they died. The description of Scrooge as a "sinner" shows that his attitude to the poor is ungodly and morally wrong.
- As the book continues, Scrooge learns to reject his selfish views: in the final chapter, he buys the Cratchits a "prize Turkey", and he makes a large donation to a charity that helps the poor. Helping those less fortunate makes him happy: he greets everyone with a "delighted smile" and repeatedly acts with a "chuckle". Scrooge's happiness at the end of the novel shows that it can be satisfying and enjoyable to help the poor. His actions also have a dramatic effect on the Cratchit family, as Tiny Tim survives thanks to Scrooge's financial help. Dickens highlights the ability of the middle and upper classes to have a huge effect on the lives of those in poverty.

9) This question requires you to think carefully about the importance of a single character, so all your points need to be clearly about that character. Don't forget to write about the extract in detail as well as the rest of the novel. Here are some points you could make:
- In the extract, Dickens's use of Pip as a first-person narrator emphasises how intimidating Miss Havisham appears. He compares her to a "ghastly waxwork" and a "skeleton"; these frightening images suggest that Miss Havisham is almost inhuman in her appearance, and reflect Pip's sense of fear. The comparison to a waxwork emphasises that Miss Havisham appears to be frozen in time on the day she was left at the altar, and describing her as a "skeleton" as well implies that perhaps she is frozen in a state similar to death. This increases the eerie atmosphere around her.

- Dickens uses bold, almost grotesque imagery to show how obsessed Miss Havisham is with her own despair: for example, she keeps her mouldy wedding cake, despite the fact that it is covered with insects and "black fungus". This indicates that she hasn't been able to move on from the past, and the unpleasant image suggests that her obsession is dangerous and unhealthy. The use of such dark imagery incites fear in the reader. By using this imagery during Miss Havisham's introduction as a character, Dickens invites the reader to associate this feeling of fear with her as a character.
- Miss Havisham is manipulative throughout the novel: she has raised Estella to "wreak revenge on all the male sex", which the reader sees when she deliberately directs Pip's attention to Estella's beauty in order to manipulate him into falling in love with her. This love hurts Pip emotionally: he says that he is "as unhappy" as Miss Havisham could "ever have meant" him to be. This makes her seem cruel and intimidating, as she had purposely intended Pip to be hurt by Estella.
- However, Miss Havisham's past allows the reader to begin to understand her cruel actions. Herbert describes her treatment at the hands of Arthur as "cruel mortification", which helps the reader to understand why she behaves in such a peculiar manner. Later, when Magwitch is revealing more about Miss Havisham's story, he only refers to her in passing as "a rich lady". This hints at the callous way in which Compeyson treated Miss Havisham as disposable, and presents her as a victim of a crime, which makes the reader feel more sympathetic and less fearful towards her.

10) This question requires you to think carefully about the importance of a single central character and how they change throughout the novel, so all your points need to be clearly about that character. Don't forget to write about the extract in detail as well as the rest of the novel. Here are some points you could make:

- Mr Rochester undergoes a series of dramatic changes over the course of the novel. In the extract, he describes his younger self as "stiff-necked" and "proud", a judgement that is supported by Jane's early encounters with him. The extract takes place after Jane has been absent from his life for some time; when she returns, he is presented as a changed man. The hardships he has gone through have made him understand and overcome the flaws in his character, and he has learned "humility".
- The most obvious change in his character that the extract reveals is his newfound respect for and worship of God: he admits that he initially "almost cursed" the fate that had taken Jane away, but believes that the hardships he went through were "chastisements" from God, which re-establish his faith in a "beneficent" God who "sees... far clearer" and "judges... far more wisely" than man. For the novel's 19th-century audience, Rochester's newfound piety would have been a sign of his virtue and goodness. Later, he regains his sight in one eye, which Jane describes as a sign of God's "mercy". This indicates that Rochester has earned forgiveness for his past sins, and has become a virtuous man.
- This newfound virtue manifests itself in Rochester's actions. Earlier in the novel, Rochester calls his younger self a "trite, commonplace sinner" for his relationship with Céline Varens. His treatment of his wife, Bertha Mason, could also be seen as sinful: he locks her in an attic and denies her existence. However, by attempting to rescue her from the Thornfield fire, Rochester demonstrates that he has already begun to change for the better. This hints that Jane's departure is a necessary step that allows him to re-evaluate his past behaviour and atone for his mistakes.
- Rochester is "humbled" by his experiences, and this is also reflected in his attitude towards wealth and material possessions: when he and Jane first become engaged, he is excited to "pour" jewels into her lap and dress her in "satin and lace". However, when Jane finds Rochester at Ferndean he is no longer interested in "fine clothes and jewels"; instead Jane is described as "the most precious thing he had". This progression of character shows that he has come to understand what is truly valuable in life, and to reject the shallow obsession with wealth and status that characterises the upper classes in the novel.
- By the end of the novel, Rochester has overcome his flaws, and the reader sees that he is now worthy of marrying Jane. This makes the novel's resolution satisfying for the reader, who sees that the characters have received the outcome they deserve.

11) For this question, you have to write about revenge, so you need to pick out important bits of the novel where the writer addresses this theme, and explain how each bit you write about relates to the question. Don't forget to write about the extract in detail as well as the rest of the novel. Here are some points you could make:

- Frankenstein's language in the extract presents revenge as a powerful and violent force: he uses emotive, visceral phrases such as "drink deep of agony" to show the strength of his anger and indicate his desire to do real harm to the monster. Similarly, the monster often speaks violently of his revenge: for example, he promises to bring about Frankenstein's "destruction" when his creator initially refuses to create a female companion.
- The idea that revenge is something unhealthy and harmful is established early on in the novel. After William's death, Alphonse begs Frankenstein to avoid "brooding thoughts of vengeance", as they will end up "festering, the wounds" of his mind. The use of the word "festering" suggests that revenge is like a disease, foreshadowing the harm it will cause.
- The monster and Frankenstein are linked by their desire for revenge, and this becomes a damaging cycle that destroys both of their lives. Revenge isolates Frankenstein permanently from society, and drives him to the Arctic, eventually leading to his death; meanwhile, the monster is made miserable, describing his quest for revenge as "deadly torture".
- The monster's idea of revenge is more complicated than Frankenstein's. Frankenstein has one goal: to kill the monster in order to avenge the deaths of his family. In contrast, the monster's revenge is more calculated: he kills Frankenstein's loved ones first, in order to inflict on Frankenstein the kind of loneliness he has suffered. This shows that his thirst for revenge has made him cruel and scheming.
- Shelley makes it clear that Frankenstein's quest for revenge has affected his sanity. In the extract, he talks about the "spirits of the departed" as if they are really there, and his exaggerated language as he describes his "deep and eternal grief" and swears an oath to "the spirits" emphasises that his behaviour is irrational. This shows the reader that he has been emotionally destroyed by the suffering he has faced, and helps them to understand his motivation in setting out on a fatal quest for revenge on the monster.
- Shelley makes it clear that revenge is an ultimately unsatisfying endeavour. Even though the monster achieves the destruction he wants, he is still "miserable" because he has been "polluted" by his crimes, so he decides that the only option is to kill himself. This suggests that he has been irrevocably tainted by the murders he has committed, and shows that even though he has been able to fulfil his revenge, it is not satisfying enough to overcome his sense of guilt and shame.

12) For this question, you have to write about Mr and Mrs Bennet's relationship, so you need to pick out important bits of the novel where the writer addresses this, and explain how each bit you write about relates to the question. Don't forget to write about the extract in detail as well as the rest of the novel. Here are some points you could make:
- The extract shows how Mr and Mrs Bennet have an unequal and often difficult relationship. When they discuss Mr Bingley's arrival at Netherfield, Mr Bennet mocks Mrs Bennet's vanity by suggesting that "Mr Bingley may like you the best of the party." This shows that Mr Bennet is more intelligent and witty than Mrs Bennet, and does not regard her as an equal, but rather makes fun of her, realising that she won't understand the joke. His behaviour is quite cruel, which also reveals his lack of affection for her. The fact that she does not appear to be offended by his teasing and lack of respect for her may be due in part to the fact that society in the early nineteenth century would not have allowed a woman like Mrs Bennet to earn a living, so she would have been entirely dependent on Mr Bennet, and could not afford to drive him away.
- Mrs Bennet switches between berating her husband for not doing as she asks, and treating him affectionately when he does what she wants. For example, in the extract she is angry and resentful when he refuses to visit Bingley, and says "You take delight in vexing me", but when she later learns that he has visited Bingley, she is delighted and immediately forgives him: "What an excellent father you have, girls". The speed with which her attitude to Mr Bennet changes shows how shallow her feelings towards him are. This highlights that their marriage isn't based on deep feelings of love, respect or equality, which reinforces the idea that they are not particularly happy together in their relationship.
- Mr and Mrs Bennet are both largely comic characters, Mr Bennet because of his quick, dry wit, and Mrs Bennet because of her ignorance and lack of decorum. However, their relationship has more serious undertones; it is clear that the marriage was a mistake and they are fundamentally unsuited to one another. For example, Mr Bennet is described as "a mixture of quick parts", whereas Mrs Bennet is "a woman of mean understanding", which illustrates the difference in their intellect. We are told that Mr Bennet was initially "captivated by youth and beauty", showing that his feelings were superficial, and all "Respect, esteem, and confidence" for his wife were quickly lost. This illustrates one of Austen's messages: that it is important to select a partner on the basis of intellect, compatibility and love, rather than on the basis of wealth or sexual attraction.
- The Bennet's unhappy marriage is echoed in other marriages in the novel that are motivated by financial or superficial reasons, namely Charlotte and Mr Collins, and Lydia and Mr Wickham. In this way, Austen uses Mr and Mrs Bennet as a way of foreshadowing what will become of these couples, and as a way of emphasising that the cycle of unhappy marriages will never be broken until people realise that the only good reason to marry is for love.

13) For this question, you have to write about Watson and Mary's relationship, so you need to pick out important bits of the novel where the writer addresses this, and explain how each bit you write about relates to the question. Don't forget to write about the extract in detail as well as the rest of the novel. Here are some points you could make:
- In the extract, Watson and Mary are finally able to admit their feelings for each other after they find out the treasure is lost. Watson says "Thank God!" when he discovers that the box is empty. This short statement, which is also punctuated with an exclamation mark, emphasises Watson's immediate joy and elation. Such a quick and emotional reaction suggests that his desire for a loving relationship with Mary is strong and genuine.
- Watson describes Mary as being within his "reach" again now that the "golden barrier" of the treasure between them has gone: describing it as a "barrier" emphasises how the treasure has kept them apart for most of the novel. This highlights the significance of the treasure in their relationship; although it is the mystery surrounding it that brings them together, their relationship is impeded by its impact.
- Mary expresses ambivalence towards the treasure. For example, she reacts "calmly" when the treasure is revealed to be lost, and says "'Thank God,' too" when Watson declares his love for her. Mary is more happy about gaining Watson than sad about losing her potential fortune, which shows that she values Watson and their loving relationship over money.
- The first meeting of Watson and Mary illustrates his immediate attraction towards her. He describes her in a positive way: she is "dainty" and "dressed in the most perfect taste". Even after she has gone, he cannot stop thinking about her "smiles" and the "deep rich tones of her voice". Such specific and detailed description highlights his attraction to her. However, while Watson describes Mary in a positive way, his observations are realistic: he notices that her face lacks both "regularity of feature" and "beauty of complexion", which suggests that the love he has for her is not just idealistic or superficial.
- Watson's position as a narrator gives the reader insight into their relationship, as he is able to narrate the events of the novel with the benefit of hindsight. For example, when Watson fails to console Mary during the cab journey, he reveals that Mary later told him he appeared "cold and distant". The phrase "She has told me since" implies that the pair stay in touch after the events of the text. As this is revealed before they admit their feelings for each other, it allows the reader to view their relationship as more likely to develop into love, despite Mary's negative impression of Watson at this point in the text.
- Part of the reason Watson is distant is his concern that he will be perceived as a "vulgar fortune-seeker" because Mary is "rich". In Victorian society, it was traditional for wives to be dependent on their husbands, and the Agra treasure threatens to reverse this. This shows that, despite their love for one another, Watson and Mary's relationship is dependent on the rules of society. It is only when the treasure is gone and their relationship conforms to these rules that they can be together.

Pages 229-231 — English Literature — Paper 2: Section A (Modern Prose or Drama)

1) This question requires you to think about a single central character, so all your points need to be about that character. You need to write about how Priestley presents Arthur Birling as a selfish character, so make sure you mention the techniques that he uses. These points give you some ideas of the kind of things you could include:
- Birling's selfish nature first becomes apparent in Act One, when he uses a congratulatory speech for Sheila and Gerald as a chance to talk about himself. He explains how their marriage means "a tremendous lot" to him, because it will bring together his company and a rival company, suggesting that his feelings about the marriage are focused on how it will benefit him in business. This portrays him as a self-interested character, who thinks about his own interests over the needs and interests of his family.
- Birling's attitude towards his workers suggests that he does not care about other people. He refused their request for a wage increase in order to "keep labour costs down", showing that he cared more about his business costs than the welfare of his employees. This indicates that his main concern in life is his own profit rather than other people. Birling's behaviour towards Eva triggers the events that lead to her death, showing that selfishness can have harmful consequences.

- Birling lacks social conscience: he doesn't feel any responsibility to society as a whole. For example, he tells Eric and Gerald that a man has to "look after himself and his own". Priestley uses dramatic irony to emphasise that this selfish opinion is misguided. During the same conversation, Birling makes false predictions about other things, saying that there "isn't a chance" of war with Germany and that the Titanic is "unsinkable". These references to famous events that hadn't occurred in early 1912, when the play is set, would have been proven wrong by 1945, when the play was first performed. This makes Birling seem foolish and implies that he could be wrong about his attitude to society too. This helps to strengthen Priestley's message in the play that the middle and upper classes should act more selflessly and do more to help those around them.
- Birling is at first shaken by the Inspector's visit, moving "hesitatingly" after he leaves. However, when Gerald reveals that the Inspector was a "hoax", he decides that the family's problems are "All over now". This shows that he wasn't upset because he and his family had acted in a way that was morally wrong, but because of the "scandal" that the information could have caused and the damage it would have done to his reputation. This shows that the Inspector's visit hasn't made him reconsider his selfishness and lack of social conscience, suggesting that he is incapable of change.

2) This question requires you to think about a central character and how they change throughout the play, so all your points need to be about that character. You're asked to write about how Mickey is presented, so make sure you write about the techniques Russell uses. These points give you some ideas of the kind of things you could include:
- As a child, Mickey is friendly, and he easily bonds with Edward: he suggests that they become "blood brothers" and promise to "always defend" each other only a short time after they first meet. As the play goes on, he starts to push away the people he loves: he denounces his bond with Edward as "kids' stuff" and refuses to listen to Linda's concerns about his medication, repeatedly telling her to "leave me alone". His desire to break these bonds reflects the fact that he feels isolated by his circumstances, and emphasises that he has been let down by society.
- Mickey loses his innocence and sense of hope for the future over the course of the play. As a child, he longs to be older because he can "go to bed dead late" and "play with matches", but later in the play he bitterly tells Eddie that he "grew up" because he had to, and he can't be a child any more, however much he might now "wish" he was. This shows that he has come to believe that adulthood doesn't bring freedom, but rather pain and loss.
- As a child, Mickey is childishly excited by naughty behaviour: he admires Sammy when he "wees straight through the letter box". This contrasts with his attitude towards the robbery he participates in later in the play: Sammy has to persuade him to take part, and he eventually only agrees to do so because of his desperate need for the "fifty notes" that Sammy promises him. This shows that as an adult, Mickey has no appetite for crime or breaking rules; it is only desperation that forces him to take part in criminal activity.
- Mickey's changes in personality are caused by the lack of opportunities that his low social class affords him: he has a menial, insecure job from which he is fired, and this leads to his criminal behaviour, imprisonment, depression and eventual death. Even though he tries hard to find another job after he is fired — he says he's been "walking around all day, every day, lookin' for a job" — he is unable to. This emphasises that he has few options, linking him to the millions of unemployed working-class men in the UK in the 1980s and reinforcing Russell's message about the unfairness of the class divide.

3) In this question, you're asked to write about cultural identity, so all your points need to be about this idea. You need to write about how Pinnock presents ideas about cultural identity, so make sure you mention the techniques that she uses. These points give you some ideas of the kind of things you could include:
- Enid's complicated relationship with her identity suggests she feels she doesn't belong anywhere. When Mai suggests Enid see a doctor in England, Enid responds "What they know about a black woman soul?", suggesting she doesn't feel understood by white English society. The unanswered rhetorical question emphasises her feeling of isolation in England. However, she also feels misunderstood by her family in Jamaica who think she's "living like a millionaire". Her family's confused perception of her lifestyle in England demonstrates that her struggles are not acknowledged by either the culture she grew up in or the one she now lives in. Pinnock thus presents Enid as a character stuck between two cultural identities, neither of which accurately reflect or understand her experiences.
- Pinnock presents Brod's relationship with his cultural identity as a contrast to Enid's. Though they shared similar experiences of emigration, Brod feels a sense of longing for life in Jamaica, which he heavily romanticises. He dreams of "the land a wood and water", with the alliteration and natural imagery showing how he idealises the Jamaican life and culture. Enid, however, says "I don't dream about back home", and distances herself from her past life. Here, Pinnock explores how people have unique and individual relationships with their cultural identity, often differing from even those close to them.
- Pinnock suggests that the negative experiences Brod faces as a migrant have made him cling to his Caribbean identity. Being forced "to pay fifty pounds to become a citizen" makes him conscious to keep his "Jamaican passport up to date", and the stage direction "Kisses his teeth" indicates his disgust at this. Of all the characters, he displays the strongest desire to feel connected to Jamaican culture, and his experience shows the way that government policies can affect the deeply personal feelings of cultural identity.
- Viv represents how second-generation migrants have complex relationships with their cultural identity. She knows very little about Jamaican culture, highlighted by her having "Never heard of" Jamaica's national heroine. As she was born in England, she identifies more with British culture, but she doesn't see herself represented in it. She searches for herself in her school books but is "never there", illustrating how the experiences of Caribbean migrant families were not reflected in books she was expected to study. Pinnock therefore shows how many second-generation migrants can struggle to identify with their family's cultural heritage, but can also feel alienated from English society, even if they have lived in England their whole lives.

4) This question requires you to write about one central character, so all your points need to be about that character. You need to show how Kelly uses Leah to explore ideas about morality, so make sure you discuss how she is connected to this theme. These points give you some ideas of the kind of things you could include:
- Leah's monologues are used by Kelly to introduce key moral questions to the play, such as whether humans are more like chimps (killing outsiders) or bonobos (welcoming them). Leah's speech uses varied sentence lengths, such as the very short "Empathy." These emphasise her main points — in this case, that humanity's nearest animal relatives are known for caring about the needs of others. The monologue comes relatively early on in the play, which encourages the audience to think about how questions of morality, and especially the importance of kindness and empathy, relate to the events of the play as they are watching.

- Leah expresses moral beliefs, in contrast with much of the group. When Phil asks "What's more important: one person or everyone?", she replies "It's Adam, Phil, Adam!" The repetition of Adam's name emphasises his humanity and individuality, suggesting that Leah disagrees with Phil's view that the welfare of the group should come first. She therefore presents an alternative view to Phil's that shows greater empathy for Adam. As the play was written in response to media concerns about 'feral' teenagers acting immorally, Kelly may be using Leah to suggest that not all teenagers are wholly immoral or unable to feel empathy.
- Leah is very dependent on Phil's opinion. This is indicated by the many times where she asks him his view, such as "Phil, what would you do?", and continues talking to him even when he doesn't answer her. She continues this pattern of speech even after Phil demonstrates how Adam could be killed in Act Three, implying that she still accepts his authority. This suggests that, at this point in the play, her morality is still limited by her obsession with Phil.
- Towards the end of the play, Kelly indicates that Leah overcomes some of her dependency on Phil. A stage direction indicates that she "Storms off." from him, suggesting that she no longer supports his behaviour. However she does not seem to inform anyone about what the group has done, which is hinted at by Mark when he explains that she has gone "without saying a thing". This makes her morality as a character ambiguous — while she protests against the group's behaviour and eventually leaves them, she does not appear to report on the group's actions or make any obvious effort to try and get help for Adam.

5) In this question, you're asked to write about hopes and dreams, so all your points need to be about these ideas. You need to write about how Odimba presents ideas about hopes and dreams, so make sure you mention the techniques that she uses. These points give you some ideas of the kind of things you could include:
- The cupboard room symbolises Princess's dream of winning the Weston-super-Mare pageant and is linked to her confidence in herself. Odimba uses "booming" voice-overs and special effects that "fill the stage" to portray what's going on in Princess's head. This enables the audience to identify when Princess becomes more doubtful of her dreams, as the special effects are more subdued. Through these techniques, the audience is given access to Princess's imagination and is encouraged to engage with Princess's fluctuating emotions regarding her dreams.
- Mavis's encouragement helps to rekindle Princess's dream of being a beauty queen. When Princess says "I don't think I can be pretty again" after experiencing racial abuse at school, Mavis tells her that as black women, "we are everything that is beautiful on this earth". By using the pronoun "we", Mavis asserts her solidarity with Princess, transforming Princess's doubt into renewed self-assurance. In a similar way, the aims of the bus boycott are successful due to the number of people who came out to support it. Therefore, Odimba suggests that the characters' dreams become more achievable with the support of others and stresses the power that this has to enact change.
- Mavis's experience of migration explores how hopes do not always match up with reality. For example, Mavis tells Margot that she saw England as a "land of Hope and Glory" when she lived in the Caribbean, but "didn't find no hope" when she arrived. This highlights the disparity between Mavis's romanticised idea of England and her actual experience, reflecting the situation of many who migrated to Britain in the 1960s. Odimba uses the patriotic British song 'Land of Hope and Glory' as an ironic contrast in order to highlight the experiences of the Windrush generation, who arrived in Britain expecting prosperity, but were often faced with racism and discrimination instead.

- Achieving hopes and dreams is shown to be challenging. Junior is "trying to learn everything" he can to get an apprenticeship as a photographer, and he's been saving up money "for nearly two years" by taking on extra hours at work. The repeated references to the obstacles that Junior faces emphasises how difficult achieving his dream will be, particularly given the position of financial and social disadvantage that the James family are in as immigrants. Odimba therefore highlights how the social situations of members of marginalised communities can impact their access to opportunities.

6) For this question, you're asked to write about women's lives, so all your points need to be about that theme. You need to discuss how Delaney uses Jo to explore this theme, so make sure you write about this character. These points give you some ideas of the kind of things you could include:
- Delaney portrays Jo as an independent character. She repeats "mine" when expressing her pleasure at having her own flat — "But it's mine. All mine", which shows her strong desire to be self-reliant. The idea of an independent woman having her own flat contrasts the typical picture of women as dependent wives, which was common in the 1950s when the play was written. In this way, Delaney uses Jo to give a alternative view of women, showing how they often do want self-reliance and independence.
- Jo also rejects traditional ideas about motherhood, for example saying "I hate babies". The powerful verb "hate" emphasises the strength of her feelings. Her attitude is very different to the one expected of women at the time the play was written, when it was commonly believed that a woman's most important role was to care for her children. This view is shown in the play through Geof's remark that motherhood was expected to be "natural" for women, which highlights Jo's lack of a maternal instinct as something unusual in the context of the play. In this way, Delaney uses Jo to show that not all women fit into 1950s social expectations of motherhood.
- Jo faces criticism because she becomes pregnant without being married. For example, she is insulted using offensive terms such as "whore", and "slut". This reflects how having sex outside of marriage, especially for women, was disapproved of in the 1950s, so those who did often faced prejudice. This shows how difficult some women's lives could be if they failed to follow society's expectations of their behaviour.
- The theatrical context of the play emphasises the idea that Delaney wanted to highlight and explore the lives of women. The play was unusual for its time, when men were usually the main characters, in having working-class women like Jo as protagonists, and for having the mother-daughter relationship between Jo and Helen as a central theme. This centrality is reflected in the play's structure, as the first and last characters on stage are Jo and Helen. This means that they are the first and last characters the audience encounter, which makes them more memorable and emphasises their experiences and relationship above those of other characters.

7) For this question, you're asked to write about the author's ideas about fear, so all your points need to be about that theme. You need to write about how Golding presents fear, so make sure you mention the techniques that he uses. These points give you some ideas of the kind of things you could include:
- There are many different types of fear in 'Lord of the Flies'. Over the course of the novel, the boys' fears shift from fear of remaining stranded on the island to fear of the unknown, and finally to fear of each other. Fear is also crucial to Golding's message, which is that evil exists inside everyone; through the events of the novel he shows how evil can be brought to the surface by fear.

- The events of the novel take place against a backdrop of fear in the form of nuclear war. Piggy suggests in the first chapter that they will never be rescued because of "the atom bomb" which means their potential rescuers are "all dead". We are reminded again about this war at the end of the novel when the naval officer arrives and behind him "another rating held a sub-machine gun." This backdrop of fear serves to remind us that fear and evil are not confined to life on the island, but exist all over the world.
- Fear of the unknown is first shown by the littluns' nightmares. They "suffered untold terrors in the dark" and Jack and Ralph agree that building shelters is important so that the littluns feel they have some sort of 'home'. At this point in the novel, the boys are trying to fight their fear of the unknown by recreating something familiar — the comforts of civilised society. The boys' feeling that creating a society can fend off fear continues throughout the novel.
- The fear of the unknown gradually shifts and becomes fear of the beast. The beast changes form during the novel — it starts off as a "snake-thing" and then the dead airman is mistaken for "something like a great ape". These changes in form indicate to the reader that the beast only exists in the boys' imaginations, although they become increasingly afraid of it.
- Only Ralph and Simon understand that the "beast" is the evil inside them, such as when the Lord of the Flies says to Simon, "You knew, didn't you? I'm part of you?" They realise that believing in the beast gives the boys a way of focusing their fear of the unknown and of each other. Ralph recognises the evil inside himself and is terrified of becoming savage, but he has little choice when he is hunted like an animal. This makes his terror when he is being hunted all the more harrowing for the reader, and Golding emphasises this by saying he "became fear," showing that he has been completely overwhelmed by fear and is no longer really human.

8) For this question, you're being asked to write about ideas about death in 'Chemistry' and another story from Telling Tales, so make sure you choose a second story that has plenty to write about on the subject. This answer is for 'Chemistry' and 'Odour of Chrysanthemums', but it gives you an idea of the kind of points you could make whichever stories you're analysing:
- In 'Odour of Chrysanthemums', Lawrence shows how Elizabeth's reaction to death is affected by the circumstances of her life. Her first reaction to her husband's possible death is to consider how her family will survive financially and how she will care for an injured husband. These thoughts are presented in a long paragraph made up of broken sentences split up with long dashes. These increase the pace of the text, reflecting how many practical concerns she has to instantly consider, and emphasising that the responsibility she has towards her husband and family outweighs any emotional reaction she has. Her worries about money may reflect the hard situation of many widows in an era when many working-class women were financially dependent on their husbands. By presenting the practical as well as emotional impacts of death, Lawrence gives a realistic picture of death in this era.
- In Lawrence's story, chrysanthemums are clearly associated with Walter and Elizabeth's marriage: Elizabeth describes how she was given chrysanthemums at their wedding. However, Walter also had "brown chrysanthemums" in his button-hole the first time he was brought home drunk. The colour of these chrysanthemums suggests they are dead, symbolising the lack of love between Elizabeth and Walter by implying that, just as he left the flowers to die, Walter did not tend to his relationship with Elizabeth properly. The traditional meaning of chrysanthemums, which are often placed at graves and are therefore associated with death, further reinforces the idea that chrysanthemums are used to symbolise the 'death' of Walter and Elizabeth's relationship.
- In 'Chemistry', death is shown to bring characters together. The narrator's father's death "reconciled" his mother and grandfather and created a "delicate equilibrium" between the three. The use of the word "equilibrium" shows that they found a balance together; because the word can be used in a scientific sense to describe a chemical reaction that is balanced, it emphasises how their relationship has become more settled. This shows how death can alter people's relationships, as well as simply causing grief and sadness. In this way, Swift shows the complexities of the impact that death can have.
- Swift also uses 'Chemistry' to show how death can provide an opportunity for new perspectives, such as the narrator's conclusion that "though things change they aren't destroyed". This idea is reinforced by the story's cyclical structure: the boat that appears at the start of the story reappears at the end, but this time it is "unstoppable" and "unsinkable". The two similar words are placed in the middle of the sentence, giving them a greater impact to emphasise that the boat's course cannot be changed. This image acts as a symbol of how the relationship between the narrator and his grandfather cannot be destroyed, even if it exists only in memory. This implies that death can offer new outlooks that are not always wholly negative.

9) In this question, you're asked to write about education and learning, so all your points need to be about these ideas. You need to write about how Orwell presents ideas about education and learning, so make sure you mention the techniques that he uses. These points give you some ideas of the kind of things you could include:
- Education is related to power in the novel: for example, the pigs are "the cleverest of the animals", so they "naturally" take over the running of the farm. The ability to read, write and reason allows the pigs to persuade the other animals that the pigs are superior to them. The less-learned animals lack the intelligence they would need to challenge the pigs' authority, leaving them powerless.
- The pigs' intelligence and education allows them to use language to repress the working classes. The way the Seven Commandments are changed to suit Napoleon's aims is an example of the pigs using language to control the less educated animals. The pigs have power because they have learned to "read and write perfectly", and therefore change the commandments to suit their own purposes. For example, the sixth commandment is changed so that it reads, "No animal shall kill any other animal without cause" to defend Napoleon's "execution of traitors". This reflects the way Stalin used propaganda to control the people of Russia and relates to the Great Purge, the killing of people thought to be traitors to instil fear in others. Because the other animals have not learned to read, they don't immediately notice when the commandments are changed, and when they do notice, they can't prove it.
- Snowball attempts to teach the other animals to read, though his attempts are frustrated because the other animals lack the intelligence or motivation to learn – most of the animals on the farm are unable to "get further than the letter A." In contrast, Napoleon chooses to concentrate his teaching on a select few, such as the puppies, who he trains to attack anyone who objects to him. He only teaches the puppies what they need to know to be useful to him, which contrasts with Snowball's attitude to education. Napoleon also teaches the sheep to loudly repeat the phrase "Four legs good, two legs bad" whenever they are agitated, which effectively "put an end to any chance of discussion." The little learning that they receive makes them a powerful tool for Napoleon, showing how he educates selectively in order to continue the oppression. They use the words without understanding what they mean, which shows how the less-educated animals simply accept the terms of the revolution and their own repression.

10) For this question, you're asked to write about the author's ideas about family, so all your points need to be about that theme. You need to write about how de Waal presents family, so make sure you mention the techniques that she uses. These points give you some ideas of the kind of things you could include:
- Leon's loyalty to his biological family can blind him to their faults. He is defensive and protective of Carol, shown by his assumption that the Zebra wants him to say "bad things" about her. He also trusts her, and generously gives her his picture of Jake. De Waal uses dramatic irony, as the reader knows that Carol will likely not take care of the photo, which is later proved correct when it's implied she has lost it. De Waal thus explores how having love for family members can make it difficult to recognise when they are doing wrong.
- Maureen and Sylvia's relationship shows how strong sibling relationships can be. Sylvia calling Maureen "Mo" or "Our Mo" suggests their relationship is comfortable and relaxed. Sylvia cares for Maureen following her illness, mirroring how Leon cares for Jake when Carol isn't well enough to do so. However, the sisters' closeness also contrasts with the way Leon and Jake are separated without being able to contact each other. As both sets of siblings have a strong bond, it allows the reader to feel optimistic that Leon "will see Jake again" as Maureen says.
- The character of Mr Devlin shows how losing family members can affect someone very negatively. As the novel progresses, it becomes clear to the reader that Mr Devlin's initial grumpiness (shown by his insistence that "No unaccompanied children" are allowed in the allotments) is a result of losing his son, Gabriel. Mr Devlin could therefore be seen as a cautionary figure who reflects the emotional toll that not addressing feelings of loss can take. However, by the novel's end, Mr Devlin's "teasing" shows he has regained a sense of humour, which suggests that building new relationships can help with processing previous losses.
- De Waal shows that people who aren't related can still be family. When Leon first meets Tufty, the domino set in Tufty's shed reminds him of Byron. By linking Byron and Tufty, de Waal foreshadows Tufty's future fatherly role. However, while Byron lets him play with the dominoes, Tufty tells him he's "too young" for them. The clear divide between who is the adult and who is the child establishes a more conventional father/son relationship between Tufty and Leon, and over the course of the novel, Tufty (and Mr Devlin) become father figures to Leon. The positive impact this has on Leon shows the benefit of building relationships with people who aren't relatives.

11) For this question, you're asked to write about the author's ideas about friendship, so all your points need to be about that theme. You need to write about how Syal presents friendship, so make sure you mention the techniques that she uses. These points give you some ideas of the kind of things you could include:
- Syal portrays two types of friends in the novel: false friends, like Anita, and true friends, such as Robert. Meena's realisation that Anita isn't a true friend is a key part of her character development throughout the novel.
- Initially, Meena values and is heavily influenced by Anita's friendship. She feels "privileged" to be her friend, thinks of her as a "kindred spirit", and tries to emulate Anita's behaviour, using coarse language such as "shag the arse off it". Because she values Anita's friendship, she is a good friend to her: for example, she tries to stop Anita finding out about the relationship between Deirdre and Dave, because she knows that Anita would feel hurt if she found out.
- In contrast, it is clear to the reader that Anita doesn't value Meena's friendship. Meena explains that "Anita talked and I listened", and Anita abuses her trust by trying to steal her belongings. This suggests that, instead of trying to engage with Meena's life and form a meaningful relationship with her, Anita simply wants to exploit Meena for her own personal gain. This emphasises the unhealthy, unbalanced nature of their friendship.
- Eventually, Meena comes to feel "pity" rather than "love" for Anita, and to understand that Anita has been using her, so she decides to "erase" her from her mind. This is an important turning point for Meena, as she starts to appreciate her own value and potential instead of trying to become someone she's not. Her realisation that her friendship with Anita wasn't healthy or fair is linked to the development of her own identity and personality.
- Syal presents examples of healthy friendships in the novel in order to highlight the inequality of Anita's relationships. For example, the Kumar family have close friendships with other people who have left India for England. Their friends are presented as a valuable source of love and support: Uncle Amman helps Shyam to find a job, and the Kumars rush to hospital to support Uncle Amman after he has a heart attack. This contrasts directly with Anita, who doesn't visit Meena at all when she's in hospital.

12) For this question, you're asked to write about the author's ideas about violence, so all your points need to be about that theme. You need to write about how Kelman presents violence, so make sure you mention the techniques that he uses. These points give you some ideas of the kind of things you could include:
- Images of violence appear regularly in the novel, creating an atmosphere of threat that builds up as the novel progresses. The first line focuses on the dead boy's blood, and Harri recalls this image at other points in the novel, such as remembering how he "saw the blood. His blood." The repetition of "blood", in these lines and throughout the novel, suggests that Harri cannot stop thinking about the boy's death. This emphasises that violence has affected him deeply on an emotional level.
- Kelman uses the structure of the novel to emphasise that Harri's violent death is not an isolated incident. For example, connections are made between Harri and the dead boy, such as when he takes on the part of the dead boy in a role-play, saying "I was the dead boy." It is not immediately clear from this sentence that Harri is acting, making the link between him and the dead boy clear and hinting that he is vulnerable to the same violence that caused the dead boy to be killed. Furthermore, the first line of the novel, starting "You could see the blood", is repeated in the final paragraph. The cyclical structure stresses the similarity between Harri and the dead boy, emphasising that he, like Harri, was an innocent victim of violence. This underlines Kelman's message that many young people have died needlessly as a result of youth violence (such as Damilola Taylor, whose death informed Kelman's novel), and that Harri's story represents just one of the lives lost due to violent acts.
- The novel's depiction of harm towards animals highlights how violence can be cruel and unnecessary. Harri describes the killing of ducklings, stating that "The babies just got crushed." The brutal verb "crushed" makes the action appear especially barbaric. The violence shown here seems particularly cruel, as the baby animals are helpless and pose no threat, which encourages the reader to sympathise with them. The ducklings act as a symbol of children such as Harri, who are also innocent, which helps the reader to understand how unjust it is that they are hurt or killed.
- Kelman uses the third-person perspective of the pigeon to reflect on the wider causes of human violence. The pigeon uses the rhetorical question "Wasn't that a sickly sweet epiphany?" to describe an infant killing an ant. The adjective "sweet" suggests that the child experiences pleasure in killing the ant. However, the adjective "sickly" suggests that there is a negative aspect to the child's joy, because it can be nauseating, implying that violence is also bad for us. Kelman's use of a child in this image implies that it is instinctive to humans to enjoy violence; however, the language he uses portrays this instinct as harmful to those who indulge in it as well as those who are victims of it.

Pages 232-235 — English Literature — Paper 2: Section B (Poetry)

13) For this question, you have to think about the way that the poets use form, structure and language to present the breakdown of a relationship, so make sure you choose a second poem that has plenty to write about on the subject. Comparing them means writing about the similarities and differences, so make some links between the poems in your answer. This answer compares 'Neutral Tones' by Thomas Hardy with 'When We Two Parted' by Lord Byron, but it gives you an idea of the kind of things you need to write whichever poems you're analysing. Here are some points you could make:

- The two poems have a similar subject matter — the end of a romantic relationship — and they use similar narrative voices to present this. Both poems are written in the first person, which gives the reader an insight into the thoughts and feelings of the narrators. Both narrators also use second-person pronouns, such as "thee" and "your", throughout the poems, which indicates that they are addressed directly to their former lovers and emphasises the fixation that both narrators have on the women they address.
- However, the two narrators express different emotions towards the breakdown of their relationships. In 'Neutral Tones', there is a time jump at the end of the third stanza, which is introduced by an ellipsis. This creates a sense of distance between the events of the past and the narrator's present-day life: although he is still haunted by the loss of his lover, he seems calm about it. The emotions that the narrator expresses in 'When We Two Parted', on the other hand, seem stronger and less controlled. For example, in line 20 he uses a rhetorical question, asking "Why wert thou so dear?" This emphasises his sense of desperation and shows how upset he is at the loss of his lover.
- Both poems have a cyclical structure that reinforces the narrator's sense of regret and loss. The final line of 'When We Two Parted' refers back to the poem's opening stanza by repeating the phrase "silence and tears". This emphasises that the breakdown of the relationship has been a traumatic experience for the narrator, as well as suggesting that he is unable to move on from it. In 'Neutral Tones', the final two lines of the poem repeat the images of the "sun", "tree" and "pond" that were introduced in the first stanza. This reflects the narrator's inability to forget the pain that his former lover inflicted on him. The return of the 'A' rhyme in the ABBA rhyme scheme reinforces this sentiment, reflecting how the narrator's memory of the break-up returns to affect him.

14) For this question, you have to think about the way that the poets use form, structure and language to describe nature, so make sure you choose a second poem that has plenty to write about on the subject. Comparing them means writing about the similarities and differences, so make some links between the poems in your answer. This answer compares 'The Prelude: Stealing the Boat' by William Wordsworth with 'Storm on the Island' by Seamus Heaney, but it gives you an idea of the kind of things you need to write whichever poems you're analysing. Here are some points you could make:

- 'The Prelude: Stealing the Boat' and 'Storm on the Island' both present nature as a powerful force, which can have a profound effect on humans. In Wordsworth's poem, the narrator experiences nature's "power" when he sees a "huge" mountain while rowing on a lake, which causes a "darkness" to hang over his thoughts for "many days" afterwards. Meanwhile, in Heaney's poem an island community experiences the violent power of nature in the form of a storm that "pummels" them. Both poems present nature as having power over humans — in Heaney's poem the impact of this power is physical, whereas in Wordsworth's poem it is psychological.
- Wordsworth and Heaney both use personification to present nature as a conscious force that can threaten humans. Wordsworth's narrator uses personification to describe how the mountain "Strode after" him with "measured motion". The word "measured" and the use of alliteration in this phrase suggest that the mountain is chasing the narrator, enabling the reader to share in his fear. Heaney also personifies nature, using language usually associated with war, such as "strafes" and "bombarded", to compare the actions of the wind to those of a fighter pilot. The use of such violent imagery emphasises the power of the storm, and suggests that the wind is deliberately attacking the island. This highlights how destructive the storm could be, which helps to clarify the islanders' fear.
- Both poems have a distinct turning point, which heightens the presentation of nature as changeable and dramatic. In 'The Prelude: Stealing the Boat', the volta in line 21 represents the moment when the narrator first encounters the "huge peak", and at this point the mood of the poem shifts from confidence to fear. Similarly, in 'Storm on the Island', the volta in line 14 represents the sudden arrival of the storm. The poem's tone is subsequently transformed by the storm's arrival — the confident opening statement, "We are prepared", now sounds empty, as the island community is powerless in the face of the storm. As in Wordsworth's poem, this change of tone reflects how changeable nature can be, and emphasises how unsettling this changeability can be for humans.

15) For this question, you have to think about the way that the poets use form, structure and language to present feelings towards places, so make sure you choose a second poem that has plenty to write about on the subject. Comparing them means writing about the similarities and differences, so make some links between the poems in your answer. This answer compares 'In a London Drawingroom' by George Eliot with 'Shall earth no more inspire thee' by Emily Brontë, but it gives you an idea of the kind of things you need to write whichever poems you're analysing. Here are some points you could make:

- 'In a London Drawingroom' and 'Shall earth no more inspire thee' both present strong feelings towards places. In Eliot's poem, the speaker's negative attitude to the city is conveyed by comparing it to "one huge prison-house". By using this comparison, Eliot gives the sense of serious confinement, which is further consolidated with the idea of people being "punished". Meanwhile, the speaker in Brontë's poem compares the natural world to "heaven". The use of positive verbs like "soothe" and "pleases" gives a far more favourable impression of a place, and suggests the positive impact that a place can have on people. While each poem has a different view of the speaker's environment, both poems show how places can provoke strong feelings and have significant impacts on their inhabitants.
- Both poems use form to reflect the speakers' feelings about places. Eliot's combination of iambic pentameter with unbroken lines of blank verse gives 'In a London Drawingroom' a relentless pace, evoking the idea of a place in constant motion, where nobody lingers, "Pauses" or rests. The form therefore reflects the city's frantic energy that the speaker seems to feel negatively about. Conversely, 'Shall earth no more inspire thee' is written in quatrains with a regular rhyme scheme and a regular metre. The effect is that the poem feels familiar and is reminiscent of a nursery rhyme, suggesting that, unlike in Eliot's poem, the place in Brontë's poem is associated with a feeling of peace.

- In both poems, the speakers feel that places have power. The speaker in Eliot's poem seems to feel the city has overpowered nature. The phrase "golden rays" is used to describe sunshine, making light seem precious. However, it is "clothed in hemp", a fibre processed for fabric. This description of the natural world being hidden by a material associated with industry implies the speaker feels negatively about the increasing industrialisation in the 19th century and its ability to overpower nature. By contrast, the use of the first person in 'Shall earth no more inspire thee' shows nature's power, as nature is the only character that gets to speak. The anaphora used as the speaker repeats "I know" implies a sense of self-confidence, which contributes to the feeling in the poem that nature is all-powerful. Therefore, while Eliot's poem presents the power of place in a negative light, Brontë's poem takes a more positive approach, as nature's power is able to "drive thy griefs away"

Pages 236-237 — English Literature — Paper 2: Section C (Unseen Poetry)

16a) For this question, you have to think about what the poet is saying about the speaker's attitude to parenthood and how she presents this attitude. Make sure you comment on how form, structure and language are used to present feelings and ideas in the poem. Here are some points you could make:
- 'For a Five-Year-Old' is about the relationship between a mother and a child, and the responsibility that the mother feels for her child's upbringing. This responsibility is emphasised using the form of the poem: it is mostly written in iambic pentameter, which creates a steady rhythm that reflects the narrator's dedication and commitment to her child.
- The poem's narrator addresses the narrative directly to the child, repeating the pronouns "you" and "your" throughout. This reflects the narrator's constant awareness of how her actions affect her child's development, and emphasises the idea that parenthood affects every aspect of a parent's life.
- The poem is structured using two distinct stanzas. In the first stanza, the narrator describes a specific interaction with the child, and then in the second stanza she describes some of the unkind things she has done at other times in her life. The child's "careful hand" in the first stanza contrasts with violent verbs such as "trapped", "shot", "drowned" and "betrayed" in the second stanza. This makes it clear that the narrator behaves differently around the child in order to set a good example, and emphasises her belief that it is important to teach children the correct lessons in life, regardless of one's personal experience.
- The snail could be seen to symbolise the child; the care and delicacy with which the narrator teaches her child to handle the snail reflects her belief that the responsibilities of parenthood must be carried out with similar care and delicacy. In the first stanza, the snail is presented as fragile using the alliterative phrase "carry it outside, with careful hand". This makes the word "careful" stand out to the reader, which shows the care and attention that the child pays to the snail, and hints at the snail's fragility. In the second stanza, the narrator refers to the child's "gentleness" and her own ability to 'mould' the child. This suggests that, like the snail, the child is fragile, and highlights the responsibility that the narrator feels to make sure that the child is treated with the same kindness and care that they show to the snail.

16b) For this question, you have to think about how the relationship between an adult and a child is presented in the two poems. Make sure you comment on how form, structure and language are used to present feelings and ideas in the poems. You're comparing the two poems, so you need to think about similarities and differences between them. Here are some points you could make:
- Adcock and Pugh both write about the process of a child learning about the world around them. Both poems are written in the first person, which allows the reader an insight into the narrators' thoughts and feelings and makes their descriptions of their relationship and experience feel more personal.
- Both poems contain characters who feel responsible for a child's moral education. In 'For a Five-Year-Old', the narrator understands that her child's "gentleness" is "moulded" by her own words; the verb "moulded" emphasises the patience and care that goes into such teaching. In 'The Beautiful Lie', the child's grandmother asks the boy, "Did you do that?", in order to teach him that his actions are wrong. The hard 'd' and 't' sounds in this phrase make the grandmother sound harsh and angry. This increases the reader's pleasure in the unexpected side-effect of her words: they "showed him" he had the "choice" of lying.
- Although both poems are about the joy of watching a child learn, the poets present different messages about what it is important for a child to learn. Adcock focuses on the innocence of the child, and the mother's pleasure in preserving this innocence. In contrast, Pugh's narrator takes pleasure in seeing a small loss of innocence, as the child learns how to lie.
- The poets reinforce their messages using their rhyme schemes. The middle six lines of each stanza of 'For a Five-Year-Old' use rhyming couplets; this careful use of form highlights the care and attention with which the narrator tries to preserve the child's "gentleness". In contrast, 'The Beautiful Lie' has no rhyme scheme and an irregular rhythm. This reflects the freedom that the narrator believes the boy gains by learning how to "tell a story": the realisation that he is able to lie opens up a world of imagination. The poem presents this as a "moving" and "momentous" occasion for the narrator, showing how an adult can experience the world afresh through a child, and hinting at how, for an adult, the achievements of a child they love can be more important than their own accomplishments.

Glossary

allegory	When the characters, settings and events of a story are used to represent something else, e.g. 'Animal Farm' is an allegory for the Russian Revolution.
alliteration	When words that are close together start with the same sound. E.g. "the beat of the band".
antithesis	A rhetorical technique where opposing words or ideas are put together to show a contrast.
aside	When a character in a play makes a short comment that reveals their thoughts to the audience, and no other character can hear it.
assonance	Using words with similar vowel sounds but different consonants. E.g. "They play in the waves."
audience	The person or group of people that read or listen to a text.
biased writing	Gives more support to one point of view than to another, due to the writer's own opinions.
blank verse	Lines from a play or poem that are written in iambic pentameter and don't rhyme.
caesura	A pause in a line of poetry. E.g. the full stop in "Over the drifted stream. My father spins".
chronological	When events are arranged in the order in which they happened.
cinematic writing	Writing that makes the reader feel like they're watching a film.
cliffhanger	When a story, or section of a story, ends in a dramatic way that introduces a new plot or idea.
colloquial language	Informal language that sounds like ordinary speech.
commentary	A type of newspaper article that expresses a writer's opinions on a theme or news event.
connotations	The suggestions that words can make beyond their obvious meaning.
context	The background to something, or the situation surrounding it, which affects the way it's understood. E.g. the context of a text from 1915 would include the First World War.
counter-argument	The opposite point of view to the writer's own view.
cyclical structure	Where key elements at the start of the text repeat themselves at the end.
direct address	When a narrator or writer speaks directly to a character or the reader, e.g. "you may recall..."
double negative	A sentence construction that incorrectly expresses a negative idea by using two negative words or phrases, e.g. "I don't want no trouble."
dramatic irony	When the reader or audience knows something that a character does not know.
dramatic monologue	A form of poetry that uses the assumed voice of a single speaker who is not the poet to address an implied audience.
embedded narrative	A story within the main story, e.g. the letters in 'The Strange Case of Dr Jekyll and Mr Hyde'.
end-stopping	Finishing a line of poetry with the end of a phrase or sentence, usually marked by punctuation.
enjambment	When a sentence or phrase runs over from one line or stanza to the next.
figurative language	Language that is used in a non-literal way to create an effect, e.g. personification.
first person	A narrative viewpoint where the narrator is one of the characters.
flashback	A writing technique where the scene shifts from the present to an event in the past.
foreshadowing	A literary device where a writer hints or gives clues about a future event.
form	The type of text (e.g. a letter, a speech) or poem (e.g. a sonnet or a ballad).

Glossary

frame narrative	An overarching story that contains other stories within it.
free verse	Poetry that doesn't rhyme and has no regular rhythm or line length.
generalisation	A statement that gives an overall impression, (sometimes misleading) without going into details.
half-rhymes	Words that have a similar, but not identical, end sound. E.g. "plough" and "follow".
hyperbole	When exaggeration is used to have an effect on the reader.
iambic pentameter	Poetry with a metre of ten syllables — five of them stressed, and five unstressed.
imagery	Language that creates a picture in your mind, e.g. metaphors, similes and personification.
inference	A conclusion reached about something, based on evidence.
internal rhyme	When two or more words rhyme, and at least one of them isn't at the end of a line.
inversion	Altering the normal word order for emphasis, e.g. "On the table sat a hedgehog."
irony	Saying one thing but meaning the opposite, e.g. "What a great idea to go for a walk in a storm."
juxtaposition	When two contrasting ideas are placed near or next to each other in a text.
linear structure	A type of narrative structure that tells the events of a story in chronological order.
list of three	Using three words (often adjectives) or phrases together to create emphasis.
metaphor	A way of describing something by saying that it is something else, e.g. "his eyes were emeralds".
metre	The arrangement of stressed and unstressed syllables to create rhythm in a line of poetry.
monologue	One person speaking alone for a long period of time.
monosyllabic	When a word only has one syllable, e.g. "had", "thought", "play".
mood	The feel or atmosphere of a text, e.g. humorous, peaceful, fearful.
motif	A recurring image or idea in a text.
narrative	Writing that tells a story or describes an experience.
narrative viewpoint	The perspective that a text is written from, e.g. first-person point of view.
narrator	The voice or character speaking the words of the narrative.
non-linear structure	A type of narrative structure that tells the events of a story in a non-chronological order.
novella	A prose text that is longer than a short story, but shorter than a novel, e.g. 'A Christmas Carol'
omniscient narrator	A narrator who knows the thoughts and feelings of all the characters in a narrative.
onomatopoeia	A word that imitates the sound it describes as you say it, e.g. 'whisper'.
oxymoron	When two opposing ideas are brought together in a word or phrase, e.g. "beautiful disaster".
pace	The speed at which the writer takes the reader through the events in a text or poem.
paradox	A statement that contradicts itself.
parenthesis	A rhetorical technique where an extra clause or phrase is inserted into a complete sentence.
pathetic fallacy	A kind of personification where nature (often weather) is given human characteristics.

Glossary

personification	Describing a non-living thing as if it's a person. E.g. "The sea growled hungrily."
phonetic spellings	When words are spelt as they sound rather than with their usual spelling.
pun	A word or phrase that's deliberately used because it has more than one meaning.
purpose	The reason someone writes a text, e.g. to persuade, to argue, to advise, to inform.
register	The specific language used to match writing to the social situation that it's for.
rhetoric	Using language techniques (e.g. repetition or hyperbole) to achieve a persuasive effect.
rhetorical question	A question that doesn't need an answer but is asked to make or emphasise a point.
rhyme scheme	A pattern of rhyming words in a poem.
rhyming couplet	A pair of rhyming lines that are next to each other.
rhythm	A pattern of sounds created by the arrangement of stressed and unstressed syllables.
sarcasm	Language that has a scornful or mocking tone, often using irony.
second person	A narrative viewpoint that is written as if the reader is one of the characters.
sensory language	Language that appeals to the five senses.
sibilance	Repeating sounds like 's' and 'sh' to create a 'hissing' or 'shushing' effect, e.g. "the slow slug".
simile	A way of describing something by comparing it to something else.
slang	Words or phrases that are informal, and often specific to one age group or social group.
soliloquy	When a character in a play speaks their thoughts aloud, but no other characters can hear them.
sonnet	A form of poem with fourteen lines, that usually follows a clear rhyme scheme.
stage directions	Written instructions in a play that describe how the play should be staged or performed.
staging	How a play appears on the stage, including the set, costumes and where the actors stand.
Standard English	English that is considered correct because it uses formal features of spelling and grammar.
stanza	A group of lines in a poem.
structure	The order and arrangement of ideas in a text. E.g. how it begins, develops and ends.
style	The way that a text is written, e.g. the type of language, sentence forms and structure used.
superlative	The most extreme form of an adjective or adverb. E.g. "Ted is the oldest man I know."
syllable	A single unit of sound within a word. E.g. "all" has one syllable, "always" has two.
symbolism	When an object stands for something else. E.g. a cross symbolises Christianity.
third person	A narrative viewpoint where the narrator remains outside the events of the story
tone	The feeling of a piece of writing, e.g. happy, sad, serious, light-hearted.
viewpoint	The attitude and beliefs that a writer is trying to convey.
voice	The characteristics of the person narrating a poem or text.
volta	A turning point in a poem, when the argument or tone changes dramatically.

Index

A
adjectives 44, 45
adverbs 44, 45
alliteration 49, 52, 86, 169
antithesis 52
asides 135
assessment objectives 12, 120
assonance 55, 169
audience 22, 74, 75, 121, 136, 137

B
bias 24, 53, 62
blank verse 143
broadsheets 73, 83, 118, 119

C
caesurae 167
characters 76, 79, 121-124, 138, 140, 143, 152
checking your work 8
chronological order 60, 151
cinematic style 43, 61
cliffhangers 61, 78, 151
colons 8
commands 64
commas 8
comparisons 21, 170, 173, 174, 191
conclusions 3, 174
conjunctions 64
context 34, 35, 50, 113, 120, 127, 138, 139, 141, 154-56, 173, 176, 178
couplets 164
cyclical structure 144, 151, 166

D
descriptions 79
descriptive language 54, 125, 152
determiners 44
dialogue 134-36
direct address 52, 76, 84, 165
double negatives 8
drama 121-44
dramatic irony 137
dramatic monologues 164

E
education 34, 138, 155
embedded narratives 61, 152
embedded quotes 5
end-stopping 167
enjambment 167
essays 3, 85
evidence 4-6, 12, 120, 175, 178
exaggeration 52, 53, 55, 140, 168
exam questions (English Language)
　paper 1, question 1
　　examples 20
　　explanation 11, 13, 94, 97
　　graded answers 97
　paper 1, question 2
　　examples 5, 25, 32, 46, 54, 65
　　explanation 11, 13, 94, 98
　　graded answers 98, 99
　paper 1, question 3
　　examples 62, 63, 68, 69
　　explanation 11, 14, 94, 100
　　graded answers 100, 101
　paper 1, question 4
　　examples 31, 42, 50, 59
　　explanation 11, 14, 95, 102
　　graded answers 102, 103
　paper 1, question 5
　　examples 72-79
　　explanation 11, 15, 95, 104
　　graded answers 104, 105
　paper 2, question 1
　　examples 24
　　explanation 11, 16, 106, 110
　　graded answers 110, 111
　paper 2, question 2
　　examples 21
　　explanation 11, 16, 106, 112
　　graded answers 112, 113
　paper 2, question 3
　　examples 26, 27, 33, 43, 45, 49, 52
　　explanation 11, 17, 107, 114
　　graded answers 114, 115
　paper 2, question 4
　　examples 31, 38, 39, 51, 53
　　explanation 11, 17, 107, 116
　　graded answers 116, 117
　paper 2, question 5
　　examples 72-75, 83-87, 90, 91
　　explanation 11, 18, 107, 118
　　graded answers 118, 119
exam structure 11, 120
exclamations 64, 86
explaining words and phrases 7

F
finding facts 13, 20, 97, 110
first person 32, 33, 59, 62, 77, 153, 165
flashbacks 61, 126, 152
foreshadowing 61, 126, 152
form 74, 83, 104, 118, 120, 121, 151, 163, 164, 170, 174, 175
frame narratives 61, 152

G
gender 34, 128, 139, 154, 155
giving opinions 4, 26, 82, 85, 102, 118
Gothic genre 155
grammar 8, 165

H
humour 140, 142
hyperbole 52, 53

I
iambic pentameter 143, 167
imagery 46, 54, 105, 124, 136, 142, 152, 169
inference 6, 112, 113
informal language 7, 124
intensifiers 44
introductions 3, 174
irony 50, 51

J
juxtaposition 61

K
key scenes 144
key words 2, 173, 191
Knowledge Organiser
　English Language exams 19
　English Literature 197-204
　exam basics 9
　language and structure 66, 67
　understanding texts 36, 37
　writing 88, 89

L
language 13, 17, 32, 98, 112, 120, 121, 124, 136, 142, 143, 152, 163, 165-70, 175, 177
　colloquial 43, 82, 124, 165
　emotive 26, 31
　figurative 32, 46

Index

leaflets 84
letters 87
linking words and phrases 7, 21, 191
list of three 52, 86
literary fiction 32, 75
  purpose 23, 73
  writing 15
literary non-fiction 33, 75
  purpose 23, 73
  writing 18

M
metaphors 46, 54, 124, 136, 142, 152, 168
metre 167
minor scenes 144
modern plays 138, 139, 148, 149
monologues 135
monosyllabic words 166
mood 134, 137, 164, 166, 168, 169, 187
motifs 61

N
narrative viewpoint 32, 59, 62, 77, 153, 165
newspaper articles 82, 83
non-standard grammar 152, 165
nouns 44

O
omniscient narrators 59, 153
onomatopoeia 49, 169
oxymoron 55

P
pace 137, 144, 164, 166, 167, 169
paradox 55, 142
paragraphs 4, 7, 60, 125, 170, 174, 191
parenthesis 52
personal response 14, 121
personification 46, 54, 124, 136, 142, 152, 168
phonetic spellings 165
planning 2, 3, 72, 170, 173
plots 123, 151
poetic techniques 165-69
poetry anthology 120, 163, 173-84
pronouns 27, 44, 72

prose 121-33, 143, 151-62
punctuation 8, 167
puns 141, 142
purpose 23, 64, 72, 73, 104, 118, 122, 187
  literary fiction 73
  literary non-fiction 60, 73
  to advise 23, 27
  to argue 23, 26, 72, 86
  to entertain 23, 25, 32, 33, 76-79, 82
  to inform 23, 24, 33, 72, 82, 84, 85
  to persuade 23, 26, 72, 86

Q
questions 64
quotations 5, 121, 129, 143, 173, 175, 185

R
register 43, 72, 74, 83
  formal 27, 34, 43, 72, 87
  informal 27, 43
religion 34, 156
Renaissance 141
repetition 32, 60, 124, 144, 152
rhetoric 26, 52, 82
rhetorical questions 52, 72, 86
rhyme 164, 166
rhythm 164, 166, 167
Romanticism 155

S
sarcasm 6, 51, 82
second person 27, 59
semi-colons 8
sensory imagery 54, 79, 169
sentence forms 64, 65, 114
sentence structure 64, 65, 120, 125
settings 125, 127, 138
sexuality 139
Shakespeare 140-44, 146, 147
sibilance 55, 169
similes 46, 54, 124, 136, 142, 152, 168
slang 7, 138, 152
social class 34, 127, 128, 138, 139, 154, 155
soliloquies 135
sonnets 164
speech 122, 124, 135, 143
speeches 86
spelling 8

spoken language 165
stage directions 134, 137, 139
stagecraft 137
Standard English 7, 43, 87
stanzas 164
statements 64
stories 76-78
structure 60, 61, 100, 119, 120, 121, 126, 136, 144, 151, 152, 163, 164, 170, 175
  linear 60, 151
  non-linear 60, 151
  of leaflets 84
  of essays 85
  of exam answers 3, 4, 7, 174
  of speeches 86
  questions about 14
style 33, 43, 60, 72, 74, 82
summarising information 16, 21, 112
superlatives 55
syllables 167
symbolism 126

T
tabloids 83
tension 76
tercets 164
themes 121, 128, 129, 140, 173, 187
third person 32, 59, 62, 77, 153, 165
tone 2, 31, 72, 74, 75, 82, 84, 169

U
unreliable narrators 59, 61, 153
unseen poetry 120, 163, 187-196

V
verbs 44, 54, 64
verse 143
vocabulary 22, 77, 120, 124, 177
voice 153, 165

W
What How Why 4, 174
word types 44
writer's attitudes 6, 17, 42, 82, 116
writer's intentions 6
writer's message 121, 128, 187